Impeachable Offenses

Impeachable Offenses

A Documentary History from 1787 to the Present

❧ ❧

Emily Field Van Tassel
Case Western Reserve University School of Law

Paul Finkelman
University of Akron School of Law

Congressional Quarterly Inc.
Washington, D.C.

Printed in the United States of America

Second Printing

Cover design: Debra Naylor

Photo credits: cover, clockwise from left, White House, Reuters, Library
of Congress, Reuters, *Washington Post*; 2, 24, 45, 57, 201, 242, 257,
Library of Congress; 75, National Archives; 207, Tennessee Historical
Society; 89, 225, Culver Pictures; 261, White House; 263, Congressional
Quarterly file photo; 269, Douglas Graham, Congressional Quarterly;
276, 289, Scott J. Ferrell, Congressional Quarterly; 296,
AP/Wide World Photos; 311, R. Michael Jenkins, Congressional Quarterly

Library of Congress Cataloging-in-Publication Data

Van Tassel, Emily Field.
    Impeachable offenses : a documentary history from 1787 to the
present / Emily Field Van Tassel, Paul Finkelman.
        p.   cm.
    Includes bibliographical references and index.
    ISBN 1-56802-479-7 (hc.) — ISBN 1-56802-480-0 (pbk.)
    1. Impeachments—United States—History. 2. Clinton, Bill, 1946–
—Impeachment. I. Finkleman, Paul, 1949–   . II. Title.
KF5075.V36   1998
342.73'062—dc21   98-54337

To our parents, with love and gratitude

❧ ❧

Helen and David Van Tassel
Ella and Simon Finkelman

Contents

Preface

ON NOVEMBER 19, 1998, independent counsel Kenneth W. Starr testified for twelve hours before the House Judiciary Committee in support of his referral to the House of eleven possible grounds for the impeachment of President Bill Clinton. Any veneer of bipartisanship that Judiciary Committee Chairman Henry Hyde hoped would overlay the committee's investigation of Clinton was stripped away within minutes of the start of the proceedings. Democrats and Republicans immediately faced off over how to conduct the hearing.

As the hearing unfolded, it also became clear that the tactics employed by Starr and his team of prosecutors and investigators were the primary focus of interest. Few committee members asked questions probing the evidence supporting Starr's allegations. The only new information to come from Starr's testimony was the revelation that he was prepared to exonerate the president in two of his investigations, those involving misuse of FBI files and the firings in the White House travel office. Starr also announced that his investigation of Clinton's involvement in the failed Arkansas Whitewater development project had turned up no provable wrongdoing by the president.

The day after Starr's appearance before the House Judiciary Committee, his ethics adviser, law professor and former Watergate majority counsel Sam Dash, resigned in protest over Starr's appearance before the committee. Dash accused Starr of unlawfully encroaching on the House's sole power of impeachment by appearing as an advocate of impeachment. Public opinion continued to veer away from removal of the president, with polls showing only 33 percent of the American people in favor of impeachment and 66 percent opposed. It may be that this particular impeachment attempt will have a greater impact on the independent counsel act under which Kenneth Starr operates than it will on the presidency. That, of course, remains to be seen.

As we put the finishing touches on this book, we are left with still unresolved issues surrounding the impeachment of President Clinton. The legal and factual question of whether the president's admitted "misleading statements" in a civil deposition amount to perjury has yet to be determined. More fundamental to the impeachment process is whether perjury in a civil deposition, if proved, amounts to a "high crime and misdemeanor" under the Constitution, subjecting the president to removal from office. The question of whether Congress can and will choose censure as an alternative to impeachment is unanswered.

For members of Congress and their constituents to make reasoned and reasonable judgments about the fate of Clinton's presidency it is important that we view the process with some historical background. In whatever fashion these questions ultimately are resolved, it is the purpose of this book to provide that backdrop of congressional precedent and history to facilitate any discussion of impeachable behavior.

Acknowledgments

This book was put together with lightning speed by publishing standards, and we would like to thank all the people who helped us to bring it together. Richard Aynes, Melvin Durchslag, Jonathan Entin, Michael Gerhardt, Dawn Kostuik, Katherine Nickras, Elizabeth Reilly, Paul Richert, and Sara Tarnow offered advice and assistance.

The editorial staff at Congressional Quarterly took on a difficult and unusual project on faith and made yeoman efforts to bring it to fruition. In particular, we would like to thank Pat Gallagher, Jon Preimesberger, Talia Greenberg, and Grace Hill.

Our spouses, Charlie Geyh and Byrgen Finkelman, made substantive contributions, offered advice, and kept us more or less on an even keel.

Finally, we would like to acknowledge the patience and forbearance of four very special people, Emily's children, Helen Hamilton "Hallie" Geyh and Sarah Gardner Van Tassel, and Paul's children, Abigail Beryl Finkelman and Isaac Chaim Finkelman.

Emily Field Van Tassel
Paul Finkelman

November 1998

Part I
INTRODUCTION

THE JUDICIARY COMMITTEE of the House of Representatives in November 1998 began considering whether to bring formal impeachment charges against President Bill Clinton. As this volume goes to press, the issue of impeachment is before the American people, and the question of what is an impeachable offense is being debated both in and out of the halls of Congress.

This is not a new debate. During the last two hundred years, Congress has launched more than sixty impeachment investigations of officers of the United States. From the Collector of the Port of New York to vice-consular officers in Shanghai, from judges and justices all the way to presidents of the United States, these investigations have been carried on under the authority of the United States Constitution, which states

The President, Vice President and all civil Officers of the United States, shall be removed from Office on Impeachment for, and Conviction of, Treason, Bribery, or other high Crimes and Misdemeanors.

But how has Congress determined what behavior constitutes "Treason, Bribery, or other high Crimes and Misdemeanors"? In all this time, and for all of its investigations, the House of Representatives has formally charged (that is, "impeached") U.S. officials only sixteen times, and only one of those was a president. Only seven times has the Senate convicted (that is, "removed") an officer on the House charges; never has a president been removed. Given the relative paucity of impeachments, figuring out what behavior should trigger the process seems very difficult. Treason is defined very specifically in the Constitution, and bribery has an accepted legal meaning.[1] But what are "other high Crimes and Misdemeanors"? Is Congress limited to removing only those officials whose misbehavior falls within those terms?

No definitive determination has ever been made about what behavior will result in impeachment. Congress has never passed a statute defining and cataloguing impeachable behavior. Arguably, it cannot. This volume provides selected documents that address the question of what has historically been considered an impeachable offense. The answer must remain am-

I

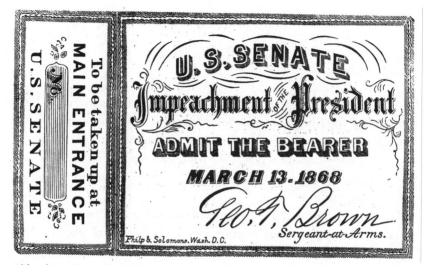

Although President Andrew Johnson did not attend, the two-and-a-half month long Senate trial drew a capacity crowd. Tickets were required for admission.

biguous, for in the end the legitimacy of the impeachment process and the outcome of impeachment trials remain deeply tied to the politics and the social context of the particular time in which individual cases arise.

Even so, these documents suggest that Congress has historically treated impeachment as more than just a moving political target. In every formal impeachment process, the House has struggled with how to proceed against the backdrop of history and its own precedents. The Senate has done the same in impeachment trials. For many members of Congress over the years, the gravity of the process has dictated seeking some principled basis on which to proceed in order to keep impeachment from being a partisan tool for removing political opponents. Principle has not always prevailed. But in decisions ranging from the refusal to remove Justice Samuel Chase for his political allegiance to an ousted party in 1804, to the refusal of a Republican Congress to remove the enormously unpopular and politically obstreperous President Andrew Johnson in 1868, members of Congress have consulted principle and their own precedents along with politics as guides.

What Is the Purpose of Impeachment?

The framers were concerned about the effects of power on those who would govern. Corruption and tyranny were the twin evils that the framers believed to be the inevitable results of excessive power. To prevent this abuse of power the framers crafted a government structure designed both to separate powers to avoid excessive concentration in any one person or group, and to blend powers to allow one branch to check and control the others. They created a system of checks and balances to allow one branch to check the power of the others. Impeachment is one checking power of the legislature to prevent corruption and tyranny from taking root in the executive or the judiciary branches.[2]

To guard against the selection or retention of unfit presidents and vice presidents, the Constitution provides for periodic elections. Frequent and regular elections mean that if the American people are unhappy with the job that these officers are doing, or disapprove of their behavior generally, they may turn them out of office. But what about a president or vice president who engages in behavior so egregious or so dangerous to the well-being of the state that the electorate ought not have to wait until the next election to be rid of him? To guard against the selection of weak, corrupt, or otherwise unfit judges, the Constitution requires the president and Congress to collaborate in the nomination and confirmation of candidates for judicial office. But what about judges who engage in odious behavior, but who ostensibly hold their offices for life? To provide a means for removing civil officers who abuse their power once in office, the impeachment process was devised as a grave remedy of last resort.

How Does the Impeachment Process Work?

Impeachment begins when the House passes a resolution to investigate the behavior of a government official. A House committee is then charged with investigating and reporting its findings back to the full House. The investigation may involve calling witnesses, examining evidence, and reviewing documents. Allegations of misbehavior have come to the attention of Congress through communications from the president, the public, members of Congress themselves, and most recently, from an independent prosecutor.

After the House committee completes its investigation, it generally makes a report to the House, recommending for or against impeachment. If the committee recommends impeachment, articles of impeachment are presented to the full House.[3] In a vote that represents the next step in the process, the House determines by majority vote whether the officer should be "impeached." A vote of impeachment means that the House has decided

to formally accuse an officer of serious misbehavior that should lead to removal if proved. Since the impeachment of Judge Robert W. Archbald in
1912 the House has elected to vote on articles of impeachment at the same
time as the vote on impeachment itself.

Much of the public drama of impeachment, as in other accusatory proceedings, occurs in the trial of the accused. This trial takes place in the
Senate. The House assigns "managers" to prosecute the accused official before the Senate sitting as a "high court of impeachments." Although managers have always been members of the House, the Constitution does not
require this, so it is possible that the House could appoint nonmembers
(such as committee staff, for instance) to prosecute an impeachment. In the
case of a presidential impeachment, the Constitution mandates that the
chief justice of the Supreme Court preside over the trial. The accused may
then appear and present evidence, summon witnesses, and cross-examine,
as in a regular trial.

If two-thirds of the senators vote to convict on any of the charges in the
bill of impeachment, the official impeached by the House stands convicted
by the Senate. The Senate cannot fine or imprison someone convicted in an
impeachment trial. As Rep. James A. Bayard, manager of the first federal
impeachment in 1798, said, "impeachment is a proceeding purely of a political nature. It is not so much designed to punish an offender, as to secure
the State. It touches neither his person nor his property, but simply divests
him of his political capacity." Conviction must result in removal under the
Constitution, which requires that officers "*shall* be removed from office"
upon impeachment and conviction, although the Senate has sometimes
cast a separate vote for removal.

In addition to removal from office, the Constitution provides that conviction may also lead to "disqualification to hold and enjoy any Office of
honor, Trust or Profit under the United States." The Senate has determined
that a simple majority, rather than a two-thirds majority, is sufficient to
vote for disqualification. The Senate has chosen to disqualify only two of
the seven officers it has removed. An officer convicted in an impeachment
process and removed from office is "nevertheless liable and subject to Indictment, Trial, Judgment and Punishment, according to Law."

The impeachment power has been rarely used, perhaps in part because
the process is lengthy, cumbersome, and inefficient. One of the most astute
chroniclers of American political culture, Englishman James Bryce,
likened impeachment to a "one hundred ton gun which needs complex ma-

chinery to bring it into position, an enormous charge of powder to fire it, and a large mark to aim at."[4] Thomas Jefferson gave up on impeachment after failing in his efforts to remove political opponents from the judiciary, calling the process "a bumbling affair" and a "mere scarecrow."[5] Yet impeachment has often served as an impressively big stick for persuading misbehaving government officials to resign.[6]

High Crimes and Misdemeanors

When the Constitution was crafted in Philadelphia in the summer of 1787, most of the debate on impeachment power was devoted to balancing the need to check unfettered power with the need to maintain the executive's independence from Congress. After tentatively agreeing to limit impeachable offenses to treason or bribery, the delegates returned to the topic to consider George Mason's proposal of adding "maladministration" to the list. Maladministration was a ground of impeachment found in some form in many of the state constitutions of the time. Mason feared that "Treason as defined in the Constitution will not reach many great and dangerous offenses," particularly "attempts to subvert the constitution." James Madison worried that "maladministration" was too vague, and would allow the Senate to remove the president at its pleasure. Madison's notes (see Document 2, p. 21) indicate that efforts to relax the impeachment standard to include "maladministration" were rebuffed on the grounds that so vague a standard would be "equivalent to tenure during pleasure of the Senate." The convention's vote to reject "maladministration" in favor of "other high Crimes and Misdemeanors" is the best evidence available that impeachable conduct must be substantively more than a job badly done.

In virtually every federal impeachment proceeding in U.S. history, the impeached officer has defended by claiming that the behavior charged has not amounted to an impeachable offense. Thus in many impeachment investigations and in most of the sixteen impeachments in U.S. history, an initial debate has occurred over what sorts of behavior should subject an official to removal from office. For instance, late in 1973 matters had come to a head for investigations of wrongdoing by President Richard Nixon. More than twenty impeachment resolutions had been introduced in the House. These were referred to the Democratic-controlled House Judiciary Committee, which was put under pressure by the Republican members to decide what constituted an impeachable offense before undertaking the investigation of the president. In response to the concerns for definition, the impeachment inquiry staff (which included twenty-six-year-old Hillary Rodham, future first lady and wife of Bill Clinton, who as president would also be a target of impeachment) submitted a memo concluding that

Because impeachment of a President is a grave step for the nation, it is to be predicated only upon conduct seriously incompatible with either the constitutional form and principles of our government or the proper performance of constitutional duties of the presidential office.[7]

President Nixon's lawyers sought a more restrictive definition, contending that "the words 'Treason, Bribery, and other high Crimes and Misdemeanors' are limited solely to indictable crimes and cannot extend to misbehavior." Addressing the contention that the word "misdemeanor" has historically meant general misbehavior rather than criminal misbehavior, the president's lawyers argued that "high Crimes and Misdemeanors"

was a unitary phrase meaning crimes against the State as opposed to those against individuals.... It is as ridiculous to say that "misdemeanor" must mean something beyond "crime" as it is to suggest that in the phrase "bread and butter issues" butter issues must be different from bread issues.[8]

This disagreement highlights only one of several recurring questions throughout the history of impeachment in America. To be impeachable, must behavior be criminally indictable? Must the behavior be done in an official capacity, or is purely private behavior impeachable? Are there different standards of behavior expected for different kinds of officers? If misbehavior does not rise to the level of impeachability, either legally or politically, is there some other action Congress may take to express disapproval, or even to punish the offending official? Can Congress arbitrarily determine what constitutes impeachable behavior? Can the courts review Congress's interpretation of what constitutes impeachable offenses?

What Is Impeachable Conduct?

Must behavior be criminally indictable to be impeachable?

It has often been contended that the phrase "high Crimes and Misdemeanors" means that impeachable behavior is only that which would subject an ordinary person to criminal indictment and prosecution. The history of impeachment suggests that Congress interprets the impeachment clause to include abuses of office that are not criminal.

For instance, District Judge Halsted L. Ritter was removed in the 1930s for misbehavior that included such things as showing favoritism in the appointment of bankruptcy receivers (see Document 20, p. 157). It may be that Congress is more comfortable removing an officer for a criminal offense, since it is easier to point to, identify, and agree on misbehavior if it has already been defined in a statute, but criminality is not a necessary component of "high Crimes and Misdemeanors."

The investigation of President Clinton presents the flip side of this question: Will any behavior that represents an ordinary crime be impeachable? What if a president committed perjury in a dismissed civil lawsuit involving an incident that occurred before he became president? Yale law professor Charles Black, in his impeachment handbook written during the investigation of Nixon in 1974, gives some possible insight. "Suppose," he asks, "a president transported a woman across a state line . . . for what is quaintly called an 'immoral purpose' " (a federal crime under the Mann Act)? "Or," he continues, "suppose the president actively assisted a young White House intern in concealing the latter's possession of three ounces of marijuana—thus himself becoming guilty of 'obstruction of justice.' "? Black concludes that it would be "preposterous" to think that this sort of behavior was what the framers contemplated when they crafted the impeachment clause to guide in the removal of high public officials. The history of impeachment suggests a mixed answer to this question, however.

Must the behavior be done in an official capacity, or is purely private behavior impeachable?
Prior to the impeachment and removal of District Judge Harry E. Claiborne in 1986 (see Document 21, p. 168), no officer had been removed for behavior that was wholly unconnected to the exercise of his or her office. Claiborne was convicted of and imprisoned for making false statements on two income tax returns. However, his removal seems clearly to have resulted from the disrepute his imprisonment brought on the office of judge, rather than from the underlying income tax issue. It is arguable, however, that unofficial behavior will be impeachable, if it is persistent enough and visible enough to bring the offender's public functions into disrepute.

Are there different standards of behavior expected for different kinds of officers?
Another question that has surfaced time and again is whether judges may be impeached for behavior that elected officials may not be impeached for, because of the constitutional statement that judges "shall hold their Offices during good Behaviour."

In 1970 Gerald R. Ford of Michigan sought the ouster of Supreme Court Justice William O. Douglas for what he considered to be disreputable, but not criminal, private behavior. In so doing, he distinguished between the standards of impeachment for judges, and all other civil officers, saying:

> In my view, one of the specific or general offenses cited in Article II [of the Constitution: Treason, bribery, or other high crimes and misdemeanors] is required for removal of the indirectly elected President and Vice President and all appointed civil officers of the executive branch of the Federal Government, whatever their terms of office. But in the case of members of the judicial branch, Federal judges and justices, I believe an additional and much stricter requirement is imposed by Article III, namely "good behavior."

For all other officials, therefore, Ford acknowledged the limits that the impeachment clause imposes.[9]

Impeachment has historically appeared to operate on different levels according to the official implicated in the process. Since impeachment is the only way, other than resignation or death, to get a federal judge off the bench, and since the Constitution mandates that federal judges hold their offices "during good behaviour," it may be that the standards for impeaching judges are different from those for officials who hold office for a limited term of years and who can be removed by the president or by voters through democratic elections.

The materials in this book allow for readers to judge whether Congress has made distinctions between officeholders. Certainly the lion's share of impeachments has been directed toward the judicial branch, suggesting a willingness on the part of Congress to allow democratic processes to weed out bad actors where the power to do so exists.

If misbehavior does not rise to the level of impeachability, either legally or politically, is there some other action Congress may take to express disapproval, or even to punish the offending official?

Another issue that has yet to be resolved is whether Congress may constitutionally punish or reprimand an officer of the United States using any method short of removal from office. Although the Constitution makes no mention of censuring or reprimanding a public official, there are precedents for such actions. In 1834 the Senate passed a resolution of censure against President Andrew Jackson (see Document 26, p. 204). Jackson argued that the resolution was unconstitutional and that if Congress disliked his behavior the only remedy was impeachment (see Document 27, p. 205). Congress later censured or condemned Presidents John Tyler and James Polk. The House Judiciary Committee has recommended censure rather than impeachment on several occasions (see p. 185). Sometimes these recommendations elicited protests similar to President Jackson's that censure of anyone outside of Congress is not a constitutional process, and denies the target of censure the opportunity to respond. Because Congress's intent in censuring federal officials has been far less clear and more ambiguous than its intent in impeachment cases, assessing the validity and utility of this alternative is difficult.

Can the courts review Congress's interpretation of what constitutes impeachable offenses?

What constitutes an impeachable offense is, to be sure, a political question, to be answered by Congress, not the courts. The Supreme Court in *Nixon v. U.S.* has so determined (see Document 35, p. 309). If the courts cannot review congressional action in impeachments, then what is to keep Congress from acting in an arbitrary fashion if it chooses to?

If there is no judicial review of the impeachment process, can Congress therefore arbitrarily determine what constitutes impeachable behavior?

By virtue of its characterization as a political question, some, such as Ford, and more recently House Majority Whip Tom DeLay, have argued that an impeachable high crime or misdemeanor is "whatever a majority of the House of Representatives considers it to be at a given moment in history." (See p. 41.) Such an argument is unassailable in the limited sense that however Congress interprets the impeachment standard, no court will likely intervene to second-guess that interpretation. But if the framers of the Constitution had intended to empower Congress to impeach and remove the president for whatever reasons it saw fit, it is unclear why they would have bothered to craft an impeachment standard limiting Congress to remove a president only upon conviction of treason, bribery, and other high crimes and misdemeanors. Debates at the Constitutional Convention underscored the framers' reluctance to give Congress free rein. Efforts to relax the impeachment standard by making civil officers liable to impeachment for "maladministration" were rebuffed. The real check on congressional arbitrariness is the democratic process. If Congress chooses to over-turn an election or an executive appointment arbitrarily, then the people will speak by removing offending members of Congress.

Impeachment in History

Notwithstanding the small number of actual impeachments that have occurred in the United States, the impeachment clause has not been one of the hidden or forgotten clauses of the U.S. Constitution. Within three years of the implementation of the new Constitution, the Capitol was ring-ing with cries for the impeachment en masse of the federal judiciary. The offense? Declaring an act of Congress unconstitutional.[10] Three years later, Congress was asked to impeach an Ohio territorial judge for "oppression and gross violations of private property under color of his office." Congress declined the invitation on grounds decidedly odd sounding to modern ears: it would be too expensive and difficult for Congress to try someone who lived so far away from the seat of government.[11]

By the end of the first decade, Congress was less concerned about dis-tance and expense, launching an impeachment trial against one of its own, Sen. William Blount (see Document 10, p. 86). In spite of the fact that Blount had already been expelled, the Senate chose to proceed with his trial, on the theory that even though he was no longer a senator, the Senate could still vote to disqualify him from holding and enjoying "any Office of honor, Trust or Profit under the United States."

Congress briefly experimented with using impeachment to remove po-litical opposition. The apparent success of this approach in the impeach-ment of Judge John Pickering (see Document 11, p. 91) was most likely a result of the judge's manifest disability (he was insane), rather than his pol-itics. Nevertheless, Congress was emboldened to move against the in-tensely partisan Supreme Court Justice Samuel Chase, voting articles of impeachment in the House on the same day that the Senate voted to con-vict Pickering. The Senate's subsequent refusal to convict Chase under-mined the validity of using impeachment for primarily partisan removals, at least for the next quarter century. Although contentious issues of eco-nomic policy and expansion caused showdowns between Congress and Presidents Jackson, Tyler, and Polk, Congress did not launch a serious im-peachment attempt in any of those cases.

The impeachment machinery was not completely dormant in the twenty-five years after the impeachment of Justice Chase; two officials resigned while under congressional investigation. The next impeachment was of Missouri district court judge James H. Peck in 1830.[12] (See Document 13, p. 107.) Peck was charged with only one offense, a noncriminal charge that he abused the contempt power. The Senate acquitted him, reinforcing the conclusion drawn from the Chase impeachment that judges ought not be removed for errors in judicial judgment. The House manager in Peck's case, future president James Buchanan, reacted to his defeat in removing Peck by successfully passing legislation to curtail the contempt power of federal judges.

No serious impeachment attempts were launched for thirty years after Judge Peck's acquittal. The next official to be impeached, Judge West H. Humphreys, was the only officer of the U.S. government who failed to resign after shifting his allegiance to the Confederacy during the Civil War. The removal of Judge Humphreys was a foregone conclusion (see Document 14, p. 114). It is an open question whether some of the things Humphreys was convicted for would be impeachable offenses if not done on behalf of an enemy government with whom the United States was at war. For instance, it is not clear that a federal official could be impeached for making a public speech in favor of the right of secession in the abstract. On the other hand, Humphreys was also convicted on the charge of failing to hold court as the law required (he was holding the district court for the Confederacy instead). It seems likely that even in peacetime, Congress would remove a judge for refusing to hold court altogether.

The impeachment of President Andrew Johnson in 1868 marked a watershed of sorts in the history of impeachment (see Document 28, p. 221). For the first time in history an American president was subjected to the full process of impeachment, all the way through trial. He escaped removal by one vote.

Short-lived and abortive impeachment moves were made against Presidents Herbert Hoover and Harry S. Truman, but another serious attempt to remove a president would not be made for over a century. For only the second time in American history the "hundred ton gun" of impeachment was brought into readiness and aimed at President Nixon in 1973–1974. Nixon resigned from office when it was clear that the House would vote articles of impeachment against him for a catalog of misdeeds in office. Although articles of impeachment were drawn up by the House Judiciary Committee, Nixon's resignation concluded the process before any votes were taken in the House. These votes might have provided precedents for further elaboration of what Congress considers to be impeachable behavior on the part of a president. Nevertheless, the Nixon impeachment investigation, in conjunction with the Johnson impeachment, provides the only historical applications of the impeachment clause to presidential behavior before the impeachment investigation of President Clinton.

In the interval between the impeachment of Johnson and the resignation of Nixon seven other officials were impeached. One cabinet officer, Secretary of War William W. Belknap, hurriedly resigned in 1876 to avoid impeachment after evidence came to light that he had effectively "sold" lucrative patronage jobs at his disposal (see Document 25, p. 191). The Senate's vote that Belknap's resignation did not deprive that body of jurisdiction to try Belknap leaves open the possibility that an official could be tried even after leaving office. As a practical matter, the fact that the Senate did not convict Belknap, suggests that except in extraordinary circumstances, resignation will bring the impeachment process to a close.[13]

The only two successful impeachment convictions of the nineteenth century resulted from circumstances unlikely to recur. Thus, they may not offer a great deal of instruction on what Congress is likely to deem impeachable in the future. Retirement and disability provisions for federal judges that have been put in place since Judge Pickering's time mean that the mental or physical disability of a judge will not bring the machinery of justice to a halt, and thus that impeachment for this reason will not be tried again.[14] The possibility of another civil war is sufficiently remote to make removing an official for failing to resign while serving an enemy government a relative curiosity. The successful twentieth-century impeachments, on the other hand, may offer more definitive clues to the meaning of "high crimes and misdemeanors." The convictions of Judge Robert W. Archbald in 1913 (see Document 17, p. 132) and Judge Halsted L. Ritter in 1936 (see Document 34, p. 304) were both based in part on abuses of their offices that were not criminal. Archbald was removed for using his office for personal gain, as was Ritter. These cases stand for the proposition that behavior need not be criminally indictable to warrant removal from office. In both cases, the behavior in question was linked to misbehavior in office either because the judge implied that litigants would receive preferential treatment for entering into business deals with him, or because the judge used the power of his office to bestow favors on friends.

The other solid precedent that has emerged is that the criminal *conviction and imprisonment* of a sitting federal judge, even for behavior that is wholly private, such as income tax evasion, will be sufficient to warrant removal. This was the case against Judge Harry E. Claiborne (see Document 21, p. 168). Although the Senate rejected an article that would have made criminal conviction and incarceration alone an impeachable offense, it nevertheless appears that in both Claiborne's case, and later, in Judge Nixon's case, that imprisonment made removal a foregone conclusion. What is not known is whether conviction alone, without incarceration, would be enough to bring behavior unrelated to the exercise of office into the realm of impeachable offenses. Had Judge Claiborne been fined instead of imprisoned, would he nevertheless have been removed? The case of Judge Alcee L. Hastings (see Document 22, p. 172) indicates that acquittal in a criminal proceeding will not save an official from impeachment, at least if the behavior is related to official functions. (Hastings had been accused of conspiring to solicit a bribe in a case appearing in his court.)

What appears to have emerged from the judicial impeachments is a two-part categorization of types of behavior that may lead to impeachment. Impeachment may follow official misbehavior that is not necessarily criminal, or personal behavior unconnected with the office that is criminal. Not all personal criminal behavior has resulted in impeachment, however. Vice President Aaron Burr presided over the impeachment trial of Justice Chase while under indictment in New York and New Jersey for the murder of Alexander Hamilton. He was not impeached. Whether personal behavior unconnected with office can be impeached if it is not criminal is unclear. In addition, there have not been enough judicial removals to say for certain whether the impeachability of private behavior is possible only because of the "good Behaviour" clause for federal judges, or whether removal for private behavior has been accomplished through an expansive interpretation of "high Crimes and Misdemeanors."

Conclusion

As *Ritter v. U.S.* (see Document 34, p. 304) and *Nixon v. U.S.* (see Document 35, p. 309) suggest, impeachment is a political process rife with "political questions" that the courts are reluctant to address. Unlike most constitutional questions, which are for the courts to decide, constitutional issues surrounding the impeachment process are ones the Constitution has assigned Congress to resolve. Hamilton explained why in *Federalist* No. 65 (see Document 3, p. 30). Removal by impeachment, argued Hamilton, is designed to remedy an "abuse or violation of some public trust." Who better than the public, through its representatives, to determine if the public trust has been abused or violated? Unlike most constitutional questions, then, where it is desirable for an independent judge to make an impartial decision, in the impeachment process, it is desirable for the decision makers to take the public's opinion into account.

Consistent with the sentiments reflected in the convention debates, Congress has declined to interpret its impeachment power as an unrestricted license to define "high Crimes and Misdemeanors" however it chooses. Instead, Congress has looked to the text of the Constitution, the intent of the framers, and the precedents it has developed over the course of previous impeachment proceedings to elucidate and limit the scope of impeachable offenses. The significance of the materials in this volume, then, goes beyond simply providing an historical context in which to better understand the impeachment process. Rather, these and related materials constitute the precedent upon which Congress can be expected to rely in defining the scope of impeachable conduct in future impeachment proceedings. In every formal impeachment process, the House of Representatives has struggled with how to proceed against the backdrop of history and its own precedents. This volume provides a substantial portion of the documentary precedents. History cannot dictate to us how to solve our problems, but it can surely help us better understand our circumstances and our options.

Whatever the ultimate outcome of the investigation of President Clinton, the question of what constitutes impeachable behavior will remain an important, although thankfully rare, issue for the American people. The documents published here are intended to inform discussion of that issue.

Notes

1. For all that, neither of these specific crimes has ever been explicitly charged in an impeachment. "Treason against the United States," the Constitution states, "shall consist only in levying War against them, or in adhering to their Enemies, giving them Aid and Comfort." For the contentious meaning of treason in the criminal context, see Paul Finkelman, "The Treason Trial of Castner Hanway," in Michal Belknap, ed., *American Political Trials,* Rev. ed. (Westport, Conn.: Greenwood, 1994), 77–96.

2. Impeachment has been thought by some to apply to members of Congress as well. However, the Constitution provides separately for congressional discipline and expulsion of its own members. Since the impeachment of Sen. William Blount in 1798, Congress has relied on expulsion rather than impeachment for removing wayward members.

3. The House may accept or not accept the committee's recommendation. In the case of Judge Harold Louderback in 1933 for instance, the committee recommended that the judge be censured, but not impeached. The House membership disagreed.

4. James Bryce, *The American Commonwealth* (1889) as quoted in Warren S. Grimes, "Hundred-Ton-Gun Control: Preserving Impeachment as the Exclusive Removal Mechanism for Federal Judges," *UCLA Law Review* 38 (1991), 1209.

5. Emily Field Van Tassel, "Resignations and Removals: A History of Federal Judicial Service and Disservice—1789 to 1992," *University of Pennsylvania Law Review* 142 (1993), 133.

6. Congress has not always accepted resignation as sufficient to stop the process, mainly because of the disqualification provision. However, since 1876 at least fourteen officers have avoided possible impeachments by resigning their offices while under investigation; Van Tassel, "Resignations and Removals," 421–422.

7. Watergate Inquiry Staff Report, 21–22.

8. "An Analysis of the Constitutional Standard for Presidential Impeachment," prepared by the attorneys for President Nixon.

9. A consensus seems to have developed about the "good Behaviour" clause and the oath of office, but too few impeachments of other officers have occurred to be able to make a reasoned judgment about whether judges are subject to a different standard, or whether Congress has developed a more expansive interpretation of high crimes and misdemeanors over time.

10. Three separate circuit courts, made up of members of the Supreme Court and district judges, had declared that an act for the relief of wounded revolutionary war veterans was unconstitutional. Charles Warren, *The Supreme Court in United States History* (Boston: Little, Brown, 1922), 70–79.

11. Van Tassel, "Resignations and Removals," 371–372.

12. Asher C. Hinds, ed. *Hinds' Precedents of the House of Representatives,* 5 vols. (Washington, D.C.: Government Printing Office, 1907).

13. Since Belknap, Congress has allowed two resignations to end formal impeachment proceedings, in the cases of Judge George W. English in 1926 and President Nixon in 1974.

14. Indeed, even before retirement and disability provisions were in place, Congress did not again try to remove a judge for mental or physical incapacity, even in the case of Supreme Court justices. Toward the end of his life, for instance, Supreme Court Justice Henry Baldwin's "intellect became deranged, and he was violent and ungovernable in his conduct on the bench." Yet he died in office in 1844 with no attempt having been made to remove him like Judge Pickering. Van Tassel, "Resignations and Removals," 395–405.

Part II

IN THE BEGINNING: THE FRAMERS'
UNDERSTANDING OF IMPEACHMENT

IMPEACHMENT AS A MEANS for removing public officials from office dates back to fourteenth-century England and was familiar to the American colonists, who incorporated impeachment procedures into their state constitutions after the Declaration of Independence. As Benjamin Franklin pointed out, the alternative form of removal, in predemocratic contexts, was assassination. Even so, some delegates to the Constitutional Convention in 1787 opposed inclusion of impeachment provisions in the proposed Constitution, on the grounds that an impeachment process would make the president dependent on whichever branch of government was delegated the impeachment power. They felt that the removal of unpopular presidents would be better achieved through the electoral process. The majority, however, thought that impeachment was essential to guard against an official who, in James Madison's words, might "pervert his administration into a scheme of peculation or oppression," or who "might betray his trust to foreign powers."

Once the delegates accepted the need for an impeachment process, two issues dominated the discussion: who was subject to impeachment, and who would possess the impeachment power. With respect to who could be impeached, some delegates recognized that the process would apply to judges, and at least one proposal explicitly applied it to members of Congress as well. The delegates were so preoccupied with the impeachment process as it pertained to the president, however, that they devoted very little discussion to the desirability of its use on members of the other branches.

With respect to who would possess the impeachment power, the initial plan provided for the national judiciary to have jurisdiction over "impeachments of any National officers." The convention ultimately abandoned this approach on the grounds that the Supreme Court, given its small size, could be too easily "warped or corrupted." The delegates also rejected other proposals empowering Congress to remove the president on the request of a majority of the state governors or legislatures, in part because they would give less populous states too much control over the presidency. The convention ultimately settled on giving the House the power to impeach, and the Senate the power to try all impeachments, notwithstanding the reluctance of some delegates to make the president so dependent on Congress.

To reduce the risk that Congress might abuse its impeachment power, some delegates made the effort to refine the definition of impeachable offenses. Characterizations of impeachable conduct offered at different stages of the convention, in debates and proposals, varied widely, and included among others: "misfeasance," "misconduct," "malpractice or neglect of duty," "mal– and corrupt conduct," "incapacity, negligence or perfidy," "treachery," and "bribery." Toward the end of the convention, however, after the delegates had decided to give Congress the impeachment power, they tentatively agreed to limit impeachable offenses to "treason or bribery."

On September 8, 1787, the delegates held a short discussion of the impeachment clause. George Mason proposed to add "maladministration" to the list, arguing that "Treason as defined in the Constitution will not reach many great and dangerous offenses," such as "attempts to subvert the constitution." James Madison, however, sharing the reservations of those reluctant to give Congress the impeachment power, objected to the Mason proposal, arguing that "so vague a term {as "maladministration"} will be equivalent to a tenure during pleasure of the Senate." In other words, without some more definite statement of what would be impeachable, the Senate might be given license to remove anyone who displeased a majority of the Senate. In response to this concern, Mason withdrew his proposal and replaced "maladministration" with "high Crimes and Misdemeanors," which was accepted. The convention thus explicitly rejected "maladministration" as a basis for impeachment, in spite of the fact that many state constitutions of the time did have maladministration as an impeachment ground.

After the Constitution was drafted, the question became whether the states would ratify it—an issue debated at conventions held in each state. Although much was written for and against the proposed Constitution, the most famous work, penned by Alexander Hamilton, John Jay, and James Madison under the pseudonym "Publius," appeared in the form of a series of newspaper articles later known as *The Federalist Papers*. These articles, which Thomas Jefferson called "the best commentary on the principles of government which was ever written," explained and defended the proposed Constitution. In the seminal case of *McCulloch v. Maryland,* Chief Justice John Marshall wrote that "the opinions expressed by the authors of {The

Federalist Papers] have been justly supposed to be entitled to great respect in expounding the Constitution," and to this day *The Federalist Papers* stand as the single most important exposition of the "original intentions" of those who framed the Constitution.

In *Federalist* No. 65, Hamilton offered an interpretive gloss on the impeachment process and the meaning of "high Crimes and Misdemeanors." He took pains to emphasize that impeachment was a remedy for offenses "which may with peculiar propriety be denominated *political,*" and which arise from "the abuse or violation of some public trust." He defended the decision to give Congress the impeachment power, on the grounds that the public's representatives were in the best position to determine when the public's trust had been violated, and hence when a high crime or misdemeanor had occurred.

In *Federalist* No. 66, Hamilton sought to answer a number of objections that had been raised against lodging the removal power in the Senate. The first objection noted that giving the Senate the power to try and convict government officials was akin to giving some of the judicial power to the Senate, an apparent violation of the separation of governmental powers into three branches. The second was that giving the Senate the removal power would make it *too* powerful; it would be able to exert excessive control over the other branches. The third noted the Senate's role in confirming presidential appointments, questioning whether pride might keep the senators from voting to remove an official they had earlier confirmed. Finally, critics of senatorial removal power objected because senators might conspire with the president to make treacherous, corrupt, or ruinous treaties, and then escape the punishment of impeachment because they would not impeach themselves.

These objections reassert themselves in various later impeachment controversies, making Hamilton's answers of consequence beyond convincing Americans to ratify the Constitution. For instance, the separation of powers issue would arise in Judge Walter L. Nixon's judicial challenge to the Senate's trial practices (see Document 35, p. 309). The question of whether members of Congress are impeachable was central in the impeachment of Sen. William Blount just six years later (see Document 10, p. 86). Implicit in Hamilton's answer to the final question is an understanding that members of Congress might be individually but not collectively impeached.

The documents from our founding period ultimately raise as many questions as they answer. The framers clearly adopted an impeachment mechanism as a means to remove corrupt public officials who abuse the trust that the electorate places in them. Beyond that, they failed to address the following issues: Which officials in what branches of government are subject to impeachment? Does an official remain subject to impeachment proceedings after leaving office? When does official conduct cease to be merely objectionable behavior—best remedied in the next election—and become a high crime or misdemeanor warranting removal by impeachment? These and other questions were left for subsequent generations to resolve.

❧ I ❧

Selected Provisions of the Constitution
(1787)

THE FOLLOWING SECTIONS of the U.S. Constitution are those that relate to impeachment. Of particular relevance, of course, is the impeachment clause itself. Article II, Section 4 states that removal from office will follow impeachment for, and conviction of, "Treason, Bribery, or other high Crimes and Misdemeanors."

Article I

SECTION 2. The House of Representatives . . . shall have the sole Power of Impeachment.

SECTION 3. The Senate shall have the sole Power to try all Impeachments. When sitting for that Purpose, they shall be on Oath or Affirmation. When the President of the United States is tried, the Chief Justice shall preside: And no Person shall be convicted without the Concurrence of two thirds of the Members present.

Judgment in Cases of Impeachment shall not extend further than to removal from Office, and disqualification to hold and enjoy any Office of honor, Trust or Profit under the United States: but the Party convicted shall nevertheless be liable and subject to Indictment, Trial, Judgment and Punishment, according to Law.

Article II

SECTION 2. The President . . . shall have Power to grant Reprieves and Pardons for Offences against the United States, except in Cases of Impeachment.

SECTION 4. The President, Vice President and all civil Officers of the United States, shall be removed from Office on Impeachment for, and Conviction of, Treason, Bribery, or other high Crimes and Misdemeanors.

Article III

SECTION 1. The Judges, both of the supreme and inferior Courts, shall hold their Offices during good Behaviour.

SECTION 2. The Trial of all Crimes, except in Cases of Impeachment, shall be by Jury. . . .

SECTION 3. Treason against the United States, shall consist only in levying War against them, or in adhering to their Enemies, giving them Aid and Comfort. No Person shall be convicted of Treason unless on the Testimony of two Witnesses to the same overt Act, or on Confession in open Court.

❧ 2 ❧

James Madison's Notes on the Constitutional Convention
(1787)

THE CONSTITUTIONAL CONVENTION that convened in Philadelphia in 1787 met in secrecy. The primary record of the convention are the notes that Virginia's James Madison took during the four months the delegates toiled. Madison's notes, published after his death, record some of the debates the framers engaged in as they crafted an entirely novel governmental structure. Most of the discussion on impeachment centered on the executive; very little was devoted to the question of removing other officers, including judges.

These debates illustrate the tensions that the framers felt about the problem of executive misconduct. They were clearly concerned about the public interest and the possible betrayal of the nation. They feared that some future president might sell out the nation for personal gain or to increase his personal power. On the other hand, they also understood the danger of legislative tyranny over the executive. Some of the delegates, especially Madison, a future president, and James Wilson of Pennsylvania, a future Supreme Court justice, understood that national success was only possible with, what Wilson calls "the vigor of the government." Indeed, he argued that the "tranquility" of the government was tied to its vigor.[1] Even Virginia delegate George Mason, who favored a weak executive, admitted that among the advantages of a strong executive were "the secresy, the dispatch, the vigor and energy which the government will derive from it."[2]

🐜 🐜 🐜

The following are excerpts from Max Farrand, ed., *The Records of the Federal Convention of 1787,* rev. ed. (New Haven, Conn.: Yale University Press, 1966).

* * *

June 1. Gunning Bedford of Delaware, opposing the seven year term for the President.

Mr. Bedford was strongly opposed to so long a term as seven years. He begged the committee to consider what the situation of the Country would be, in case the magistrate should be saddled on it for such period and it should be found on trial that he did not possess the qualifications ascribed to him, or should lose them after his appointment. An impeachment he said would be no cure for this evil, as an impeachment would reach misfeasance only, not incapacity. He was for a triennial election, and for an ineligibility after a period of nine years.

* * *

June 2. In a debate over how the President should be chosen, and removed from office the Convention rejected John Dickinson's suggestion that the state governors be able to ask for the removal of the president by a simple majority of the national legislature. Instead, the Convention adopts an "impeachment" scheme.

Mr. Dickenson moved "that the Executive be made removeable by the National Legislature on the request of a majority of the Legislatures of individual States." It was necessary he said to place the power of removing somewhere. He did not like the plan of impeaching the Great Officers of State. He did not know how provision could be made for removal of them in a better mode than that which he had proposed. He had no idea of abolishing the State Governments as some gentlemen seemed inclined to do. The happiness of this Country in his opinion required considerable powers to be left in the hands of the States.

Mr. Bedford seconded the motion.

Mr. Sherman contended that the National Legislature should have power to remove the Executive at pleasure. . . .

Mr. Mason. Some mode of displacing an unfit magistrate is rendered indispensable by the fallibility of those who choose, as well as by the corruptibility of the man chosen. He opposed decidedly the making the Executive the mere creature of the Legislature as a violation of the fundamental principle of good Government.

Mr. [Madison] & Mr. Wilson Observed that it would leave an equality of agency in the small with the great States; that it would enable a minority of the people to prevent ye removal of an officer who had rendered himself justly criminal in the eyes of a majority; that it would open a door for intrigues agst. him in States where his administration tho' just might be unpopular, and might tempt him to pay court to particular States whose leading partizans he might fear, or wish to engage as his partizans. They both thought it bad policy <to introduce such a mixture> of the State authorities, when their agency could be otherwise supplied. . . .

A motion, being made to strike out "on request by a majority of the Legislatures of the individual States" and rejected, Connecticut. S. Carol: & Geo. being ay. the rest no: the question was taken—

On Mr. Dickenson's motion for making Executive removeable by Natl. Legislature at request of majority of State Legislatures <was also rejected. all the States <being in the negative> except Delaware which <gave an> affirmative vote.

The Question for making ye. Executive ineligible after seven years, (was next taken, and agreed to:)

Massts. ay. Cont. no. N Y—ay Pa. divd. Del. ay. Maryd. ay. Va. ay. N.C. ay. S.C. ay. Geo. no: [Ayes—7; noes—2; divided—1.]

Mr. Williamson 2ded. by Mr. Davie moved to add to the last Clause, the words— "and to be removeable on impeachment & conviction of mal-practice or neglect of duty"—which was agreed to.

* * *

June 13. During the debate over the national judiciary:

It was moved by Mr Randolph seconded by Mr Madison to adopt the following resolution respecting the national Judiciary namely "That the jurisdiction of the national Judiciary shall extend to cases which respect the collection of the national revenue, impeachments of any national officers, and questions which involve the national peace and harmony"

passed in the affirmative

* * *

July 18. The Convention turned to the way judges should be chosen.

Mr Mason. The mode of appointing the Judges may depend in some degree on the mode of trying impeachments, of the Executive. If the Judges were to form a tribunal for that purpose, they surely ought not to be appointed by the Executive. There were insuperable objections besides agst. referring the appointment to the Executive. He mentioned as one, that as the seat of Govt. must be in some one State, and the Executive would remain in office for a considerable time, for 4, 5, or 6 years at least he would insensibly form local & personal attachments within the particular State that would deprive equal merit elsewhere, of an equal chance of promotion.

The Constitution lays out the powers and duties of the three branches of government and outlines the causes for impeachment. Here the framers take turns signing their names to the Constitution.

Mr. Govr. Morris supposed it would be improper for an impeachmt. Of the Executive to be tried before the Judges. The latter would in such case be drawn into intrigues with the Legislature and an impartial trial would be frustrated. As they wd. be much about the seat of Govt they might even be previously consulted & arrangements might be made for a prosecution of the Executive. He thought therefore that no argument could be drawn from the probability of such a plan of impeachments agst. the motion before the House.

Mr. M(adison), suggested that the Judges might be appointed by the Executives with the concurrence of (1/3 at least) of the 2d. branch. This would unite the advantage of responsibility in the Executive with the security afforded in the 2d. branch agst. any incautious or corrupt nomination by the Executive.

* * *

July 18 (later in the day). After some debate (see above) the Convention took impeachment out of the hands of the judges.

13. Resol: ("Impeachments of national officers" were struck out on motion for the purpose.) "The jurisdiction of Natl. Judiciary." Several criticisms having been made on the definition; it was proposed by Mr (Madison) so to alter as to read thus—"that the jurisdiction shall extend to all cases arising under the Natl. laws: And to such other questions as may involve the Natl. peace & harmony." which was agreed to nem. con.

* * *

July 19. The Convention reconsidered its decision of the previous day to allow the executive to be eligible for more than one term in office. This led to a long speech by Gouverneur Morris in which he discussed impeachments.

Mr. Governeur Morris. . . . The Executive is also to be impeachable. This is a danger-ous part of the plan. It will hold him in such dependence that he will be no check on the Legislature, will not be a firm guardian of the people and of the public interest. He will be the tool of a faction, of some leading demagogue in the Legislature. These then are the faults of the Executive establishment as now proposed. Can no better es-tablishmt. be devised? If he is to be the Guardian of the people let him be appointed by the people? If he is to be a check on the Legislature let him not be impeachable. Let him be of short duration, that he may with propriety be re-eligible.—It has been said that the candidates for this office will not be known to the people. If they be known to the Legislature, they must have such a notoriety and eminence of Charac-ter, that they cannot possibly be unknown to the people at large. It cannot be possi-ble that a man shall have sufficiently distinguished himself to merit this high trust without having his character proclaimed by fame throughout the Empire. As to the danger from an unimpeachable magistrate he could not regard it as formidable. There must be certain great officers of State; a minister of finance, of war, of foreign affairs &c. These he presumes will exercise their functions in subordination to the Executive, and will be amenable by impeachment to the public Justice. Without these ministers the Executive can do nothing of consequence. He suggested a bien-nial election of the Executive at the time of electing the 1st. branch, and the Execu-tive to hold over, so as to prevent any interregnum in the Administration. . . .

* * *

July 19 (later in the day). Morris argued that short terms for the executive would prevent the need for impeachments.

Mr. Govr Morris was for a short term, in order to avoid impeachts. which wd. be oth-erwise necessary.

* * *

July 20. The Convention had a long and heated debate over the impeach-ment of the executive. It was on the resolution that the executive should be "removable on impeachment and conviction." After the debate a motion to pospone lost 2 to 8 and then the clause passed 8 to 2.

"to be removeable on impeachment and conviction (for) malpractice or neglect of duty." See Resol: 9:

Mr. Pinkney & Mr Govr. Morris moved to strike out this part of the Resolution.

Mr P. observd. he (ought not to) be impeachable whilst in office

Mr. Davie. If he be not impeachable whilst in office, he will spare no efforts or means whatever to get himself re-elected. He considered this as an essential security for the good behaviour of the Executive.

Mr Wilson concurred in the necessity of making the Executive impeachable whilst in office.

Mr. Govr. Morris. He can do no criminal act without Coadjutors who may be pun-ished. In case he should be re-elected, that will be sufficient proof of his innocence. Be-sides who is to impeach? Is the impeachment to suspend his functions. If it is not the mischief will go on. If it is the impeachment will be nearly equivalent to a displace-ment, and will render the Executive dependent on those who are to impeach

Col. Mason. No point is of more importance than that the right of impeachment should be continued. Shall any man be above Justice? Above all shall that man be above it, who can commit the most extensive injustice? When great crimes were committed he was for punishing the principal as well as the Coadjutors. There had been much debate & difficulty as to the mode of chusing the Executive. He approved of that which had been adopted at first, namely of referring the appointment to the Natl. Legislature. One objection agst. Electors was the danger of their being corrupted by the Candidates: & this furnished a peculiar reason in favor of impeachments whilst in office. Shall the man who has practised corruption & by that means procured his appointment in the first instance, be suffered to escape punishment, by repeating his guilt?

Docr. Franklin was for retaining the clause as favorable to the executive. History furnishes one example only of a first Magistrate being formally brought to public Justice. Every body cried out agst this as unconstitutional. What was the practice before this in cases where the chief Magistrate rendered himself obnoxious? Why recourse was had to assassination in wch. he was not only deprived of his life but of the opportunity of vindicating his character. It wd. be the best way therefore to provide in the Constitution for the regular punishment of the Executive when his misconduct should deserve it, and for his honorable acquittal when he should be unjustly accused.

Mr. Govr Morris admits corruption & some few other offences to be such as ought to be impeachable; but thought the cases ought to be enumerated & defined:

Mr. (Madison)—thought it indispensable that some provision should be made for defending the Community agst the incapacity, negligence or perfidy of the chief Magistrate. The limitation of the period of his service, was not a sufficient security. He might lose his capacity after his appointment. He might pervert his administration into a scheme of peculation or oppression. He might betray his trust to foreign powers. The case of the Executive Magistracy was very distinguishable, from that of the Legislative or of any other public body, holding offices of limited duration. It could not be presumed that all or even a majority of the members of an Assembly would either lose their capacity for discharging, or be bribed to betray, their trust. Besides the restraints of their personal integrity & honor, the difficulty of acting in concert for purposes of corruption was a security to the public. And if one or a few members only should be seduced, the soundness of the remaining members, would maintain the integrity and fidelity of the body. In the case of the Executive Magistracy which was to be administered by a single man, loss of capacity or corruption was more within the compass of probable events, and either of them might be fatal to the Republic.

Mr. Pinkney did not see the necessity of impeachments. He was sure they ought not to issue from the Legislature who would in that case hold them as a rod over the Executive and by that means effectually destroy his independence. His revisionary power in particular would be rendered altogether insignificant.

Mr. Gerry urged the necessity of impeachments. A good magistrate will not fear them. A bad one ought to be kept in fear of them. He hoped the maxim would never be adopted here that the chief Magistrate could do (no) wrong.

Mr. King expressed his apprehensions that an extreme caution in favor of liberty might enervate the Government we were forming. He wished the House to recur to the primitive axiom that the three great departments of Govts. should be separate & independent: that the Executive & Judiciary should be so as well as the Legislative: that the Executive should be so equally with the Judiciary. Would this be the case if the Executive should be impeachable? It had been said that the Judiciary would be impeachable. But it should have been remembered at the same time that the Judiciary hold their places not for a limited time, but during good behaviour. It is necessary therefore that a forum should be established for trying misbehaviour. Was the Executive to hold his place during good behaviour?—The Executive was to hold his place for a limited term like the members of the Legislature; Like them particularly the Senate whose members would continue in appointmt the same term of 6 years. he would periodically be tried for his behaviour by his electors, who would continue or discontinue him in trust according to the manner in which he had discharged it. Like them therefore, he ought to be subject to no intermediate trial, by impeachment. He ought not to be impeachable unless he hold his office during good behavior, a tenure which would be most agreeable to him; provided an independent and effectual forum could be devised; But under no circumstances ought he to be impeachable by the Legislature. This would be destructive of his independence and of the principles of the Constitution. He relied on the vigor of the Executive as a great security for the public liberties.

Mr. Randolph. The propriety of impeachments was a favorite principle with him; Guilt wherever found ought to be punished. The Executive will have great opportunitys of abusing his power; particularly in time of war when the military force, and in some respects the public money will be in his hands. Should no regular punishment be provided, it will be irregularly inflicted by tumults & insurrections. He is aware of the necessity of proceeding with a cautious hand, and of excluding as much as possible the influence of the Legislature from the business. He suggested for consideration an idea which had fallen (from Col Hamilton) of composing a forum out of the Judges belonging to the States: and even of requiring some preliminary inquest whether just grounds of impeachment existed.

Doctr. Franklin mentioned the case of the Prince of Orange during the late war. An agreement was made between France & Holland; by which their two fleets were to unite at a certain time & place. The Du<t>ch fleet did not appear. Every body began to wonder at it. At length it was suspected that the Statholder was at the bottom of the matter. This suspicion prevailed more & more. Yet as he could not be impeached and no regular examination took place, he remained in his office, and strengtheing his own party, as the party opposed to him became formidable, he gave birth to the most violent animosities & contentions. Had he been impeachable, a regular & peaceable inquiry would have taken place and he would if guilty have been duly punished, if innocent restored to the confidence of the public.

Mr. King remarked that the case of the Statholder was not applicable. He held his place for life, and was not periodically elected. In the former case impeachments are proper to secure good behaviour. In the latter they are unnecessary; the periodical responsibility to the electors being an equivalent security.

Mr Wilson observed that if the idea were to be pursued, the Senators who are to hold their places during the same term with the Executive. ought to be subject to impeachment & removal.

Mr. Pinkney apprehended that some gentlemen reasoned on a supposition that the Executive was to have powers which would not be committed to him: (He presumed) that his powers would be so circumscribed as to render impeachments unnecessary.

Mr. Govr. Morris's opinion had been changed by the arguments used in the discussion. He was now sensible of the necessity of impeachments, if the Executive was to continue for any time in office. Our Executive was not like a Magistrate having a life interest, much less like one having an hereditary interest in his office. He may be bribed by a greater interest to betray his trust; and no one would say that we ought to expose ourselves to the danger of seeing the first Magistrate in foreign pay without being able to guard agst it by displacing him. One would think the King of England well secured agst bribery. He has as it were a fee simple in the whole Kingdom. Yet Charles II was bribed by Louis XIV. The Executive ought therefore to be impeachable for treachery; Corrupting his electors, and incapacity were other causes of impeachment. For the latter he should be punished not as a man, but as an officer, and punished only by degradation from his office. This Magistrate is not the King but the prime-Minister. The people are the King. When we make him amenable to Justice however we should take care to provide some mode that will not make him dependent on the Legislature.

(It was moved & 2ded. to postpone the question of impeachments which was negatived. Mas. & S. Carolina only being ay.)

On ye. Question, Shall the Executive be removeable on impeachments? Mas. no. Ct. ay. N.J. ay. Pa. ay. Del. ay. Md. ay. Va. ay. N.C. ay. S.C. no. Geo ay- [Ayes—8; noes—2.]

* * *

Sept. 4. Report of the Committee of Eleven.

The latter part of the 2 sect 10 art to read as follows.

He shall be removed from his office on impeachment by the House of representatives, and conviction by the Senate, for treason or bribery, and in case of his removal as aforesaid, death, absence, resignation or inability to discharge the powers or duties of his office the Vice President shall exercise those powers and duties until another President be chosen, or until the inability of the President be removed.

On the question to agree to the first clause of the report.

it passed in the affirmative

* * *

September 8. The final wording of the impeachment clause created at the last moment.

The clause referring to the Senate, the trial of impeachments agst. the President, for Treason & bribery, was taken up.

Col. Mason. Why is the provision restrained to Treason & bribery only? Treason as defined in the Constitution will not reach many great and dangerous offences.

Hastings is not guilty of Treason. Attempts to subvert the Constitution may not be Treason as above defined—As bills of attainder which have saved the British Constitution are forbidden, it is the more necessary to extend: the power of impeachments. He movd. to add after "bribery" "or maladministration."

Mr. Gerry seconded him—

Mr Madison So vague a term will be equivalent to a tenure during pleasure of the Senate.

Mr Govr Morris, it will not be put in force & can do no harm—An election of every four years will prevent maladministration.

Col. Mason withdrew "maladministration" & substitutes "other high crimes & misdemeanors" (agst. the State)

On the question thus altered

N.H—ay. Mas. ay—Ct. ay. (N.J. no) Pa no. Del. no. Md ay. Va. ay. N.C. ay. S.C. ay. Geo. ay. [Ayes—8; noes—3.]

Mr. Madison, objected to a trial of the President by the Senate especially as he was to be impeached by the other branch of the Legislature, and for any act which might be called a misdemesnor. The President under these circumstances was made improperly dependent. He would prefer the supreme Court for the trial of impeachments, or rather a tribunal of which that should form a part.

Mr Govr Morris thought no other tribunal than the Senate could be trusted. The Supreme Court were too few in number and might be warped or corrupted. He was agst. a dependence of the Executive on the Legislature, considering the Legislative tyranny the great danger to be apprehended; but there could be no danger that the Senate would say untruly on their oaths that the President was guilty of crimes or facts, especially as in four years he can be turned out.—

Mr Pinkney disapproved of making the Senate the Court of Impeachments, as rendering the President too dependent on the Legislature. If he opposes a favorite law, the two Houses will combine agst him, and under the influence of heat and faction throw him out of office.

Mr. Williamson thought there was more danger of too much lenity than of too much rigour towards the President, considering the number of cases in which the Senate was associated with the President—

Mr Sherman regarded the Supreme Court as improper to try the President, because the Judges would be appointed by him.

On motion by Mr. Madison to strike out the words—"by the Senate" after the word "Conviction"

N–H. no. Mas—no. Ct. no. N.J. no—Pa. ay—Del—no. Md. no. Va. ay—N.C. no. S.C.—no. Geo. no. (Ayes—2; noes—9.]

In the amendment of Col: Mason just agreed to, the word "State" after the words "misdemeanors against" was struck out, and the words "United States" inserted, (unanimously) in order to remove ambiguity—

On the question to agree to clause as amended,

N.H. ay. Mas. ay. (Cont ay) N.J. ay. Pa. no. (Del. ay) Md. ay—Va. ay. N.C. ay. S.C. ay. Geo. ay [Ayes—10; noes—1.]

* * *

Mr. Govr Morris moved to add to clause (3) of the report made on Sept. 4. the words "and every member shall be on oath" which being agreed to, and a question taken on the clause (so amended) viz—"The Senate of the U.S. shall have power to try all impeachments: but no person shall be convicted without the concurrence of two thirds of the members present: and every member shall be on oath"
    N.H. ay.—Mas. ay. Ct. ay. N.J.—ay. Pa. no—Del—(p. 553) ay—
    Md ay. Va. no. N.C. ay. S.C. ay. Geo. ay. [Ayes—9; noes—2.]

* * *

September 14. Even at the last days of the convention Rutledge and Morris were unhappy with the impeachment provisions.

Mr Rutledge and Mr. Govr. Morris moved "that persons impeached be suspended from their office until they be tried and acquitted"
    Mr. Madison—The President is made too dependent already on the Legislature, by the power of one branch to try him in consequence of an impeachment by the other. This intermediate suspension, will put him in the power of one branch only— They can at any moment, in order to make way for the functions of another who will be more favorable to their views, vote a temporary removal of the existing magis-trate—Mr. King (concurred) in the opposition to the amendment
    On the question to agree to it: N.H. no. Mas. no—Ct. ay— N.J. no. Pa. no. Del—no. Md no. Va. no. N.C. no. S.C. ay, Geo. ay, [Ayes—3; noes—8.]

Notes

1. Max Farrand, ed., *The Records of the Federal Convention of 1787* (New Haven, Conn.: Yale University Press, 1913), 1:96.
    2. Farrand, 1:112.

≈§ 3 §≈

The Federalist Papers, Nos. 65 and 66

(1788)

A FTER THE CONSTITUTION was drafted, attention shifted to the states, where individual ratifying conventions were held to consider the proposed new government. Alexander Hamilton, John Jay, and James Madison wrote a series of newspaper articles, eighty-five in all, to explain and defend the Constitution. These would later be gathered together and published as *The Federalist Papers. Federalist* No. 65 and No. 66, were written by Alexander Hamilton to the citizens of New York to explain the impeachment clause and answer objections that had been raised to it.

FEDERALIST NO. 65

To the People of the State of New York:

The remaining powers which the plan of the convention allots to the Senate, in a distinct capacity, are comprised in their participation with the executive in the appointment to offices, and in their judicial character as a court for the trial of impeachments. As in the business of appointments the executive will be the principal agent, the provisions relating to it will most properly be discussed in the examination of that department. We will, therefore, conclude this head with a view of the judicial character of the Senate.

A well-constituted court for the trial of impeachments is an object not more to be desired than difficult to be obtained in a government wholly elective. The subjects of its jurisdiction are those offenses which proceed from the misconduct of public men, or, in other words, from the abuse or violation of some public trust. They are of a nature which may with peculiar propriety be denominated *political,* as they relate chiefly to injuries done immediately to the society itself. The prosecution of them, for this reason, will seldom fail to agitate the passions of the whole community, and to divide it into parties more or less friendly or inimical to the accused. In many cases it will connect itself with the pre-existing factions, and will enlist all their animosities, partialities, influence, and interest on one side or on the other; and in such cases there will always be the greatest danger that the decision will be regulated more by the comparative strength of parties, than by the real demonstrations of innocence or guilt.

The delicacy and magnitude of a trust which so deeply concerns the political reputation and existence of every man engaged in the administration of public affairs, speak for themselves. The difficulty of placing it rightly, in a government resting entirely on the basis of periodical elections, will as readily be perceived, when it is considered that the most conspicuous characters in it will, from that circumstance, be too often the leaders or the tools of the most cunning or the most numerous faction, and on this account, can hardly be expected to possess the requisite neutrality towards those whose conduct may be the subject of scrutiny.

The convention, it appears, thought the Senate the most fit depositary of this important trust. Those who can best discern the intrinsic difficulty of the thing, will be least hasty in condemning that opinion, and will be most inclined to allow due weight to the arguments which may be supposed to have produced it.

What, it may be asked, is the true spirit of the institution itself? Is it not designed as a method of *national inquest* into the conduct of public men? If this be the design of it, who can so properly be the inquisitors for the nation as the representatives of the nation themselves? It is not disputed that the power of originating the inquiry, or, in other words, of preferring the impeachment, ought to be lodged in the hands of one branch of the legislative body. Will not the reasons which indicate the propriety of this arrangement strongly plead for an admission of the other branch of that body to a share of the inquiry? The model from which the idea of this institution has been borrowed, pointed out that course to the convention. In Great Britain it is the province of the House of Commons to prefer the impeachment, and of the House of Lords to decide upon it. Several of the State constitutions have followed the example. As well the latter, as the former, seem to have regarded the practice of impeachments as a bridle in the hands of the legislative body upon the executive servants of the government. Is not this the true light in which it ought to be regarded?

Where else than in the Senate could have been found a tribunal sufficiently dignified, or sufficiently independent? What other body would be likely to feel *confidence enough in its own situation,* to preserve, unawed and uninfluenced, the necessary impartiality between an *individual* accused, and the *representatives of the people, his accusers?*

Could the Supreme Court have been relied upon as answering this description? It is much to be doubted, whether the members of that tribunal would at all times be endowed with so eminent a portion of fortitude, as would be called for in the execution of so difficult a task; and it is still more to be doubted, whether they would possess the degree of credit and authority, which might, on certain occasions, be indispensable towards reconciling the people to a decision that should happen to clash with an accusation brought by their immediate representatives. A deficiency in the first, would be fatal to the accused; in the last, dangerous to the public tranquillity. The hazard in both these respects, could only be avoided, if at all, by rendering that tribunal more numerous than would consist with a reasonable attention to economy. The necessity of a numerous court for the trial of impeachments, is equally dictated by the nature of the proceeding. This can never be tied down by such strict rules, either in the delineation of the offense by the prosecutors, or in the construction of it by the judges, as in common cases serve to limit the discretion of courts in favor of personal security. There will be no jury to stand between the judges who are to pronounce the sentence of the law, and the party who is to receive or suffer it. The awful discretion which a court of impeachments must necessarily have, to doom to honor or to infamy the most confidential and the most distinguished characters of the community, forbids the commitment of the trust to a small number of persons.

These considerations seem alone sufficient to authorize a conclusion, that the Supreme Court would have been an improper substitute for the Senate, as a court of impeachments. There remains a further consideration, which will not a little strengthen this conclusion. It is this: The punishment which may be the consequence of conviction upon impeachment, is not to terminate the chastisement of the offender. After having been sentenced to a perpetual ostracism from the esteem and confidence, and honors and emoluments of his country, he will still be liable to prosecution and punishment in the ordinary course of law. Would it be proper that the persons who had disposed of his fame, and his most valuable rights as a citizen in one trial, should, in another trial, for the same offense, be also the disposers of his life and his fortune? Would there not be the greatest reason to apprehend, that error, in the first sentence, would be the parent of error in the second sentence? That the strong bias of one decision would be apt to overrule the influence of any new lights which might be brought to vary the complexion of another decision? Those who know anything of human nature, will not hesitate to answer these questions in the affirmative; and will be at no loss to perceive, that by making the same persons judges in both cases, those who might happen to be the objects of prosecution would, in a great measure, be deprived of the double security intended them by a double trial. The loss of life and estate would often be virtually included in a sentence which, in its terms, imported nothing more than dismission from a present, and disqualification for a future, office. It may be said, that the intervention of a jury, in the second instance, would obviate the danger. But juries are frequently influenced by the opinions of judges. They are sometimes induced to find special verdicts, which refer the main question to the decision of the court. Who would be willing to stake his life and his estate upon the verdict of a jury acting under the auspices of judges who had predetermined his guilt?

Would it have been an improvement of the plan, to have united the Supreme Court with the Senate, in the formation of the court of impeachments? This union would certainly have been attended with several advantages; but would they not have been overbalanced by the signal disadvantage, already stated, arising from the agency of the same judges in the double prosecution to which the offender would be liable? To a certain extent, the benefits of that union will be obtained from making the chief justice of the Supreme Court the president of the court of impeachments, as is proposed to be done in the plan of the convention; while the inconveniences of an entire incorporation of the former into the latter will be substantially avoided. This was perhaps the prudent mean. I forbear to remark upon the additional pretext for clamor against the judiciary, which so considerable an augmentation of its authority would have afforded.

Would it have been desirable to have composed the court for the trial of impeachments, of persons wholly distinct from the other departments of the government? There are weighty arguments, as well against, as in favor of, such a plan. To some minds it will not appear a trivial objection, that it could tend to increase the complexity of the political machine, and to add a new spring to the government, the utility of which would at best be questionable. But an objection which will not be thought by any unworthy of attention, is this: a court formed upon such a plan, would either be attended with a heavy expense, or might in practice be subject to a variety of casualties and inconveniences. It must either consist of permanent officers, stationary at the seat of government, and of course entitled to fixed and regular stipends, or of certain officers of the State governments to be called upon whenever an impeachment was actually depending. It will not be easy to imagine any third mode materially different, which could rationally be proposed. As the court, for reasons already given, ought to be numerous, the first scheme will be reprobated by every man who can compare the extent of the public wants with the means of supplying them. The second will be espoused with caution by those who will seriously consider the difficulty of collecting men dispersed over the whole Union; the injury to the innocent, from the procrastinated determination of the charges which might be brought against them; the advantage to the guilty, from the opportunities which delay would afford to intrigue and corruption; and in some cases the detriment to the State, from the prolonged inaction of men whose firm and faithful execution of their duty might have exposed them to the persecution of an intemperate or designing majority in the House of Representatives. Though this latter supposition may seem harsh, and might not be likely often to be verified, yet it ought not to be forgotten that the demon of faction will, at certain seasons, extend his sceptre over all numerous bodies of men.

But though one or the other of the substitutes which have been examined, or some other that might be devised, should be thought preferable to the plan in this respect, reported by the convention, it will not follow that the Constitution ought for this reason to be rejected. If mankind were to resolve to agree in no institution of government, until every part of it had been adjusted to the most exact standard of perfection, society would soon become a general scene of anarchy, and the world a desert. Where is the standard of perfection to be found? Who will undertake to unite the discordant opinions of a whole community, in the same judgment of it; and to prevail upon one conceited projector to renounce his *infallible* criterion for the *fallible* criterion of his more *conceited neighbor?* To answer the purpose of the adversaries of the Constitution, they ought to prove, not merely that particular provisions in it are not the best which might have been imagined, but that the plan upon the whole is bad and pernicious.

PUBLIUS.

FEDERALIST NO. 66

To the People of the State of New York:

A review of the principal objections that have appeared against the proposed court for the trial of impeachments, will not improbably eradicate the remains of any unfavorable impressions which may still exist in regard to this matter.

The *first* of these objections is, that the provision in question confounds legislative and judiciary authorities in the same body, in violation of that important and well established maxim which requires a separation between the different departments of power. The true meaning of this maxim has been discussed and ascertained in another place, and has been shown to be entirely compatible with a partial intermixture of those departments for special purposes, preserving them, in the main, distinct and unconnected. This partial intermixture is even, in some cases, not only proper but necessary to the mutual defense of the several members of the government against each other. An absolute or qualified negative in the executive upon the acts of the legislative body, is admitted, by the ablest adepts in political science, to be an indispensable barrier against the encroachments of the latter upon the former. And it may, perhaps, with no less reason be contended, that the powers relating to impeachments are, as before intimated, an essential check in the hands of that body upon the encroachments of the executive. The division of them between the two branches of the legislature, assigning to one the right of accusing, to the other the right of judging, avoids the inconvenience of making the same persons both accusers and judges; and guards against the danger of persecution, from the prevalency of a factious spirit in either of those branches. As the concurrence of two thirds of the Senate will be requisite to a condemnation, the security to innocence, from this additional circumstance, will be as complete as itself can desire.

It is curious to observe, with what vehemence this part of the plan is assailed, on the principle here taken notice of, by men who profess to admire, without exception, the constitution of this State; while that constitution makes the Senate, together with the chancellor and judges of the Supreme Court, not only a court of impeachments, but the highest judicatory in the State, in all causes, civil and criminal. The proportion, in point of numbers, of the chancellor and judges to the senators, is so inconsiderable, that the judiciary authority of New York, in the last resort, may, with truth, be said to reside in its Senate. If the plan of the convention be, in this respect, chargeable with a departure from the celebrated maxim which has been so often mentioned, and seems to be so little understood, how much more culpable must be the constitution of New York?*

A *second* objection to the Senate, as a court of impeachments, is, that it contributes to an undue accumulation of power in that body, tending to give to the government a countenance too aristocratic. The Senate, it is observed, is to have concurrent authority with the Executive in the formation of treaties and in the appointment to offices: if, say the objectors, to these prerogatives is added that of deciding in all cases of impeachment, it will give a decided predominancy to senatorial influence. To an objection so little precise in itself, it is not easy to find a very precise answer. Where is the measure or criterion to which we can appeal, for determining what will give the Senate too much, too little, or barely the proper degree of influence? Will it not be more safe, as well as more simple, to dismiss such vague and uncertain calculations, to examine each power by itself, and to decide, on general principles, where it may be deposited with most advantage and least inconvenience?

If we take this course, it will lead to a more intelligible, if not to a more certain result. The disposition of the power of making treaties, which has obtained in the plan of the convention, will, then, if I mistake not, appear to be fully justified by the considerations stated in a former number, and by others which will occur under the next head of our inquiries. The expediency of the junction of the Senate with the Executive, in the power of appointing to offices, will, I trust, be placed in a light not less satisfactory, in the disquisitions under the same head. And I flatter myself the observations in my last paper must have gone no inconsiderable way towards proving that it was not easy, if practicable, to find a more fit receptacle for the power of determining impeachments, than that which has been chosen. If this be truly the case, the hypothetical dread of the too great weight of the Senate ought to be discarded from our reasonings.

But this hypothesis, such as it is, has already been refuted in the remarks applied to the duration in office prescribed for the senators. It was by them shown, as well on the credit of historical examples, as from the reason of the thing, that the most *popular* branch of every government, partaking of the republican genius, by being generally the favorite of the people, will be as generally a full match, if not an overmatch, for every other member of the Government.

But independent of this most active and operative principle, to secure the equilibrium of the national House of Representatives, the plan of the convention has provided in its favor several important counterpoises to the additional

---

* In that of New Jersey, also, the final judiciary authority is in a branch of the legislature. In New Hampshire, Massachusetts, Pennsylvania, and South Carolina, one branch of the legislature is the court for the trial of impeachments.

authorities to be conferred upon the Senate. The exclusive privilege of originating money bills will belong to the House of Representatives. The same house will possess the sole right of instituting impeachments: is not this a complete counterbalance to that of determining them? The same house will be the umpire in all elections of the President, which do not unite the suffrages of a majority of the whole number of electors; a case which it cannot be doubted will sometimes, if not frequently, happen. The constant possibility of the thing must be a fruitful source of influence to that body. The more it is contemplated, the more important will appear this ultimate though contingent power, of deciding the competitions of the most illustrious citizens of the Union, for the first office in it. It would not perhaps be rash to predict, that as a mean of influence it will be found to outweigh all the peculiar attributes of the Senate.

A *third* objection to the Senate as a court of impeachments, is drawn from the agency they are to have in the appointments to office. It is imagined that they would be too indulgent judges of the conduct of men, in whose official creation they had participated. The principle of this objection would condemn a practice, which is to be seen in all the State governments, if not in all the governments with which we are acquainted: I mean that of rendering those who hold offices during pleasure, dependent on the pleasure of those who appoint them. With equal plausibility might it be alleged in this case, that the favoritism of the latter would always be an asylum for the misbehavior of the former. But that practice, in contradiction to this principle, proceeds upon the presumption, that the responsibility of those who appoint, for the fitness and competency of the persons on whom they bestow their choice, and the interest they will have in the respectable and prosperous administration of affairs, will inspire a sufficient disposition to dismiss from a share in it all such who, by their conduct, shall have proved themselves unworthy of the confidence reposed in them. Though facts may not always correspond with this presumption, yet if it be, in the main, just, it must destroy the supposition that the Senate, who will merely sanction the choice of the Executive, should feel a bias, towards the objects of that choice, strong enough to blind them to the evidences of guilt so extraordinary, as to have induced the representatives of the nation to become its accusers.

If any further arguments were necessary to evince the improbability of such a bias, it might be found in the nature of the agency of the Senate in the business of appointments.

It will be the office of the President to *nominate,* and, with the advice and consent of the Senate, to *appoint.* There will, of course, be no exertion of *choice* on the part of the Senate. They may defeat one choice of the Executive, and oblige him to make another; but they cannot themselves *choose*—they can only

ratify or reject the choice of the President. They might even entertain a preference to some other person, at the very moment they were assenting to the one
proposed, because there might be no positive ground of opposition to him; and
they could not be sure, if they withheld their assent, that the subsequent nomination would fall upon their own favorite, or upon any other person in their
estimation more meritorious than the one rejected. Thus it could hardly happen, that the majority of the Senate would feel any other complacency towards
the object of an appointment than such as the appearances of merit might inspire, and the proofs of the want of it destroy.

A *fourth* objection to the Senate in the capacity of a court of impeachments, is
derived from its union with the Executive in the power of making treaties.
This, it has been said, would constitute the senators their own judges, in every
case of a corrupt or perfidious execution of that trust. After having combined
with the Executive in betraying the interests of the nation in a ruinous treaty,
what prospect, it is asked, would there be of their being made to suffer the punishment they would deserve, when they were themselves to decide upon the accusation brought against them for the treachery of which they have been guilty?

This objection has been circulated with more earnestness and with greater
show of reason than any other which has appeared against this part of the plan;
and yet I am deceived if it does not rest upon an erroneous foundation.

The security essentially intended by the Constitution against corruption
and treachery in the formation of treaties, is to be sought for in the numbers
and characters of those who are to make them. The *joint agency* of the Chief
Magistrate of the Union, and of two thirds of the members of a body selected
by the collective wisdom of the legislatures of the several States, is designed to
be the pledge for the fidelity of the national councils in this particular. The
convention might with propriety have meditated the punishment of the Executive, for a deviation from the instructions of the Senate, or a want of integrity
in the conduct of the negotiations committed to him; they might also have had
in view the punishment of a few leading individuals in the Senate, who should
have prostituted their influence in that body as the mercenary instruments of
foreign corruption: but they could not, with more or with equal propriety,
have contemplated the impeachment and punishment of two thirds of the Senate, consenting to an improper treaty, than of a majority of that or of the other
branch of the national legislature, consenting to a pernicious or unconstitutional law, a principle which, I believe, has never been admitted into any government. How, in fact, could a majority in the House of Representatives impeach themselves? Not better, it is evident, than two thirds of the Senate
might try themselves. And yet what reason is there, that a majority of the
House of Representatives, sacrificing the interests of the society by an unjust

and tyrannical act of legislation, should escape with impunity, more than two thirds of the Senate, sacrificing the same interests in an injurious treaty with a foreign power? The truth is, that in all such cases it is essential to the freedom and to the necessary independence of the deliberations of the body, that the members of it should be exempt from punishment for acts done in a collective capacity; and the security to the society must depend on the care which is taken to confide the trust to proper hands, to make it their interest to execute it with fidelity, and to make it as difficult as possible for them to combine in any interest opposite to that of the public good.

So far as might concern the misbehavior of the Executive in perverting the instructions or contravening the views of the Senate, we need not be apprehensive of the want of a disposition in that body to punish the abuse of their confidence or to vindicate their own authority. We may thus far count upon their pride, if not upon their virtue. And so far even as might concern the corruption of leading members, by whose arts and influence the majority may have been inveigled into measures odious to the community, if the proofs of that corruption should be satisfactory, the usual propensity of human nature will warrant us in concluding that there would be commonly no defect of inclination in the body to divert the public resentment from themselves by a ready sacrifice of the authors of their mismanagement and disgrace.

PUBLIUS.

Part III
THE SCOPE OF IMPEACHABLE OFFENSES: SOME RECURRING ISSUES

T HE DOCUMENTS IN THIS SECTION introduce some of the major issues that surface time and again as the House exercises its "sole power of impeachment" and the Senate tries those impeachments. These documents address questions about the impeachability of private behavior, the claim that behavior must be criminal to be impeachable, and the question of whether the "good Behaviour" clause of the Constitution that defines judicial tenure gives Congress wider latitude in impeaching judges than other officers. Documents 4 and 5, relating to the behavior of the first secretary of the Treasury, Alexander Hamilton, suggest that the framers did not perceive private behavior to be impeachable, even private behavior that raised serious suspicions of official misconduct, as Hamilton's payments to a known speculator certainly did.

The next set of three documents relate to an attempt to impeach Supreme Court Justice William O. Douglas in 1970. Rep. Gerald Ford's speech supporting impeachment draws a distinction between life-tenured federal judges and all other federal officers. Ford concludes that the limited terms of presidents and vice presidents under which they can be voted out of office every four years, "would indeed require crimes of the magnitude of treason and bribery" for removal. For judges, however, conduct failing to meet general standards of "good behavior" would be enough to warrant removal. Both Rep. Paul McCloskey's reply to Ford and the excerpt from the subcommittee report exonerating Douglas, indicate an alternative conclusion: that conduct that fails to meet the standard of "good behavior" but that does not come within the definition of "high Crimes and Misdemeanors," is not subject to impeachment.

The final document in this section is an excerpt from *Deschler's Precedents of the House of Representatives,* a compendium of House actions, showing what practices have occurred in the House during specific cases. This selection addresses the question of what are impeachable offenses, most notably as discussed in the House Judiciary Committee during the impeachment investigation of President Richard Nixon from 1973 to 1974.

Alexander Hamilton in Defense of Himself
(1797)

I N REPLYING to impeachment charges brought before Congress by inde-
pendent counsel Kenneth W. Starr (see Document 31, p. 267), President
Bill Clinton's lawyers pointed to an incident involving President George
Washington's secretary of the Treasury, Alexander Hamilton, as a precedent for the proposition that private behavior has historically been understood not to fall within the realm of impeachable offenses. The "Reynolds
Affair" as this incident became known, has some eerie parallels to President
Clinton's travails. Its precedential value is uncertain, however, for no official action by the House of Representatives was involved, and no vote was
ever held on whether Hamilton's behavior and its aftermath constituted
impeachable offenses.

The following document was drafted by Hamilton years after the
events, in response to publication of accusations that, while in office, he had
maintained a corrupt relationship with shady securities speculator James
Reynolds. The *Observations* gave Hamilton's side of the story, which most biographers have accepted as true. However, contemporaries such as Thomas
Jefferson and James Monroe and later biographers felt that Hamilton's
adulterous affair was either manufactured or publicized by Hamilton for
the purpose of drawing attention away from the charge that he used Treasury information to engage in speculation.

The Reynolds Affair had its roots in the intensely partisan, but not particularly titillating, controversy between Treasury secretary Hamilton and
Secretary of State Jefferson. Hamilton, a proponent of a strong national
government, advocated completely paying off the infant country's Revolutionary War debt, as well as the states' war debts. He argued that paying off
the debts at face value would give the United States credibility and would
give potential creditors confidence enough to lend more money to the new
government. Thomas Jefferson, on the other hand, believed that Hamilton's fiscal policies, particularly the creation of a national bank, unconstitutionally aggregated power to the federal government at the expense of the
states and of the "agricultural interests" that Jefferson supported. The ani-

mosity between the two men over what were ultimately two fundamentally different visions for the country's future would result in Jefferson's drafting of a resolution to place before Congress seeking Hamilton's ouster from the cabinet.

Virginia Rep. William Branch Giles presented this resolution to the House just weeks after the Reynolds Affair came to light. His resolution (see Document 5, p. 52) was watered down from Jefferson's into a request for an investigation of Treasury accounting practices and would contain no whisper of the Reynolds Affair, although Jefferson was well aware of it.

As the First Congress considered Hamilton's funding plan in 1790, it was widely known that well-informed individuals could profit enormously from speculation on war debts. Notes issued by the Continental Congress to finance the Revolutionary War had fallen precipitously in value. Speculators had already bought up most of these notes from small farmers and others at a fraction of their face value, some apparently doing so on the basis of information about the funding plan. Speculators stood to make a great deal of money if Hamilton's funding plan was adopted. Because friends and relatives of Hamilton's were among those heavily engaged in speculation, the secretary of the Treasury was quickly suspected of supplying inside information. When information that Hamilton might be engaged in speculation himself came to the attention of three members of Congress—including Thomas Jefferson's friend Sen. James Monroe of Virginia—they took the charges seriously and began their own investigation.

The investigation turned up correspondence and claims by small-time speculator James Reynolds, suggesting that Hamilton was supplying Reynolds with lists of soldiers to whom the government owed back pay. With these lists Reynolds, as Hamilton's agent, could buy up the soldiers' claims. Corroboration of this relationship came in the form of letters in Hamilton's disguised hand showing payments made to Reynolds. Hamilton explained that the payments were not for the purpose of speculation, but blackmail payments to keep Reynolds from disclosing Hamilton's adulterous relationship with Reynolds' wife Maria. The members of Congress accepted Hamilton's explanation (although Monroe apparently continued to be skeptical). When Congress began investigating Hamilton's handling of the Treasury Department the following month, no mention was made of either Hamilton's admission of adultery, or the charges of improper speculation.

The issue did not surface publicly until some years later when journalist James Callender—the same Callender whose seditious libel trial would figure prominently in the impeachment of Supreme Court Justice Samuel Chase—published a pamphlet in which he resurrected the speculation charges and, referring to statements made by Maria Reynolds, expressed disbelief in Hamilton's adultery explanation. Hamilton responded by publishing his innocuously titled *Observations*.

The whole affair was tangled and complicated. A complete and interesting account of it can be found in an appendix to Volume 18 of the published papers of Thomas Jefferson. The editor of the papers, Julian Boyd, did not believe Hamilton and concluded that Hamilton himself wrote the letters from Maria (not published here) that he put forth as corroboration of his story. Boyd included the reported response of Maria Reynolds upon hearing Hamilton's claim that adultery and blackmail, rather than speculation had been the basis of their relationship:

Mrs. Reynolds . . . appeared much shocked at it and wept immoderately—That she denied the imputation and declared that it had been a fabrication of Colo. Hamilton and that her husband had joined in it, who had told her so, and that he had given him receipts for money and written letters, so as to give the countenance to the pretence. . . .[1]

James Monroe recorded this testimony at the time; his skepticism about Hamilton's veracity was based in part on this. The editor of Hamilton's papers, Harold Syrett, seemed less sure of which offense Hamilton was guilty, but he also detailed the affair in Volume XXI of *The Papers of Alexander Hamilton*. Whatever the truth of the Reynolds Affair, it did not result in any official action against Hamilton. However, because Monroe and the other two members did not report back to Congress concerning their suspicions, and because others who knew of Hamilton's adultery defense did not press for an official investigation, the only precedential claim that can reasonably be made about the Reynolds Affair is that these individual members of Congress did not perceive Hamilton's private misbehavior to warrant removal from office.

OBSERVATIONS, &C.

. . . I dare appeal to my immediate fellow citizens of whatever political party for the truth of the assertion, that no man ever carried into public life a more unblemished pecuniary reputation, than that with which I undertook the office of Secretary of the Treasury; a character marked by an indifference to the acquisition of property rather than by an avidity for it. . . .

Merely because a member of the House of Representatives entertained a different idea from me, as to the legal effect of appropriation laws, and did not understand accounts, I was exposed to the imputation of having committed a deliberate and criminal violation of the laws and to the suspicion of being a defaulter for millions; so as to have been driven to the painful necessity of calling for a formal and solemn inquiry.

The inquiry took place. It was conducted by a committee of fifteen members of the House of Representatives—a majority of them either my decided political enemies or in-

Alexander Hamilton

clined against me, some of them the most active and intelligent of my opponents, without a single man, who being known to be friendly to me, possessed also such knowledge and experience of public affairs as would enable him to counteract injurious intrigues. Mr. GILES of Virginia who had commenced the attack was of the committee.

The officers and books of the treasury were examined. The transactions between the several banks and the treasury were scrutinized. Even my *private accounts* with those institutions were laid open to the committee; and every possible facility given to the inquiry. The result was a complete demonstration that the suspicions which had been entertained were groundless. . . .

Of all the vile attempts which have been made to injure my character that which has been lately revived in No. V and VI, of the history of the United States for 1796 is the most vile. This it will be impossible for any *intelligent,* I will not say *candid,* man to doubt, when he shall have accompanied me through the examination.

I owe perhaps to my friends an apology for condescending to give a public explanation. A just pride with reluctance stoops to a formal vindication against so despicable a contrivance and is inclined rather to oppose to it the uniform evidence of an upright character. This would be my conduct on the present occasion, did not the tale seem to derive a sanction from the names of three men of some weight and consequence in the society: a circumstance, which I trust will excuse me for paying attention to a slander that without this prop, would defeat itself by intrinsic circumstances of absurdity and malice.

The charge against me is a connection with one James Reynolds for purposes of improper pecuniary speculation. My real crime is an amorous connection with his wife for a considerable time with his privity and connivance, if not originally brought on by a combination between the husband and wife with the design to extort money from me.

This confession is not made without a blush. I cannot be the apologist of any vice because the ardour of passion may have made it mine. I can never cease to condemn myself for the pang, which it may inflict in a bosom eminently intitled to all my gratitude, fidelity and love. But that bosom will approve, that even at so great an expence, I should effectually wipe away a more serious stain from a name, which it cherishes with no less elevation than tenderness. The public too will I trust excuse the confession. The necessity of it to my defence against a more heinous charge could alone have extorted from me so painful an indecorum. . . .

I proceed in the next place to offer a frank and plain solution of the enigma, by giving a history of the origin and progress of my connection with Mrs. Reynolds, of its discovery, real and pretended by the husband, and of the disagreeable embarrassments to which it exposed me. This history will be supported by the letters of Mr. and Mrs. Reynolds, which leave no room for doubt of the principal facts, and at the same time explain with precision the objects of the little notes from me which have been published, shewing clearly that such of them as have related to money had no reference to any concern in speculation. As the situation which will be disclosed, will fully explain every ambiguous appearance, and meet satisfactorily the written documents, nothing more can be requisite to my justification. For frail indeed will be the tenure by which the most blameless man will hold his reputation, if the assertions of three of the most abandoned characters in the community, two of them stigmatized by the discrediting crime which has been mentioned, are sufficient to blast it—The business of accusation would soon become in such a case, a regular trade, and men's reputations would be bought and sold like any marketable commodity.

Some time in the summer of the year 1791 a woman called at my house in the city of Philadelphia and asked to speak with me in private. I attended her into a room apart from the family. With a seeming air of affliction she informed that she was a daughter of a Mr. Lewis, sister to a Mr. G. Livingston of the State of New-York, and a wife to a Mr. Reynolds whose father was in the

Commissary Department during the war with Great Britain, that her husband, who for a long time had treated her very cruelly, had lately left her, to live with another woman, and in so destitute a condition, that though desirous of returning to her friends she had not the means—that knowing I was a citizen of New-York, she had taken the liberty to apply to my humanity for assistance.

I replied, that her situation was a very interesting one—that I was disposed to afford her assistance to convey her to her friends, but this at the moment not being convenient to me (which was the fact) I must request the place of her residence, to which I should bring or send a small supply of money. She told me the street and the number of the house where she lodged. In the evening I put a bank-bill in my pocket and went to the house. I inquired for Mrs. Reynolds and was shewn up stairs, at the head of which she met me and conducted me into a bed room. I took the bill out of my pocket and gave it to her. Some conversation ensued from which it was quickly apparent that other than pecuniary consolation would be acceptable.

After this, I had frequent meetings with her, most of them at my own house; Mrs. Hamilton with her children being absent on a visit to her father. In the course of a short time, she mentioned to me that her husband had solicited a reconciliation, and affected to consult me about it. I advised to it, and was soon after informed by her that it had taken place. She told me besides that her husband had been engaged in speculation, and she believed could give information respecting the conduct of some persons in the department which would be useful. I sent for Reynolds who came to me accordingly.

In the course of our interview, he confessed that he had obtained a list of claims from a person in my department which he had made use of in his speculations. I invited him, by the expectation of my friendship and good offices, to disclose the person. After some affectation of scruple, he pretended to yield, and ascribed the infidelity to Mr. Duer from whom he said he had obtained the list in New-York, while he (Duer) was in the department.

As Mr. Duer had resigned his office some time before the seat of government was removed to Philadelphia; this discovery, if it had been true, was not very important—yet it was the interest of my passions to appear to set value upon it, and to continue the expectation of friendship and good offices. Mr. Reynolds told me he was going to Virginia, and on his return would point out something in which I could serve him. I do not know but he said something about employment in a public office. . . .

The intercourse with Mrs. Reynolds, in the mean time continued; and, though various reflections, (in which a further knowledge of Reynold's character and the suspicion of some concert between the husband and wife bore a part) induced me to wish a cessation of it; yet her conduct, made it extremely difficult to disentangle myself. All the appearances of violent attachment, and of agonising distress at the idea of a relinquishment, were played with a most imposing art. This, though it did not make me entirely the dupe of the plot, yet kept me in a state of irresolution. My sensibility, perhaps my vanity, admitted the possibility of a real fondness; and led me to adopt the plan of a gradual discontinuance rather than of a sudden interruption, as least calculated to give pain, if a real partiality existed.

Mrs. Reynolds, on the other hand, employed every effort to keep up my attention and visits—Her pen was freely employed, and her letters were filled with those tender and pathetic effusions which would have been natural to a woman truly fond and neglected.

One day, I received a letter from her . . . intimating a discovery by her husband. It was a matter of doubt with me whether there had been really a discovery by accident, or whether the time for the catastrophe of the plot was arrived.

The same day, being the 15th of December 1791, I received from Mr. Reynolds the letter . . . by which he informs me of the detection of his wife in the act of writing a letter to me, and that he had obtained from her a discovery of her connection with me, suggesting that it was the consequence of an undue advantage taken of her distress. . . .

On the 19th, I received the promised letter . . . the essence of which is that he was willing to take a thousand dollars as the plaister for his wounded honor.

I determined to give it to him, and did so in two payments, as per receipts . . . dated the 22nd of December and 3rd of January. It is a little remarkable, that an avaricious speculating secretary of the treasury should have been so straitened for money as to be obliged to satisfy an engagement of this sort by two different payments!

On the 17th of January, I received the letter No. V. by which Reynolds invites me to *renew my visits to his wife.* He had before requested that I would see her no more. The motive to this step appears in the conclusion of the letter, *"I rely* upon your befriending me, *if there should any thing offer that should be to my advantage,* as you *express a wish to befriend me."* Is the pre-existence of a speculating connection reconcileable with this mode of expression? . . .

These letters collectively, furnish a complete elucidation of the nature of my transactions with *Reynolds.* They resolve them into an amorous connection with his wife, detected, or pretended to be detected by the husband, imposing on me the necessity of a pecuniary composition with him, and leaving me afterwards under a duress for fear of disclosure, which was the instrument of levying upon me from time to time *forced loans*—They apply directly to this state of things, the notes which *Reynolds* was so careful to preserve, and which had been employed to excite suspicion. . . .

It has been seen that an explanation on the subject was had cotemporarily that is in December 1792, with three members of Congress—F. A. Muhlenberg. J. Monroe, and A. Venable. It is proper that the circumstances of this transaction should be accurately understood. . . .

. . . [O]n the morning of the 15th of December, 1792, the above mentioned gentlemen presented themselves at my office. Mr. Muhlenberg was then speaker. He introduced the subject by observing to me, that they *had discovered a very improper connection* between me and a Mr. Reynolds: extremely hurt by this mode of introduction, I arrested the progress of the discourse by giving way to very strong expressions of indignation. The gentlemen explained, telling me in substance that I had misapprehended them—that they did not take the fact for established—that their meaning was to apprise me that unsought by them, information had been given them of an improper pecuniary connection between Mr. Reynolds and myself; that they had thought it their duty to pursue it and had become possessed of some documents of a suspicious complexion—that they had contemplated laying the matter before the President, but before they did this they thought it right to apprise me of the affair and to afford an opportunity of explanation; declaring at the same time that their agency in the matter was influenced solely by a sense of public duty and by no motive of personal ill will. If my memory be correct, the notes from me in a disguised hand were now shewn to me which without a moment's hesitation I acknowledged to be mine.

I replied, that the affair was now put upon a different footing—-that I always stood ready to meet fair inquiry with frank communication—that it happened, in the present instance, to be in my power by written documents to remove all doubts as to the real nature of the business, and fully to convince, that nothing of the kind imputed to me did in fact exist. The same evening at my house was by mutual consent appointed for an explanation.

I immediately after saw Mr. Wolcott, and for the first time informed him of the affair and of the interview just had; and delivering into his hands for perusal the documents of which I was possessed, I engaged him to be present at the intended explanation in the evening.

In the evening the proposed meeting took place, and Mr. Wolcott according to my request attended. The information, which had been received to that time, from *Clingman, Reynolds* and his wife, was communicated to me and the notes were I think again exhibited.

I stated in explanation, the circumstances of my affair with Mrs. Reynolds and the consequences of it and in confirmation produced the documents. . . . One or more of the gentlemen . . . was struck with so much conviction, before I had gotten through the communication that they delicately urged me to discontinue it as necessary. I insisted upon going through the whole and did so. The result was a full and unequivocal acknowledgment on the part of the three gentlemen of perfect satisfaction with the explanation and expressions of regret at the trouble and embarrassment which had been occasioned to me. Mr. Muhlenberg and Mr. Venable, in particular manifested a degree of sensibility on the occasion. Mr. Monroe was more cold but intirely explicit.

One of the gentlemen, I think, expressed a hope that I also was satisfied with their conduct in conducting the inquiry—I answered, that they knew I had been hurt at the opening of the affair—that this excepted, I was satisfied with their conduct and considered myself as having been treated with candor or with fairness and liberality, I do not now pretend to recollect the exact terms. I took the next morning a memorandum of the substance of what was said to me, which will be seen by a copy of it transmitted in a letter to each of the gentlemen. . . .

I deny absolutely, as alleged by the editor of the publication in question, that I intreated a suspension of the communication to the President, or that from the beginning to the end of the inquiry, I asked any favour or indulgence whatever, and that I discovered any symptom different from that of a proud consciousness of innocence.

Some days after the explanation I wrote to the three gentlemen. . . . That letter evinces the light in which I considered myself as standing in their view. . . .

Thus the affair remained 'till the pamphlets No. V and VI of the history of the U. States for 1796 appeared; with the exception of some dark whispers, which were communicated to me by a friend in Virginia, and to which I replied by a statement of what had passed. . . .

But the turn which *Clingman* gives to the matter must necessarily fall to the ground. It is, that Mrs. Reynolds denied her amorous connection with me, and represented the suggestion of it as a mere contrivance between *her husband* and *myself* to cover me, alleging that there had been a fabrication of letters and receipts to countenance it—The plain answer is that Mrs. Reynolds' own letters contradict absolutely this artful explanation of hers; if indeed she ever made it, of which *Clingman's* assertion is no evidence whatever. . . . They shew explicitly the connection with her, the discovery of it by her husband and the pains she took to prolong it when I evidently wished to get rid of it—This cuts up, by the root, the pretence of a contrivance between the husband and myself to fabricate the evidences of it.

The variety of shapes which this woman could assume was endless. In a conversation between her and a gentleman whom I am not at liberty publicly to name, she made a voluntary confession of her belief and even knowledge, that I was innocent of all that had been laid to my charge by *Reynolds* or any other person of her acquaintance, spoke of me in exalted terms of esteem and respect, declared in the most solemn manner her extreme unhappiness lest I should suppose her accessory to the trouble which had been given me on that account, and expressed her fear that the resentment of Mr. Reynolds on a *particular score,* might have urged him to improper lengths of revenge—appearing at the same time extremely agitated and unhappy. With the gentleman who gives this information, I have never been in any relation personal or political that could be supposed to bias him—His name would evince that he is an impartial witness. And though I am not permitted to make a public use of it, I am permitted to refer any gentleman to the perusal of his letter in the hands of William Bingham, Esquire; who is also so obliging as to permit me to deposit with him for similar inspection all the original papers which are contained in the appendix to this narrative. The letter from the gentleman above alluded to has been already shewn to *Mr. Monroe.* . . .

But it is observed that the dread of the disclosure of an amorous connection was not a sufficient cause for my humility, and that I had nothing to lose as to my reputation for chastity; concerning which the world had fixed a previous opinion.

I shall not enter into the question what was the previous opinion entertained of me in this particular—nor how well founded, for it was indeed such as it is represented to have been. It is sufficient to say that there is a wide difference between vague rumours and suspicions and the evidence of a positive fact—no man not indelicately unprincipled, with the state of manners in this country, would be willing to have a conjugal infidelity fixed upon him with positive certainty—He would know that it would justly injure him with a considerable and respectable portion of the society—and especially no man, tender of the happiness of an excellent wife could without extreme pain look forward to the affliction which she might endure from the disclosure, especially a *public disclosure,* of the fact. Those best acquainted with the interior of my domestic life will best appreciate the force of such a consideration upon me.

The truth was, that in both relations and especially the last, I dreaded extremely a disclosure—and was willing to make large sacrifices to avoid it. It is true, that from the acquiescence of Reynolds, I had strong ties upon his secrecy, but how could I rely upon any tie upon so base a character. How could I know, but that from moment to moment he might, at the expence of his own disgrace, become the *mercenary* of a party, with whom to blast my character in *any way* is a favourite object! . . .

If after the recent confessions of the gentlemen themselves, it could be useful to fortify the proof of the full conviction my explanation had wrought, I might appeal to the total silence concerning this charge, when at a subsequent period, in the year 1793, there was such an active legislative persecution of me. It might not even perhaps be difficult to establish, that it came under the eye of Mr. Giles, and that he discarded it as the plain case of a private amour unconnected with any thing that was the proper subject of a public attack. . . .

ALEXANDER HAMILTON.
Philadelphia, July, 1797.

Note

1. Julian Boyd, ed., *Papers of Thomas Jefferson*. Vol. 18.

≈ 5 ≈
Giles's Resolutions Criticizing Hamilton
(1793)

VIRGINIA REPRESENTATIVE William Branch Giles introduced the following resolutions in the House as a means to begin an investigation
of Treasury secretary Alexander Hamilton, accused of making payments to
a speculator. The goal of Giles and other like-minded government leaders,
including Secretary of State Thomas Jefferson, was to convince President
George Washington to remove Hamilton from the cabinet.

Jefferson had actually written the first draft of these resolutions. While
writing his draft, Jefferson was aware of both the charges of speculation
against Hamilton and of Hamilton's defense that his secret payments to
speculator James Reynolds had been blackmail payments to keep Reynolds
quiet about Hamilton's adultery. (This would not become public knowledge until five years later when Hamilton published his *Observations*.) In
Jefferson's draft, the tenth resolution read:

Resolved, That the Secretary of the Treasury has been guilty of maladministration in
the duties of his office, and should, in the opinion of Congress, be removed from his
office by the President of the United States.

In the Giles resolutions, as introduced in the House, the wording was
softened to ask merely that the preceding resolutions be transmitted to the
president. Similarly deleted from Jefferson's draft was an accusation that
Hamilton had violated the instructions of the president "for the benefit of
speculators." No mention of blackmail or adultery appeared in Jefferson's
draft. Had Jefferson believed that Hamilton's adultery and blackmail payments were offenses that would support removal from office, he most likely
would have included them in his draft. After intensive congressional investigation, Hamilton was completely vindicated by the House.

The resolutions brought forward yesterday by Mr. GILES, were called for by that gentleman. The reading being finished, Mr. AMES moved that the resolutions should be taken up.

Mr. MURRAY suggested the necessity of giving a preference to the Judiciary Bill reported by him some days since. He was seconded by Mr. KEY.

The motion for taking up the resolutions was carried, forty members rising in favor of it. The resolutions were accordingly read by the Clerk, and are as follow, viz:

1. *Resolved,* That it is essential to the due administration of the Government of the United States, that laws making specific appropriations of money should be strictly observed by the administrator of the finances thereof.

2. *Resolved,* That a violation of a law making appropriations of money, is a violation of that section of the Constitution of the United States which requires that no money shall be drawn from the Treasury but in consequence of appropriations made by law.

3. *Resolved,* That the Secretary of the Treasury has violated the law passed the 4th of August, 1790, making appropriations of certain moneys authorized to be borrowed by the same law, in the following particulars, viz: *First,* By applying a certain portion of the principal borrowed to the payment of interest falling due upon that principal, which was not authorized by that or any other law. *Secondly,* By drawing part of the same moneys into the United States, without the instructions of the President of the United States.

4. *Resolved,* That the Secretary of the Treasury has deviated from the instructions given by the President of the United States, in exceeding the authorities for making loans under the acts of the 4th and 12th of August, 1790.

5. *Resolved,* That the Secretary of the Treasury has omitted to discharge an essential duty of his office, in failing to give Congress official information in due time, of the moneys drawn by him from Europe into the United States; which drawing commenced December, 1790, and continued till January, 1793; and of the causes of making such drafts.

6. *Resolved,* That the Secretary of the Treasury has, without the instructions of the President of the United States, drawn more moneys borrowed in Holland into the United States than the President of the United States was authorized to draw, under the act of the 12th of August, 1790: which act appropriated two millions of dollars only, when borrowed, to the purchase of the Public Debt: And that he has omitted to discharge an essential duty of his office, in failing to give official information to the Commissioners for purchasing the Public Debt, of the various sums drawn from time to time, suggested by him to have been intended for the purchase of the Public Debt.

7. *Resolved,* That the Secretary of the Treasury did not consult the public interest in negotiating a Loan with the Bank of the United States, and drawing therefrom four hundred thousand dollars, at five per cent, per annum, when a greater sum of public money was deposited in various banks at the respective periods of making the respective drafts.

8. *Resolved,* That the Secretary of the Treasury has been guilty of an indecorum to this House, in undertaking to judge of its motives in calling for information which was demandable of him, from the constitution of his office; and in failing to give all the necessary information within his knowledge, relatively to the subjects of the reference made to him of the 19th January, 1792, and of the 22d November, 1792, during the present session.

9. *Resolved,* That a copy of the foregoing resolutions be transmitted to the President of the United States. . . .

❧ 6 ❧
Gerald Ford on Impeachment of William O. Douglas
(1970)

IN APRIL 1970 Rep. Gerald Ford, the Michigan Republican and future president, rose in the House chamber to speak in support of the impeachment of Supreme Court Justice William O. Douglas. Ford's speech came in the midst of intense national turmoil and divisive debates over what appeared at the time to be revolutionary changes in public morality that were seen, depending on one's perspective, as either the doom or salvation of American civilization. Violence as a tool of political change or as a reflection of frustration with the political system had become more common. Riots, assassinations, and bombings had brought a more-than-ordinary level of fearfulness and distrust between those of opposing political views.

As Ford indicates in the beginning of his speech, another member of the Supreme Court, Associate Justice Abe Fortas, had only recently withdrawn himself from consideration for chief justice, and subsequently resigned from the Court altogether. His withdrawal from the confirmation process was the result of intense conservative opposition that brought much of his nonjudicial life into the public spotlight. Publication of allegations of financial improprieties against Fortas and a reputed threat of criminal prosecution by the Justice Department prompted Fortas's resignation. Although there was impeachment talk in Congress, President Richard Nixon apparently convinced members of Congress not to proceed, arguing that impeachment hearings would tear the country apart and that Fortas could be persuaded to resign. After Fortas's resignation, Sen. Strom Thurmond of South Carolina put out a news release saying "Douglas is next."[1]

Ford's attack on Douglas arose in part as retaliation for the Senate's rejection of two of President Nixon's earlier Supreme Court nominees, conservative southerners G. Harrold Carswell and Clement Haynesworth. The attack on Douglas also reflected a specific Republican distaste for the justice, who had come under attack at earlier points for dissenting in the Rosenberg espionage case during the McCarthy anticommunism era, and whose multiple marriages and divorces seemed to put him beyond the acceptable social pale. Much of Ford's attack on Douglas centered on nonjudicial activities, such as speechmaking and publication of nonlegal materials.

It was in this speech that Ford uttered what has become one of the most quoted definitions of the meaning of "high crimes and misdemeanors" in the annals of American impeachment: "An impeachable offense is whatever a majority of the House of Representatives considers it to be at any given moment in history." In a portion of his speech that is seldom quoted, however, Ford made it clear that such an expansive and arbitrary interpretation of the impeachment power applied only to federal judges, for whom no other means than impeachment exists for removal. Presidents, vice presidents, and other officers of the federal government could be removed by other means, including frequent elections, and thus Congress was not warranted in interjecting its judgment except in cases of extreme official misbehavior. Because there is no other means for removing judges, and because the Constitution states that judges shall hold their offices during good behavior, Ford argued that bad behavior, however Congress chooses to define it, should be sufficient for the removal of federal judges. Rep. Paul N. McCloskey in his reply and the investigating subcommittee in its report (see Document 7, p. 60), interpreted the impeachment clause and House precedents very differently.

☙ ☙ ☙

Mr. Speaker. . . . Following the public disclosure last year of the extrajudicial activities and moonlighting employment of Justices Fortas and Douglas, which resulted in the resignation from the Supreme Bench of Mr. Justice Fortas but not of Mr. Justice Douglas, I received literally hundreds of inquiries and protests from concerned citizens and colleagues.

In response to this evident interest I quietly undertook a study of both the law of impeachment and the facts about the behavior of Mr. Justice Douglas. I assured inquirers that I would make my findings known at the appropriate time. That preliminary report is now ready.

Let me say by way of preface that I am a lawyer, admitted to the bar of the U.S. Supreme Court. I have the most profound respect for the U.S. Supreme Court. I would never advocate action against a member of that Court because of his political philosophy or the legal opinions which he contributes to the decisions of the Court. Mr. Justice Douglas has been criticized for his liberal opinions and because he granted stays of execution to the convicted spies, the Rosenbergs, who stole the atomic bomb for the Soviet Union. Probably I would disagree, were I on the bench, with most of Mr. Justice Douglas' views, such as his defense of the filthy film, "I Am Curious (Yellow)." But a judge's right to his legal views, assuming they are not improperly influenced or corrupted, is fundamental to our system of justice.

I should say also that I have no personal feeling toward Mr. Justice Douglas. His private life, to the degree that it does not bring the Supreme Court into disrepute, is his own business. One does not need to be an ardent admirer of any judge or justice, or an advocate of his life style, to acknowledge his right to be elevated to or remain on the bench.

. . . There has not been sufficient consideration given, in my judgment, to the qualifications which a person should possess to remain upon the U.S. Supreme Court.

For, contrary to a widespread misconception, Federal judges and the Justices of the Supreme Court are not appointed for life. The Founding Fathers would have been the last to make such a mistake; the American Revolution was waged against an hereditary monarchy in which the King always had a life term and, as English history bloodily demonstrated, could only be removed from office by the headsman's ax or the assassin's dagger.

No, the Constitution does not guarantee a lifetime of power and authority to any public official. The terms of Members of the House are fixed at 2 years; of the President and Vice President at 4; of U.S. Senators at 6. Members of the Federal judiciary hold their offices only "during good behavior."

Let me read the first section of article III of the Constitution in full:

The judicial power of the United States shall be vested in one supreme Court, and in such inferior Courts as the Congress may from time to time ordain and establish. The Judges, both of the supreme and inferior Courts, shall hold their Offices *during good Behavior*, and shall, at stated Times, receive for their Services, a Compensation, which shall not be diminished during their Continuance in Office.

... To me the Constitution is perfectly clear about the tenure, or term of office, of all Federal judges—it is "during good behavior." It is implicit in this that when behaviour ceases to be good, the right to hold judicial office ceases also. Thus, we come quickly to the central question: What constitutes

William O. Douglas

"good behaviour" or, conversely, ungood or disqualifying behaviour?

The words employed by the Framers of the Constitution were, as the proceedings of the Convention detail, chosen with exceedingly great care and precision. Note, for example, the word "behaviour." It relates to action, not merely to thoughts or opinions; further, it refers not to a single act but to a pattern or continuing sequence of action. We cannot and should not remove a Federal judge for the legal views he holds—this would be as contemptible as to exclude him from serving on the Supreme Court for his ideology or past decisions. Nor should we remove him for a minor or isolated mistake—this does not constitute behaviour in the common meaning.

What we should scrutinize in sitting Judges is their continuing pattern of action, their behaviour. The Constitution does not demand that it be "exemplary" or "perfect." But it does have to be "good."

Naturally, there must be orderly procedure for determining whether or not a Federal judge's behaviour is good.

... In this seldom-used procedure, called impeachment, the legislative branch exercises both executive and judicial functions. The roles of the two bodies differ dramatically. The House serves as prosecutor and grand jury; the Senate serves as judge and trial jury.

Article I of the Constitution has this to say about the impeachment process:

The House of Representatives—shall have the sole power of Impeachment.

The Senate shall have the sole Power to try all Impeachments. When sitting for that Purpose, they shall be on Oath or Affirmation. When the President of the United States is tried, the Chief Justice shall preside: And no Person shall be convicted without the Concurrence of two-thirds of the Members present.

Article II, dealing with the executive branch, states in section 4:

The President, Vice President, and all civil Officers of the United States, shall be removed from office on impeachment for, and conviction of, Treason, Bribery or other high crimes and misdemeanors.

This has been the most controversial of the constitutional references to the impeachment process. No con[s]ensus exists as to whether, in the case of Federal judges, impeachment must depend upon conviction of one of the two specified crimes of treason or bribery or be within the nebulous category of "other high crimes and misdemeanors." There are pages upon pages of learned argument whether the adjective "high" modifies "misdemeanors" as well as "crimes," and over what, indeed constitutes a "high misdemeanor."

In my view, one of the specific or general offenses cited in article II is required for removal of the indirectly elected President and all appointed civil officers of the executive branch of the Federal Government, whatever their terms of office. But in the case of members of the judicial branch, Federal judges and Justices, I believe an additional and much stricter requirement is imposed by article II, namely, "good behaviour." . . .

With this brief review of the law of the constitutional background for impeachment, I have endeavored to correct two common misconceptions: first, that Federal judges are appointed for life and, second, that they can be removed only by being convicted, with all ordinary protections and presumptions of innocence to which an accused is entitled, of violating the law.

This is not the case. Federal judges can be and have been impeached for improper personal habits such as chronic intoxication on the bench, and one of the charges brought against President Andrew Johnson was that he delivered "intemperate, inflammatory, and scandalous harangues."

I have studied the principal impeachment actions that have been initiated over the years and frankly, there are too few cases to make very good law. About the only thing the authorities can agree upon in recent history, though it was hotly argued up to President Johnson's impeachment and the trial of Judge Swayne, is that an offense need not be indictable to be impeachable. In other words, something less than a criminal act or criminal dereliction of duty may nevertheless be sufficient grounds for impeachment and removal from public office.

What, then, is an impeachable offense?

The only honest answer is that an impeachable offense is whatever a majority of the House of Representatives considers to be at a given moment in history; conviction results from whatever offense or offenses two-thirds of the other body considers to be sufficiently serious to require removal of the accused from office. Again, the historical context and political climate are important; there are few fixed principles among the handful of precedents.

I think it is fair to come to one conclusion, however, from our history of impeachments: a higher standard is expected of Federal judges than of any other "civil officers" of the United States.

The President and Vice President, and all persons holding office at the pleasure of the President, can be thrown out of office by the voters at least every 4 years. To remove them in midterm—it has been tried only twice and never done—would indeed require crimes of the magnitude of treason and bribery. Other elective officials, such as Members of the Congress, are so vulnerable to public displeasure that their removal by the complicated impeachment route has not even been tried since 1798. But nine Federal judges, including one Associate Justice of the Supreme Court, have been impeached by this House and tried by the Senate; four were acquitted; four convicted and removed from office; and one resigned during trial and the impeachment was dismissed.

In the most recent impeachment trial conducted by the other body, that of U.S. Judge Halsted L. Ritter of the southern district of Florida, who was removed in 1936, the point of judicial behavior was paramount, since the criminal charges were admittedly thin. This case was in the context of F.D.R.'s effort to pack the Supreme Court with Justices more to his liking; Judge Ritter was a transplanted conservative Colorado Republican appointed to the Federal bench in solidly Democratic Florida by President Coolidge. He was convicted by a coalition of liberal Republicans, New Deal Democrats, and Farmer-Labor and Progressive Party Senators in what might be called the northwestern strategy of that era. Nevertheless, the arguments were persuasive:

In a joint statement, Senators Borah, La Follette, Frazier, and Shipstead said:

We therefore did not, in passing upon the facts presented to us in the matter of the impeachment proceedings against Judge Halsted L. Ritter, seek to satisfy ourselves as to whether technically a crime or crimes had been committed, or as to whether the acts charged and proved disclosed criminal intent or corrupt motive; we sought only to ascertain from these facts whether his conduct has been such as to amount to misbehavior, misconduct—as to whether he had conducted himself in a way that was calculated to undermine public confidence in the courts and to create a sense of scandal.

There are a great many things which one must readily admit would be wholly unbecoming, wholly intolerable, in the conduct of a judge, and yet these things might not amount to a crime.

Note

1. Laura Kalman, *Abe Fortas: A Biography* (New Haven, Conn.: Yale University Press, 1990), 374–375; Van Tassel, 382–385.

❧ 7 ❧

Paul N. McCloskey's Reply to Ford

(1970)

I N REPLY TO Rep. Gerald Ford's speech requesting an investigation of Associate Justice William O. Douglas, Rep. Paul N. McCloskey, a Republican from California, concludes that for conduct to be subject to an impeachment inquiry, and potential removal from office, it must be either official misconduct, which may or may not be criminal, or unofficial but criminal misconduct. In McCloskey's view, there is no basis in precedent for the conclusion that purely private behavior that is not criminal can be the basis for impeachment.

🐜 🐜 🐜

CONGRESS OF THE UNITED STATES
HOUSE OF REPRESENTATIVES,
Washington, D.C., August 18, 1970.
HON. EMANUEL CELLER,
Chairman, Committee on the Judiciary, House of Representatives,
Rayburn House Office Building, Washington, D.C.

DEAR MR. CHAIRMAN: Jerry Ford has been kind enough for furnish me a copy of his letter to you dated August 5, enclosing the Memorandum of Dykema, Wheat, Spencer, Goodnow & Trigg, on the congressional impeachment power.

I have reviewed this brief but do not believe that its arguments go to the primary points I raised in my answer to Mr. Ford's comments on the floor of the House of April 21, as follows:

1. Impeachment should be considered in the nature of a criminal proceeding, since its end result is "conviction" and the debates in the Constitutional Convention of 1787 infer a common understanding of the delegates that impeachment was analogous to a criminal proceeding. This is noteworthy in that, under traditional American principles of justice, we customarily require that the *prosecutor* be himself convinced that the potential accused is guilty before filing the complaint or urging an indictment. Thus, the House, before bringing impeachment proceedings, should collectively reach the conclusion by a majority vote that the accused is guilty of the charges filed, not just that he *may* be guilty.

2. Conduct of a Judge, while it may be less than criminal in nature to constitute "less than good behavior", has never resulted in a successful impeachment unless the judge was acting in his *judicial* capacity or misusing his *judicial* power. In other words the precedents suggest that misconduct must either be *"judicial* misconduct" or conduct which constitutes a crime. There is no basis for impeachment on charges of *non*-judicial misconduct which [occurs] off the bench and does *not* constitute a crime. The key conclusion of the Dykema, et al. brief goes back to the Ritter proceeding in 1963:

"Where a judge *on the bench,* by his own conduct, arouses a substantial doubt as to his judicial integrity he commits the highest crime that a judge can commit under the Constitution." (Emphasis added)

3. The primary difficulty with the charges outlined by Mr. Ford is that all but one relate to personal *off-the-bench* conduct which is not criminal in nature. There is no precedent cited which would justify impeachment of Justice Douglas unless he is determined to have given legal advice in violation of the U.S. Code.

Respectfully,

PAUL N. MCCLOSKEY, Jr.

HOUSE DEBATE ON
DOUGLAS IMPEACHMENT

The SPEAKER pro tempore. Under a previous order of the House, the gentleman from California (Mr. McCloskey) is recognized for 60 minutes.

Mr. MCCLOSKEY. Mr. Speaker, I rise in response to the remarks of my distinguished leader, the gentleman from Michigan (Mr. GERALD R. FORD) last Wednesday evening, when he set forth his views of the constitutional power of impeachment and stated certain facts and opinions which, in his judgment, justified his vote for the immediate impeachment of Associate Supreme Court Justice William O. Douglas. The dialog which ensued is reported in the CON-GRESSIONAL RECORD of April 15, 1970, at pages H3112 through H3127.

I respectfully disagree with the basic premise "that an impeachable offense is whatever a majority of the House of Representatives considers it to be at a given moment in history."

To accept this view, in my judgment would do grave damage to one of the most treasured cornerstones of our liberties, the constitutional principle of an independent judiciary, free not only from public passions and emotions, but also free from fear of executive or legislative disfavor except under already-defined rules and precedents.

The arguments presented last Wednesday raise grave constitutional issues, and I hope my colleagues will understand that I speak not in derogation of my leader's judgment, but to express a differing view of the law of impeachment and the criteria to be applied by the House to conduct attributed to a member of the Judiciary. I do not speak in defense of Justice Douglas, whom I have met but once many years ago. I would like to speak, however, for the principle of judicial independence and the concept that Congress should not challenge a sitting judge except under the clearest showing of misconduct.

Also, in view of the fact that the issues are those of law and precedent, I think it especially incumbent on those of us who are lawyers to discuss all aspects of the case from the various points of view traditional to our profession.

The first two sentences of the canons of ethics of the American Bar Association impose a special duty on lawyers:

It is the duty of the lawyer to maintain towards the courts a respectful attitude, not for the sake of the temporary incumbent of the judicial office, but for the maintenance of its supreme importance. Judges, not being wholly free to defend themselves, are peculiarly entitled to receive the support of the bar against unjust criticism and clamor.

In my State of California, the attorney's duty to the courts has been referred to as among the foremost of his obligations.

The members of the legal profession should, above all other members of society, be the first to uphold the dignity of judicial tribunals and to protect them against falling into that disrepute to which they would be hastened if proceedings before them were conducted without order or decorum * * * *Platnauer* v. *Superior Court*, 32 Cal. App. 463, 473 (1917).

Attorneys must observe the principles of truth, honesty, and fairness, especially in criticism of the courts. In re Humphrey, 174 Cal. 290, 295 (1917).

No one would question that our duties to the Nation as Members of Congress supersede any duty to the courts occasioned by our professional background, but I do think the canons and court decisions lend support to the tradition of this Nation that our courts are not to be attacked in the same manner that we might criticize political opponents or members of the executive branch.

It also seems appropriate for Members of the House who are also privileged to be members of the bar to lay before the House such historical facts, interpretations, and legal argument as may warrant a stricter construction of the term "good behavior" than those urging impeachment have suggested.

First, I should like to discuss the concept of an impeachable offense as "whatever the majority of the House of Representatives considers it to be at any given time in history." If this concept is accurate, then of course there are no limitations on what a political majority might determine to be less than good behavior. It follows that judges of the Court could conceivably be removed whenever the majority of the House and two-thirds of the Senate agreed that a better judge might fill the position. But this concept has no basis, either in our constitutional history or in actual case precedent.

The intent of the framers of the Constitution was clearly to protect judges from political disagreement, rather than to simplify their ease of removal.

The Original Colonies had had a long history of difficulties with the administration of justice under the British Crown. The Declaration of Independence listed as one of its grievances against the King:

He has made Judges dependent on his Will alone, for the tenure of their offices and the amount and payment of their salaries.

The signers of the Declaration of Independence were primarily concerned about preserving the independence of the judiciary from direct or indirect pressures, and particularly from the pressure of discretionary termination of their jobs or diminution of their salaries.

In the debates which took place in the Constitutional Convention 11 years later, this concern was expressed in both of the major proposals presented to the delegates. The Virginia and New Jersey plans both contained language substantively similar to that finally adopted, as follows:

Article III, Section 1 states "The Judges, both of the Supreme and inferior Courts, shall hold their offices during good Behavior, and shall, at stated times, receive for their Services, a Compensation, which shall not be diminished during their Continuance in Office."

The "good behavior" standard thus does not stand alone. It must be read with reference to the clear intention of the [framers] to protect the independence of the judiciary against executive or legislative action on their compensation, presumably because of the danger of political disagreement.

If, in order to protect judicial independence, Congress is specifically precluded from terminating or reducing the salaries of Judges, it seems clear that Congress was not intended to have the power to designate "as an impeachable offense whatever a majority of the House of Representatives considers it to be at a given moment."

If an independent judiciary is to be preserved, the House must exercise decent restraint and caution in its definition of what is less than good behavior. As we honor the Court's self-imposed doctrine of judicial restraint, so we might likewise honor the principle of legislative restraint in considering serious charges against members of a coequal branch of Government which we have wished to keep free from political tensions and emotions. . . .

There is a far graver question, however, with the argument that "good behavior," or lack of it, is whatever the majority of the House wants to make it.

The term "good behavior," as the Founding Fathers considered it, must be taken together with the specific provisions limiting cause for impeachment of executive branch personnel to treason, bribery or other high crimes and misdemeanors. The higher standard of good behavior required of Judges might well be considered as applicable solely to their judicial performance and capability and not to their private and nonjudicial conduct unless the same is violative of the law. Alcoholism, arrogance, nonjudicial temperament, and senility of course interfere with judicial performance and properly justify impeachment. I can find no precedent, however, for impeachment of a Judge for nonjudicial conduct which falls short of violation of law.

In looking to the nine cases of impeachment of Judges spanning 181 years of our national history, in every case involved, the impeachment was based on either improper judicial conduct or nonjudicial conduct which was considered as criminal in nature.

Mr. GROSS. Mr. Speaker, will the gentleman yield?

Mr. MCCLOSKEY. I will yield.

Mr. GROSS. What is nonjudicial conduct of a judge? Conduct that takes place when he is not sitting as a judge? How can there be nonjudicial conduct?

Mr. MCCLOSKEY. In the sense I use these terms, judicial conduct would be in the conduct of his office on the bench and nonjudicial conduct would be his private and personal life off the bench and utterances unconnected with the performance of his judicial duties. That is the sense I use it in this discussion.

Mr. GROSS. What the gentleman is saying, then, is if he wants to be a Lothario, that is all right as long as it does not involve what he is actually doing on the bench. Is that what the gentleman is saying?

Mr. McCLOSKEY. If his private or personal life should constitute a violation of criminal or civil law, then, in my judgment, it would justify impeachment for the failure of good behavior. If, on the other hand, his private life might be such as to cause blame to fall on him on the part of some, but not others, then I think that the Congress a[t] its peril goes into the question of reaching for the first time a definition of what is different, rather than good, behavior.

Let me continue, if I may, and I will yield further as I try to ring out this point. . . .

From the brief research I have been able to do on these nine cases, and as reflected in the Congressional Quarterly of April 17, 1970, the charges were as follows:

District Judge John Pickering, 1804: Loose morals, intemperance, and irregular judicial procedure.

Associate Supreme Court Justice Samuel Chase, 1805: Partisan, harsh, and unfair conduct during trials.

District Judge James H. Peck, 1831: Imposing an unreasonably harsh penalty for contempt of court.

District Judge West H. Humphreys, 1862: Supported secession and served as a Confederate judge.

District Judge Charles Swayne, 1905: Padding expense accounts, living outside his district, misuse of property and of the contempt power.

Associate Court of Commerce Judge Robert Archbald, 1913: Improper use of influence, and accepting favors from litigants.

District Judge George W. English, 1926: Tyranny, oppression, and partiality.

District Judge Harold Louderback, 1933: Favoritism, and conspiracy.

District Judge Halsted L. Ritter, 1936; Judicial improprieties, accepting legal fees while on the bench, bring his court into scandal and disrepute, and failure to pay his income tax.

The bulk of these challenges to the court were thus on judicial misconduct, with scattered instances of nonjudicial behavior. In all cases, however, insofar as I have been able to thus far determine, the nonjudicial behavior involved clear violations of criminal or civil law, and not just a "pattern of behavior" that others might find less than "good."

If the House accept precedent as a guide, then, an [impeachment] of a Justice of the Supreme Court based on charges which are neither unlawful in nature nor connected with the performance of his judicial duties would represent a highly dubious break with custom and tradition at a time when, as the gentleman from New York, (Mr. Horton) stated last Wednesday:

We are living in an era when the institutions of government and the people who man them are undergoing the severest tests in history.

There is merit, I think, in a strict construction of the words "good behavior" as including conduct which complies with judicial ethics while on the bench and with the criminal and civil laws while off the bench. Any other construction of the term would make judges vulnerable to any majority group in the Congress which held a common view of impropriety of conduct which was admittedly lawful. If lawful conduct can nevertheless be deemed an impeachable offense by a majority of the House, how can any Judge feel free to express opinions on controversial subjects off the bench? Is there anything in our history to indicate that the framers of our Constitution intended to preclude a judge from stating political views publicly, either orally or in writing? I have been unable to find any constitutional history to so indicate.

The gentleman from New Hampshire (Mr. Wyman) suggests that a judge should not publicly declare his personal views on controvers[ies] likely to come before the Court. This is certainly true. But it certainly does not preclude a judge from voicing personal political views, since political issues are not within the jurisdiction of the court and thus a judge's opinions on political matters would generally not be prejudicial to interpretations of the law which his jurisdiction is properly limited.

To subject a Judge to impeachment for controversial political views stated off the Bench has a ring of ex post facto unless there is some precedent which can be found in our own rather colorful history as a Nation. . . .

I have tried to point out the fact that we must balance the disrespect that we may feel that the Justice has brought upon himself against the need to preserve an independent judiciary because long after a personality may have been forgotten, we must have an independent judiciary free to deliberate on the issues of law which is far more desirable than the temporary disappointment we may feel against an individual whom we may feel has brought this upon us.

Mr. PUCINSKI. Mr. Speaker, if the gentleman will yield further, this is why I think this dissertation by the gentleman is so necessary and is deserving of the in-depth study which the gentleman has made. However, I think it proves what we have been saying, and that is that the Founding Fathers did draw a distinction between the executive, the legislative, and the Supreme Court to the effect that the conduct of those nine Justices, unlike any other American, must be of extraordinary prudence.

Mr. McCLOSKEY. We are in agreement, but if we ask judicial restraint we should as Members of Congress exercise legislative restraint when we criticize the Court. We also must not bring disrespect upon the law and the institutions of this country. And, when we ask the young people of the land to obey the law and respect it, at the same time we may contribute ourselves to a great disaffection between the public and the law and the Government that administers that law.

Mr. FOLEY. Mr. Speaker, I want to compliment the gentleman on his presentation and the legal research that he has so carefully undertaken. I think he has added a new scope and dimension to this question. In view of an earlier comment by the gentleman from Iowa (Mr. Gross), I want to say on my own behalf, that I think I understand very clearly why the gentleman from California has made his statement. I do not regard his remarks as being a personal defense of Justice Douglas. I believe the gentleman is deeply concerned, as I am with the independence of the judiciary. I think the gentleman is saying that regardless of the personal feelings or attitudes of individual Members, the question of impeachment of a Justice is one that should be approached with the most serious caution and restraint, with the deepest concern for precedent and then only on compelling evidence of judicial or other misconduct justifies so grave a remedy.

As I understand the gentleman, he is stating that allegations made earlier this week by the distinguished minority leader, are not of themselves and without additional evidence of misconduct sufficient to justify impeachment.

⁂ 8 ⁂

Subcommittee Report on Douglas Impeachment

(1970)

THE SUBCOMMITTEE INVESTIGATING Associate Justice William O. Douglas's behavior devoted several introductory pages of its report to the issue of how to define impeachable conduct. As an initial matter, the subcommittee concluded that "the term 'misdemeanors' requires a showing of misconduct which is inherently serious in relation to social standards." The subcommittee elaborated on this understanding, stating that:

When such misbehavior occurs in connection with the federal office, actual criminal conduct should not be a requisite to impeachment of a judge or any other federal official. While such conduct need not be criminal, it nonetheless must be sufficiently serious to be offenses against good morals and injurious to the social body.

The subcommittee developed two concepts of impeachment, under either of which private conduct that was not criminal could not be subject to impeachment. On the other hand, misconduct involving an officer's official duties could be impeachable even if not criminal.

爲 爲 爲

FINAL REPORT BY THE SPECIAL SUBCOMMITTEE ON H. RES. 920 OF THE COM-
MITTEE ON THE JUDICIARY HOUSE OF REPRESENTATIVES NINETY-FIRST CONGRESS
SECOND SESSION

... The desire of the American people to assure independence of the judiciary and to emphasize the exalted station assigned to the judge by our society,
have erected pervasive constitutional and statutory safeguards. The judge of a
United States court holds office "during good behavior." Further his salary may
not be reduced while he is in office by any branch of Government. A judge may
be removed from office only by the cumbersome procedure of impeachment.

Accordingly, when the public is confronted with allegations of dishonesty
or venality, and is forced to recognize that judges are human, and hence fallible, the impact is severe. Exposure of infirmities in the judicial system is undertaken only with reluctance. It is an area in which the bar, the judiciary, and
the executive and legislative branches alike have seen fit to move cautiously
and painstakingly. There must be full recognition of the necessity to proceed
in such a manner that will result in the least damage possible to judicial independence, but which, at the same time, will result in correction or elimination
of any condition that brings discredit to the judicial system.

Removal of a Federal judge, for whatever reason, historically has been difficult. Constitutional safeguards to assure a free and independent judiciary make
it difficult to remove a Federal judge who may be unfit, whether through in-
competence, insanity, senility, alcoholism, or corruption.

For a judge to be impeached, it must be shown that he has committed treason, accepted a bribe, or has committed a high crime or misdemeanor. All conduct that can be impeached must at least be a "misdemeanor." A judge is
entitled to remain a judge as long as he holds his office "during good behavior." The content of the word "misdemeanor" must encompass some activities
which fall below the standard of "good behavior." Conduct which fails to meet
the standard of "good behavior" but which does not come within the definition
of "misdemeanor" is not subject to impeachment.

In each of the nine impeachments involving judges, there has been controversy as to the meaning of the word "misdemeanor." Primarily the controversy
concerned whether the activities being attacked must be criminal or whether the
word "misdemeanor" encompasses less serious departures from society norms.

In his memorandum "Opinion on the Impeachment of Halsted L. Ritter,"
Senator H. W. Johnson described the confusion of thought prevailing in the
Senate on these concepts. He stated:

"The confusion of thought prevailing among Senators is evidenced by their varying
expressions. One group eloquently argued any gift to a judge, under any circum-

stances, constituted misbehavior, for which he should be removed from office—and moreover that neither corrupt motive or evil intent need be shown in the acceptance of a gift or in any so-called misbehavior. Another prefaced his opinion with the statement: 'I do not take the view that an impeachment proceeding of a judge of the inferior Federal courts under the Constitution of the United States is a criminal proceeding. The Constitution itself has expressly denuded impeachment proceedings of every aspect or characteristic of a criminal proceeding.'

"And yet another flatly takes a contrary view, and states although finding the defendant guilty on the seventh count: 'The procedure is criminal in its nature, for upon conviction, requires the removal of a judge, which is the highest punishment that could be administered such an officer. The Senate, sitting as a court, is required to conduct its proceedings and reach its decisions in accordance with the customs of our law. In all criminal cases the defendant comes into court enjoying the presumption of innocence, which presumption continues until he is proven guilty beyond a reasonable doubt.'

"And again we find this: 'Impeachment, though, must be considered as a criminal proceeding.' "

In his April 15, 1970, speech, Representative Ford articulated the concept that an impeachable offense need not be indictable and may be something less than a criminal act or criminal dereliction of duty. He said:

"What, then, is an impeachable offense?

"The only honest answer is that an impeachable offense is whatever a majority of the House of Representatives considers to be at a given moment in history; conviction results from whatever offense or offenses two-thirds of the other body considers to be sufficiently serious to require removal of the accused from office. Again, the historical context and political climate are important; there are few fixed principles among the handful of precedents.

"I think it is fair to come to one conclusion, however, from our history of impeachments: a higher standard is expected of Federal judges than of any other 'civil officers' of the United States." (First Report, p. 31)

The "Kelley Memorandum" submitted by Mr. Ford enforces this position. The Kelley Memorandum asserts that misbehavior by a Federal judge may constitute an impeachable offense though the conduct may not be an indictable crime or misdemeanor. The Kelley Memorandum concludes:

"In conclusion, the history of the constitutional provisions relating to the impeachment of Federal judges demonstrates that only the Congress has the power and duty to remove from office any judge whose proven conduct, either in the administration of justice or in his personal behavior, casts doubt on his personal integrity and thereby on the integrity of the entire judiciary. Federal judges must maintain the highest standards of conduct to preserve the independence of and respect for the judicial system and the rule of law."

On the other hand, Counsel for Associate Justice Douglas, Simon H. Rifkind, has submitted a memorandum that contends that a Federal judge may not be impeached for anything short of criminal conduct. Mr. Rifkind also contends that the other provisions of the Constitution, i.e., the prohibition of *ex post facto* laws, due process notice requirement and the protection of the First Amendment prevent the employment of any other standard in impeachment proceedings. In conclusion Mr. Rifkind stated:

"The constitutional language, in plain terms, confines impeachment to 'Treason, Bribery, or other high Crimes and Misdemeanors.' The history of those provisions reinforces their plain meaning. Even when the Jeffersonians sought to purge the federal bench of all Federalist judges, they felt compelled to at least assert that their political victims were guilty of 'high Crimes and Misdemeanors.' The unsuccessful attempt to remove Justice Chase firmly established the proposition that impeachment is for *criminal* offenses only, and is not a 'general inquest' into the behavior of judges. There has developed the consistent practice, rigorously followed in every case in this century, of impeaching federal judges only when criminal offenses have been charged. Indeed, the House has *never* impeached a judge except with respect to a 'high Crime' or 'Misdemeanor.' Characteristically, the basis for impeachment has been the soliciting of bribes, selling of votes, manipulation of receivers' fees, misappropriation of properties in receivership, and willful income tax evasion."

A vast body of literature has been developed concerning the scope of the impeachment power as it pertains to federal judges. The precedents show that the House of Representatives, particularly in the arguments made by its Managers in the Senate trials, favors the conclusion that the phrase "high crimes and misdemeanors" encompasses activity which is not necessarily criminal in nature.

Although there may be divergence of opinion as to whether impeachment of a judge requires conduct that is criminal in nature in that it is proscribed by specific statutory or common law prohibition, all authorities hold that for a judge to be impeached, the term "misdemeanors" requires a showing of misconduct which is inherently serious in relation to social standards. No respectable argument can be made to support the concept that a judge could be impeached if his conduct did not amount at least to a serious dereliction of his duty as a member of society.

The punishment imposed by the Constitution measures how serious misconduct need be to be impeachable. Only serious derelictions of duty owed to society would warrant the punishment provided. An impeachment proceeding is a trial which results in punishment after an appropriate finding by the trier of facts, the Senate. Deprivation of office is a punishment. Disqualification to hold any future office of honor, trust and profit is a greater punishment. The judgment of the Senate confers upon that body discretion, in the words of the

Federalist Papers ". . . to doom to honor or to infamy the most influential and the most distinguished characters of the community. . . ."

Reconciliation of the differences between the concept that a judge has a right to his office during "good behavior" and the concept that the legislature has a duty to remove him if his conduct constitutes a "misdemeanor" is facilitated by distinguishing conduct that occurs in connection with the exercise of his judicial office from conduct that is non-judicially connected. Such a distinction permits recognition that the content of the word "misdemeanor" for conduct that occurs in the course of exercise of the power of the judicial office includes a broader spectrum of action than is the case when non-judicial activities are involved.

When such a distinction is made, the two concepts on the necessity for judicial conduct to be criminal in nature to be subject to impeachment becomes defined and may be reconciled under the overriding requirement that to be a "misdemeanor", and hence impeachable, conduct must amount to a serious dereliction of an obligation owed to society.

To facilitate exposition, the two concepts may be summarized as follows:

Both concepts must satisfy the requirements of Article II, Section 4, that the challenged activity must constitute " . . . Treason, Bribery or High Crimes and Misdemeanors."

Both concepts would allow a judge to be impeached for acts which occur in the exercise of judicial office that (1) involve criminal conduct in violation of law, or (2) that involve serious dereliction from public duty, but not necessarily in violation of positive statutory law or forbidden by the common law. Sloth, drunkenness on the bench or unwarranted and unreasonable impartiality manifest for a prolonged period are examples of misconduct, not necessarily criminal in nature that would support impeachment. When such misbehavior occurs in connection with the federal office, actual criminal conduct should not be a requisite to impeachment of a judge or any other federal official. While such conduct need not be criminal, it nonetheless must be sufficiently serious to be offenses against good morals and injurious to the social body.

Both concepts would allow a judge to be impeached for conduct not connected with the duties and responsibilities of the judicial office which involve criminal acts in violation of law.

The two concepts differ only with respect to impeachability of judicial behavior not connected with the duties and responsibilities of the judicial office. Concept 2 would define "misdemeanor" to permit impeachment for serious derelictions of public duty but not necessarily violations of statutory or common law.

In summary, an outline of the two concepts would look this way:

A judge may be impeached for " . . . Treason, Bribery, or High Crimes or Misdemeanors."

A. Behavior, connected with judicial office or exercise of judicial power.
Concept I
1. Criminal conduct.
2. Serious dereliction from public duty.
Concept II
1. Criminal conduct.
2. Serious dereliction from public duty.
B. Behavior not connected with the duties and responsibilities of the judicial office.
Concept I
1. Criminal conduct.
Concept II
1. Criminal conduct.
2. Serious dereliction from public duty.

[Chapter III] Disposition of Charges sets forth the Special Subcommittee's analysis of the charges that involve activities of Associate Justice William O. Douglas. Under this analysis it is not necessary for the members of the Judiciary Committee to choose between Concept I and II.

The theories embodied in Concept I have been articulated by Representative Paul N. McCloskey, Jr. In his speech to the House on April 21, 1970, Mr. McCloskey stated:

"The term 'good behavior,' as the Founding Fathers considered it, must be taken together with the specific provisions limiting cause for impeachment of executive branch personnel to treason, bribery or other high crimes and misdemeanors. The higher standard of good behavior required of judges might well be considered as applicable solely to their judicial performance and capacity and not to their private and nonjudicial conduct unless the same is violative of the law. Alcoholism, arrogance, nonjudicial temperament, and senility of course interfere with judicial performance and properly justify impeachment. I can find no precedent, however, for impeachment of a Judge for nonjudicial conduct which falls short of violation of law.

"In looking to the nine cases of impeachment of Judges spanning 181 years of our national history, in every case involved, the impeachment was based on either improper judicial conduct or non-judicial conduct which was considered as criminal in nature." Cong. Rec. 91st Cong., 2nd Sess., H 3327.

In his August 18, 1970, letter to the Special Subcommittee embodying his comments on the "Kelley Memorandum", Mr. McCloskey reaffirmed this concept. He stated:

"Conduct of a Judge, while it may be less than criminal in nature to constitute 'less than good behavior', has never resulted in a successful impeachment unless the judge was acting in his *judicial* capacity or misusing his *judicial* power. In other words the precedents suggest that misconduct must either be *'judicial* misconduct' or conduct which constitutes a crime. There is no basis for impeachment on charges of *non-judicial* misconduct which occurs off the bench and does *not* constitute a crime.". . .

IV. Recommendations of Special Subcommittee to
Judiciary Committee

1. It is not necessary for the members of the Judiciary Committee to take a position on either of the concepts of impeachment that are discussed in Chapter II.

2. Intensive investigation of the Special Subcommittee has not disclosed creditable evidence that would warrant preparation of charges on any acceptable concept of an impeachable offense.

EMANUEL CELLER,
BYRON G. ROGERS,
JACK BROOKS.

⛬ 9 ⛬
Deschler's Precedents of
the House of Representatives
(1977)

BECAUSE THE CONSTITUTIONAL phrase "high Crimes and Misdemeanors" has no obvious meaning, it has been a focus of debate in almost every impeachment controversy during the past two hundred years. The following document is an excerpt from the *Precedents of the House of Representatives,* which is a compendium of House actions compiled by House parliamentarian Lewis Deschler. It includes the majority and minority views of the House Judiciary Committee on what constitutes impeachable offenses, developed in the context of the Watergate investigation of President Richard Nixon. The impeachment of President Andrew Johnson in 1867 is also discussed here. (For more on Nixon and Watergate, see Document 30, p. 253; for more on the impeachment of Johnson, see Document 28, p. 221.)

Grounds for Impeachment 3.0

The various grounds for impeachment and the form of impeachment articles have been document during recent investigations. Following the inquiry into charges against President Nixon, the Committee on the Judiciary reported to the House a report recommending impeachment, which report included the text of a resolution and articles impeaching the President. As indicated by the articles, and by the conclusions of the report as to the specific articles, the Committee on the Judiciary determined that the grounds for Presidential impeachment need not be indictable or criminal; articles II and III impeached the President for a course of conduct constituting an abuse of power and for failure to comply with subpenas issued by the committee during the impeachment inquiry. The committee also concluded that an article of impeachment could cumulate charges and facts constituting a course of conduct, as in article II.

The grounds for impeachment of federal judges were scrutinized in 1970, in the inquiry into the conduct of Associate Justice Douglas of the Supreme Court. Concepts of impeachment were debated on the floor of the House, as to the ascertainability of the definition of an impeachable offense, and as to whether a federal judge could be impeached for conduct not related to the performance of his judicial function or for judicial conduct not criminal in nature.

A special subcommittee of the Committee on the Judiciary was created to investigate and report on the charges of impeachment against Justice Douglas, and submitted to the committee a final report recommending against impeachment, finding the evidence insufficient. The report concluded that a federal judge could be impeached for judicial conduct which is either criminal or a serious abuse of public duty, or for non-judicial conduct which is criminal. . . .

[§ 3.6] With respect to the conduct of President Richard Nixon, the impeachment inquiry staff of the Committee on the Judiciary reported to the committee on "Constitutional Grounds for Presidential Impeachment," which included references to the value of historical precedents.

During an inquiry into impeachable offenses against President Nixon in the 93d Congress by the Committee on the Judiciary, the committee's impeachment inquiry staff reported to the committee on grounds for impeachment of the President. The report discussed in detail the historical bases and origins, in both English parliamentary practice and in the practice of the U.S. Congress, of the impeachment power, and drew conclusions as to the grounds for impeachment of the President and of other federal civil officers from the history of impeachment proceedings and from the history of the U.S. Constitution.

EXHIBIT
CRIM 1827-72
WATERGATE

This photo of the Watergate complex in 1972 was introduced during the first trial of the seven men accused of breaking into the Democratic National Committee headquarters.

Grounds for Presidential Impeachment

[§ 3.7] The Committee on the Judiciary concluded, in recommending articles impeaching President Richard Nixon to the House, that the President could be impeached not only for violations of federal criminal statutes, but also for (1) serious abuse of the powers of his office, and (2) refusal to comply with proper subpenas [sic] of the committee for evidence relevant to its impeachment inquiry.

In its final report to the House pursuant to its impeachment inquiry into the conduct of President Nixon in the 93d Congress, the Committee on the Judiciary set forth the following conclusions (footnotes omitted) on the three articles of impeachment adopted by the committee and included in its report:

[Article I]
Conclusion

After the Committee on the Judiciary had debated whether or not it should recommend Article I to the House of Representatives, 27 of the 38 Members of the Committee found that the evidence before it could only lead to one conclusion; that Richard M. Nixon, using the powers of his high office, engaged, personally and through his subordinates and agents, in a course of conduct or plan designed to delay, impede, and obstruct the investigation of the unlawful entry, on June 17, 1972, into the headquarters of the Democratic National Committee; to cover up, conceal and protect those responsible; and to conceal the existence and scope of other unlawful covert activities. . . .

President Nixon's actions resulted in manifest injury to the confidence of the nation and great prejudice to the cause of law and justice, and was subversive of constitutional government. His actions were contrary to his trust as President and unmindful of the solemn duties of his high office. It was this serious violation that Richard M. Nixon's constitutional obligations as President, and not the fact that violations of Federal criminal statutes occurred, that lies at the heart of Article I.

The Committee finds, based upon clear and convincing evidence, that this conduct, detailed in the foregoing pages of this report, constitutes "high crimes and misdemeanors" as that term is used in Article II, Section 4 of the Constitution. Therefore, the Committee recommends that the House of Representatives exercise its constitutional power to impeach Richard M. Nixon. . . .

[Article II]

Conclusion

In recommending Article II to the House, the Committee finds clear and convincing evidence that Richard M. Nixon, contrary to his trust as President and unmindful of the solemn duties of his high office, has repeatedly used his power as President to violate the Constitution and the law of the land.

In so doing, he has failed in the obligation that every citizen has to live under the law. But he has done more, for it is the duty of the President not merely to live by that law but to see that law faithfully applied. Richard M. Nixon has repeatedly and willfully failed to perform that duty. He has failed to perform it by authorizing and directing actions that violated or disregarded the rights of citizens and that corrupted and attempted to corrupt the lawful functioning of executive agencies. He has failed to perform it by condoning and ratifying, rather than acting to stop, actions by his subordinates that interfered with lawful investigations and impeded the enforcement of the laws.

Article II, section 3 of the Constitution requires that the President "shall take Care that the Laws be faithfully executed." Justice Felix Frankfurter described this provision as "the embracing function of the President"; President Benjamin Harrison called it "the central idea of the office." "[I]n a republic," Harrison wrote, "the thing to be executed is the law, not the will of the ruler as in despotic governments. The President cannot go beyond the law, and cannot stop short of it.". . .

Our Constitution provides for a responsible Chief Executive, accountable for his acts. The framers hoped, in the words of Elbridge Gerry, that "the maxim would never be adopted here that the chief Magistrate could do no wrong." They provided for a single executive because, as Alexander Hamilton wrote, "the executive power is more easily confined when it is one" and "there should be a single object for the . . . watchfulness of the people."

The President, said James Wilson, one of the principal authors of the Constitution, "is the dignified, but accountable magistrate of a free and great people." Wilson said, "The executive power is better to be trusted when it has no screen . . . [W]e have a responsibility in the person of our President . . . he cannot roll upon any other person the weight of his criminality . . ." As both Wilson and Hamilton pointed out, the President should not be able to hide behind his counsellors; he must ultimately be accountable for their acts on his behalf. James Iredell of North Carolina, a leading proponent of the proposed Constitution and later a Supreme Court Justice, said that the President "is a very different nature from a monarch. He is to be . . . personally responsible for any abuse of the great trust reposed in him.". . .

The abuse of a President's powers poses a serious threat to the lawful and proper functioning of the government and the people's confidence in it. For just such Presidential misconduct the impeachment power was included in the Constitution. The impeachment provision, wrote Justice Joseph Story in 1833, "holds out a deep and immediate responsibility, as a check upon arbitrary power; and compels the chief magistrate, as well as the humblest citizen, to bend to the majesty of the law." And Chancellor James Kent wrote in 1826:

If . . . neither the sense of duty, the force of public opinion, nor the transitory nature of the seat, are sufficient to secure a faithful exercise of the executive trust, but the President will use the authority of his station to violate the Constitution or law of the land, the House of Representatives can arrest him in his career, by resorting to the power of impeachment.

. . . The Committee finds that, in the performance of his duties as President, Richard M. Nixon on many occasions has acted to the detriment of justice, right, and the public good, in violation of his constitutional duty to see to the faithful execution of the laws. This conduct has demonstrated a contempt for the rule of law; it has posed a threat to our democratic republic. The Committee finds that this conduct constitutes "high crimes and misdemeanors" within the meaning of the Constitution, that it warrants his impeachment by the House, and that it requires that he be put to trial in the Senate. . . .

[Article III]

Conclusion

The undisputed facts, historic precedent, and applicable legal principles support the Committee's recommendation of Article III. There can be no question that in refusing to comply with limited, narrowly drawn subpoenas—issued only after the Committee was satisfied that there was other evidence pointing to the existence of impeachable offenses—the President interfered with the exercise of the House's function as the "Grand Inquest of the Nation." Unless the defiance of the Committee's subpoenas under these circumstances is considered grounds for impeachment, it is difficult to conceive of any President acknowledging that he is obligated to supply the relevant evidence necessary for Congress to exercise its constitutional responsibility in an impeachment proceeding. If this were to occur, the impeachment power would be drained of its vitality. Article III, therefore, seeks to preserve the integrity of the impeachment process itself and the ability of Congress to act as the ultimate safeguard against improper presidential conduct.

[§ 3.8] In the report of the Committee on the Judiciary recommending the impeachment of President Richard Nixon, the minority took the view that grounds for Presidential impeachment must be criminal conduct or acts with criminal intent.

On Aug. 20, 1974, the Committee on the Judiciary submitted a report recommending the impeachment of President Nixon. In the minority views set out below (footnotes omitted), Messrs. Hutchinson, Smith, Sandman, Wiggins, Dennis, Mayne, Lott, Moorhead, Maraziti, and Latta discussed the grounds for presidential impeachment:

B. Meaning of "Treason, Bribery or other high Crimes and Misdemeanors"

The Constitution of the United States provides that the President "shall be removed from Office on Impeachment for, and Conviction of, Treason, Bribery, or other high Crimes and Misdemeanors." Upon impeachment and conviction, removal of the President from office is mandatory. The offenses for which a President may be impeached are limited to those enumerated in the Constitution, namely "Treason, Bribery, or other high Crimes and Misdemeanors." We do not believe that a President or any other civil officer of the United States government may constitutionally be impeached and convicted for errors in the administration of his office.

1. Adoption of "Treason, Bribery, or Other High Crimes and Misdemeanors" at Constitutional Convention

The original version of the impeachment clause at the Constitutional Convention of 1787 had made "malpractice or neglect of duty" the grounds for impeachment. On July 20, 1787, the Framers debated whether to retain this clause, and decided to do so.

Gouverneur Morris, who had moved to strike the impeachment clause altogether, began by arguing that it was unnecessary because the executive "can do no criminal act without Coadjutors who may be punished." George Mason disagreed, arguing that "When great *crimes* were committed he [favored] punishing the principal as well as the Coadjutors." Fearing recourse to assassinations, Benjamin Franklin favored impeachment "to provide in the Constitution for the regular *punishment* of the executive when his misconduct should deserve it, and for his honorable acquittal when he should be unjustly accused." Gouverneur Morris then admitted that "corruption & some few other offenses" should be impeachable, but thought "the case ought to be enumerated & defined."

Rufus King, a co-sponsor of the motion to strike the impeachment clause, pointed out that the executive, unlike the judiciary, did not hold his office during good behavior, but during a fixed, elective term; and accordingly ought not be impeachable, like the judiciary, for "misbehaviour:" this would be "destructive of his independence and of the principles of the Constitution.". . .

[2]c. *American impeachment practice*

The impeachment of President Andrew Johnson is the most important precedent for a consideration of what constitutes grounds for impeachment of a President, even if it has been historically regarded (and probably fairly so) as an excessively partisan exercise of the impeachment power.

The Johnson impeachment was the product of a fundamental and bitter split between the President and the Congress as to Reconstruction policy in the Southern states following the Civil War. Johnson's vetoes of legislation, his use of pardons, and his choice of appointees in the South made it all impossible for the Reconstruction Acts to be enforced in the manner which Congress not only desired, but thought urgently necessary.

On March 7, 1867, the House referred to the Judiciary Committee a resolution authorizing it

to inquire into the *official conduct of* Andrew Johnson . . . and to report to this House whether, in their opinion, the said Andrew Johnson, while in said office, has been guilty of acts which were *designed or calculated to overthrow or corrupt the government of the United States* . . . and whether the said Andrew Johnson has been guilty of any act, or has conspired with others to do acts, which, in contemplation of the Constitution, are high crimes and misdemeanors, requiring the interposition of the constitutional powers of this House.

On November 25, 1867, the Committee reported to the full House a resolution recommending impeachment, by a vote of 5 to 4. A minority of the Committee, led by Rep. James F. Wilson of Iowa, took the position that there could be no impeachment because the President had committed no crime:

In approaching a conclusion, we do not fail to recognize two standpoints from which this case can be viewed—the legal and the political.

. . . Judge him politically, we must condemn him. But the day of political impeachments would be a sad one for this country. Political unfitness and incapacity must be tried at the ballot-box, not in the high court of impeachment. A contrary rule might leave to Congress but little time for other business than the trial of impeachments.

. . . [C]rimes and misdemeanors are now demanding our attention. Do these, within the meaning of the Constitution, appear? Rest the case upon political offenses, and we are prepared to pronounce against the President, for such offenses are numerous and grave . . . [yet] we still affirm that the conclusion at which we have arrived is correct.

The resolution recommending impeachment was debated in the House on December 5 and 6, 1867, Rep. George S. Boutwell of Massachusetts speaking for the Committee majority in favor of impeachment, and Rep. Wilson speaking in the negative. Aside from characterization of undisputed facts discovered by the Committee, the only point debated was whether the commission of a crime was an essential element of impeachable conduct by the President. Rep. Boutwell began by saying, "If the theory of the law submitted by the minority of the committee be in the judgement of this House a true theory, then the majority have no case whatsoever." "The country was disappointed, no doubt, in the report of the committee," he continued, "and very likely this House participated in the disappointment, that there was no specific, heinous, novel offense charged upon and proved against the President of the United States." And again, "It may not be possible, by specific charge, to arraign him for this great crime, but is he therefore to escape?"

The House of Representatives answered this question the next day, when the majority resolution recommending, impeachment was defeated by a vote of 57 to 108. The issue of impeachment was thus laid to rest for the time being.

Earlier in 1867, the Congress had passed the Tenure-of-Office Act, which took away the President's authority to remove members of his own Cabinet, and provided that violation of the Act should be punishable by imprisonment of up to five years and a fine of up to ten thousand dollars and "shall be deemed a high misdemeanor"—fair notice that Congress would consider violation of the statute an impeachable, as well as a criminal, offense. It was generally known that Johnson's policy toward Reconstruction was not shared by his Secretary of War, Edwin M. Stanton. Although Johnson believed the Tenure-of-Office Act to be unconstitutional, he had not infringed its provisions at the time the 1867 impeachment attempt against him failed by such a decisive margin.

Two an a half months later, however, Johnson removed Stanton from office, in apparent disregard of the Tenure-of-Office Act. The response of Congress was immediate: Johnson was impeached three days later, on February 24, 1868, by a vote of 128 to 47—an even greater margin than that by which the first impeachment vote had failed.

The reversal is a dramatic demonstration that the House of Representatives believe it had to find the President guilty of a crime before impeaching him. The nine articles of impeachment which were adopted against Johnson, on March 2, 1868, all related to his removal of Secretary Stanton, allegedly in deliberate violation of the Tenure-of-office Act, the Constitution, and certain other related statutes. The vote had failed less than three months before; and except for Stanton's removal and related matters, nothing in the new Articles charged Johnson with any act committed subsequent to the previous vote.

The only other case of impeachment of an officer of the executive branch is that of Secretary of War William W. Belknap in 1876. All five articles alleged that Belknap "corruptly" accepted and received considerable sums of money in exchange for exercising his authority to appoint a certain person as a military post trader. The facts alleged would have sufficed to constitute the crime of bribery. Belknap resigned before the adoption of the Articles and was subsequently indicted for the conduct alleged.

It may be acknowledged that in the impeachment of federal judges, as opposed to executive officers, the actual commission of a crime does not appear always to have been thought essential. However, the debates in the House and opinions filed by Senators have made it clear that in impeachments of federal judges, Congress has placed great reliance upon the "good behavior" clause. The distinction between officers tenured during good behavior and elected officers, for purpose of grounds for impeachment, was stressed by Rufus King at the Constitutional Convention of 1787. A judge's impeachment or conviction resting upon "general misbehavior," in whatever degree, cannot be an appropriate guide for the impeachment or conviction of an elected officer serving for a fixed term.

The impeachments of federal judges are also different from the case of a President for other reasons: (1) Some of the President's duties, *e.g.,* as chief of a political party, are sufficiently dissimilar to those of the judiciary that conduct perfectly appropriate for him, such as making a partisan political speech, would be grossly improper for a judge. An officer charged with the continual adjudication of disputes labors under a more stringent injunction against the appearance of partisanship than an officer directly charged with the formulation and negotiation of public policy in the political arena—a fact reflected in the adoption of Canons of Judicial Ethics. (2) The phrase "and all civil Officers" was not added until after the debates on the impeachment clause had taken place. The words "high crimes and misdemeanors" were added while the Framers were debating a clause concerned exclusively with the impeachment of the President. There was no discussion during the Convention as to what would constitute impeachable conduct for judges. (3) Finally, the removal of a President from office would obviously have a far greater impact upon the equilibrium of our system of government than the removal of a single federal judge.

d. The need for a standard: criminal intent

When the Framers included the power to impeach the President in our Constitution, they desired to "provide some mode that will not make him dependent on the Legislature." To this end, they withheld from the Congress many of the powers enjoyed by Parliament in England; and they defined the grounds for impeachment in their written Constitution. It is hardly conceivable that the Framers wished the new Congress to adopt as a starting point the record of all the excesses to which desperate struggles for power had driven Parliament, or to use the impeachment power freely whenever Congress might deem it desirable. The whole tenor of the Framer's discussions, the whole purpose of their many careful departures from English impeachment practice, was in the direction of limits and of standards. An impeachment power exercised without extrinsic and objective standards would be tantamount to the use of bills of attainder and *ex post facto* laws, which are expressly forbidden by the Constitution and are contrary to the American spirit of justice.

It is beyond argument that a violation of the President's oath or a violation of his duty to take care that the laws be faithfully executed, must be impeachable conduct or there would be no means of enforcing the Constitution. However, this elementary proposition is inadequate to define the impeachment power. It remains to determine what kind of conduct constitutes a violation of the oath or the duty. Furthermore, reliance on the summary phrase, "violation of the Constitution," would not always be appropriate as a standard, because actions constituting an apparent violation of one provision of the Constitution may be justified or even required by other provisions of the Constitution.

There are types of misconduct by public officials—for example, ineptitude, or unintentional or "technical" violations of rules or statutes, or "maladministration"—which would not be criminal; nor could they be made criminal, consonant with the Constitution, because the element of criminal intent or *mens rea* would be lacking. Without a requirement of criminal acts or at least criminal intent, Congress would be free to impeach these officials. The loss of this freedom should not be mourned; such a use of the impeachment power was never intended by the Framers, is not supported by the language of our Constitution, and, if history is to guide us, would be seriously unwise as well.

As Alexander Simpson stated in his *Treatise on Federal Impeachments* (1916):

The Senate must find an intent to do wrong. It is, of course, admitted that a party will be presumed to intend the natural and necessary results of his voluntary acts, but that is a presumption only, and it is not always inferable from the act done. So ancient is this principle, and so universal is its application, that it has long since ripened into the maxim, *Actus non facit reun, {nisi} mens sit rea,* and has come to be regarded as one of the fundamental legal principles of our system of jurisprudence.

The point was thus stated by James Iredell in the North Carolina ratifying convention: "I beg leave to observe that, when any man is impeached, it must be for an error of the heart, and not of the head. God forbid that a man, in any country in the world, should be liable to be punished for want of judgement. This is not the case here. . . ."

Part IV

JUDGES, LEGISLATORS, AND CABINET
OFFICIALS: OFFENSES SUBJECT TO
IMPEACHMENT OR CENSURE

T HE DOCUMENTS IN THIS SECTION provide a window into the major historical precedents available for determining what behavior falls within the compass of high crimes and misdemeanors. These include articles of impeachment brought against a member of Congress, a cabinet officer, and twelve federal judges. (The thirteenth judge resigned before articles of impeachment could be drawn, so what is published here is a synopsis of the proceedings against him.)

The nonjudicial impeachments ended inconclusively. Sen. William Blount was the first person impeached by the House; he was simultaneously expelled by the Senate, another "first." Blount was caught plotting a military action against Spain in cooperation with the British government. Clearly both houses of Congress believed that his actions were inconsistent with his office as senator and merited removal. However, because Blount was no longer a member of the government by the time of his impeachment trial, and because it was unclear that members of Congress are officers subject to removal by impeachment, the Senate voted to dismiss the charges. Secretary of War William Belknap is the only other nonjudicial officer, besides President Andrew Johnson, to have been impeached. Like Blount, Belknap was no longer a member of the government at the time of his impeachment. Belknap resigned just hours before the House impeached him. A majority of the Senate—but not a two-thirds majority—voted to try him anyway. When it came time to vote on conviction, the number of senators unconvinced of the Senate's power to try a private citizen was sufficient to deny a two-thirds majority for guilty on any of the charges against Belknap, so he was acquitted.

The judicial impeachments represent the largest group of precedents for what Congress has considered to be impeachable behavior. They must be treated carefully, for the peculiar circumstances under which some of them were brought may make any conclusion about impeachability applicable only to the particular facts of those cases. For instance, Judge John Pickering was insane and drunk on the bench, at a time when no means existed for relieving him of his duty to hold court, and when no other judge could legally hold court in his place. Impeachment was the only solution, other than resignation. Congress went ahead and removed Judge Pickering, but enough senators believed that drunkenness and insanity were not high crimes and misdemeanors that the Senate voted to remove him without finding that his behavior fell within the impeachment clause. Judge West Humphreys was removed during the Civil War when he failed to resign after joining the Confederacy. The charges against him were such that his removal probably should have been done under the treason prong of the impeachment clause, but at this point in the war, the government was uncertain of the legal status of the conflict, that is, was the U.S. government at war with a sovereign enemy government or merely engaged in putting down an insurrection? The circumstances under which Congress chose to call Humphreys's offenses high crimes and misdemeanors rather than treason suggest that caution should be used in interpreting this precedent.

CONGRESSIONAL IMPEACHMENT

❦ 10 ❦
Senator William Blount
(1797–1799)

WILLIAM BLOUNT was a speculator in the newly opened western lands after American independence. William Masterson, Blount's biographer, described him as "a businessman in politics for business." Blount was elected to the U.S. Senate in 1796 as a member of the first congressional delegation from the newly admitted state of Tennessee. What should have been a full term lasted less than a year. In July 1797 he was expelled from the Senate and impeached by the House. The conclusion of his Senate trial, however, did not occur until 1799.

SENATOR WILLIAM BLOUNT   Case Dismissed

CHARGES: Conspiracy to mount a military expedition in violation of American neutrality contrary to duty and trust as a senator.

MAJOR ISSUES: Whether Blount's expulsion from the Senate made him no longer subject to impeachment; and whether a senator is an officer of the United States within the meaning of the Constitution's impeachment clause.

HOUSE VOTE ON IMPEACHMENT: Voice Vote

SENATE VOTE TO DISMISS BECAUSE OF LACK OF JURISDICTION: 14–11

After war broke out between Spain and England in October 1796, Blount began scheming to mount a military expedition to secure Louisiana and the Floridas (then in the possession of Spain) for England, hoping to benefit himself in the process. Westerners feared that Spain would cede its southern and western territory to the French, as the price of French military assistance against the British. Control of the territory by the powerful French would end westerners' dreams of seizing the land from the weak Spanish crown, a seizure that would allow Americans to control the vital Mississippi River. Having England in control of the territory would increase the value of the vast tracts of land that Blount hoped to sell to the British.

On July 3, 1797, President John Adams sent to Congress a letter in Blount's handwriting laying out the plot. By July 7 the House had voted to impeach Senator Blount without having drafted articles of impeachment. At the same time, the Senate voted, 25 to 1, to expel Blount for "having been guilty of a high misdemeanor entirely inconsistent with his public trust and duty as a Senator." The House did not adopt articles of impeachment until January 29, 1798, long after Blount's expulsion from the Senate. His trial did not begin until December 1798.

In the meantime, Blount skipped town and headed back to Tennessee, where he was warmly welcomed. He briefly considered seeking a new senatorial post in defiance of the Senate's expulsion but ended up running for the state senate instead. Ironically, while his own impeachment trial was taking place in Philadelphia, Blount was engaged in impeaching a state judge in Tennessee.

In 1799 the Senate voted to discontinue the trial because of lack of jurisdiction. It is not clear whether the decision was based on Blount's argument that senators were not government officers or on his argument that he was not an officer because he had been expelled. Nevertheless, in congressional practice, Blount's impeachment has come to stand for the proposition that members of Congress are not "officers of the United States" subject to impeachment under the Constitution.

ARTICLES OF IMPEACHMENT

The Secretary then read the articles of impeachment in the words following:

Articles exhibited by the House of Representatives of the United States, in the name of themselves, and of all the people of the United States, against William Blount, in maintenance of their impeachment against him for high crimes and misdemeanors.

ARTICLE 1. That, whereas the United States, in the months of February, March, April, May, and June, in the year of our Lord one thousand seven hundred and ninety seven, and for many years then past, were at peace with his Catholic Majesty, the king of Spain; and whereas, during the months aforesaid, his said Catholic Majesty and the king of Great Britain were at war with each other; yet the said William Blount, on or about the months aforesaid, then being a Senator of the United States, and well knowing the premises, but disregarding the duties and obligations of his high station, and designing and intending to disturb the peace and tranquillity of the United States, and to violate and infringe the neutrality thereof, did conspire, and contrive to create, promote, and set on foot, within the Jurisdiction and territory of the United States, and to conduct and carry on, from thence, a military hostile expedition against the territories and dominions of his said Catholic Majesty in the Floridas and Louisiana, or a part thereof, for the purpose of wresting the same from his Catholic Majesty, and of conquering the same for the king of Great Britain, with whom his said Catholic Majesty was then at war as aforesaid, contrary to the duty of his trust and station as a Senator of the United States, in violation of the obligation of neutrality, and against the laws of the United States, and the peace and interests thereof.

ARTICLE 2. That, whereas, . . . William Blount, on or about the months of February, March, April, May, and June, in the year of our Lord one thousand seven hundred and ninety-seven, then being a Senator of the United States, . . . but disregarding the duties of his high station, and the stipulations of the [treaty with the King of Spain which pledged to keep peace among the Indians], and the obligations of neutrality, did conspire and contrive to excite the

Creek and Cherokee nations of Indians, then inhabiting within the territorial boundary of the United States, to commence hostilities against the subjects and possessions of his Catholic majesty, in the Floridas and Louisiana, for the purpose of reducing the same to the dominion of the King of Great Britain, with whom his Catholic majesty was then at war as aforesaid: contrary to the duty of his trust and station as a Senator of the United States, in violation of the said treaty of friendship, limits, and navigation, and of the obligations of neutrality, and against the laws of the United States, and the peace and interests thereof.

William Blount

ARTICLE 3. That . . . William Blount, on or about the said twenty-first day of April, in the year of our Lord one thousand seven hundred and ninety-seven, then being a Senator of the United States, and well knowing the premises, did, in the prosecution of his criminal designs and of his conspiracies aforesaid, and the more effectually to accomplish his intention of exciting the Creek and Cherokee nations of Indians to commence hostilities against the subjects of his Catholic majesty, further conspire and contrive to alienate and divert the confidence of the said Indian tribes or nations from the said Benjamin Hawkins, the principal temporary agent [for Indian affairs], and to diminish, impair, and destroy the influence of the said Benjamin Hawkins with the said Indian tribes, and their friendly intercourse and understanding with him, contrary to the duty of his trust and station as a Senator of the United States, and against the ordinances and laws of the United States, and the peace and interests thereof.

ARTICLE 4. That . . . William Blount, on or about the said twenty-first day of April, in the year last aforesaid, then being a Senator of the United States, and well knowing the premises, did, in prosecution of his criminal designs, and in furtherance of his conspiracies aforesaid, conspire and contrive to seduce . . . James Carey from the duty and trust of his said appointments [as "interpreter for the United States to the said Cherokee nation of Indians, and assistant at the public trading house established at the Tellico blockhouse, in the state of Tennessee"], and to engage the said James Carey to assist in the promotion and execution of his said criminal intentions and conspiracies aforesaid, contrary to the duty of his trust and station as a Senator of the United States, and against the laws and treaties of the United States, and the peace and interests thereof.

ARTICLE 5. That . . . to separate the lands and possessions of the said Indians from the lands and possessions of the United States, and the citizens hereof: . . . William Blount, on or about the twenty-first day of April, in the year of our Lord one thousand seven hundred and ninety-seven, then being a Senator of the United States, and well knowing the premises, in further prosecution of his said criminal designs, and of his conspiracies aforesaid, and the more effectually to accomplish his intention of exciting the said Indians to commence hostilities against the subjects of his Catholic majesty, did further conspire and contrive to diminish and impair the confidence of the said Cherokee nation in the government of the United States, and to create and foment discontents and disaffection among the said Indians towards the government of the United States in relation to the ascertainment and marking of the said boundary line, contrary to the duty of his trust and station as a Senator of the United States, and against the peace and interests thereof.

And the House of Representatives, by protestation, saving to themselves the liberty of exhibiting, at any time hereafter, any further articles, or other accusation, or impeachment, against the said William Blount, and also of replying to his answers, which he shall make unto the said articles, or any of them and of offering proof to all and every the aforesaid articles, and to all and every other articles of impeachment, or accusation which shall be exhibited by them, as the case shall require, do demand that the said William Blount may be put to answer the said crimes and misdemeanors, and that such proceedings, examinations, trials, and judgments, may be thereupon had and given as are agreeable to law and justice.

Signed by order and in behalf of the House.

JONATHAN DAYTON, *Speaker.*
Attest, JONATHAN W. CONDY, *Clerk.*

❧ II ❧

District Judge John Pickering

(1803–1804)

THE IMPEACHMENT OF JOHN PICKERING, District Judge for the District of New Hampshire, the first in which a federal official was removed from office, had two important features. One was that it revealed the fact that the Constitution made no provision for removing a judge because of disability (in Pickering's case drunkenness and insanity). The other was that it occurred in part as a test of a theory of impeachment held by the newly dominant states-rights party of Thomas Jefferson—known as Jeffersonian Republicans. The Federalist Party, standing for commercial expansion and a strong national government, had held sway over all three branches of government during the administrations of George Washington and John Adams; the election of Jefferson to the presidency brought with it Jeffersonian control of both houses of Congress for the first time. In light of this circumstance, the Jeffersonian theory of impeachment looked to the process as a means of bringing the judicial branch into partisan alignment with the two political branches of government.

When Thomas Jefferson became the first non-Federalist president in 1801, he faced a federal judiciary that included not a single member of his own party. Jefferson's political ally, Rep. William Branch Giles of Virginia, told Jefferson that the only way to get judges with the proper political outlook on the bench would be to remove "all of [the judges] . . . indiscriminately." New Hampshire district court judge John Pickering seemed to provide a good first case.

For some time complaints had been mounting about his erratic behavior on the bench. In fact, under a disability provision in the Judiciary Act of 1801—the so-called midnight judges act that had allowed outgoing president John Adams to appoint sixteen more Federalists to newly created circuit courts—Judge Pickering's duties had been taken over by one of the

---

DISTRICT JUDGE JOHN PICKERING   Convicted and Removed

CHARGES: Making decisions contrary to law; failure to hear witnesses or allow an appeal contrary to law; intoxication on the bench.

MAJOR ISSUE: Whether official misbehavior caused by insanity is a "high crime and misdemeanor."

HOUSE VOTE ON IMPEACHMENT: 45–8

SENATE VOTE FOR CONVICTION:

	Guilty	Not Guilty
All Articles	19	1

SENATE VOTE FOR REMOVAL: 20–6

---

new circuit judges. The Jeffersonians' repeal of the 1801 act put Pickering back on the bench.

Judge Pickering's very inability to do his job, an apparent result of insanity, made his impeachment questionable. Sen. William Plumer, a Federalist also from New Hampshire, noted that

some of our democrats feel uneasy. They do not wish to act either as the accuser or judges of a madman; but one of my brother Senators told me he was resolved *not* to believe Pickering insane; but if the facts alledged [sic] in the impeachments were proved to remove him from office. This is the case with several of them. But still they feel embarrassed [and] fear to meet the shaft of ridicule, should the accused attend, the trial would be farcical indeed!

When it came time for the Senate to vote on the charges against Pickering, the senators could not bring themselves to vote him guilty "of high crimes and misdemeanors." Instead they voted him "guilty as charged." The debate over this issue follows Pickering's article of impeachment. As a consequence, after Pickering it cannot be said that the Senate thought that behavior that resulted from insanity fit the definition of "high crime and misdemeanor."

Although Pickering was removed, his manifest disability undercut the precedential value his removal had for establishing the validity of the Jeffersonian theory of impeachment. That would be tested in the next impeachment proceeding, against Federalist Supreme Court justice Samuel Chase in 1804–1805.

ARTICLES OF IMPEACHMENT

Articles exhibited by the House of Representatives of the United States, in the name of themselves and of all the people of the United States, against John Pickering, judge of the district court of the district of New Hampshire, in maintenance and support of their impeachment against him for high crimes and misdemeanors.

ARTICLE 1. That whereas George Wentworth, surveyor of the district of New Hampshire, did, in the port of Portsmouth . . . on the 15th day of October, in the year 1802, seize the ship called the *Eliza,* . . . alleging that there had been unladen from on board of said ship, contrary to law, sundry goods, wares, and merchandise, of foreign growth and manufacture, of the value of $400 and upwards, and did likewise seize on land within the said district . . . two cables of the value of $250, . . . and whereas Thomas Chadbourn, a deputy marshal of the said district of New Hampshire, did, on the 16th day of October, in the year 1802 . . . arrest and detain in custody for trial before the said John Pickering, judge of the said district court, the said ship, called the *Eliza,* with her furniture, tackle, and apparel, and also the two cables aforesaid;

And whereas by an act of Congress, passed on the 2d day of March, in the year 1789, it is among other things provided that [claimant to a ship must produce a certificate showing that the duties have been paid] . . . yet the said John Pickering, judge of the said district court of the said district of New Hampshire, the said act of Congress not regarding, but with intent to evade the same, did order the said ship called the *Eliza,* with her furniture, tackle, and apparel, and the said two cables, to be delivered to a certain Eliphalet Ladd, who claimed the same, without his, the said Eliphalet Ladd, producing any certificate from the collector and naval officer of the said district that the tonnage duty on the said ship or the duties on the said cables had been paid or secured, contrary to his trust and duty as judge of the said district court, against the law of the United States and to the manifest injury of their revenue.

ARTICLE 2. That whereas, at a special district court of the United States, begun and held at Portsmouth on the 11th day of November, in the year 1802, by John Pickering, judge of said court, the United States, by Joseph Whipple, the collector of said district, . . . having prayed . . . that the said ship, with her furniture, tackle, and apparel, might by the said court be adjudged to be forfeited to the United States and be disposed of according to law; and a certain Eliphalet Ladd, by his proctor and attorney, having come into the said court, and having claimed the said ship *Eliza,* with her tackle, furniture, and apparel, . . . and having prayed the said court that the said ship, with her furniture, tackle, and apparel, might be restored to him; . . . and whereas John S. Sherburne, attorney for the United States in and for the said district of New Hampshire, did appear in the said district, as his special duty it was by law, to prosecute the said cause in behalf of the United States, and did produce sundry witnesses to prove the facts charged by the United States . . . to show that the said ship *Eliza,* with her tackle, furniture, and apparel, was justly forfeited to the United States, . . . yet the said John Pickering, being then judge of the said district court, and then in court sitting, with intent to defeat the just claims of the United States, did refuse to hear the testimony of the said witnesses so as aforesaid, produced in behalf of the United States, and without hearing the said testimony so adduced in behalf of the United States in the trial of the said cause did order and decree the said ship *Eliza,* with her furniture, tackle, and apparel, to be restored to the said Eliphalet Ladd, the claimant, contrary to his trust and duty as judge of the said district court, in violation of the laws of the United States and to the manifest injury of the revenue.

ARTICLE 3. That whereas it is provided by an act of Congress, passed on the 24th day of September, in the year 1789, "that from all final decrees of the district court in cases of admiralty and maritime jurisdiction, where the matter in dispute exceeds the sum or value of $300 exclusive of costs, an appeal shall be allowed to the next circuit court to be held in such district;" and whereas on the 12th day of November, in the year 1802, . . . the said John Pickering, judge of the said district of New Hampshire, did decree that the said ship *Eliza,* with her furniture, tackle, and apparel, should be restored to the said Eliphalet Ladd, the claimant; and whereas the said John S. Sherburne, attorney for the United States in and for the said district of New Hampshire, . . . did, in the name and behalf of the United States, claim an appeal from said decree of the district court . . . in conformity to the provisions of the act of Congress last aforesaid, yet the said John Pickering, judge of the said district court, disregarding the authority of the laws and wickedly meaning and intending to injure the revenues of the United States and thereby to impair their public credit, did absolutely and positively refuse to allow the said appeal, as prayed for and claimed by the said John S. Sherburne in behalf of the United States, contrary to his trust and duty of judge of the district court, against the laws of the United States, to the great injury of the public revenue, and in violation of the solemn oath which he had taken to administer equal and impartial justice.

ARTICLE 4. That whereas for the due, faithful, and impartial administration of justice, temperance, and sobriety are essential qualities in the character of a judge, yet the said John Pickering, being a man of loose morals and intemperate habits, on the 11th and 12th days of November, in the year 1802, being then judge of the district court in and for the district of New Hampshire, did appear on the bench of the said court for the administration of justice in a state of total intoxication, produced by the free and intemperate use of intoxicating liquors; and did then and there frequently, in a most profane and indecent manner, invoke the name of the Supreme Being, to the evil example of all the good citizens of the United States; and was then and there guilty of other high misdemeanors, disgraceful to his own character as a judge and degrading to the honor of the United States.

And the House of Representatives, by protestation, saving to themselves the liberty of exhibiting at any time hereafter any further articles or other accusation or impeachment against the said John Pickering; and also of replying to his or any answers which he shall make to the said articles, or any of them; and of offering proof to all and every other articles, impeachment, or accusation which shall be exhibited by them as the case shall require, do demand that the said John Pickering may be put to answer the said high crimes and misdemeanors; and that such proceedings, examinations, trials, and judgments may be thereupon had and given as may be agreeable to law and justice.

PETITION FROM JACOB PICKERING

The House of Representatives of the United States *v.* John Pickering, judge of the district court for the district of New Hampshire.

Jacob S. Pickering, of Portsmouth, in the district of New Hampshire, and son of the said John Pickering, against whom articles of impeachment have been exhibited by the House of Representatives of the United States, conceives it his duty most respectfully to state to this high and honorable court the real situation of the said John Pickering, the facts and circumstances relative to said articles, wherein he stands charged of supposed high crimes and misdemeanors, and to request that this court would grant him such term of time as they shall think fit and reasonable to substantiate this statement.

Your petitioner will be able to show that all the time when the crimes wherewith the said John stands charged are supposed to have been committed, the said John was, and for more than two years before, and ever since has been, and now is, insane, his mind wholly deranged, and altogether incapable of transacting any kind of business which requires the exercise of judgment, or the faculties of reason; and, therefore, that the said John Pickering is incapable of corruption of judgment, no subject of impeachment, or amenable to any tribunal for his action.

That this derangement has been constant and permanent, every day of his life completely demonstrating his insanity; every attempt for his relief, which has been prescribed by the faculty who have been consulted on his case, has proved unavailing, and his disorder has baffled all medical aid.

Your petitioner is well aware that the most conclusive evidence of the aforegoing fact would result from an actual view of the respondent, which unfortunately, by reason of his great infirmities can not now be, but at the hazard of his life—he is wholly unable at this inclement season to support the fatigue of so long a journey; yet if the respondent's life be spared, and his health in any degree restored, it will be the endeavor of your petitioner that the said John shall make his personal appearance before this honorable court at any future day they shall think proper to assign.

Your petitioner will be able to show, any pretense to the contrary notwithstanding, that the decisions made in the cause stated in the first article of impeachment, although not the result of reflection, or grounded on any deductions of reason, were, nevertheless, correct, perfectly consonant to the principles of justice, and conformable to the laws of the land; and the refusal of the said judge to grant the appeal claimed by the said John S. Sherburne, in behalf of the United States, was not against law, or to the injury of the public revenue, as the third article of the impeachment supposes; there being no law to warrant such appeal in such a case.

While, with deep humility, your petitioner admits and greatly laments the indecorous and improper expressions used by the said judge on the seat of justice, as mentioned in the last article of impeachment, he will clearly evince the injustice of that part thereof which respects his moral character, and show abundantly, that from his youth upward, through a long, laborious and useful life, and until he was visited by the most awful dispensation of Providence, and the most deplorable of all human calamities, the loss of reason, he was unexceptionable in his morals, remarkable for the purity of his language, and the correctness of his habits, and the deviations in these particulars now complained of, are irresistible evidence of the deranged state of his mind. . . .

Audi alteram partem is a maxim held in reverence wherever liberty yet remains. The Senate of America will be the last tribunal on earth that will cease to respect it; they will never condemn unheard; they will never refuse time for a full and impartial trial.

That time, that impartial trial, your petitioner prays for; the charity of the law presumes the innocence of the respondent; and your petitioner, also, respectfully entreats that, in the meantime, and more especially as the evidence on which the impeachment is founded, was taken ex parte, no unfavorable impressions may be made on the minds of this honorable court, by any report or extrajudicial representations which may have been made on the subject before them.

JACOB S. PICKERING.

SYNOPSIS OF SENATE DEBATE

The court determined to confine the question in the judgment on Judge Pickering to the simple question of guilt on the charges. The court, in the

Pickering judgment, declined to permit an expression as to whether the offenses constituted high crimes and misdemeanors.

In conformity with English precedents the Senate pronounced judgment, article by article, in the Pickering case.

The final question in the Pickering judgment was on the removal of the accused from office.

Meanwhile, on the same day, the Court of Impeachment had convened, and Mr. Samuel White, of Delaware, inquired whether the question was to be taken on each article separately, as practiced in the House of Lords, or on the whole together. He hoped upon each separately, as gentlemen might wish to vote affirmatively on some and negatively on others, from which privilege they must be precluded by giving but one general vote of guilty or not guilty. He would, therefore, beg leave to submit to the consideration of the court the following as the form of the question to be put to each member upon each article of impeachment, viz:

Is John Pickering, district judge of the district of New Hampshire, guilty of high crimes and misdemeanors upon the charges contained in the—article of impeachment or not guilty?

For this form of question, Mr. White observed, he could adduce precedent. It was nearly the same as was used in the very celebrated case of Warren Hastings, and he presumed would collect the sense of the court with as much certainty as any that could be proposed, which was his only object. . . .

Mr. Joseph Anderson, of Tennessee, mentioned that he had objections to the form of question proposed by the gentleman from Delaware, and moved to strike out the words "of high crimes and misdemeanors."

On motion, the galleries were cleared and the doors closed. After some debate, Mr. White's form of question was lost—only 10 voting in favor of it and 18 against it.

Mr. Anderson's form was then adopted—yeas 18, nays 9.

Mr. White stated that he believed Judge Pickering had practiced much of the indecent and improper conduct charged against him in the articles of impeachment; that he had been seen intoxicated and heard to use very profane language upon the bench; that he had acted illegally and very unbecoming a judge in the case of the ship *Eliza*, as charged against him in the articles, but that he was very far from believing that any part of his conduct amounted to high crimes and misdemeanors or that he was in any degree capable of such an offense, because, after the testimony the court had heard, scarcely a doubt could remain in the mind of any gentleman but that the judge was actually insane at the time; and Mr. White wished to know whether it was to be understood by the two last votes just taken that the court intended only to find the facts and to avoid pronouncing the law upon them; that they could have it in view to say merely that Judge Pickering had committed the particular acts charged against him in the articles of impeachment and upon such a conviction, to remove him, without saying directly or indirectly whether those acts amounted to high crimes and misdemeanors or not; for in the several articles they are not so charged, though judgment is demanded upon them as such. Upon such a principle and by such a mode of proceeding good behavior, he observed, would be no longer the tenure of office; every officer of the Government must be at the mercy of a majority of Congress, and it would not hereafter be necessary that a man should be guilty of high crimes and misdemeanors in order to render him liable to removal from office by impeachment, but a conviction upon any facts stated in articles exhibited against him would be sufficient.

Mr. Jonathan Dayton, of New Jersey, observed that the honorable gentleman from Virginia seemed to be offended at the language of his honorable friend from Delaware, who, in speaking of the proceedings on the impeachment, had called them a mere mockery of trial. To such terms, however, the ears of that honorable gentleman must be accustomed and accommodated, for, whilst either he or his friend had the honor of a seat in that body, they should designate this trial by no other character. It deserved no better appellation and would be thus characterized in all parts of the United States where these proceedings could be seen and understood.

That the conclusion of this exhibition might perfectly correspond with its commencement and progress, that the catastrophe might comport with the other parts of the piece, the Senate were now to be compelled, by a determined majority, to take the question in a manner never before heard of on similar occasions. They were simply to be allowed to vote, whether Judge Pickering was guilty as charged—that is, guilty of the facts charged in each article—aye or no. If voted guilty of the facts, the Senate was to follow, without any previous question whether these facts amounted to a high crime and misdemeanor. The latest reason of this course was, Mr. Dayton said, too obvious. There were numbers who were disposed to give sentence of removal against this unhappy judge, upon the ground of the facts alleged and proved, who could not, however, conscientiously vote that they amounted to high crimes and misdemeanors, especially when committed by a man proved at the very time to be insane and to have been so ever since, even to the present moment. The Constitution gave no power to the Senate, and the High Court of Impeachments, to pass such a sentence of removal and disqualification, except upon charges and conviction of high crimes and misdemeanors. The House of Representatives had so charged the judge and had exhibited articles in maintenance and support, as they themselves declared, of those charges. The Senate had received and heard the evidence adduced by the managers and had gone through certain forms of a trial, and they now, by a majority, dictated the form of a final question the most extraordinary, unprecedented, and unwarrantable. For himself, Mr. Dayton said, he felt at a loss how to act. He was free to declare he believed the respondent guilty of most of the facts stated in the articles, but, considering the deranged state of intellect of that unfor[t]unate man, he could not declare him guilty of the words of the Constitution; he could not vote it a conviction under the impeachment. Let the question be stated, as had been proposed by his honorable friend from Delaware, agreeably to the form observed in the well recollected case of Warren Hastings:

Is John Pickering guilty of a high crime and misdemeanor upon the charge contained in the first, the second, the third, or the fourth article of the impeachment, or not guilty?

Or, if the court preferred it, he should have no objection against taking the preliminary question, whether guilty of the facts charged in each article, provided they would allow it to be followed by another most important question, viz: Whether those facts, thus proved and found, amounted to a conviction of high crimes and misdemeanors, as charged in the impeachment, and expressly required by the Constitution. Both these forms of stating the question were, it was now too evident, intended to be refused by the majority, and thus a precedent established for removing a judge in a manner unauthorized by that charter.

Mr. White asked whether, after the question now before the court—which goes merely to settle, as gentlemen themselves believe, the point whether Judge Pickering has committed the particular acts charged against him in the articles of impeachment or not—should be decided, it would then be in his power to obtain a vote of the court upon another question which, without presenting at present, he would state in his place, viz: Is it the opinion of this court that John Pickering is guilty of high crimes and misdemeanors, upon the charges exhibited against him in the articles of impeachment preferred by the House of Representatives?

The President pro tempore replied that he thought such a motion could not be received after the vote had been taken.

Mr. Wright submitted the following as the final question, viz:

Is the court of opinion that John Pickering be removed from the office of judge of the district court of the district of New Hampshire?

This form was agreed to.

In the Pickering impeachment certain Senators retired from the court because dissatisfied with form of the question on final judgment.

Messrs. John Armstrong, of New York; Stephen R. Bradley, of Vermont; David Stone, of North Carolina; Jonathan Dayton, of New Jersey; and Samuel White, of Delaware, retired from the court. The two last not because they believed Judge Pickering guilty of high crimes and misdemeanors, but because they did not choose to be compelled to give so solemn a vote upon a form of question which they considered an unfair one, and calculated to preclude them from giving any distinct and explicit opinion upon the true and most important point in the case, viz, as to the insanity of Judge Pickering, and whether the charges contained in the articles of impeachment, if true, amounted in him to high crimes and misdemeanors or not.

In final judgment the court found Judge Pickering guilty in all the articles and decreed his removal from office.

Final judgment being pronounced, the court of impeachment in Pickering's case adjourned sine die.

The question was then taken in the presence of the managers and of the House of Representatives, and decided as follows:

On the question—

Is John Pickering, district judge of New Hampshire, guilty as charged in the first article of impeachment exhibited against him by the House of Representatives?

It was determined in the affirmative, yeas 19, nays 7.

The same question was put, in the same way, on the three remaining articles, and decided by a like result.

On the question—

Is the court of opinion that John Pickering be removed from office of judge of the district court of the district of New Hampshire?

It was determined in the affirmative, yeas 20, nays 6.

The court then adjourned sine die.

The Senate Journal records simply the fact of the sitting and adjournment of the court, as on other days, and makes no mention of the result of the trial.

Supreme Court Justice Samuel Chase

(1804–1805)

THE IMPEACHMENT OF Supreme Court Justice Samuel Chase arose from a sense of political crisis that gripped the United States in its early years. Just twelve years after the country's adoption of the constitutional experiment, and after the first two presidential administrations under the Federalists, a party that favored a strong central government, power was passed from President John Adams to a man who represented a party with a radically different political outlook. When Thomas Jefferson took over the presidency in 1801 and brought his states-rights party—known as the Jeffersonian Republicans—into power in Congress, no one knew whether the carefully crafted but untried governmental structure would survive the transition. Turmoil had marked Adams's presidency, and partisan animosities had reached a fever pitch.

The federal judiciary was highly unpopular with the Jeffersonians. Under the Adams administration, the judiciary had been charged with administering controversial laws (some of which targeted the political opposition) and had done so with zeal. Perceived as an engine in opposition to the states, and already a symbol of a centralizing government, the federal judiciary became an immediate focus of Jeffersonian reform. In 1803, after the removal of John Pickering, a district judge who was insane (see Document 11, p. 91), the Jeffersonians turned their attention to Samuel Chase, a volatile and intensely partisan Supreme Court justice. Chase represented an extreme form of Federalism that viewed the common people—and indeed democracy itself—with distrust and sought dominance by the federal government over the authority of the states. Chase's politics and his intemperate behavior on the bench made him an ideal test for the legitimacy of partisan impeachment. In one case he chastised the defense lawyers so much and made such apparently unfair rulings that they withdrew from the case. The same day that the Senate voted to remove Judge Pickering from office the House voted to impeach Justice Chase.

Chase had earned impressive credentials as a patriot and statesman. A signer of the Declaration of Independence and an active participant in the politics of the revolutionary period, Chase noted that his accusers in the

---

SUPREME COURT JUSTICE SAMUEL CHASE   Acquitted

CHARGES: "Arbitrary, unjust and oppressive" behavior in conducting trials; improperly instructing a grand jury; subjecting a grand jury to a "political harangue."

MAJOR ISSUE: Whether an offense need be criminally indictable to be impeachable.

HOUSE VOTE ON IMPEACHMENT: 73–32

SENATE VOTE FOR ACQUITTAL:

	Guilty	Not Guilty
Article I	16	18
Article II	10	24
Articles III–IV	18	16
Article V	0	34
Article VI	4	30
Article VII	10	24
Article VIII	19	15

House were "'puling in their nurses' arms' whilst I was contributing my utmost aid to lay the groundwork of American liberty." No stranger to controversy, Chase had been the target of an impeachment attempt earlier in his career as a state court judge in Maryland. His vocal Federalism and his judicial excesses in handling politically sensitive trials led the House to draft eight articles of impeachment against him. The complaints against Chase stemmed from four events, which arose from his duties as a circuit-riding trial judge rather than from his behavior while sitting on the Supreme Court. The first six articles called into question his handling of the treason trial of John Fries, who was accused of resisting a U.S. revenue act, and the seditious libel trial of James Callender, who maligned President Adams and his administration. (This was the same Callender whose accusations against Alexander Hamilton led Hamilton to publish his *Observations.* See Document 4, p. 42.) The last two articles questioned Chase's insertion of partisan politics into grand jury charges.

Chase's defense lay chiefly in his counsel's argument "that no judge can be impeached and removed from office for any act or offense for which he could not be indicted." When it came time to vote on the articles, a motion was made to use the wording that had been used in the Pickering impeachment, that is, was the judge "guilty as charged?" In this case, the Senate voted 17 to 16 to consider whether the judge was "guilty of high crimes and misdemeanors." This judgment gives further support to the interpretation of the Pickering impeachment as an aberration, which came about primarily as a result of a constitutional omission, that is, the failure to provide guidance for situations in which a judge was unable to perform judicial functions. An interesting note to Chase's trial is the fact that Vice President Aaron Burr, who presided over Chase's trial as president of the Senate, was at the time under indictment for the murder of Alexander Hamilton in New Jersey and New York. No attempt was ever made to impeach Burr. The Senate voted not guilty on five of the eight articles charged against Chase; a majority voted him guilty on three articles, but not by the two-thirds margin necessary for conviction. As a result, the Jeffersonians sought other means to curb the federal judiciary. It would be twenty-five years before another impeachment trial.

ARTICLES OF IMPEACHMENT

Articles exhibited by the House of Representatives of the United States, in the name of themselves and of all the people of the United States, against Samuel Chase, one of the associate justices of the Supreme Court of the United States, in maintenance and support of their impeachment against him for high crimes and misdemeanors.

ARTICLE 1. That unmindful of the solemn duties of his office, and contrary to the sacred obligation by which he stood bound to discharge them, "faithfully and impartially, and without respect to persons," the said Samuel Chase, on the trial of John Fries, charged with treason, before the circuit court of the United States, held for the district of Pennsylvania, in the city of Philadelphia, during the months of April and May, one thousand eight hundred, whereat the said Samuel Chase presided, did, in his judicial capacity, conduct himself in a manner highly arbitrary, oppressive, and unjust, viz:

1. In delivering an opinion in writing, on the question of law, on the construction of which the defense of the accused materially depended, tending to prejudice the minds of the jury against the case of the said John Fries, the prisoner, before counsel had been heard in his defense;

2. In restricting the counsel for the said Fries from recurring to such English authorities as they believed apposite, or from citing certain statutes of the United States, which they deemed illustrative of the positions upon which they intended to rest the defense of their client;

3. In debarring the prisoner from his constitutional privilege of addressing the jury (through his counsel) on the law, as well as on the fact, which was to determine his guilt or innocence, and at the same time endeavoring to wrest from the jury their indisputable right to hear argument and determine upon the question of law, as well as the question of fact, involved in the verdict which they were required to give.

In consequence of which irregular conduct of the said Samuel Chase, as dangerous to our liberties as it is novel to our laws and usages, the said John Fries was deprived of the right, secured to him by the eighth article amendatory of the Constitution, and was condemned to death without having been heard

Samuel Chase

by counsel, in his defense, to the disgrace of the character of the American bench, in manifest violation of law and justice, and in open contempt of the right of juries, on which ultimately rest the liberty and safety of the American people.

ARTICLE 2. That, prompted by a similar spirit of persecution and injustice, at a circuit court of the United States, held at Richmond, in the month of May, 1800, for the district of Virginia, whereat the said Samuel Chase presided, and before which a certain James Thompson Callender was arraigned for a libel on John Adams, then President of the United States, the said Samuel Chase, with intent to oppress and procure the conviction of the said Callender, did overrule the objection of John Basset, one of the jury, who wished to be excused from serving on the trial, because he had made up his mind as to the publication from which the words, charged to be libelous in the indictment, were extracted; and the said Basset was accordingly sworn, and did serve on the said jury, by whose verdict the prisoner was subsequently convicted.

ARTICLE 3. That with intent to oppress and procure the conviction of the prisoner, the evidence of John Taylor, a material witness on behalf of the aforesaid Callender, was not permitted by the said Samuel Chase to be given in, on pretense that the said witness could not prove the truth of the whole of one of the charges contained in the indictment, although the said charge embraced more than one fact.

ARTICLE 4. That the conduct of the said Samuel Chase was marked, during the whole course of the said trial, by manifest injustice, partiality, and intemperance, viz:

1. In compelling the prisoner's counsel to reduce to writing, and submit to the inspection of the court, for their admission or rejection, all questions which the said counsel meant to propound to the above-named John Taylor, the witness.

2. In refusing to postpone the trial, although an affidavit was regularly filed stating the absence of material witnesses on behalf of the accused; and although it was manifest that, with the utmost diligence, the attendance of such witnesses could not have been procured at that term.

3. In the use of unusual, rude, and contemptuous expressions toward the prisoner's counsel; and in falsely insinuating that they wished to excite the public fears and indignation, and to produce that insubordination to law to which the conduct of the judge did at the same time manifestly tend.

4. In repeated and vexatious interruptions of the said counsel, on the part of the said judge, which at length induced them to abandon their cause and their client, who was thereupon convicted and condemned to fine and imprisonment.

5. In an indecent solicitude, manifested by the said Samuel Chase, for the conviction of the accused, unbecoming even a public prosecutor, but highly disgraceful to the character of a judge, as it was subversive of justice.

ARTICLE 5. And whereas it is provided by the act of Congress passed on the 24th day of September, 178[9], entitled "An act to establish the judicial courts of the United States," that for any crime or offense against the United States the offender may be arrested, imprisoned, or bailed, agreeably to the usual mode of process in the State where such offender may be found; and whereas it is provided by the laws of Virginia that upon presentment by any grand jury of an offense not capital the court shall order the clerk to issue a summons against the person or persons offending to appear and answer such presentment at the next court; yet the said Samuel Chase did, at the court aforesaid, award a capias against the body of the said James Thompson Callender, indicted for an offense not capital, whereupon the said Callender was arrested and committed to close custody, contrary to law in that case made and provided.

ARTICLE 6. And whereas it is provided by the thirty-fourth section of the aforesaid act, entitled "An act to establish the judicial courts of the United States," that the laws of the several States, except where the Constitution, treaties, or statutes of the United States shall otherwise require or provide, shall be regarded as the rules of decision in trials at common law in the courts of the United States in cases where they apply; and whereas by the laws of Virginia it is provided that in cases not capital the offender shall not be held to answer any presentment of a grand jury until the court next succeeding that during which such presentment shall have been made, yet the said Samuel Chase, with intent to oppress and procure the conviction of the said James Thompson Callender, did, at the court aforesaid, rule and adjudge the said Callender to trial during the term at which he, the said Callender, was presented and indicted, contrary to law in that case made and provided.

ARTICLE 7. That at a circuit court of the United States for the district of Delaware, held at Newcastle, in the month of June, 1800, whereat the said Samuel Chase presided, the said Samuel Chase, disregarding the duties of his office, did descend from the dignity of a judge and stoop to the level of an informer by refusing to discharge the grand jury, although entreated by several of the said jury so to do; and after the said grand jury had regularly declared through their foreman that they had found no bills of indictment, nor had any presentments to make, by observing to the said grand jury that he, the said Samuel Chase, understood "that a highly seditious temper had manifested itself in the State of Delaware among a certain class of people, particularly in Newcastle County, and more especially in the town of Wilmington, where lived a most seditious printer, unrestrained by any principle of virtue, and regardless of social order, that the name of this printer was"—but checking himself, as if sensible of the indecorum which he was committing, added "that it might be assuming too much to mention the name of this person, but it becomes your duty, gentlemen, to inquire diligently into this matter," or words to that effect; and that with intention to procure the prosecution of the printer in question the said Samuel Chase did, moreover, authoritatively enjoin on the district attorney of the United States the necessity of procuring a file of the papers to which he alluded (and which were understood to be those published under the title of "Mirror of the Times and General Advertiser"), and, by a strict examination of them, to find some passage which might furnish the groundwork of a prosecution against the printer of the said paper, thereby degrading his high judicial functions and tending to impair the public confidence in and respect for the tribunals of justice so essential to the general welfare.

ARTICLE 8. And whereas mutual respect and confidence between the Government of the United States and those of the individual States, and between the people and those governments, respectively, are highly conducive to that public harmony without which there can be no public happiness, yet the said Samuel Chase, disregarding the duties and dignity of his judicial character, did, at a circuit court for the district of Maryland, held at Baltimore in the month of May, 1803, pervert his official right and duty to address the grand jury then and there assembled on the matters coming within the province of the said jury, for the purpose of delivering to the said grand jury an intemperate and inflammatory political harangue, with intent to excite the fears and resentment of the said grand jury and of the good people of Maryland against their State government and constitution, a conduct highly censurable in any, but peculiarly indecent and unbecoming in a judge of the Supreme Court of the United States; and, moreover, that the said Samuel Chase then and there, under pretense of exercising his judicial right to address the said grand jury, as aforesaid, did, in a manner highly unwarrantable, endeavor to excite the odium of the said grand jury and of the good people of Maryland against the Government of the United States by delivering opinions which, even if the judicial authority were competent to their expression on a suitable occasion and in a proper manner, were at that time, and as delivered by him, highly indecent, extrajudicial, and tending to prostitute the high judicial character with which he was invested to the low purpose of an electioneering partisan.

And the House of Representatives, by protestation, saving to themselves the liberty of exhibiting, at any time hereafter, any further articles, or other accusation or impeachment against the said Samuel Chase, and also of replying to his answers which he shall make unto the said articles, or any of them, and of offering proof to all and every the aforesaid articles, and to all and every other articles, impeachment, or accusation, which shall be exhibited by them as the case shall require, do demand that the said Samuel Chase may be put to answer the said crimes and misdemeanors, and that such proceedings, examinations, trials, and judgments may be thereupon had and given as are agreeable to law and justice.

❧ 13 ❧
District Judge James H. Peck
(1830)

THE IMPEACHMENT CASE against Judge James H. Peck of Missouri originated in animosities over land titles in the transition of the Louisiana Territory from French control to U.S. control. Just four years after Missouri was admitted to statehood in 1821, as part of the "Missouri Compromise" over the westward spread of slavery, Judge Peck decided a land case against the claimants—the Soulards—and in favor of the United States.

DISTRICT COURT JUDGE JAMES H. PECK   Acquitted

CHARGES: Abuse of the contempt power.

MAJOR ISSUE: Whether errors in judgment are high crimes and misdemeanors if committed with bad motive.

HOUSE VOTE ON IMPEACHMENT: 123–49

SENATE VOTE FOR ACQUITTAL:

	Guilty	Not Guilty
Article I	21	22

The claimants' attorney, Luke Lawless, dismayed at the implication this case had for other land claimants he represented, published a detailed criticism of Judge Peck's opinion under the name "A Citizen" in a local newspaper. Outraged at this show of disrespect to his court, Judge Peck hauled Lawless into court for contempt and sentenced him to a twenty-four-hour stay in jail. The truly punitive part of Judge Peck's sentence, however, was to bar Lawless from practicing law in Peck's court for eighteen months.

Lawless was not about to take this treatment lying down. Less than a year after Judge Peck had decided the Soulard case and sentenced Lawless for contempt, Lawless convinced a member of Congress to petition for Peck's impeachment. It would take three years and repeated petitions before Lawless could get the rest of Congress to go along with him, but finally, in December 1829, the House Judiciary Committee began investigating Peck and in March 1830 recommended impeachment. Peck's trial before the Senate began in May.

In discussing what defines an impeachable offense by a judge, one of the House managers stated that "A judicial misdemeanor consists, in my opinion, in doing an illegal act, [in an official capacity] . . . with bad motives, or in doing an act within the competency of the court or judge in some cases, but unwarranted in a particular case from the facts existing in that case, with bad motives." In other words, a judge should be impeached for "exceeding a just and lawful discretion" if the judge did so from "bad motives." Another House manager dismissed the notion that "no act, judicial or otherwise, unless indictable, is impeachable," maintaining that "any official act committed or omitted by the judge, which is in violation of the condition upon which he holds his office, is an impeachable offense under the Constitution." Finally, another House manager and future president, James Buchanan, told the Senate, "I freely admit that we are bound to prove that the respondent has violated the Constitution or some known law of the land. . . . But this violation of law may consist in the abuse, as well as in the usurpation of authority."

The managers referred back to the trial and acquittal of Justice Samuel Chase for precedent, but they seem not to have interpreted the precedent to foreclose impeaching judges for making bad decisions. Indeed, Buchanan, preferring the Pickering impeachment, took as its precedent "that if the charge against a judge be merely an illegal decision on a question of property, in a civil cause, his error ought to be gross and palpable, indeed, to justify the inference of a criminal intention and to convict him upon an impeachment." In Judge Peck's case, Buchanan believed that the error was indeed "gross and palpable" enough to indicate criminal intent and to justify conviction by the Senate on the basis of an inference of criminal intent rather than actual proof.

In defense of Judge Peck, his counsel, William Wirt, argued that "a mere mistake of law is no crime or misdemeanor in a judge. It is the intention that is the essence of every crime." According to Wirt, the House managers had properly included as part of the charge against Judge Peck the fact that he had acted with bad intent. Wirt contended that bad intent had to be proved in order to remove Judge Peck. Wirt concluded that

He might have been mistaken in considering that as a contempt, which in truth was not one. But this would have been a mere error of judgment, for which he was not answerable either civilly much less criminally. If he knew it was not a contempt, and still punished it as one, it would have been an intentional violation of the law, which would have been an impeachable offense.

The doctrine that Wirt wished the Senate to acknowledge was that "it is the guilty intention which forms the gist of the charge in every impeachment, and that a mere mistake of judgment is not an impeachable offense." Twenty-one senators voted "guilty" on the charge; twenty-two voted "not guilty."

ARTICLE OF IMPEACHMENT

Article exhibited by the House of Representatives of the United States, in the name of themselves, and of all the people of the United States, against

James H. Peck, judge of the district court of the United States for the district of Missouri, in maintenance and support of their impeachment against him for high misdemeanors in office.

Article

That the said James H. Peck, judge of the district court of the United States for the district of Missouri, at a term of the said court, holden at St. Louis, in the State of Missouri, on the 4th Monday in December, 1825, did, under and by virtue of the power and authority vested in the said court, by [t]he act of the Congress of the United States, entitled "An act enabling the claimants to lands within the limits of the State of Missouri and Territory of Arkansas to institute proceedings to try the validity of their claims," approved on the 26th day of May, 1824, render a final decree of the said court in favor of the United States, and against the validity of the claim of the petitioners, in a certain matter or cause depending in the said court, under the said act, and before that time prosecuted in the said court, before the said judge, by Julie Soulard, widow of Antoine Soulard, and James G. Soulard, Henry G. Soulard, Eliza Soulard, and Benjamin A. Soulard, children and heirs at law of the said Antoine Soulard, petitioners against the United States, praying for the confirmation of their claim, under the said act, to certain lands situated in the said State of Missouri; and the said court did, thereafter, on the 30th day of December, in the said year, adjourn to sit again on the third Monday in April, 1826.

And the said petitioners did, and at the December term of the said court, holden by and before the said James H. Peck, judge as aforesaid, in due form of law, under the said act, appeal against the United States from the judgment and decree so made and entered in the said matter, to the Supreme Court of the United States; of which appeal, so made and taken in the said district court, the said James H. Peck, judge of the said court, had then and there full notice. And the said James H. Peck, after the said matter or cause had so been duly appealed to the Supreme Court of the United States, and on or about the 30th day of March, 1826, did cause to be published, in a certain public newspaper, printed at the city of St. Louis, called "The Missouri Republican," a certain communication, prepared by the said James H. Peck, purporting to be the opinion of the said James H. Peck, as judge of the said court, in the matter or cause aforesaid, and purporting to set forth the reasons of the said James H. Peck, as such judge, for the said decree; and that Luke Edward Lawless, a citizen of the United States, and an attorney and counsellor at law in the said district court, and who had been of counsel for the petitioners in the said court, in the matter aforesaid, did, thereafter, and on or about the 8th day of April, 1826, cause to be published in a certain other newspaper, printed at the city of St. Louis, called "The Missouri Advocate and St. Louis Enquirer," a certain article signed "A Citizen," and purporting to contain an exposition of certain errors of doctrine and fact alleged to be contained in the opinion of the said James H. Peck, as before that time so published, which publication by the said Luke Edward Lawless was to the effect following, viz:

"*To the Editor:*

"SIR: I have read, with the attention which the subject deserves, the opinion of Judge Peck on the claim of the widow and heirs of Antoine Soulard, published in the Republican of the 30th ultimo. I observe that, although the judge has thought proper to decide against the claim, he leaves the grounds of his decree open for further discussion.

"Availing myself, therefore, of this permission, and considering the opinion so published to be a fair subject of examination to every citizen who feels himself interested in, or aggrieved by, its operation, I beg leave to point the attention of the public to some of the principal errors which I think I have discovered in it. In doing so, I shall confine myself to little more than an enumeration of those errors, without entering into any demonstration or developed reasoning on the subject. This would require more space than a newspaper allows, and, besides, is not, as regards most of the points, absolutely necessary.

"Judge Peck, in this opinion, seems to me to have erred in the following assumptions, as well of fact as of doctrine:

"1. That, by the ordinance of 1754, a subdelegate was prohibited from making a grant in consideration of services rendered or to be rendered.

"2. That a subdelegate in Louisiana was not a subdelegate, as contemplated by the said ordinance.

"3. That O'Reily's regulations, made in February, 1770, can be considered as demonstrative of the extent of the granting power of either the governor-general or the subdelegates, under the royal order of August, 1790.

"4. That the royal order of August, 1770 (as recited or referred to in the preamble to the regulations of Morales, of July, 1799), related exclusively to the governor-general.

"5. That the word 'mercedes,' in the ordinance of 1754, which, in the Spanish language, means 'gifts,' can be narrowed, by anything in that ordinance, or in any other law, to the idea of a grant to an Indian, or a reward to an informer, and much less to a mere sale for money.

"6. That O'Reily's regulations were in their terms applicable, or ever were in fact applied to, or published in, upper Louisiana.

"7. That the regulations of O'Reily have any bearing on the grant to Antoine Soulard, or that such a grant was contemplated by them.

"8. That the limitations to a square league of grants to new settlers in Opelousas, Attakapas, and Natchitoches (in eighth article of O'Reily's regulations) prohibits a larger grant in upper Louisiana.

"9. That the regulations of the governor-general, Gayoso, dated 9th September, 1797, entitled 'Instructions to be observed for the admission of new settlers,' prohibit, in future, a grant for services, or have the effect of annulling that to Antoine Soulard, which was made in 1796, and not located or surveyed until February, 1804.

"10. That the complete titles made by Gayoso are not to be referred to as affording the construction made by Gayoso himself, of his own regulations.

"11. That, although the regulations of Morales were not promulgated as law in upper Louisiana, the grantee in the principal case was bound by them, inasmuch as he had notice, or must be presumed, 'from the official station which he held,' to have had notice, of their terms.

"12. That the regulations of Morales 'exclude all belief that any law existed under which a confirmation of the title in question could have been claimed.'

"13. That the complete titles (produced to the court) made by the governor-general, or the intendant-general, though based on incomplete titles, not conformable to the regulations of O'Reily, Gayoso, or Morales, afford no inference in favor of the power of the lieutenant-governor, from whom these incomplete titles emanated, and must be considered as anomalous exercises of power in favor of individual grantees.

"14. That the language of Morales himself, in the complete titles issued by him, on concessions made by the lieutenant-governor of upper Louisiana, anterior to the date of his regulations, ought not to be referred to as furnishing the construction which he, Morales, put on his own regulations.

"15. That the uniform practice of the subdelegates, or lieutenant-governor of upper Louisiana, from the first establishment of that province to the 10th March, 1804, is to be disregarded as proof of law, usage, or custom therein.

"16. That the historical fact that nineteen-twentieths of the titles to lands in upper Louisiana were not only incomplete but not conformable to the regulations of O'Reily, Gayoso, or Morales at the date of the cession to the United States, affords no inference in favor of the general legality of those titles.

"17. That the fact that incomplete concessions, whether floating or located, were, previous to the cession, treated and considered by the Government and population of Louisiana as property, salable, transferable, and the subject of inheritance and distribution ab intestato, furnishes no inference in favor of those titles, or to their claim to the protection of the treaty of cession, or of the law of nations.

"18. That the laws of Congress heretofore passed in favor of incomplete titles furnish no argument or protecting principle in favor of those titles of a precisely similar character, which remain unconfirmed.

"In addition to the above, a number of other errors, consequential on those indicated, might be stated. The judge's doctrine as to the forfeiture which he contends is inflicted by Morales's regulations, seems to me to be peculiarly pregnant with grievous consequences. I shall, however, not tire the reader with any further enumeration, and shall detain him only to observe, by way of conclusion, that the judge's recollection of the argument of the counsel for the petitioner, as delivered at the bar, differs materially from what I can remember, who also heard it. In justice to the counsel I beg to observe that all that I have now submitted to the public has been suggested by that argument as spoken, and by the printed report of it, which is even now before me.

"A CITIZEN."

And the said James H. Peck, judge as aforesaid, unmindful of the solemn duties of his station, and that he held the same, by the Constitution of the United States, during good behavior only, with intention wrongfully and unjustly to oppress, imprison, and otherwise injure the said Luke Edward Lawless, under color of law, did, thereafter, at a term of the said district court of the United States for the district of Missouri, begun and held at the city of St. Louis, in the State of Missouri, on the 3d Monday in April, 1826, arbitrarily, oppressively, and unjustly, and under the further color and pretense that the said Luke Edward Lawless was answerable to the said court for the said publication signed "A Citizen," as for a contempt thereof, institute, in the said court, before him, the said James H. Peck, judge as aforesaid, certain proceedings against the said Luke Edward Lawless, in a summary way, by attachment issued for that purpose by the order of the said James H. Peck, as such judge, against the person of the said Luke Edward Lawless, touching the said pretended contempt, under and by virtue of which said attachment the said Luke Edward Lawless was, on the 21st day of April, 1826, arrested, imprisoned, and brought into the said court, before the said judge, in the custody of the marshal of the said State; and the said James H. Peck, judge as aforesaid, did, afterwards, on the same day, under the color and pretenses aforesaid, and with the intent aforesaid, in the said court, then and there, unjustly, oppressively, and arbitrarily, order and adjudge that the said Luke Edward Lawless, for the cause aforesaid, should be committed to prison for the period of twenty-four hours, and that he should be suspended from practicing as an attorney or counsellor at law in the said district court for the period of eighteen calendar months from that day, and did then and there further cause the said unjust and oppressive sentence to be carried into execution; and the said Luke Edward Lawless was, under color of the said sentence, and by the order of the said James H. Peck, judge as aforesaid, thereupon suspended from practicing as such attorney or counsellor in the said court for the period aforesaid, and immediately committed to the common prison in the said city of St. Louis, to the great disparagement of public justice, the abuse of judicial authority, and to the subversion of the liberties of the people of the United States.

And the House of Representatives, by protestation, saving to themselves the liberty of exhibiting, at any time hereafter, any further articles, or other accusations or impeachment, against the said James H. Peck, and also of replying to his answers which he shall make unto the article herein preferred against him, and of offering proof to the same, and every part thereof, and to all and every other articles, accusation, or impeachment, which shall be exhibited by them as the case shall require, do demand that the said James H. Peck may be put to answer the misdemeanors herein charged against him, and that such proceedings, examinations, trials, and judgments, may be thereupon had and given, as may be agreeable to law and justice.

A. STEVENSON,
Speaker of the House of Representatives, United States.

Attest:
M. ST. CLAIR CLARKE,
Clerk House of Representatives, United States.

The Vice-President then informed the managers that the Senate would take proper order thereon, of which the House of Representatives should have due notice.

The managers, by their chairman, delivered the article of impeachment at the table of the Secretary, and then withdrew.

On motion by Mr. Tazewell, it was

Resolved, That the Secretary be directed to issue a summons, in the usual form, to James H. Peck, judge of the district court of the United States for the district of Missouri, to answer a certain article of impeachment exhibited against him by the House of Representatives on this day; that the said summons be returnable here on Tuesday next, the 11th instant, and be served by the Sergeant-at-Arms, or some person to be deputed by him, at least three days before the return day thereof; and that the Secretary communicate this resolution to the House of Representatives.

❊ 14 ❊
District Judge West H. Humphreys
(1862)

THE LONG NATIONAL TURMOIL over slavery, westward expansion, and sectional economic supremacy erupted into the Civil War after Abraham Lincoln was elected president in 1860. As 1861 unfolded, the slave

---

DISTRICT JUDGE WEST H. HUMPHREYS   Convicted and Disqualified

CHARGES: Supporting the Confederacy; failing to hold court.

MAJOR ISSUE: Whether the constitutional requirement that "No Person shall be convicted of Treason unless on the Testimony of two witnesses to the same overt Act" applies in an impeachment trial. Whether the Senate must vote separately for removal and for disqualification.

HOUSE VOTE ON IMPEACHMENT: Voice Vote

SENATE VOTE FOR CONVICTION:

	Guilty	Not Guilty
Article 1	39	0
Article 2	36	1
Article 3	33	4
Article 4	28	10
Article 5	39	0
Article 6, specification 1	36	1
Article 6, specification 2	12	24
Article 6, specification 3	35	1
Article 7	35	1

Senate Vote for Disqualification: 36–0

---

states of the lower South, and later the upper South, followed South Carolina in declaring their secession from the Union. With secession came masses of resignations as members of the U.S. government loyal to the Southern cause threw their lot with the newly organized Confederate States of America.

One Supreme Court justice resigned his office, as did thirteen district court judges from the Southern states. One judge, West H. Humphreys of Tennessee, failed to resign his post, even after accepting appointment as the Confederate district judge for Tennessee. Why Humphreys alone among the judges loyal to the Confederacy should have failed to resign is not clear. Although his appointment to the Confederate bench came before his state officially voted to secede, it would be hard to argue that Humphreys thought he could act simultaneously for two governments.

Once Humphreys was appointed to the Confederate bench, he ceased to hold court for the United States, although he used the same facilities to hold court under the Confederacy. Perhaps he simply neglected to return his commission, figuring that failing to hold court and accepting a conflicting

appointment with the Confederacy was sufficient and that formal resignation was pointless. This was the explanation he offered when he applied for
amnesty after the war was over in 1865. Whatever the reason, the Lincoln
administration and Congress clearly declined to assume that Humphreys's
failure to hold court and his adherence to the Confederacy amounted to a
resignation.

One hallmark of the Civil War was the Union's attempt to operate as
much as possible under normal constitutional processes. The attempt
would not always succeed, but in Humphrey's case, the formal process of
impeachment moved forward on the assumption that even abandoning
one's post and serving an enemy government at war with the United States
would not short-circuit the constitutional protection that forbade the removal of a federal officer by any means other than conviction on an impeachment for "Treason, Bribery, or other high Crimes and Misdemeanors."
Until Humphreys was removed from his judgeship by impeachment, Lincoln would be unable to appoint a loyal unionist to take his place and re-
open the U.S. district court.

In the circumstances, Humphreys's removal was a foregone conclusion.
The House impeached him on a voice vote and drew up seven articles of
impeachment. Article 3 accused him of levying war on the United States,
an act that falls within the constitutional definition of treason. Arguably,
many, if not all, of the other articles could fit within the alternative portion
of the constitutional definition of treason: "adhering to [the United States's]
Enemies, giving them Aid and Comfort." Even Article 5, which charged
Humphreys with failing to hold court, did so in terms that implied adherence to the Confederacy, giving them "Aid and Comfort."

Still, the word "treason" was never used in the articles of impeachment,
and when it came time for the Senate to vote on Humphreys's guilt, the
question was not whether he was guilty of treason. Instead, as in the earlier
cases of Samuel Chase and James Peck, the question put to each senator was
whether Humphreys was guilty or not guilty of "the high crimes and misdemeanors as charged." As a result of this wording and the overwhelming
guilty vote on all but two of the articles, Humphreys's impeachment has on
occasion been cited as support for removing officers for less than criminal
behavior. The circumstances of Humphreys's removal and the open question of whether his behavior amounted to treason dilute the force of such a
judgment.

ARTICLES OF IMPEACHMENT

Articles exhibited by the House of Representatives of the United States in the name of themselves and of all the people of the United States against West H. Humphreys, judge of the district court of the United States for the several districts of the State of Tennessee, in maintenance and support of their impeachment against him for high crimes and misdemeanors.

ARTICLE 1. That, regardless of his duties as a citizen of the United States, and unmindful of the duties of his said office, and in violation of the sacred obligation of his official oath "to administer justice without respect to persons," "and faithfully and impartially discharge all the duties incumbent upon him as judge of the district court of the United States for the several districts of the State of Tennessee agreeable to the Constitution and laws of the United States," the said West H. Humphreys, on the 29th day of December, A.D. 1860, in the city of Nashville . . . did endeavor by public speech to incite revolt and rebellion within said State against the Constitution and Government of the United States, and did then and there publicly declare that it was the right of the people of said State, by an ordinance of secession, to absolve themselves from all allegiance to the Government of the United States, the Constitution and laws thereof.

ARTICLE 2. That, in further disregard of his duties as a citizen of the United States, and unmindful of the solemn obligations of his office as judge of the district court of the United States for the several districts of the State of Tennessee, and that he held his said office, by the Constitution of the United States, during good behavior only . . . did, together with other evil-minded persons within said State, openly and unlawfully support, advocate, and agree to an act commonly called an ordinance of secession, declaring the State of Tennessee independent of the Government of the United States, and no longer within the jurisdiction thereof.

ARTICLE 3. That in the years of our Lord 1861 and 1862, within the United States, and in said State of Tennessee, the said West H. Humphreys, then owing allegiance to the United States of America, and then being district judge of the United States, as aforesaid, did then and there, to wit: within said State, unlawfully, and in conjunction with other persons, organize armed rebellion against the United States and levy war against them.

ARTICLE 4. That on the 1st day of August, A.D. 1861, and on divers other days since that time, within said State of Tennessee, the said West H. Humphreys, then being judge of the district court of the United States, as aforesaid, and J. C. Ramsay, and Jefferson Davis, and others, did unlawfully conspire together "to oppose by force the authority of the Government of the United States," contrary to his duty as such judge and to the laws of the United States.

ARTICLE 5. That said West H. Humphreys, with intent to prevent the due administration of the laws of the United States within said State of Tennessee, and to aid and abet the overthrow of "the authority of the Government of the United States" within said State, has, in gross disregard of his duty as judge of the district court of the United States, as aforesaid, and in violation of the laws of the United States, neglected and refused to hold the district court of the United States, as by law he was required to do, within the several districts of the State of Tennessee, ever since the 1st day of July, A.D. 1861.

ARTICLE 6.[1.] That the said West H. Humphreys, in the year of our Lord 1861, within the State of Tennessee, and with intent to subvert the authority of the Government of the United States, to hinder and delay the due execution of the laws of the United States, and to oppress and injure citizens of the United States, did unlawfully act as judge of an illegally constituted tribunal within said State, called the district court of the Confederate States of America, and as judge of said tribunal last named said West H. Humphreys, with the intent aforesaid, then and there assumed and exercised powers unlawful and unjust, to wit, in causing one Perez Dickinson, a citizen of said State, to be unlawfully arrested and brought before him, as judge of said alleged court of said Confederate States of America, and required him to swear allegiance to the pretended government of said Confederate States of America; and upon the refusal of said Dickinson so to do, the said Humphreys, as judge of said illegal tribunal, did unlawfully, and with the intent to oppress said Dickinson, require and receive of him a bond, conditioned that while he should remain within said State he would keep the peace, and as such judge of said illegal tribunal, and without authority of law, said Humphreys there and then decreed that said Dickinson should leave said State.

2. In decreeing within said State, and as judge of said illegal tribunal, the confiscation to the use of said Confederate States of America of property of citizens of the United States, and especially of property of one Andrew Johnson and one John Catron.

3. In causing, as judge of said illegal tribunal, to be unlawfully arrested and imprisoned within said State citizens of the United States because of their fidelity to their obligations as citizens of the United States, and because of their rejection of, and their resistance to, the unjust and assumed authority, of said Confederate States of America.

ARTICLE 7. That said West H. Humphreys, judge of the district court of the United States as aforesaid, assuming to act as judge of said tribunal known as the district court of the Confederate States of America, did, in the year of our Lord 1861, without lawful authority, and with intent to injure one William G. Brownlow, a citizen of the United States, cause said Brownlow to be unlawfully arrested and imprisoned within said State in violation of the rights of said Brownlow as a citizen of the United States, and of the duties of said Humphreys as a district judge of the United States.

And the House of Representatives, by protestation, saving to themselves the liberty of exhibiting at any time hereafter any further articles, or other accusation or impeachment against the said West H. Humphreys, and also of replying to his answers which he shall make unto the articles herein preferred against him, and of offering proof to the same and every part thereof, and to all and every other article, accusation, or impeachment which shall be exhibited by them as the case shall require, do demand that the said West H. Humphreys may be put to answer the high crimes and misdemeanors herein charged against him, and that such proceedings, examinations, trials, and judgments may be thereupon had and given as may be agreeable to law and justice.

GALUSHA A. GROW,
Speaker House of Representatives.

Attest:
EMERSON ETHERIDGE,
Clerk House of Representatives.

⋇ 15 ⋇

District Judge Mark H. Delahay
(1873)

PRESIDENT ABRAHAM LINCOLN appointed Mark H. Delahay to the federal bench in Kansas in 1863. Ten years later the House impeached him, with the "most grievous charge" being "that his personal habits unfitted him for the judicial office; that he was intoxicated off the bench as well as on the bench." The Delahay impeachment indicates again a willingness on the part of the House to impeach for behavior that was not indictable. Judge John Pickering's impeachment was cited as precedent for removing a judge for intoxication.

The case of Judge Delahay is the only impeachment in U.S. history in which articles were never drafted. After Judge Delahay was impeached, but before articles could be drawn up, he resigned. Because Delahay resigned, the Senate did not see a reason for holding a trial. For this case, only the in-

DISTRICT JUDGE MARK H. DELAHAY   Resigned

CHARGES: No articles were drafted because of the judge's resignation; the
charges articulated in the House investigation centered on "intoxication off
the bench as well as on the bench."

MAJOR ISSUES: Whether "improper" personal habits exhibited while on the
bench are sufficient to impeach.

HOUSE VOTE ON IMPEACHMENT: Voice vote

SENATE VOTE: None

dividual House members' statements serve as a guide to the impeachable
offenses in question.

During the 1870s, a period marked by corruption and scandal throughout public life, Congress launched more serious investigations of judges
than during any other time in our history. Of the eight judges investigated,
five (including Judge Delahay) would resign under a cloud.

Judge Delahay's impeachment was sandwiched between two nonjudicial
impeachments. President Johnson's impeachment (see Document 28, p.
221) had occurred five years before, and three years after Delahay left office,
Congress would impeach Secretary of War William W. Belknap for selling
army post traderships in 1876 (see Document 25, p. 191).

SYNOPSIS OF HOUSE DEBATE ON IMPEACHMENT

The impeachment of Mark H. Delahay, United States district judge for
Kansas.

The House voted to investigate the conduct of Judge Delahay after the
Judiciary Committee had examined the charges in a memorial.

The Judiciary Committee was empowered in the Delahay case to take testimony in Kansas through a subcommittee.

In the investigation into the conduct of Judge Delahay he was permitted to
present testimony.

On March 19, 1872, Mr. Benjamin F. Butler, of Massachusetts, from the
Committee on the Judiciary, proposed a resolution, which was agreed to without debate:

Resolved, That the Committee on the Judiciary be, and they are hereby, authorized to
send for persons and papers, to administer oaths, and to take testimony in the matter

of the memorial and charges against Mark H. Delahay, district judge of the United States district for the State of Kansas.

On May 28 Mr. John A. Bingham, of Ohio, from the Judiciary Committee, reported the following resolution, which was agreed to:

Resolved, That the Committee on the Judiciary be directed to further investigate the charges against the character and official conduct of M. H. Delahay, United States district judge for the district of Kansas, and for that purpose a subcommittee shall be authorized to sit during the recess of Congress, and may proceed to Kansas, subpoena witnesses, send for persons and papers, administer oaths, take testimony, and employ a clerk and reporter, the expense of which shall be paid from the contingent fund of the House on the order of the chairman.

In another case, relating to Judge Charles T. Sherman, Mr. Butler, citing the case of Judge Delahay, said that this subcommittee heard in Kansas such witnesses as Judge Delahay chose to have summoned.

The House, without division, voted to impeach Judge Delahay for improper personal habits.

The House voted the impeachment of Judge Delahay at the end of one Congress, intending to present articles in the next.

Forms and ceremonies for carrying of the impeachment of Judge Delahay to the Senate.

The Speaker gave the minority party representation on the committee to carry the impeachment of Judge Delahay to the Senate.

The impeachment of Judge Delahay was carried to the Senate by a committee of three.

On February 28, 1873, Mr. Butler reported this resolution from the Judiciary Committee:

Resolved, That a committee of three be appointed to go to the Senate, and at the bar thereof, in the name of the House of Representatives, and of all the people of the United States, to impeach Mark H. Delahay, judge of the United States district court for the district of Kansas, of high crimes and misdemeanors in office, and acquaint the Senate that the House of Representatives will, in due time, exhibit particular articles of impeachment against him and make good the same, and that the committee do demand that the Senate take order for the appearance of said Mark H. Delahay to answer to said impeachment.

Two questions arose from this report:

1. Mr. Henry L. Dawes, of Massachusetts, asked if the Judiciary Committee, in view of the fact that the Congress was about to expire, had settled the question whether or not the next House of Representatives could present the articles of impeachment, of which this House might notify them. Mr. Butler said:

The Committee on the Judiciary do not expect to prepare articles of impeachment against Judge Delahay and present them for trial at this session. In the earliest case of impeachment of a judge in this country, in 1803, the case of Judge Pickering, which was in all respects like this, this exact question arose and was settled. One House presented articles of impeachment to the Senate and another House at the next session prosecuted those articles, as will be done in this case. We do not expect any other action except the formal presentation of the articles of impeachment to the Senate. The Senate is a perpetual court of impeachment, and in presenting these articles we act only as a grand jury.

2. As to the offense for which the impeachment was to be the remedy, Mr. Butler stated that—

The most grievous charge, and that which is beyond all question, was that his personal habits unfitted him for the judicial office; that he was intoxicated off the bench as well as on the bench. This question has also been decided by precedent. That was the exact charge against Judge Pickering, of New Hampshire, who, with one exception, is the only judge who has been impeached.

Mr. Butler then had read testimony showing that the judge had sentenced prisoners when intoxicated, to the great detriment of judicial dignity.

There was also a question as to certain alleged corrupt transactions, but Mr. Daniel W. Voorhees, of Indiana, said it was not proven to the satisfaction of several members of the committee that there was any malfeasance. Mr. Butler said:

The committee agree that there is enough in his personal habits to found a charge upon, and that is all there is in this resolution.

The resolution of impeachment was then agreed to without division.

On March 3 the Speaker announced the appointment of Mr. Butler, Mr. John A. Peters, of Maine, and Mr. Clarkson N. Potter, of New York, members of the committee. Two of these were members of the majority party in the House, and the third represented the minority.

On the same day the committee appeared at the bar of the Senate and, having been announced, advanced toward the area in front of the Secretary's desk, and Mr. Butler said:

Mr. President, in obedience to the order of the House of Representatives, this committee of the House appear at the bar of the Senate of the United States, and do impeach Mark H. Delahay, district judge of the United States district court for the district of Kansas, in the name of the House of Representatives and all the people of the United States, for high crimes and misdemeanors in office. And we do further acquaint the Senate, by the order of the House, that the House will in due time furnish particular articles against said Delahay and make good the same. And this committee is further charged by the House to demand of the Senate that they will take order for the appearance of Mark H. Delahay, as such judge, to answer the same.

The Presiding Officer said:

The Senate will take order in the premises, of which due notice shall be given to the House of Representatives.

Later, on the same day, on motion of Mr. George F. Edmunds, of Vermont, it was

Ordered, That the Secretary inform the House of Representatives that the Senate will receive articles of impeachment against Mark H. Delahay, judge of the district court of the United States for the district of Kansas, this day impeached by the House of Representatives before it of high crimes and misdemeanors, whenever the House of Representatives shall be ready to receive the same.

Meanwhile, the committee had returned to the House of Representatives, where Mr. Butler, the chairman, submitted the following written report:

That, in obedience to the order of the House, the committee have been to the Senate, and, in the name of the House of Representatives and of all the people of the United States, have impeached Mark H. Delahay, district judge of the United States for the district of Kansas, of high crimes and misdemeanors; and have acquainted the Senate that the House of Representatives will, in due time, exhibit particular articles against him, and make good the same. And further, that the committee have de-manded that the Senate take order for the appearance of the said Mark H. Delahay to answer to the said impeachment.

A message was also received in the House from the Senate in these terms:

The Senate is ready to receive articles of impeachment against Mark H. Delahay, judge of the United States district court for the State of Kansas.

No further proceedings took place. On March 10, 1874, as shown by the records of the State Department, Cassius G. Foster was appointed judge to fill a vacancy in this district.

❧ 16 ❧
District Judge Charles Swayne
(1904–1905)

SINCE THE FEDERAL JUDICIARY was first organized in 1789, federal district court judges have been required to live in their districts. In 1812 Congress added to the residency requirement the proviso that "any

DISTRICT JUDGE CHARLES SWAYNE   Acquitted

CHARGES: Failure to live in district as required by law; use of private railroad car; overstating expenses while sitting away from home; abusing contempt power.

MAJOR ISSUE: Whether Congress can make an action (or inaction) a high crime and misdeameanor by statute if it was not so at the time of the adoption of the Constitution.

HOUSE VOTE ON IMPEACHMENT: Voice Vote

SENATE VOTE FOR ACQUITTAL:

	Guilty	Not Guilty
Article 1	33	49
Articles 2–3	50	1
Articles 4–5	13	69
Article 6	31	51
Article 7	19	63
Articles 8–11	31	51
Article 12	35	47

person offending against the injunction or prohibition of this act shall be deemed guilty of a high misdemeanor." When the impeachability of a judge for nonresidence came up in the case of Alabama district court judge Richard Busteed in 1873, one member of the House raised the question of whether Congress could by law designate behavior a "high misdemeanor" if it was not such when the Constitution was framed. The question was not resolved: Judge Busteed resigned before a vote to impeach could be taken. The question came up again in the impeachment and trial of Florida district court judge Charles Swayne in 1904–1905.

Swayne was appointed to the federal bench by Republican president Benjamin Harrison in 1890. A native of Delaware, Swayne had practiced law for ten years in Philadelphia before moving to Florida in 1885. He apparently angered Democrats in Florida by his handling of cases involving election frauds allegedly committed by the Democratic Party. In 1903 the Florida legislature asked the state's congressional delegation to set the impeachment machinery in motion so that Swayne could be removed from office. The House eventually complied with a voice vote for impeachment and appointed a committee to draw up articles of impeachment on December 13, 1904.

The committee did not return with articles until more than a year later. By then some members of Congress developed significant reservations about the impeachability of all the charges against Swayne except those relating to abuse of the contempt power. The articles drawn up against Swayne—twelve in all—charged him with a conglomeration of offenses: overstating his expenses while sitting in other districts, accepting the use of a private railroad car from a railroad in receivership, abusing the contempt power, and failing to live in his district as required by law. The House adopted the five articles relating to contempt "without division." But on the three articles charging overstatement of expenses the House was almost evenly divided, with 160 members voting against those articles and only 165 voting in favor. Similarly, on the two articles charging improper use of a railway car, 138 voted against adoption. On other charges, 159 members thought Swayne should be tried for nonresidence in his district (Articles 6 and 7), while 136 thought he should not be tried.

Swayne did not deny the facts of any of the charges except the two relating to nonresidence. Instead, he argued that his behavior was neither unlawful nor impeachable. The Senate acquitted Swayne on all articles; not even a majority voted guilty on any article. Interestingly, for the first time since the impeachment of Judge John Pickering one hundred years earlier, the Senate voted on whether the judge was "guilty or not guilty as charged in this article." The decision to drop the language that the judge was guilty of a "high crime and misdemeanor as charged" was made in secret session. It is not known why the Senate made this change. However, from this point forward the practice has been to include the accusation of violation of a high crime and misdemeanor directly into the individual impeachment articles.

ARTICLES OF IMPEACHMENT

Articles exhibited by the House of Representatives of the United States of America, in the name of themselves and of all the people of the United States of America, against Charles Swayne, a judge of the United States, in and for the northern district of Florida, in maintenance and support of their impeachment against him for high crimes and misdemeanor in office.

ARTICLE 1. That the said Charles Swayne, at Waco, in the State of Texas, on the 20th day of April, 1897, being then and there a United States district judge in and for the northern district of Florida, did then and there, as said judge, make and present to R. M. Love, then and there being the United States marshal in and for the northern district of Texas, a false claim against the Government of the United States in the sum of $230, then and there knowing said claim to be false, and for the purpose of obtaining payment of said false claim, did then and there as said judge, make and use a certain false certificate then and there knowing said certificate to be false, said certificate being in the words and figures following:

"UNITED STATES OF AMERICA, *Northern District of Texas, ss:*

"I, Charles Swayne, district judge of the United States for the northern district of Florida, do hereby certify that I was directed to and held court at the city of Waco, in the northern district of Texas, twenty-three days, commencing on the 20th day of April, 1897; also, that the time engaged in holding said court, and in going to and returning from the same, was twenty-three days, and that my reasonable expenses for travel and attendance amounted to the sum of two hundred and thirty dollars and cents, which sum is justly due me for such attendance and travel.

"CHAS. SWAYNE, *Judge.*
"Waco, *May 15, 1897.*

"Received of R. M. Love, United States marshal for the northern district of Texas, the sum of 230 dollars and no cents in full payment of the above account.
"$230.   " CHAS. SWAYNE."

when in truth and in fact, as the said Charles Swayne then and there well knew, there was then and there justly due the said Swayne from the Government of the United States and from said United States marshal a far less sum, whereby he has been guilty of a high crime and misdemeanor in his said office.

ARTICLE 2. That the said Charles Swayne, having been duly appointed, confirmed, and commissioned as judge of the United States in and for the northern district of Florida, entered upon the duties of his office, and while in the exercise of his office as judge, as aforesaid, the said Charles Swayne was entitled by law to be paid his reasonable expenses for travel and attendance when lawfully directed to hold court outside of the northern district of Florida, not to exceed $10 per diem, to be paid upon his certificate by the United States marshal for the district in which the court was held, and was forbidden by law to receive compensation for such services. Yet the said Charles Swayne, well knowing these provisions, falsely certified that his reasonable expenses for travel and attendance were $10 per diem while holding court at Tyler, Tex., twenty-four days commencing December 3, 1900, and seven days going to and returning from said Tyler, Tex., and received therefor from the Treasury of the United States, by the hand of John Grant, the United States marshal for the eastern district of Texas, the sum of $310, when the reasonable expenses incurred and paid by the said Charles Swayne for travel and attendance did not amount to the sum of $10 per diem.

Wherefore the said Charles Swayne, judge as aforesaid, misbehaved himself and was and is guilty of a high crime, to wit, the crime of obtaining money from the United States by a false pretense, and of a high misdemeanor in office.

ARTICLE 3. That the said Charles Swayne having been duly appointed, confirmed, and commissioned as judge of the United States in and for the northern district of Florida, entered upon the duties of his office, and while in the exercise of his office of judge as aforesaid was entitled by law to be paid his reasonable expenses for travel and attendance when lawfully directed to hold court outside of the northerns [sic] district of Florida, not to exceed $10 per diem, to be paid upon his certificate by the United States marshal of the district in which the court was held, and was forbidden by law to receive any compensation for such services. Yet the said Charles Swayne, well knowing these provisions, falsely certified that his reasonable expenses for travel in going to and coming from and attendance were $10 per diem while holding court at Tyler, Tex., thirty-five days from January 12, 1903, and six days going to and returning from said Tyler, Tex., and received therefor from the Treasury of the United States, by the hand of A. J. Houston, the United States marshal for the eastern district of Texas, the sum of $410, when the reasonable expenses of the said Charles Swayne incurred and paid by him during said period were much less than said sum.

Wherefore the said Charles Swayne, judge as aforesaid, misbehaved himself and was and is guilty of a high crime, to wit, obtaining money from the United States by a false pretense, and of a high misdemeanor in office.

ARTICLE 4. That the said Charles Swayne having been duly appointed, confirmed, and commissioned as judge of the United States in and for the northern district of Florida, entered upon the duties of his office, and while in the exercise of his office as judge as aforesaid heretofore, to wit, A.D. 1893, did unlawfully appropriate to his own use, without making compensation to the owner, a certain railroad car, belonging to the Jacksonville, Tampa and Key West Railroad Company, for the purpose of transporting himself, his family, and friends from Guyencourt, in the State of Delaware, to Jacksonville, Fla., the said railroad company being at the time in the possession of a receiver appointed by said Charles Swayne, judge as aforesaid, on the petition of creditors.

The said car was supplied with provisions by the said receiver, which were consumed by said Swayne and his friends, and was provided with a conductor or porter at the cost and expense of said railroad company, and with transportation over connecting lines. The expenses of the trip were paid by the said receiver out of the funds of the said Jacksonville, Tampa and Key West Railroad

Company, and the said Charles Swayne, acting as judge, allowed the credit claimed by the said receiver for and on account of the said expenditure as a part of the necessary expenses of operating said road. The said Charles Swayne, judge as aforesaid, used the said property without making compensation to the owner, and under a claim of right, for the reason that the same was in the hands of a receiver appointed by him.

Wherefore the said Charles Swayne, judge as aforesaid, was and is guilty of an abuse of judicial power and of a high misdemeanor in office.

ARTICLE 5. That the said Charles Swayne was duly appointed, commissioned, and confirmed as judge of the United States in and for the northern district of Florida, and entered upon the duties of said office, and while in the exercise of his office of judge as aforesaid heretofore, to wit, A.D. 1893, did unlawfully appropriate to his own use, without making compensation to the owner, a certain railroad car belonging to the Jacksonville, Tampa and Key West Railroad Company for the purpose of transporting himself, his family, and friends from Jacksonville, Fla., to California, said railroad company being at the time in the possession of a receiver appointed by the said Charles Swayne, judge as aforesaid, on the petition of creditors.

The car was supplied with some provisions by the said receiver, which were consumed by the said Swayne and his friends, and it was provided with a porter at the cost and expense of the railroad company and also with transportation over connecting lines. The wages of said porter and the cost of said provisions were paid by the said receiver out of the funds of the Jacksonville, Tampa and Key West Railroad Company, and the said Charles Swayne, acting as judge as aforesaid, allowed the credits claimed by the said receiver for and on account of the said expenditures as a part of the necessary expenses of operating the said railroad. The said Charles Swayne, judge as aforesaid, used the said property without making compensation to the owner under a claim of right, alleging that the same was in the hands of a receiver appointed by him and he therefore had a right to use the same.

Wherefore the said Charles Swayne, judge as aforesaid, was and is guilty of an abuse of judicial power and of high misdemeanor in office.

ARTICLE 6. That the said Charles Swayne, having been duly appointed and confirmed, was commissioned district judge of the United States in and for the northern district of Florida on the 1st day of April, A.D. 1890, to serve during good behavior, and thereafter, to wit, on the 22d day of April, A.D. 1890, took the oath of office and assumed the duties of his appointment, and established his residence at the city of St. Augustine, in the State of Florida, which was at that time within the said northern district. That subsequently, by an act of Congress approved the 23d of July, A.D. 1894, the boundaries of the said northern district of Florida were changed, and the city of St. Augustine and contiguous territory were transferred to the southern district of Florida; whereupon it became and was the duty of the said Charles Swayne to change his residence and reside in the northern district of Florida and to comply with the five hundred and fifty-first section of the Revised Statutes of the United States, which provides that—

"A district judge shall be appointed for each district, except in cases hereinafter provided. Every judge shall reside in the district for which he is appointed, and for offending against this provision shall be deemed guilty of a high misdemeanor."

Nevertheless the said Charles Swayne, judge as aforesaid, did not acquire a residence, and did not, within the intent and meaning of said act, reside in his said district, to wit, the northern district of Florida, from the 23d day of July, A.D. 1894, to the 1st day of October, A.D. 1900, a period of about six years.

Wherefore the said Charles Swayne, judge as aforesaid, willfully and knowingly violated the aforesaid law and was and is guilty of a high misdemeanor in office.

ARTICLE 7. That the said Charles Swayne, having been duly appointed and confirmed, was commissioned district judge of the United States in and for the northern district of Florida on the 1st day of April, A.D. 1890, to serve during good behavior, and thereafter, to wit, on the 22d day of April, A.D. 1890, took the oath of office and assumed the duties of his appointment, and established his residence at the city of St. Augustine, in the State of Florida, which was at that time within the said northern district. That subsequently, by an act of Congress of the United States approved the 23d day of July, A.D. 1894, the boundaries of the said northern district of Florida were changed, and the city of St. Augustine, with the contiguous territory, was transferred to the southern district of Florida, whereupon it became and was the duty of the said Charles Swayne to change his residence and reside in the northern district of Florida, as defined by said act of Congress, and to comply with section 551 of the Revised Statutes of the United States, which provides that—

"A district judge shall be appointed for each district, except in cases hereinafter provided. Every judge shall reside in the district for which he is appointed, and for offending against this provision shall be deemed guilty of a high misdemeanor."

Nevertheless, the said Charles Swayne, judge as aforesaid, totally disregarding his duty as aforesaid, did not acquire a residence, and within the intent and meaning of said act did not reside in his said district, to wit, the northern district of Florida, from the 23d day of July, A.D. 1894, to the 1st day of January, A.D. 1903, a period of about nine years.

Wherefore the said Charles Swayne, judge as aforesaid, willfully and knowingly violated the aforesaid law, and was and is guilty of a high misdemeanor in office.

ARTICLE 8. That the said Charles Swayne, having been appointed, confirmed, and duly commissioned as judge of the district court of the United States in and for the northern district of Florida, entered upon the duties of said office, and while in the exercise of his office as judge, as aforesaid, to wit, while performing the duties of a judge of a circuit court of the United States, heretofore, to wit, on the 12th day of November, A.D. 1901, at the city of Pensacola, in the county of Escambia, in the State of Florida, did maliciously and unlawfully adjudge guilty of a contempt of court and impose a fine of $100 upon and commit to prison for a period of ten days E. T. Davis, an attorney and counselor at law, for an alleged contempt of the circuit court of the United States.

Wherefore the said Charles Swayne, judge as aforesaid, misbehaved himself in his office of judge, and was and is guilty of an abuse of judicial power and of a high misdemeanor in office.

ARTICLE 9. That the said Charles Swayne, having been appointed, confirmed, and duly commissioned as judge of the district court of the United States in and for the northern district of Florida, entered upon the duties of said office, and while in the exercise of his office as judge as aforesaid, to wit, while performing the duties of a judge of a circuit court of the United States heretofore, to wit, on the 12th day of November, A.D. 1901, at the city of Pensacola, in the county of Escambia, in the State of Florida, did knowingly and unlawfully adjudge guilty of a contempt of court and impose a fine of $100 upon and commit to prison for a period of ten days E. T. Davis, an attorney and counselor at law, for an alleged contempt of the circuit court of the United States.

Wherefore the said Charles Swayne, judge as aforesaid, misbehaved himself in his office of judge and was and is guilty of an abuse of judicial power and of a high misdemeanor in office.

ARTICLE 10. That the said Charles Swayne, having been appointed, confirmed, and duly commissioned as judge of the district court of the United States in and for the northern district of Florida, entered upon the duties of said office, and while in the exercise of his office as judge as aforesaid, to wit, while performing the duties of a judge of a circuit court of the United States heretofore, to wit, on the 12th day of November, A.D 1901, at the city of Pensacola, in the county of Escambia, in the State of Florida, did maliciously and unlawfully adjudge guilty of a contempt of court and impose a fine of $100 upon and commit to prison for a period of ten days Simeon Belden, an attorney and counselor at law, for an alleged contempt of the circuit court of the United States.

Wherefore the said Charles Swayne, judge as aforesaid, misbehaved himself in his office of judge and was and is guilty of an abuse of judicial power and of a high misdemeanor in office.

ARTICLE 11. That the said Charles Swayne, having been appointed, confirmed, and duly commissioned as judge of the district court of the United States in and for the northern district of Florida, entered upon the duties of said office, and while in the exercise of his office as judge as aforesaid, to wit, while performing the duties of a circuit judge of the United States heretofore, to wit, on the 12th day of November, A.D. 1901, at the city of Pensacola, in the county of Escambia, in the State of Florida, did knowingly and unlawfully adjudge guilty of contempt of court and impose a fine of $100 upon and commit to prison for a period of ten days Simeon Belden, an attorney and counselor at law, for an alleged contempt of the circuit court of the United States.

Wherefore the said Charles Swayne, judge as aforesaid, misbehaved himself in his office as judge and was and is guilty of an abuse of judicial power and of a high misdemeanor in office.

ARTICLE 12. That the said Charles Swayne, having been duly appointed, confirmed, and commissioned as judge of the United States in and for the northern district of Florida, entered upon the duties of his office, and while in the exercise of his office of judge heretofore, to wit, on the 9th day of December, A.D. 1902, at Pensacola, in the county of Escambia, in the State of Florida, did unlawfully and knowingly adjudge guilty of contempt and did commit to prison for the period of sixty days one W. C. O'Neal, for an alleged contempt of the district court of the United States for the northern district of Florida.

Wherefore the said Charles Swayne, judge as aforesaid, misbehaved himself in his office of judge, as aforesaid, and was and is guilty of an abuse of judicial power and of a high misdemeanor in office.

And the House of Representatives by protestation, saving to themselves the liberty of exhibiting at any time hereafter any further articles of accusation or impeachment against the said Charles Swayne, judge of the United States court for the northern district of Florida, and also of replying to his answers which he shall make unto the articles herein preferred against him, and of offering proof to the same and every part thereof, and to all and every other article or accusation or impeachment which shall be exhibited by them as the case shall require, do demand that the said Charles Swayne may be put to answer the high crimes and misdemeanors in office herein charged against him, and that such proceedings, examinations, trials, and judgments may be thereupon had and given as may be agreeable to law and justice.

J. G. CANNON,
Speaker of the House of Representatives.

Attest:
A. McDOWELL, *Clerk.*

❧ 17 ❧
Circuit Judge Robert W. Archbald
(1912)

WHEN CONGRESS IMPEACHED Judge Robert W. Archbald in 1912, the court on which he sat, the U.S. Commerce Court, was only two years old and under serious attack. Created to deal with "the railroad problem," the Commerce Court was unpopular from its inception, in part because many thought it would favor the railroads in disputes with the Interstate Commerce Commission. Within months of Archbald's removal, Congress abolished the Commerce Court. The court had lasted for only three years. Archbald's fate was not directly tied to the fate of his court, but the unseemly behavior that led to his ouster was seen by many as symptomatic of the problems to be expected from a court that was perceived as biased.

> The impeachment of Judge Archbald justly cast no reflection against the Court as an institution nor any of its other members. Hence we find that during the final stage of the movement for abolition of the Court, the Archbald impeachment does not figure in the debate. Yet the mere fact of the impeachment was a weighty, even if inarticulate, factor. For the conviction of one of the judges . . . because it involved the use of his influence to secure favors from carriers litigating before him, confirmed the widespread claim of railroad bias and partisanship deemed inevitable in the very nature of so specialized and concentrated a tribunal as the Commerce Court.[1]

This assessment reveals the basis of the charges against Judge Archbald as well as his defense. Archbald was accused of using his position as a federal judge to enter into profitable business arrangements with potential litigants before his court. He was accused of behavior that was an abuse of his office, but which would not subject him to criminal prosecution. Were he an ordinary businessman, nothing that Archbald was accused of would be indictable, and, at the time, nothing he did appeared to violate any laws regulating judges. Yet the House committee that drafted the articles of impeachment argued that the constitutional clause stating that judges shall hold their offices during "good Behaviour" gave legitimacy to impeachment for noncriminal offenses. If judges hold their offices "during good Behaviour," the committee claimed, then *bad* behavior is a violation of the condition for holding office, and an additional basis for removal:

JUDGE ROBERT W. ARCHBALD   Convicted and Disqualified

CHARGES: Improperly using his influence as a judge to enter into business dealings with potential litigants before his court; improper acceptance of gifts from litigants; improper appointment of a jury commissioner.

MAJOR ISSUE: Whether a federal judge's noncriminal private behavior that suggests an improper use of the office is a "high crime and misdemeanor."

HOUSE VOTE ON IMPEACHMENT: 223–1

SENATE VOTE FOR CONVICTION:

	Guilty	Not Guilty
Article 1	68	5
Article 2	46	25
Article 3	60	11
Article 4	52	20
Article 5	66	6
Article 6	24	45
Article 7	29	36
Article 8	22	42
Article 9	23	39
Article 10	1	65
Article 11	11	51
Article 12	19	46
Article 13	42	20

SENATE VOTE FOR DISQUALIFICATION: 39–35

Your committee is of opinion that Judge Archbald's sense of moral responsibility has become deadened. He has prostituted his high office for personal profit. He has attempted by various transactions to commercialize his potentiality as judge. He has shown an overweening desire to make gainful bargains with parties having cases before him or likely to have cases before him. To accomplish this purpose he has not hesitated to use his official power and influence. He has degraded his high office and has destroyed the confidence of the public in his judicial integrity. He has forfeited the condition upon which he holds his commission and should be removed from office by impeachment.

The thirteen articles of impeachment voted by the House detailed a series of financial dealings and improper communications between Archbald and litigants or potential litigants in his court. Article 13 summarized the gist of the charges against Archbald that were detailed in the preceding twelve articles. The alleged misdeeds dealt primarily with Archbald's private business dealings; the impeachability issue seemed to hinge on the fact that he used his position as federal judge hearing railroad cases to imply that benefits might accrue from doing business with him. No bribery was actually alleged, however. Apparently in anticipation of possible defenses, the impeachment inquiry committee attacked head-on the question of whether actions not taken in an official capacity can be impeachable. In what might be a foreshadowing of arguments propounded in the attempt to impeach Supreme Court Justice William O. Douglas fifty-eight years later, the committee declared that

> Any conduct on the part of a judge which reflects on his integrity as a man or his fitness to perform the judicial functions should be sufficient to sustain his impeachment. It would be both absurd and monstrous to hold that an impeachable offense must needs be committed in an official capacity. If such an atrocious doctrine should receive the sanction of the congressional authority, there is no limit to the variety and viciousness of the offenses which a Federal judge might commit with perfect immunity from effective impeachment.

Archbald did not deny the facts of most of the charges against him; he simply denied that what he had done was against the law and denied that he entered into the business deals with any bad intent. He argued that bad behavior that was not criminal could not subject him to impeachment. The Senate did not agree. He was convicted by the required two-thirds majority on Articles 1, 3, 4, 5, and the catchall thirteenth article. The Senate went on to conclude, for only the second time in U.S. history, to disqualify a judge from holding any office of honor, trust, or profit under the United States. This case represents the first solid precedent for the proposition that behavior need not be criminally indictable in order to be impeachable, at least with regard to federal judges.

ARTICLES OF IMPEACHMENT

Articles of impeachment of the House of Representatives of the United States of America in the name of themselves and of all of the people of the United States of America against Robert W. Archbald, additional circuit judge of the United States from the third judicial circuit, appointed pursuant to the act of June 18, 1910 (U.S. Stat. L., vol. 36, 540), and having duly qualified and having been duly commissioned and designated on the 31st day of January, 1911, to serve for four years in the Commerce Court:

Article 1

That the said Robert W. Archbald, at Scranton, in the State of Pennsylvania, being a United States circuit judge, and having been duly designated as one of the judges of the United States Commerce Court on March 31, 1911, entered into an agreement with one Edward J. Williams whereby the said Robert W. Archbald and the said Edward J. Williams agreed to become partners in the purchase of a certain culm dump, commonly known as the Katydid culm dump, near Moosic, Pa., owned by the Hillside Coal & Iron Co., and of the Erie Railroad Co., a corporation, which owned all of the stock of said coal company, to enter into an agreement with the said Robert W. Archbald and the said Edward J. Williams to sell the interest of the said Hillside Coal & Iron Co., a corporation, and one John M. Robertson, for the purpose of disposing of said property at a profit. That pursuant to said agreement, and in furtherance thereof, the said Robert W. Archbald . . . did undertake . . . to induce and influence, the officers of the said Hillside Coal & Iron Co. in the Katydid culm dump for a consideration of $4,500. That . . . at the time aforesaid and during the time the aforesaid negotiations were in progress the said Erie Railroad Co. was a common carrier engaged in interstate commerce and was a party litigant in certain suits, . . . then pending in the United States Commerce Court; and the said Robert W. Archbald, judge as aforesaid, well knowing these facts, willfully, unlawfully, and corruptly took advantage of his official position as such judge to induce and influence the officials of the said Erie Railroad Co., and the said Hillside Coal & Iron Co., a subsidiary corporation thereof, to enter into a contract with him and the said Edward J. Williams, as aforesaid, for profit to themselves and that the said Robert W. Archbald, then and there, through the influence exerted by reason of his position as such judge, willfully, unlawfully, and corruptly did induce the officers of said Erie Railroad Co. and Hillside Coal & Iron Co. to enter into said contract for the consideration aforesaid.

Wherefore the said Robert W. Archibald was and is guilty of misbehavior as such judge and of a high crime and misdemeanor in office.

Article 2

That the said Robert W. Archbald . . . being judge as aforesaid . . . did, then and there, engage, for a consideration, to assist the said George M. Watson to settle the aforesaid case then pending before the Interstate Commerce Commission and to sell to the said Delaware, Lackawanna & Western Railroad Co. the said two-thirds of the stock of the said Marian Coal Co., and in pursuance of said engagement the said Robert W. Archbald, on or about the 10th day of August, 1911, and at divers other times and at different places, did undertake, by correspondence, by personal conferences, and otherwise, to induce and influence the officers of the Delaware, Lackawanna & Western Railroad Co. to enter into an agreement with the said George M. Watson for the settlement of the aforesaid case and the sale of said stock of the Marian Coal Co.; and the said Robert W. Archbald thereby willfully, unlawfully, and corruptly did use his influence as such judge in the attempt to settle said case and to sell said stock of the said Marian Coal Co. to the Delaware, Lackawanna & Western Railroad Co.

Wherefore the said Robert W. Archbald was and is guilty of misbehavior as such judge and of a high crime and misdemeanor in office.

Article 3

That the said Robert W. Archbald, being a United States circuit judge and a judge of the United States Commerce Court, on or about October 1, 1911, did secure from the Lehigh Valley Coal Co., a corporation, which coal company was then and there owned by the Lehigh Valley Railroad Co., a common carrier engaged in interstate commerce, and which railroad company was at that time a party litigant in certain suits then pending in the United States Commerce Court . . . all of which was well known to said Robert W. Archbald, an agreement which permitted said Robert W. Archbald and his associates to lease a culm dump, known as Packer No. 3, near Shenandoah, in the State of Pennsylvania, which said culm dump contained a large amount of coal, to wit, 472,670 tons, and which said culm dump the said Robert W. Archbald and his associates agreed to operate and to ship the product of the same exclusively over the lines of the Lehigh Valley Railroad Co.; and that the said Robert W. Archbald unlawfully and corruptly did use his official position and influence as such judge to secure from the said coal company the said agreement.

Wherefore the said Robert W. Archbald was and is guilty of misbehavior as such judge and of a misdemeanor in such office.

Article 4

That the said Robert W. Archbald, while holding the office of United States circuit judge and being a member of the United States Commerce Court, was and is guilty of gross and improper conduct, and was and is guilty of a misdemeanor as said circuit judge and as a member of said Commerce Court in manner and form as follows, to wit: Prior to and on the 4th day of April, 1911, there was pending in said United States Commerce Court the suit of Louisville and Nashville Railroad Co. v. The Interstate Commerce Commission. Said suit was argued and submitted to said United States Commerce Court on the 4th day of April, 1911; that afterwards, to wit, on the 22d day of August, 1911, while said suit was still pending in said court, and before the same had been decided, the said Robert W. Archbald, as a member of said United States Commerce Court, secretly, wrongfully, and unlawfully did write a letter to the attorney for the said Louisville & Nashville Railroad Co. requesting said attorney to see one of the witnesses who had testified in said suit on behalf of said company and to get his explanation and interpretation of certain testimony that the said witness had given in said suit, and communicate the same to the said Robert W. Archbald, which request was complied with by said attorney; that afterwards, to wit, on the 10th day of January, 1912, while said suit was still pending, and before the same had been decided by said court, the said Robert W. Archbald, as judge of said court, secretly, wrongfully, and unlawfully again did write to the said attorney that other members of said United States Commerce Court has discovered evidence on file in said suit detrimental to the said railroad company and contrary to the statements and contentions made by the said attorney, and the said Robert W. Archbald, judge of said United States Commerce Court as aforesaid, in said letter requested the said attorney to make to him, the said Robert W. Archbald, an explanation and an answer thereto; and he, the said Robert W. Archbald, as a member of said United States Commerce Court aforesaid, did then and there request and solicit the said attorney for the said railroad company to make and deliver to the said Robert W. Archbald a further argument in support of the contentions of the said attorney so representing the railroad company, which request was complied with by said attorney, all of which on the part of said Robert W. Archbald was done secretly, wrongfully, and unlawfully, and which was without the knowledge or consent of the said Interstate Commerce Commission or its attorneys.

Wherefore the said Robert W. Archbald was and is guilty of misbehavior in office, and was and is guilty of a misdemeanor.

Article 5

That in the year 1904 one Frederick Warnke, of Scranton, Pa., purchased a two-thirds interest in a lease on certain coal lands owned by the Philadelphia & Reading Coal & Iron Co., located near Lorberry Junction, in said State, and put up a number of improvements thereon and operated a culm dump located on said property for several years thereafter; that operations were carried on at a loss; that said Frederick Warnke thereupon applied to the Philadelphia & Reading Coal & Iron Co. for the mining maps of the said land covered by the said lease, and was informed that the lease under which he claimed had been forfeited two years before it was assigned to him, and his application for said maps was therefore denied; that said Frederick Warnke then made a proposition to George F. Baer, president of the Philadelphia & Reading Railroad Co. and president of the Philadelphia & Reading Coal & Iron Co., to relinquish any claim that he might have in this property under the said lease, provided that the Philadelphia & Reading Coal & Iron Co. would give him an operating lease on what was known as the Lincoln culm bank located near Lorberry; that said George F. Baer referred said proposition to one W. J. Richards, vice president and general manager of the Philadelphia & Reading Coal & Iron Co., for consideration and action; that the general policy of the said coal company being adverse to the lease of any of its culm banks, the said George F. Baer and the said W. J. Richards declined to make the lease, and the said Frederick Warnke was so advised; that the said Frederick Warnke then made several attempts, through his attorneys and friends, to have the said George F. Baer and the said W. J. Richards reconsider their decision in the premises, but without avail; that on or about November 1, 1911, the said Frederick Warnke called upon Robert W. Archbald, who was then and now is a United States circuit judge, having been duly designated as one of the judges of the United States Commerce Court, and asked him, the said Robert W. Archbald, to intercede in his behalf with the said W. J. Richards; that on November 24, 1911, the said Robert W. Archbald, judge as aforesaid, pursuant to said request, did write a letter to the said W. J. Richards requesting an appointment with the said W. J. Richards; that several days thereafter the said Robert W. Archbald called at the office of the said W. J. Richards to intercede for the said Frederick Warnke; that the said W. J. Richards then and there informed the said Robert W. Archbald that the decision which he had given to the said Warnke must be considered as final, and the said Archbald so informed the said Warnke; that the entire capital stock of the Philadelphia & Reading Coal & Iron Co. is owned by the Reading Co., which also owns the entire capital stock of the Philadelphia & Reading Railroad Co., which last-named company is a common carrier engaged in interstate commerce.

That the said Robert W. Archbald, judge as aforesaid, well knowing all of the aforesaid facts, did wrongfully attempt to use his influence as such judge to aid and assist the said Frederick Warnke to secure an operating lease of the said Lincoln culm dump owned by the Philadelphia & Reading Coal & Iron Co., as aforesaid, which lease the officials of the said Philadelphia & Reading Coal & Iron Co. had theretofore refused to grant, which said fact was also well known to the said Robert W. Archbald.

That the said Robert W. Archbald, judge as aforesaid, shortly after the conclusion of his attempted negotiations with the officers of the Philadelphia & Reading Railroad Co. and of the Philadelphia & Reading Coal & Iron Co. aforesaid in behalf of the said Frederick Warnke, and on or about the 31st day of March, 1912, willfully, unlawfully, and corruptly did accept as a gift, reward, or present from the said Frederick Warnke, tendered in consideration of favors shown him by said judge in his efforts to secure a settlement and agreement with the said railroad company and the said coal company, and for other favors shown by said judge to the said Frederick Warnke, a certain promissory note for $500 executed by the firm of Warnke & Co., of which the said Frederick Warnke was a member.

Wherefore the said Robert W. Archbald was and is guilty of misbehavior as a judge and high crimes and misdemeanor in office.

Article 6

That the said Robert W. Archbald, being a United States circuit judge and a judge of the United States Commerce Court, on or about the 1st day of December, 1911, did unlawfully, improperly, and corruptly attempt to use his influence as such judge with the Lehigh Valley Coal Co. and the Lehigh Valley Railway Co. to induce the officers of said companies to purchase a certain interest in a tract of coal land containing 800 acres, which interest at said time belonged to certain persons known as the Everhardt heirs.

Wherefore the said Robert W. Archbald was and is guilty of misbehavior in office, and was and is guilty of a misdemeanor.

Article 7

That during the months of October and November, A.D. 1908, there was pending in the United States district court, in the city of Scranton, State of Pennsylvania, over which court Robert W. Archbald was then presiding as the duly appointed judge thereof, a suit or action at law wherein the Old Plymouth Coal Co. was plaintiff and the Equitable Fire & Marine Insurance Co. was defendant. That the said coal company was principally owned and entirely controlled by one W. W. Rissinger, which fact was well known to said Robert W. Archbald; that on or about November 1, 1908, and while said suit was pending, the said Robert W. Archbald and the said W. W. Rissinger wrongfully and corruptly agreed together to purchase stock in a gold-mining scheme in Honduras, Central America, for the purpose of speculation and profit; that in order to secure the money with which to purchase said stock the said Rissinger executed his promissory note in the sum of $2,500, payable to Robert W. Archbald and Sophia J. Hutchison, which said note was indorsed then and there by the said Robert W. Archbald for the purpose of having same discounted for cash; that one of the attorneys for said Rissinger in the trial of said suit was one John T. Lenahan; that on the 23d day of November, 1908, said suit came on for trial before said Robert W. Archbald, judge presiding, and a jury, and after the plaintiff's evidence was presented the defendant insurance company demurred to the sufficiency of such evidence and moved for a nonsuit, and after extended argument by attorneys for both plaintiff and defendant the said Robert W. Archbald ruled against the defendant and in favor of the plaintiff, and thereupon the defendant proceeded to introduce evidence, before the conclusion of which the jury was dismissed and a consent judgment rendered in favor of the plaintiff for $2,500, to be discharged upon the payment of $2,129.63 if paid within 15 days from November 23, 1908, and on the same day judgments were entered in a number of other like suits against different insurance companies, which resulted in the recovery of about $28,000 by the Old Plymouth Coal Co.; that before the expiration of said 15 days the said Rissinger, with the knowledge and consent of said Robert W. Archbald, presented said note to the said John T. Lenahan for discount, which was refused and which was later discounted by a bank and has never been paid.

All of which acts on the part of the said Robert W. Archbald were improper, unbecoming, and constituted misbehavior in his said office as judge and render him guilty of a misdemeanor.

Article 8

That during the summer and fall of the year 1909 there was pending in the United States district court for the middle district of Pennsylvania, in the city of Scranton, over which court the said Robert W. Archbald was then and there presiding as the duly appointed judge thereof, a civil action wherein the Marian Coal Co. was defendant, which action involved a large sum of money, and which defendant coal company was principally owned and controlled by one Christopher G. Boland and one William P. Boland, all of which was well known to said Robert W. Archbald; and while said suit was so pending the said Robert W. Archbald drew a note for $500, payable to himself, and which note was signed by one John Henry Jones and indorsed by the said Robert W. Archbald, and then and there during the pendency of said suit as aforesaid the said Robert W. Archbald wrongfully agreed and consented that the said note should be presented to the said Christopher G. Boland and the said William P. Boland, or one of them, for the purpose of having the said note discounted, corruptly intending that his name on said note would coerce and induce the said Christopher G. Boland and the said William P. Boland, or one of them to discount the same because of the said Robert W. Archbald's position as judge, and because the said Bolands were at that time litigants in his said court.

Wherefore the said Robert W. Archbald was and is guilty of gross misconduct in his office as judge, and was and is guilty of misdemeanor in his said office as judge.

Article 9

That the said Robert W. Archbald, of the city of Scranton and State of Pennsylvania, on or about November 1, 1909, being then and there a United

States district judge in and for the middle district of Pennsylvania, in the city of Scranton and State aforesaid, did draw a note in his own proper handwriting, payable to himself, in the sum of $500, which said note was signed by one John Henry Jones, which said note the said Robert W. Archbald indorsed for the purpose of securing the sum of $500, and the said Robert W. Archbald, well knowing that his indorsement would not secure money in the usual commercial channels, then and there wrongfully did permit the said John Henry Jones to present said note for discount, at his law office, to one C. H. Von Storch, attorney at law and practitioner in said district court, which said Von Storch, a short time prior thereto, was a party defendant in a suit in the said district court presided over by said Robert W. Archbald, which said suit was decided in favor of the said Von Storch upon a ruling by the said Robert W. Archbald; and when the said note was presented to the said Von Storch for discount, as aforesaid, the said Robert W. Archbald wrongfully and improperly used his influence as such judge to induce the said Von Storch to discount the same; that the said note was then and there discounted by the said Von Storch, and the same has never been paid, but is still due and owning.

Wherefore the said Robert W. Archbald was and is guilty of gross misconduct in his said office, and was and is guilty of a misdemeanor in his said office as judge.

Article 10

That the said Robert W. Archbald, while holding the office of United States district judge, in and for the middle district of the State of Pennsylvania, on or about the 1st day of May, 1910, wrongfully and unlawfully did accept and receive a large sum of money, the exact amount of which is unknown to the House of Representatives, from one Henry W. Cannon; that said money so given by the said Henry W. Cannon and so unlawfully and wrongfully received and accepted by the said Robert W. Archbald, judge as aforesaid, was for the purpose of defraying the expenses of a pleasure trip of the said Robert W. Archbald to Europe; that the said Henry W. Cannon, at the time of the giving of said money and the receipt thereof by the said Robert W. Archbald, was a stockholder and officer in various and divers interstate railway corporations, to wit: A director in the Great Northern Railway, a director in the Lake Erie & Western Railroad Co., and a director in the Fort Wayne, Cincinnati & Louisville Railroad Co.; that the said Henry W. Cannon was president and chairman of the board of directors of the Pacific Coast Co., a corporation which owned the entire capital stock of the Columbus & Puget Sound Railroad Co., the Pacific Coast Railway Co., the Pacific Coast Steamship Co., and various other corporations engaged in the mining of coal and in the development of agricultural and timber land in various parts of the United States; that the acceptance by the said Robert W. Archbald, while holding said office of the United States district judge, of said favors from an officer and official of the said corporations, any of which in the due course of business was liable to be interested in litigation pending in the said court over which he presided as such judge, was improper and had a tendency to and did bring his said office of district judge into disrepute.

Wherefore the said Robert W. Archbald was and is guilty of misbehavior in office, and was and is guilty of a misdemeanor.

Article 11

That the said Robert W. Archbald, while holding the office of United States district judge in and for the middle district of the State of Pennsylvania, did, on or about the 1st day of May, 1910, wrongfully and unlawfully accept and receive a sum of money in excess of $500, which sum of money was contributed and given to the said Robert W. Archbald by various attorneys who were practitioners in the said court presided over by the said Robert W. Archbald; that said money was raised by subscription and solicitation from said attorneys by two of the officers of said court, to wit, Edward R. W. Searle, clerk of said court, and J. B. Woodward, jury commissioner of said court, both the said Edward R. W. Searle and the said J. B. Woodward having been appointed to the said positions by the said Robert W. Archbald, judge aforesaid.

Wherefore said Robert W. Archbald was and is guilty of misbehavior in office, and was and is guilty of a misdemeanor.

Article 12

That on the 9th day of April, 1901, and for a long time prior thereto, one J. B. Woodward was a general attorney for the Lehigh Valley Railroad Co., a corporation and common carrier doing a general railroad business; that on said day the said Robert W. Archbald, being then and there a United States district judge in and for the middle district of Pennsylvania, and while acting as such judge, did appoint the said J. B. Woodward as a jury commissioner in and for said judicial district, and the said J. B. Woodward, by virtue of said appointment and with the continued consent and approval of the said Robert W. Archbald, held such office and performed all the duties pertaining thereto during all the time that the said Robert W. Archbald held said office of United States district judge, and that during all of said time the said J. B. Woodward continued to act as a general attorney for the said Lehigh Valley Railroad Co.; all of which was at all times well known to the said Robert W. Archbald.

Wherefore the said Robert W. Archbald was and is guilty of misbehavior in office, and was and is guilty of a misdemeanor.

Article 13

That Robert W. Archbald, on the 29th day of March, 1901, was duly appointed United States district judge for the middle district of Pennsylvania and held such office until the 31st day of January, 1911, on which last-named date he was duly appointed a United States circuit judge and designated as a judge of the United States Commerce Court.

That during the time in which the said Robert W. Archbald has acted as such United States district judge and judge of the United States Commerce Court he, the said Robert W. Archbald, at divers times and places, has sought wrongfully to obtain credit from and through certain persons who were interested in the result of suits then pending and suits that had been pending in the court over which he presided as judge of the district court, and in suits pending in the United States Commerce Court, of which the said Robert W. Archbald is a member.

That the said Robert W. Archbald, being United States circuit judge and being then and there a judge of the United States Commerce Court, at Scranton, in the State of Pennsylvania, on the 31st day of March, 1911, and at divers other times and places, did undertake to carry on a general business for speculation and profit in the purchase and sale of culm dumps, coal lands, and other coal properties, and for a valuable consideration to compromise litigation pending before the Interstate Commerce Commission, and in the furtherance of his efforts to compromise such litigation and of his speculations in coal properties, willfully, unlawfully, and corruptly did use his influence as a judge of the said United States Commerce Court to induce the officers of the Erie Railroad Co., the Delaware, Lackawanna & Western Railroad Co., the Lackawanna & Wyoming Valley Railroad Co., and other railroad companies engaged in interstate commerce, respectively, to enter into various and divers contracts and agreements in which he was then and there financially interested with divers persons, to wit, Edward J. Williams, John Henry Jones, Thomas H. Jones, George M. Watson, and others, without disclosing his said interest therein on the face of the contract, but which interest was well known to the officers and agents of said railroad companies.

That the said Robert W. Archbald did not invest any money or other thing of value in consideration of any interest acquired or sought to be acquired by him in securing or in attempting to secure such contracts or agreements or properties as aforesaid, but used his influence as such judge with the contracting parties thereto, and received an interest in said contracts, agreements, and properties in consideration of such influence in aiding and assisting in securing same.

That the said several railroad companies were and are engaged in interstate commerce, and at the time of the execution of the several contracts and agreements aforesaid and of entering into negotiations looking to such agreements had divers suits pending in the United States Commerce Court, and that the conduct and efforts of the said Robert W. Archbald in endeavoring to secure and in securing such contracts and agreements from said railroad companies was continuous and persistent from the said 31st day of March, 1911, to about the 15th day or April, 1912.

Wherefore the said Robert W. Archbald was and is guilty of misbehavior as such judge and of misdemeanors in office.

Note

1. Felix Frankfurter and James Landis, *The Business of the Supreme Court: A Study in the Federal Judicial System* (New York: MacMillian, 1928), 171.

◄§ 18 ◊►
District Judge George W. English
(1926)

WHEN ILLINOIS DISTRICT COURT judge George W. English resigned his post less than one week before his impeachment trial was to begin in the Senate, he managed to do what neither Sen. William Blount nor Secretary of War William W. Belknap had been able to do. He avoided trial. The Senate quickly dismissed all charges against him. Perhaps the Senate looked back at the Belknap trial and concluded that it lacked jurisdiction or that it simply was not worth the time required to try an official who was already out of office. By the time he resigned, Judge English was sixty-one years old; perhaps this also influenced the Senate, because the only possible punishment—disqualification from future officeholding—may have seemed unnecessary.

When Congress began its investigation of Judge English in 1926, the 1920s were beginning to look a lot like the scandal-ridden 1870s, when Ulysses S. Grant was president. During the Grant era there were two impeachments and countless congressional investigations of corrupt govern-

DISTRICT JUDGE GEORGE W. ENGLISH   Resigned

CHARGES: Abuse of power; favoritism; tyrannical and oppressive behavior.

MAJOR ISSUE: In the first resignation during the impeachment process since 1876 the Senate agreed to dismiss the charges.

HOUSE VOTE ON IMPEACHMENT: 306–62

SENATE VOTE TO DISMISS CHARGES: 70–9

ment officials. In the 1920s, the Teapot Dome scandal, involving secret leases of government property to private oil companies, became the hallmark of the administration of President Warren G. Harding. Improprieties in the Justice Department, the Veterans Bureau, and the Interior Department resulted in suicides, resignations, and the first prison term for a cabinet officer in American history. Justice Oliver Wendell Holmes, who claimed not to follow politics, was nevertheless moved to write to his friend Sir Frederick Pollock in England that "we are investigating everybody and I daresay fostering a belief too readily accepted that public men generally are corrupt."

In the years between Judge Robert Archbald's impeachment and English's resignation, three other judges resigned either while under investigation or after allegations of misbehavior surfaced. In 1914 a district court judge for the District of Columbia resigned after Congress launched an impeachment investigation. In 1915 a district judge in Utah resigned after he was accused in a scandal involving the "cleaning lady" in his courtroom. And in 1921 a member of Congress asked that Judge Kennesaw Mountain Landis, a district court judge in Illinois, be impeached for serving as the first commissioner of baseball at a salary of $42,500 per year while still a federal judge. (This was at a time when the salary of a district court judge was less than $5,000 per year.)

In hopes that he might help clean up the sport, Landis had been appointed in the wake of the Black Sox scandal that involved the fixing of the 1919 World Series. One of the grounds suggested for impeachment was that Landis had injured "the national sport of baseball by permitting the use of his office as district judge of the United States because the impression will prevail that gambling and other illegal acts in baseball will not be punished in the open forum as in other cases." Because Congress was nearing the end of the session, the investigating committee concluded that Landis's behavior indicated that serious improprieties existed that should be more thoroughly investigated by the next Congress. Landis resigned a year later.

Although the Senate dismissed the charges against English, the articles of impeachment as drafted by the House indicate that had the trial gone forward, it would have been more interesting than the Archbald impeachment tales of coal dump purchases. The first article alone makes the startling claim that the judge sent the U.S. marshall to round up all the Illinois state sheriffs and state attorneys in his district, along with the mayor of Wamac, and herded them into his court for an imaginary case. English is then alleged to have put them in the jury box and "in a loud angry voice, using improper, profane, and indecent language, denounced said officials, . . . and [did] threaten to remove said State officials from their said offices, and when addressing them used obscene and profane language, and thereupon then and there dismissed said officials from his said court and denied them any explanation or hearing. . . ."

Among the impeachable offenses listed by the House were charges of oppressive and tyrannical conduct; favoritism; placement of bankruptcy funds in favored banks for the purpose of gaining personal financial advantage; and acquiring financial advantages for friends and relatives by bestowing bankruptcy funds under his control in particular banks. Like Judge Robert W. Archbald before him, and Judges Harold Louderback and Halsted Ritter after, English was also accused in a final "omnibus" article of bringing "scandal and disrepute" to his court and the administration of justice, by all the behavior specified in the previous articles. If the House's accusations were true, Judge English was certainly a tyrannical and improper judge who engaged in unseemly and censurable behavior. None of it appeared to be criminal, however, which once again revealed the belief of the House that indictable behavior is not required for impeachment.

ARTICLES OF IMPEACHMENT

Articles of impeachment of the House of Representatives of the United States of America in the name of themselves and of all of the people of the United States of America against George W. English, who was appointed, duly qualified, and commissioned to serve during good behavior in office, as United States District Judge for the Eastern District of Illinois, on May 3, 1918

Article I

That the said George W. English, having been nominated by the President of the United States, confirmed by the Senate of the United States, duly qualified and commissioned, and while acting as the district judge for the eastern district of Illinois, did on divers and various occasions so abuse the powers of his high office that he is hereby charged with tyranny and oppression, whereby he has brought the administration of justice in said district in the court of which he is judge into disrepute, and by his tyrannous and oppressive course of conduct is guilty of misbehavior falling under the constitutional provision as ground for impeachment and removal from office.

In that the said George W. English . . . did willfully, tyrannically, oppressively, and unlawfully suspend and disbar one Thomas M. Webb . . . without due process of law; and also,

In that the said George W. English . . . did willfully tyrannically, oppressively, and unlawfully suspend and disbar one Charles A. Karch . . . without due process of law; and also in that the said George W. English, judge as aforesaid, restored the said Karch to membership of the bar in said district, but willfully, tyrannically, oppressively, and unlawfully deprived the said Charles A. Karch of the right to practice in said court or try any case before him, the said George W. English, while sitting or holding court in said eastern district of Illinois; and also,

In that the said George W. English, judge as aforesaid, on the 1st day of August, 1922, unlawfully and deceitfully issued a summons from the said district court of the United States, and had the same served by the marshal of said district, summoning the State sheriffs and State attorneys then and there in the said eastern district of Illinois, being duly elected and qualified officials of the sovereign State of Illinois, and the mayor of the city of Wamac, also a duly elected and qualified municipal office of said State of Illinois, residing in said district, to appear before him in an imaginary case of "the United States against one Gourley and one Daggett," when in truth and fact no such case was then and there pending in said court, and in placing the said State officials and mayor of Wamac in the jury box, and when they came into court, in answer to said summons, then and therein a loud, angry voice, using improper, profane, and indecent language, denounced said officials without any lawful or just cause or reason, and without naming any act of misconduct or offense committed by the said officials and without permitting said officials or any of them to be heard, and without having any lawful authority or control over said officials, and then and there did unlawfully, improperly, oppressively, and tyrannically threaten to remove said State officials from their said offices, and when addressing them used obscene and profane language, and thereupon then and there dismissed said officials from his said court and denied them any explanation or hearing; and also,

In that the said George W. English, judge aforesaid, on the 8th day of May, 1922, in the trial of the case of the United States against Hall, then and there pending before said George W. English, as judge, the said George W. English, judge as aforesaid, from the bench and in open court, did willfully, unlawfully, tyrannically, and oppressively, and intending thereby to coerce the minds of the jurymen in the said court in the performance of their duty as jurors, stated in open court and in the presence of said jurors, parties and counsel in said case, that if he told them (thereby then and there meaning said jurymen) that a man was guilty and they did not find him guilty that he would send them to jail; and also,

In that the said George W. English, judge aforesaid, on the 15th day of August, 1922, willfully, unlawfully, tyrannically, and oppressively did summon Michael L. Munie, of East St. Louis, a member of the editorial staff of the East St. Louis Journal, a newspaper published in said East St. Louis, and Samuel A. O'Neal, a reporter of the St. Louis Post-Dispatch, a newspaper published at St. Louis, in the State of Missouri, and when said Munie and the said O'Neal appeared before him did willfully, unlawfully, tyrannically, and oppressively, and with angry and abusive language attempt to coerce and did threaten them as members of the press from truthfully publishing the facts in relation to the disbarment of Charles A. Karch by said George W. English, judge as aforesaid, and then and there used the power of his office tyrannically, in violation of the freedom of the press guaranteed by the Constitution, to suppress the publication of the facts about the official conduct of said George W. English, judge aforesaid, and did then and there forbid the said Munie and the said O'Neal to publish any facts whatsoever in relation to said disbarment under threats of imprisonment; and also,

In that the said George W. English, judge aforesaid, on the 15th day of August, 1922, at East St. Louis, in the State of Illinois, did unlawfully summon before him one Joseph Maguire, being then and there the editor and publisher of the Carbondale Free Press, a newspaper published in Carbondale, in said eastern district of Illinois, and then and there, on the appearance before him of said Joseph Maguire in open court, did violently threaten said Joseph Maguire with imprisonment for having printed in his said paper a lawful editorial from the columns of the St. Louis Post-Dispatch, a newspaper published at St. Louis, in the state of Missouri, and in a very angry and improper manner did threaten said Maguire with imprisonment for having also printed some lawful handbills—said handbills having no allusion to said judge or to his conduct of the said court—and then and there did threaten this member of the press with imprisonment.

Wherefore the said George W. English was and is guilty of a course of conduct tyrannous and oppressive and is guilty of a misdemeanor in office as such judge, and was and is guilty of a misdemeanor in office.

Article II

That George W. English, judge as aforesaid, was guilty of a course of improper and unlawful conduct as said judge, filled with partiality and favoritism, resulting in the creation of a combination to control and manage in collusion with Charles B. Thomas, referee in bankruptcy, in and for the eastern district of Illinois for their own interests and profit and that of the relatives and friends of said George W. English, judge as aforesaid, and of Charles B. Thomas, referee, the bankruptcy affairs of the eastern district of Illinois. . . .

The said George W. English, judge aforesaid, well knowing the facts and premises, then and there did willfully, improperly, and unlawfully take advantage of his said official position as judge aforesaid, and did aid and assist said Charles B. Thomas, referee, aforesaid, in the establishment, maintenance, and operation of said unlawful and improper organization as above set forth, for the purpose of obtaining improper and unlawful personal gains and profits for the said George W. English, judge aforesaid, and his family and friends;

Wherefore, the said George W. English was and is guilty of a course of conduct as aforesaid constituting misbehavior as such judge and was and is guilty of a misdemeanor in office.

Article III

That George W. English, judge aforesaid, was guilty of misbehavior in office is [sic] that he corruptly extended partiality and favoritism in diverse other matters hereinafter set forth to Charles B. Thomas, said sole referee in bankruptcy in the said eastern district of Illinois, and by his conduct and partiality as judge brought the administration of justice into discredit and disrepute, degraded the dignity of the court, and destroyed the confidence of the public in its integrity;

. . . [T]hat with full knowledge that said referee, Charles B. Thomas, was neglecting his duties as referee in bankruptcy in his office at East St. Louis in spending six months of his time 290 miles away from his office at East St. Louis, George W. English, judge as aforesaid, did then and there, despite this knowledge and these facts, approve said negligence on the part of said Charles B. Thomas and said neglect of duty without criticism or rebuke by then and there reappointing him for another term.

Wherefore the said George W. English was and is guilty of misbehavior as such judge and was and is guilty of a misdemeanor in office.

Article IV

That George W. English, while serving as judge as aforesaid, in the District Court of the United States for the Eastern District of Illinois, did in conjunction with Charles B. Thomas, sole referee in bankruptcy aforesaid, corruptly and improperly handle and control the deposit of bankruptcy and other funds under his control in said court, by depositing, transferring, and using said funds for the pecuniary benefit of himself and said Charles by Thomas, sole referee in bankruptcy, thus prostituting his official power and influence for the purpose of securing benefits to himself and to his family and to the said Charles B. Thomas and his family; . . .

In that George W. English, judge as aforesaid, did improperly designate the Merchants State Bank, of Centralia, Ill., to be a Government depository of bankruptcy funds, in which bank he, the said George W. English, and he the said Charles B. Thomas, were then and there depositors and stockholders and George W. English was then and there director; and, also,

. . . [T]hat said George W. English, judge as aforesaid, and Charles B. Thomas, sole referee in bankruptcy aforesaid, acting in concert with officers and directors of said Merchants State Bank of Centralia, Ill., did borrow with said directors sums of money in the total equal to all of the surplus, assets, and capital of said bank and at a low rate of interest and without security.

Wherefore the said George W. English was and is guilty of a course of conduct constituting misbehavior as such judge and that said George W. English was and is guilty of a misdemeanor in office.

Article V

That George W. English, on the 3d day of May, 1918, was duly appointed United States district judge for the eastern district of Illinois, and has held such office to the present day.

That during the time in which said George W. English has acted as such United States district judge, he, the said George W. English, at divers times and places, has repeatedly, in his judicial capacity, treated members of the bar, in a manner coarse, indecent, arbitrary, and tyrannical, and has so conducted himself in court and from the bench as to oppress and hinder members of the bar in the faithful discharge of their sworn duties to their clients, and to deprive such clients of their right to appear and be protected in their liberty and property by counsel, and in the above and other ways has conducted himself in a manner unbecoming the high position which he holds and thereby did bring the administration of justice in his said court into contempt and disgrace, to the great scandal and reproach of the said court.

That said George W. English, as judge aforesaid, during his said term of office, at divers times and places, while acting as such judge, did disregard the authority of the laws, and, wickedly meaning and intending so to do, did refuse to allow parties lawfully in said court the benefit of trial by jury, contrary to his said trust and duty as judge of said district court, against the laws of the United States, and in violation of the solemn oath which had taken to administer equal and impartial justice.

That the said George W. English, as judge aforesaid, during his said term of office, at divers times and places, when acting as such judge, did so conduct himself in his said court, in making decisions and orders in actions pending in his said court and before him as said judge, as to excite fear and distrust and to inspire a widespread belief, in and beyond said eastern district of Illinois that causes were not decided in said court according to their merits but were decided with partiality and with prejudice and favoritism to certain individuals, particularly to one Charles B. Thomas, referee in bankruptcy for said eastern district.

That the said George W. English, as judge aforesaid, during his said term of office, at divers time and places, while acting as said judge, did improperly and unlawfully intent [sic] to favor and prefer Charles B. Thomas, his referee in bankruptcy for said eastern district, and to make for said Thomas large and improper gains and profits, continually and habitually prefer said Thomas in his appointments, rulings, and decrees.

That said George W. English, as judge aforesaid, during his said term of office, at divers times and places while acting as said judge, from the bench and in open court, did interfere with and usurp the authority and power and privileges of the sovereign State of Illinois, and usurp the rights and powers of said State over its State officials, and set at naught the constitutional rights of said sovereign State of Illinois, to the great prejudice and scandal of the cause of justice and of his said court and the rights of the people to have and receive due process of law.

That said George W. English, as judge aforesaid, during his said term of office, at divers times and places, did, while acting as said judge, unlawfully and improperly attempt to secure the approval, cooperation, and assistance of his associate upon the bench in said eastern district of Illinois, Judge Walter C. Lindley, by suggesting to said Walter C. Lindley, judge as aforesaid, that he appoint George W. English, jr., son of said George W. English, judge as aforesaid, to receiverships and other appointments in the said district court for said eastern district of Illinois, in consideration that said George W. English, judge as aforesaid, would appoint to like positions in his said court a cousin of said Judge Walter C. Lindley, and thereby unlawfully and improperly avoid the law in such case made and provided; all to the disgrace and prejudice of the administration of justice in the court of George W. English, judge as aforesaid.

That said George W. English, as judge aforesaid, during his said term of office, at divers times and places, did, while serving as said judge, seek from a large railroad corporation, to wit, the Missouri Pacific Railroad Co., which had large trackage, in said eastern district of Illinois, the appointment of his son, George W. English, jr., as attorney for said railroad.

All to the scandal and disrepute of said court and the administration of justice therein.

Wherefore, the said George W. English was and is guilty of misbehavior as such judge and of a misdemeanor in office.

❧ 19 ❧

District Judge Harold Louderback

(1933)

THE GREAT DEPRESSION that gripped the country in the 1930s brought with it massive business failures. One of the side effects of these failures was increased bankruptcies and the consequent need for people to supervise the operations of businesses in bankruptcy. These supervisors, known as receivers, received fees for their services that could be very large, and certainly were welcome at a time when employment generally was precarious. Federal judges controlled these coveted appointments. Suspicions and complaints of favoritism in appointing receivers were not unusual; in the atmosphere of the Depression, they flourished.

District Judge Harold Louderback was accused of favoritism in the appointment of bankruptcy receivers. One of the impeachment charges against Judge George W. English in 1926 likewise involved favoritism in appointing receivers; and Congress investigated three other judges between English and Louderback for improprieties involved with bankruptcies receivers. What is interesting about the Louderback case is that, as with two of the three cases that Congress investigated prior to Judge Louderback, the investigating committee recommended against impeachment, voting 17 to 3 in favor of censuring rather than impeachment. The committee did not believe that Louderback's behavior rose to the level of "high crime and misdemeanor." Yet unlike the other cases, the House rejected the committee's recommendation and voted to impeach Louderback.

In the end, it appears that the full House should have listened to the committee, since the first four articles brought against Louderback could not even elicit a majority vote for guilt, and the final article fell seven votes shy of

---

DISTRICT JUDGE HAROLD LOUDERBACK   Acquitted

CHARGES: Favoritism and official financial improprieties.

MAJOR ISSUE: Whether it is permissable to aggregate all of the specific charges against an officer into one final "catch-all" or "omnibus" article.

HOUSE VOTE ON IMPEACHMENT: 183–142

SENATE VOTE FOR ACQUITTAL:

	Guilty	Not Guilty
Article I	34	42
Article II	23	47
Article III	11	63
Article IV	30	47
Article V (as amended)	45	34

---

the two-thirds needed to convict. The first four articles all involved appointments of receivers; none alleged any criminal behavior on the part of the judge. As with the case against Judge Robert W. Archbald, and as would be the case in the next impeachment trial (of Judge Halsted L. Ritter in 1936), the final article was an amalgam of the preceding articles, charging that Judge Louderback by a series of actions had brought his court into disrepute.

ARTICLES OF IMPEACHMENT

. . . Articles of impeachment of the House of Representatives of the United States of America in the name of themselves and of all of the people of the United States of America against Harold Louderback, who was appointed, duly qualified, and commissioned to serve during good behavior in office, as United States district judge for the northern district of California, on April 17, 1928.

Article I

That the said Harold Louderback, having been nominated by the President of the United States, confirmed by the Senate of the United States, duly qualified and commissioned and while acting as a district judge for the northern district of California did on diverse and various occasions so abuse the power of his high office, that he is hereby charged with tyranny and oppression, favoritism and conspiracy, whereby he has brought the administration of justice in said district in the court of which he is a judge into disrepute, and by his conduct is guilty of misbehavior, falling under the constitutional provision as ground for impeachment and removal from office.

In that the said Harold Louderback on or about the 13th day of March, 1930, at his chambers and in his capacity as judge aforesaid, did willfully, tyrannically, and oppressively discharge one Addison G. Strong, whom he had on the 11th day of March, 1930, appointed as equity receiver in the matter of Olmstead against Russell-Colvin Co. after having attempted to force and coerce the said Strong to appoint one Douglas Short as attorney for the receiver in said case.

In that the said Harold Louderback improperly did attempt to cause the said Addison G. Strong to appoint the said Douglas Short as attorney for the receiver by promises of allowance of large fees and by threats of reduced fees did he refuse to appoint said Douglas Short.

In that the said Harold Louderback improperly did use his office and power of district judge in his own personal interest by causing the appointment of the said Douglas Short as attorney for the receiver, at the instance, suggestion, or demand of one Sam Leake, to whom the said Harold Louderback was under personal obligation, the said Sam Leake having entered into a certain arrangement and conspiracy with the said Harold Louderback to provide him, the said Harold Louderback, with a room at the Fairmont Hotel in the city of San Francisco, Calif., and made arrangements for registering said room in his, Sam Leake's name and paying all bills therefor in cash under an arrangement with the said Harold Louderback, to be reimbursed in full or in part in order that the said Harold Louderback might continue to actually reside in the city and county of San Francisco after having improperly and unlawfully established a fictitious residence in Contra Costa County for the sole purpose of improperly removing for trial to said Contra Costa County a cause of action which the said Harold Louderback expected to be filed against him; and that the said Douglas Short did receive large and exorbitant fees for his services as attorney for the receiver in said action, and the said Sam Leake did receive certain fees, gratuities, and loans directly or indirectly from the said Douglas Short amounting approximately to $1,200.

In that the said Harold Louderback entered into a conspiracy with the said Sam Leake to violate the provisions of the California Political Code in establishing a residence in the county of Contra Costa when the said Harold Louderback in fact did not reside in said county and could not have established a residence without the concealment of his actual residence in the county of San Francisco, covered and concealed by means of the said conspiracy with the said Sam Leake, all in violation of the law of the State of California.

In that the said Harold Louderback, in order to give color to his fictitious residence in the county of Contra Costa, all for the purpose of preparing and falsely creating proof necessary to establish himself as a resident of Contra Costa County in anticipation of an action he expected to be brought against him, for the sole purpose of meeting the requirements of the Code of Civil Procedure of the State of California providing that all causes of action must be tried in the county in which the defendant resides at the commencement of the action, did in accordance with the conspiracy entered into with the said Sam Leake unlawfully register as a voter in said Contra Costa County, when in law and in fact he did not reside in said county and could not so register, and that the said acts of Harold Louderback constitute a felony defined by section 42 of the Penal Code of California.

Wherefore the said Harold Louderback was and is guilty of a course of conduct improper, oppressive, and unlawful and is guilty of misbehavior in office as such judge and was and is guilty of a misdemeanor in office.

Article II

That Harold Louderback, judge as aforesaid, was guilty of a course of improper and unlawful conduct as a judge, filled with partiality and favoritism in improperly granting excessive, exorbitant, and unreasonable allowances as disbursements to one Marshall Woodward and to one Samuel Shortridge, jr., as receiver and attorney, respectively, in the matter of the Lumbermen's Reciprocal Association. . . .

In that the said Harold Louderback did not give his fair, impartial, and judicial consideration to the objections of the said State commissioner of insurance against the allowance of excessive fees and unreasonable disbursements to the said Marshall Woodward the Samuel Shortridge, jr., receiver and attorney, respectively, in the case of the Lumbermen's Reciprocal Association, in order to favor and enrich his friends at the expense of the litigants and parties in interest in said matter, and did thereby cause said State commissioner of insurance and the parties in interest additional delay, expense, and labor in taking an appeal to the United States Circuit Court of Appeals in order to protect their rights and property in the matter against the partial, oppressive, and unjudicial conduct of said Harold Louderback.

Wherefore, said Harold Louderback was and is guilty of a course of conduct oppressive and unjudicial and is guilty of misbehavior in office as such judge and was and is guilty of a misdemeanor in office.

Article III

The said Harold Louderback, judge aforesaid, was guilty of misbehavior in office resulting in expense, disadvantage, annoyance, and hindrance to litigants in his court in the case of the Fageol Motor Co., for which he appointed one Guy H. Gilbert receiver, knowing that the said Gilbert was incompetent, unqualified, and inexperienced to act as such receiver in said case. . . .

Wherefore the said Harold Louderback was and is guilty of a course of conduct constituting misbehavior as said judge and that said Harold Louderback was and is guilty of a misdemeanor in office.

Article IV

That the said Harold Louderback, judge aforesaid, was guilty of misbehavior in office, filled with partiality and favoritism, in improperly, willfully, and unlawfully granting on insufficient and improper papers an application for the appointment of a receiver in the Prudential Holding Co. case for the sole purpose of benefiting and enriching his personal friends and associates. . . .

In that the said Harold Louderback did on or about the 15th day of August, 1931, on insufficient and improper application, appoint one Guy H. Gilbert receiver of the Prudential Holding Co. case when as a matter of fact and law and under conditions then existing no receiver should have been appointed; . . . that the said Harold Louderback in an attempt to benefit and enrich the said Guy H. Gilbert and his attorneys, Dinkelspiel and Dinkelspiel, failed to give his fair, impartial, and judicial consideration to the application of the said Prudential Holding Co. for a dismissal of the petition and a discharge of the receiver; . . . that during the pendency of the application for the dismissal of the petition and for the discharge of the receiver a petition in bankruptcy was filed against the said Prudential Holding Co. based entirely and solely on an allegation that a receiver in equity had been appointed for the said Prudential Holding Co., and the said Harold Louderback then and there willfully, improperly, and unlawfully, sitting in a part of the court to which he had not been assigned at the time, took jurisdiction of the case in bankruptcy and though knowing the facts in the case and of the application then pending before him for the dismissal of the petition and the discharge of the equity receiver, granted the petition in bankruptcy and did on the 2d day of October, 1930, appoint the same Guy H. Gilbert receiver in bankruptcy and the said Dinkelspiel and Dinkelspiel attorneys for the receiver, knowing all of the time that the said Prudential Holding Co. was entitled as a matter of law to have the said petition in equity dismissed; in that through the oppressive, deliberate, and willful action of the said Harold Louderback acting in his capacity as a judge and misusing the powers of his judicial office for the sole purpose of benefiting and enriching said Guy H. Gilbert and Dinkelspiel and Dinkelspiel, did cause the said Prudential Holding Co. to be put to unnecessary delay, expense, and labor and did deprive them of a fair, impartial, and judicial consideration of their rights and the protection of their property, to which they were entitled.

Wherefore the said Harold Louderback was, and is, guilty of a course of conduct constituting misbehavior as said judge and that said Harold Louderback was, and is, guilty of a misdemeanor in office.

Article V

That Harold Louderback, on the 17th day of April, 1928, was duly appointed United States district judge for the northern district of California, and has held such office to the present day.

That the said Harold Louderback as judge aforesaid, during his said term of office, at diverse times and places when acting as such judge, did so conduct himself in his said court and in his capacity as judge in making decisions and orders in actions pending in his said court and before him as said judge, and in the method of appointing receivers and attorneys for receivers, in appointing incompetent receivers, and in displaying a high degree of indifference to the litigants in equity receiverships, as to excite fear and distrust and to inspire a widespread belief in and beyond said northern district of California that causes were not decided in said court according to their merits, but were decided with partiality and with prejudice and favoritism to certain individuals, particularly to receivers and attorneys for receivers by him so appointed, all of which is prejudicial to the dignity of the judiciary.

All to the scandal and disrepute of said court and the administration of justice therein.

Wherefore the said Harold Louderback was, and is, guilty of misbehavior as such judge and of a misdemeanor in office.

[SEAL.] JNO. N. GARNER.
Speaker of the House of Representatives.
Attest: SOUTH TRIMBLE, *Clerk.*

◄ 20 ►

District Judge Halsted L. Ritter
(1936)

THE ARTICLES OF IMPEACHMENT against Judge Halsted L. Ritter included charges that he failed to dismiss a foreclosure suit so that he could appoint a colleague of his former law partner as receiver; received a kickback from his former law partner in return for making him a receiver; practiced law in violation of the prohibition on judges practicing law; failed to report his fees from practicing law on his income tax returns; and, finally, brought disrepute to his court by the sum total of his behavior. The Senate, which acquitted Ritter of all of the specific charges detailed in the first six

---

DISTRICT JUDGE HALSTED L. RITTER   Convicted

CHARGES: Favoritism in appointments of receivers; practicing law; bringing disrepute on the federal judiciary.

MAJOR ISSUE: Whether an official can be removed on a guilty vote for an article aggregating specific offenses, for each of which he had been individually acquitted.

HOUSE VOTE ON IMPEACHMENT: 181–146

SENATE VOTE FOR CONVICTION:

	Guilty	Not Guilty
Article I	55	29
Article II	52	32
Article III	44	39
Articles IV–V	36	48
Article VI	46	37
Article VII	56	28

SENATE VOTE AGAINST DISQUALIFICATION: 76–0

---

articles, mustered a two-thirds majority to convict him on the final article that concerned bringing discredit to his office. Texas Democrat Hatton Sumners, the House manager who prosecuted the case in the Senate, indicated in his opening statement that "the last impeachment charge deals with the man as a judge on the bench, while the first six to some extent deal with him individually."

One of the recurring issues in virtually every impeachment hearing and trial in U.S. history has been whether behavior need be criminal to be impeachable. By the time of Judge Ritter's impeachment in 1936, the House seemed to have settled into an interpretation of the removal power, at least regarding judges, that combined "high crimes and misdemeanors" with the "good Behaviour" clause of the U.S. Constitution, governing the tenure of judges.[1] Eventually the House reached the conclusion that official bad behavior alone was sufficient for removal of judges. Ten years before the Ritter impeachment, the House had approved the impeachment report for Judge George W. English, which contained the following exposition of what warrants impeachment:

Although frequently debated, and the negative advocated by some high authorities, it is now, we believe, considered that impeachment is not confined alone to acts which are forbidden by the Constitution or Federal statutes. The better sustained and modern view is the provision for impeachment in the Constitution applies not only to high crimes and misdemeanors as those words were understood at common law but also acts which are not defined as criminal and made subject to indictment, but also to those which affect the public welfare. Thus an official may be impeached for offenses of a political character and for gross betrayal of public interests. Also, for abuses or betrayal of trusts, for inexcusable negligence of duty, for the tyrannical abuse of power, or, as one writer puts it, for a "breach of official duty by malfeasance or misfeasance, including conduct such as drunkenness when habitual, or in the performance of official duties, gross indecency, profanity, obscenity, or other language used in the discharge of an official function, which tends to bring the office into disrepute, or for an abuse or reckless exercise of discretionary power as well as the breach of an official duty imposed by statute or common law."[2]

However, the Senate did not have a chance to vote on this definition because English resigned and the Senate dismissed the case. In the case against Judge Harold Louderback, which also seemed to rely on generally bad behavior rather than any implication of crime, the Senate voted to acquit. The Ritter case also solidified the precedent begun by the impeachment of Robert W. Archbald, that criminal behavior was not required for removal, at least of a federal judge. Unlike Archbald, when it came time to decide whether Ritter should be barred from future office, the Senate voted unanimously against disqualifying him. The Ritter case did result in a historical milestone: the first court challenge to Congress's interpretation of what constitutes an impeachable offense (see Document 34, p. 304). It would also be the last time that Congress would impeach a public official for fifty years.

ARTICLES OF IMPEACHMENT

ARTICLES IMPEACHING JUDGE HALSTED L. RITTER WERE REPORTED TO THE HOUSE IN TWO SEPARATE RESOLUTIONS.

In March 1936, articles of impeachment against Judge Ritter were reported to the House:

. . . Articles of Impeachment of the House of Representatives of the United States of America in the name of themselves and of all of the people of the United States of America against Halsted L. Ritter, who was appointed, duly qualified, and commissioned to serve, during good behavior in office, as

United States district judge for the southern district of Florida, on February 15, 1929.

Article I

That the said Halsted L. Ritter, having been nominated by the President of the United States, confirmed by the Senate of the United States, duly qualified and commissioned, and while acting as a United States district judge for the southern district of Florida, was and is guilty of misbehavior and of a high crime and misdemeanor in office in manner and form as follows, to wit: On or about October 11, 1929, A. L. Rankin (who had been a law partner of said judge immediately before said judge's appointment as judge), as solicitor for the plaintiff, filed in the court of the said Judge Ritter a certain foreclosure suit and receivership proceeding, the same being styled "Bert E. Holland and others against Whitehall Building and Operating Company and others" (Number 678-M-Eq.). On or about May 15, 1930, the said Judge Ritter allowed the said Rankin an advance of $2,500 on his fee for his services in said case. On or about July 2, 1930, the said Judge Ritter by letter requested another judge of the United States district court for the southern district of Florida, to wit, Honorable Alexander Akerman, to fix and determine the total allowance for the said Rankin for his services in said case for the reason as stated by Judge Ritter in said letter, that the said Rankin had formerly been the law partner of the said Judge Ritter, and he did not feel that he should pass upon the total allowance made said Rankin in that case and that if Judge Akerman would fix the allowance it would relieve the writer, Judge Ritter, from any embarrassment if thereafter any question should arise as to his, Judge Ritter's, favoring said Rankin with an exorbitant fee.

Thereafterward, notwithstanding the said Judge Akerman, in compliance with Judge Ritter's request, allowed the said Rankin a fee of $15,000 for his services in said case, from which sum the said $2,500 theretofore allowed the said Rankin by Judge Ritter as an advance on his fee was deducted, the said Judge Ritter, well knowing that at his request compensation had been fixed by Judge Akerman for the said Rankin's services in said case, and notwithstanding the restraint of propriety expressed in his said letter to Judge Akerman, and ignoring the danger of embarrassment mentioned in said letter, did fix an additional and exorbitant fee for the said Rankin in said case. On or about December 24, 1930, when the final decree in said case was signed, the said Judge Ritter allowed the said Rankin, additional to the total allowance of $15,000 theretofore allowed by Judge Akerman, a fee of $75,000 for his services in said case, out of which allowance the said Judge Ritter directly profited. On the same day, December 24, 1930, the receiver in said case paid the said Rankin, as part of his said additional fee, the sum of $25,000, and the said Rankin on the same day privately paid and delivered to the said Judge Ritter the sum of $2,500 in cash; $2,000 of said $2,500 was deposited in bank by Judge Ritter on, to wit, December 29, 1930, the remaining $500 being kept by Judge Ritter and not deposited in bank until, to wit, July 10, 1931. Between the time of such initial payment on said additional fee and April 6, 1931, the said receiver paid said Rankin thereon $5,000. On or about April 6, 1931, the said Rankin received the balance of the said additional fee allowed him by Judge Ritter, said balance amounting to $45,000. Shortly thereafter, on or about April 14, 1931, the said Rankin paid and delivered to the said Judge Ritter, privately, in cash, an additional sum of $2,000. The said Judge Halsted L. Ritter corruptly and unlawfully accepted and received for his own use and benefit from the said A. L. Rankin the aforesaid sums of money, amounting to $4,500.

Wherefore, the said Judge Halsted L. Ritter was and is guilty of misbehavior and was and is guilty of a high crime and misdemeanor.

Article II

That the said Halsted L. Ritter, while holding the office of United States district judge for the southern district of Florida, having been nominated by the President of the United States, confirmed by the Senate of the United States, duly qualified and commissioned, and while acting as a United States district judge for the southern district of Florida, was and is guilty of misbehavior and of high crimes and misdemeanors in office in manner and form as follows, to wit:

On the 15th day of February 1929 the said Halsted L. Ritter, having been appointed as United States district judge for the southern district of Florida, was duly qualified and commissioned to serve as such during good behavior in office. Immediately prior thereto and for several years the said Halsted L. Ritter had practiced law in said district in partnership with one A. L. Rankin, which partnership was dissolved upon the appointment of said Ritter as said United States district judge.

On the 18th day of July 1928 one Walter S. Richardson was elected trustee in bankruptcy . . . and as such trustee took charge of the assets of said Whitehall Building and Operating Company, which consisted of a hotel property located in Palm Beach in said district. . . . That before the discharge of said Walter S. Richardson as such trustee, said Richardson, together with said A. L. Rankin, one Ernest Metcalf, one Martin Sweeney, and the said Halsted L. Ritter, entered into an arrangement to secure permission of the holder or holders of at least $50,000 of first-mortgage bonds on said hotel property for the purpose of filing a bill to foreclose the first mortgage on said premises in the court of said Halsted L. Ritter, by which means the said Richardson, Rankin, Metcalf, Sweeney, and Ritter were to continue said property in litigation before said Ritter.

On the 30th day of August 1929, the said Walter S. Richardson, in furtherance of said arrangement and understanding, wrote a letter to the said Martin Sweeney, in New York, suggesting the desirability of contacting as many first-mortgage bondholders as possible in order that their cooperation might be secured, directing special attention to Mr. Bert E. Holland, an attorney, whose address was in the Tremont Building in Boston, and who, as cotrustee, was the holder of $50,000 of first-mortgage bonds, the amount of bonds required to institute the contemplated proceedings in Judge Ritter's court.

On October 3, 1929, the said Bert E. Holland [cotrustee], being solicited by the said Sweeney, requested the said Rankin and Metcalf to prepare a complaint to file in said Judge Ritter's court for foreclosure of said first mortgage and the appointment of a receiver. . . .

On October 28, 1929, a hearing on the complaint and petition for receivership was heard before Judge Halsted L. Ritter at Miami, at which hearing the said Bert E. Holland appeared in person before said Judge Ritter and advised the judge that he wished to withdraw the suit and asked for dismissal of the bill of complaint on the ground that the bill was filed without his authority.

But the said Judge Ritter, fully advised of the facts and circumstances hereinbefore recited, wrongfully and oppressively exercised the powers of his office to carry into execution said plan and agreement theretofore arrived at, and refused to grant the request of the said Holland and made effective the champertuous undertaking of the said Richardson and Rankin and appointed the said Richardson receiver of the said hotel property, notwithstanding that objection was made to Judge Ritter that said Richardson had been active in fomenting this litigation and was not a proper person to act as receiver.

On October 15, 1929, said Rankin made oath to each of the bills for intervenors which were filed the next day.

On October 16, 1929, bills for intervention in said foreclosure suit were filed by said Rankin and Metcalf in the names of holders of approximately $5,000 of said first-mortgage bonds, which intervenors did not possess the said requisite $50,000 in bonds required by said first mortgage to bring foreclosure proceedings on the part of the bondholders.

The said Rankin and Metcalf appeared as attorneys for complainants and intervenors, and in response to a suggestion of the said Judge Ritter, the said Metcalf withdrew as attorney for complainants and intervenors and said Judge Ritter thereupon appointed said Metcalf as attorney for the said Richardson, the receiver.

And in the further carrying out of said arrangement and understanding, the said Richardson employed the said Martin Sweeney and one Bemis, together with Ed Sweeney, as managers of said property, for which they were paid the sum of $60,000 for the management of said hotel for the two seasons the property remained in the custody of said Richardson as receiver. . . .

While the Whitehall Hotel was being operated in receivership under said proceeding pending in said court (and in which proceeding the receiver in charge of said hotel by appointment of said Judge was allowed large compensation by said judge) the said judge stayed at said hotel from time to time without cost to himself and received free rooms, free meals, and free valet service, and, with the knowledge and consent of said judge, members of his family, including his wife, his son, Thurston Ritter, his daughter, Mrs. M. R. Walker, his secretary, Mrs. Lloyd C. Hooks, and her husband, Lloyd C. Hooks, each likewise on various occasions stayed at said hotel without cost to themselves or to said judge, and received free rooms, and some or all of them received from said hotel free meals and free valet service; all of which expenses were borne by the said receivership to the loss and damage of the creditors whose interests were involved therein.

The said judge willfully failed and neglected to perform his duty to conserve the assets of the Whitehall Building and Operating Company in receivership in his court, but to the contrary, permitted waste and dissipation of its assets, to the loss and damage of the creditors of said corporation, and was a party to the waste and dissipation of such assets while under the control of his said court, and personally profited thereby, in the manner and form hereinabove specifically set out.

Wherefore, the said Judge Halsted L. Ritter was and is guilty of misbehavior, and was and is guilty of a high crime and misdemeanor in office. . . .

Article III

That the said Halsted L. Ritter, having been nominated by the President of the United States, confirmed by the Senate of the United States, duly qualified and commissioned, and, while acting as a United States District judge for the southern district of Florida, was and is guilty of a high crime and misdemeanor in office in manner and form as follows, to wit:

That the said Halsted L. Ritter, while such judge, was guilty of a violation of section 258 of the Judicial Code of the United States of America (U.S.C., Annotated title 28, sec. 373) making it unlawful for any judge appointed under the authority of the United States to exercise the profession of employment of counsel or attorney, or to be engaged in the practice of the law, . . . Judge Ritter on, to wit, March 11, 1929, wrote a letter to Charles A. Brodek, of counsel for Mulford Realty Corporation (the client which his former law firm had been representing in said litigation), stating that there had been much extra and unanticipated work in the case, that he was then a Federal

Judge; that his partner, A. L. Rankin, would carry through further proceedings in the case, but that he, Judge Ritter, would be consulted about the matter until the case was all closed up; . . . and further that he was "of course primarily interested in getting some money in the case", and that he thought "$2,000 more by way of attorneys' fees should be allowed". . . .

Which acts of said judge were calculated to bring his office into disrepute, constitute a violation of section 258 of the Judicial Code of the United States of America (U.S.C., Annotated, title 28, sec. 373), and constitute a high crime and misdemeanor within the meaning and intent of section 4 of article II of the Constitution of the United States.

Wherefore, the said Judge Halsted L. Ritter was and is guilty of a high misdemeanor in office.

Article IV

. . . [T]hat Judge Ritter did exercise the profession or employment of counsel or attorney, or engage in the practice of the law, representing J. R. Francis, with relation to the Boca Raton matter and the segregation and saving of the interest of J. R. Francis herein, or in obtaining a deed or deeds to J. R. Francis from the Spanish River Land Company to certain pieces of realty, and in the Edgewater Ocean Beach Development Company matter for which services the said Judge Ritter received from the said J. R. Francis the sum of $7,500.

Which acts of said judge were calculated to bring his office into disrepute constitute a violation of the law above recited, and constitute a high crime and misdemeanor within the meaning and intent of section 4 of article II of the Constitution of the United States.

Wherefore, the said Judge Halsted L. Ritter was and is guilty of a high misdemeanor in office.

Article V

. . . That the said Halsted L. Ritter, while such judge, was guilty of violation of section 146(h) of the Revenue Act of 1928, making it unlawful for any person willfully to attempt in any manner to evade or defend the payment of the income tax levied in and by said Revenue Act of 1928, in the during the year 1929 said Judge Ritter received gross taxable income—over and above his salary as judge—to the amount of some $12,000, yet paid no income tax thereon.

Among the fees included in said gross taxable income for 1929 were the extra fee of $2,000 collected and received by Judge Ritter in the Brazilian court case as described in article III, and the fee of $7,500 received by Judge Ritter from J. R. Francis.

Wherefore the said Judge Halsted L. Ritter was and is guilty of a high misdemeanor in office.

Article VI

That the said Halsted L. Ritter, while such judge, was guilty of violation of section 146(b) of the Revenue Act of 1928, making it unlawful for any person willfully to attempt in any manner to evade or defeat the payment of the income tax levied in and by said Revenue Act of 1928, in the during the year 1930 the said Judge Ritter received gross taxable income—over and above his salary as judge—to the amount of to wit, $5,300, yet failed to report any part thereof in his income-tax return for the year 1930, and paid no income tax thereon.

Two thousand five hundred dollars of said gross taxable income for 1930 was that amount of cash paid Judge Ritter by A. L. Rankin on December 24, 1930, as described in article I.

Wherefore the said Judge Halsted L. Ritter was and is guilty of a high misdemeanor in office.

Article VII

. . . The reasonable and probable consequence of the actions or conduct of Halsted L. Ritter, hereunder specified or indicated in this article, since he became judge of said court, as an individual or as such judge, is to bring his court into scandal and disrepute, to the prejudice of said court and public confidence in the administration of justice therein, and to the prejudice of public respect for and confidence in the Federal judiciary, and to render him unfit to continue to serve as such judge:

1. In that the Florida Power Company case (Florida Power and Light Company against City of Miami and others, numbered 1138-M-Eq.) which was a case wherein said judge had granted the complainant power company a temporary injunction restraining the enforcement of an ordinance of the city of Miami, which ordinance prescribed a reduction in the rates for electric current being charged in said city, said judge improperly appointed one Cary T. Hutchinson, who had long been associated with and employed by power and utility interests, special master in chancery in said suit, and refused to revoke his order so appointing said Hutchinson. Thereafter, when criticism of such action had become current in the city of Miami, and within two weeks after a resolution (H. Res. 163, Seventy-third Congress) had been agreed to in the House of Representatives of the Congress of the United States, authorizing and directing the Judicial Committee thereof to invest the official conduct of said judge and to make a report concerning said conduct to said House of Repre-

sentatives an arrangement was entered into with the city commissioners of the city of Miami or with the city attorney of said city by which the said city commissioners were to pass a resolution expressing faith and confidence in the integrity of said judge, and the said judge recuse himself as judge in said power suit. The said agreement was carried out by the parties thereto, and said judge, after the passage of such resolution, recused himself from sitting as judge in said power suit, thereby bartering his judicial authority in said case for a vote of confidence. Nevertheless, the succeeding judge allowed said Hutchinson as special master in chancery in said case a fee of $5,000, although he performed little, if any, service as such, and in the order making such allowance recited: "And it appearing to the court that a minimum fee of $5,000 was approved by the court for the said Cary T. Hutchinson, special master in this cause."

2. In that in the Trust Company of Florida cases (Illick against Trust Company of Florida and others numbered 1043-M-Eq., and Edmunds Committee and others against Marion Mortgage Company and others, numbered 1124-M-Eq.) after the State banking department of Florida, through its comptroller, Honorable Ernest Amos, had closed the doors of the Trust Company of Florida and appointed J. H. Therrell liquidator for said trust company, and had intervened in the said Illick case, said Judge Ritter wrongfully and erroneously refused to recognize the right of said State authority to administer the affairs of the said trust company and appointed Julian E. Eaton and Clark D. Stearns as receivers of the property of said trust company. On appeal, the United States Circuit Court of Appeals for the Fifth Circuit reversed the said order or decree of Judge Ritter and ordered the said property surrendered to the State liquidator. Thereafter, on, to wit, September 12, 1932, there was filed in the United States District Court for the Southern District of Florida the Edmunds Committee case, supra. Mario Mortgage Company was a subsidiary of the Trust Company of Florida. Judge Ritter being absent from his district at the time of the filing of said case, an application for the appointment of receivers therein was presented to another judge of said district, namely, Honorable Alexander Akerman. Judge Ritter, however, prior to the appointment of such receivers, telegraphed Judge Akerman, requesting him to appoint the aforesaid Eaton and Stearns as receivers in said case, which appointments were made by Judge Akerman. Thereafter the United States Circuit Court of Appeals for the Fifth Circuit reversed the order of Judge Akerman, appointing said Eaton and Stearns as receivers in said case. In November 1932, J. H. Therrell, as liquidator, filed a bill of complaint in the Circuit Court of Dade County, Florida—a court of the State of Florida—alleging that the various trust properties of the Trust Company of Florida were burdensome to the liquidator to keep, and asking that the court appoint a succeeding trustee. Upon petition for removal of said cause from said State court into the United States District Court for the Southern District of Florida, Judge Ritter took jurisdiction, notwithstanding

the previous rulings of the United States Circuit Court of Appeals above referred to, and again appointed the said Eaton and Stearns as the receivers of the said trust properties. In December 1932 the said Therrell surrendered all of the trust properties to said Eaton and Stearns as receivers, together with all records of the Trust Company of Florida pertaining thereto. During the time said Eaton and Stearns, as such receivers, were in control of said trust properties, Judge Ritter wrongfully and improperly approved their accounts without notice or opportunity for objection thereto to be heard.

With the knowledge of Judge Ritter, said receivers appointed the sister-in-law of Judge Ritter, namely, Mrs. G. M. Wickard, who had had no previous hotel-management experience, to be manager of the Julia Tuttle Hotel and Apartment Building, one of said trust properties. On, to wit, January 1, 1933, Honorable J. M. Lee succeeded Honorable Ernest Amos as comptroller of the State of Florida and appointed M. A. Smith liquidator in said Trust Company of Florida cases to succeed J. H. Therrell. An appeal was again taken to the United States Circuit Court of Appeals for the Fifth Circuit from the then latest order or decree of Judge Ritter, and again the order or decree of Judge Ritter appealed from was reversed by the said circuit court of appeals which held that the State officer was entitled to the custody of the property involved and that said Eaton and Stearns as receivers were not entitled to such custody. Thereafter, and with the knowledge of the decision of the said circuit court of appeals, Judge Ritter wrongfully and improperly allowed said Eaton and Stearns and their attorneys some $26,000 as fees out of said trust-estate properties and endeavored to require, as a condition precedent to releasing said trust properties from the control of his court, a promise from counsel for the said State liquidator not to appeal from his order allowing the said fees to said Eaton and Stearns and their attorneys.

3. In that the said Halsted L. Ritter, while such Federal judge, accepted, in addition to $4,500 from his former law partner as alleged in article I hereof other large fees or gratuities, to wit, $7,500 from J. R. Francis, on or about April 19, 1929, J. R. Francis at this time having large property interests within the territorial jurisdiction of the court of which Judge Ritter was a judge; and on, to wit, the 4th day of April 1929 the said Judge Ritter accepted the sum of $2,000 from Brodek, Raphael and Eisner, representing Mulford Realty corporation, as its attorneys, through Charles A. Brodek, senior member of said firm and a director of said corporation, as a fee or gratuity, at which time the said Mulford Realty Corporation held and owned large interests in Florida real estate and citrus groves, and a large amount of securities of the Olympia Improvement Corporation, which was a company organized to develop and promote Olympia, Florida, said holding being within the territorial jurisdiction of the United States District Court of which Judge Ritter was a judge from, to wit, February 15, 1929.

4. By his conduct as detailed in articles I, II, III, and IV hereof, and by his income-tax evasions as set forth in articles V and VI hereof.

Wherefore, the said Judge Halsted L. Ritter was and is guilty of misbehavior, and was and is guilty of high crimes and misdemeanors in office.

Notes

1. Article III, section 1, of the Constitution states that judges "both of the supreme and inferior Courts, shall hold their Offices during good Behaviour. . . ."

2. Lewis Deschler, *Precedents of the House of Representatives.* Vol. III (Washington, D.C.: Government Printing Office, 1977).

District Judge Harry E. Claiborne
(1986)

ON MARCH 16, 1986, District Judge Harry E. Claiborne of Nevada entered the federal penitentiary at Maxwell Air Force Base in Alabama. Two years earlier he had been convicted of making false statements on his income tax returns. With his appeals process exhausted, he reported to prison to serve his two-year sentence. Two months later, in May 1986, the U.S. House of Representatives found itself engaged in the first full-blown impeachment proceedings in fifty years, and the first impeachment hearings since Richard Nixon's resignation from the presidency stopped the process twelve years earlier. In the words of Wisconsin representative James Sensenbrenner, Judge Claiborne had "challenged the Congress of the United States to impeach him and to place him on trial in the U.S. Senate." What had the judge done to affront Congress? Claiborne had gone to prison without resigning his office as judge and was continuing to receive his salary of $78,700 a year. Worse, he had vowed to return to the bench when he emerged from prison.

Judge Claiborne's refusal to resign brought into sharp focus the same truth that had prompted the first judicial impeachment (the removal of the insane Judge John Pickering) nearly two centuries before: the Constitution allows for only one method of removing a federal judge, and that is impeachment. Although Claiborne received the formal trappings of an impeachment

---

DISTRICT JUDGE HARRY E. CLAIBORNE   Convicted

CHARGES: Under reporting income for 1979 and 1980; making false statements on tax returns for 1979 and 1980; having been convicted of the crime of filing false income tax returns, and for having been sentenced to two years in jail; bringing his court into scandal and disrepute.

MAJOR ISSUE: Whether the mere fact of having been imprisoned for private criminal conduct is a high crime and misdemeanor.

HOUSE VOTE ON IMPEACHMENT: 406–0

SENATE VOTE FOR CONVICTION:

	Guilty	Not Guilty
Article 1	87	10
Article 2	90	7
Article 3	46	17
Article 4	89	8

---

investigation in Congress, it was clear to all involved that the embarrassment and unseemliness of having a federal judge in prison made his removal a foregone conclusion. The House hearings did not consider whether Claiborne's conviction was proper. Claiborne claimed it was not. The House did not meaningfully consider whether income tax evasion rose to the level of high crime and misdemeanor. After less than a day of hearings, the judiciary committee reported impeachment articles to the House, which promptly sent them to the Senate for trial. One of the four articles made the mere fact of his conviction and prison sentence an impeachable offense.

Judge Claiborne's impeachment trial was the first in which the Senate used a rule that had passed in 1935. This rule allowed the Senate to designate a committee to hear evidence and then report to the full Senate for a vote. After closing arguments, the Senate quickly voted to impeach Claiborne but resoundingly rejected, by a vote 46 to 17, the charge that conviction and imprisonment is a "high Crime and Misdemeanor."

Claiborne's trial was the first in a series of three rapid-fire judicial impeachments that occurred over as many years. These three trials seemed to forecast an end to impeachment as it had evolved over the previous 180 years. The ultimate meaning of the Claiborne impeachment was tied up in what happened in the next two impeachments, of Judges Alcee Hastings and Walter Nixon.

Articles of Impeachment

Resolved, . . . That Harry E. Claiborne, a judge of the United States District Court for the District of Nevada, be impeached for misbehavior and for high crimes and misdemeanors; that the evidence heretofore taken by a subcommittee of the Committee on the Judiciary of the House of Representatives sustains articles of impeachment, which are hereinafter set out; and that the articles be adopted by the House of Representatives and exhibited to the Senate:

Articles of Impeachment exhibited by the House of Representatives of the United States of America in the name of itself and all of the people of the United States of America, against Judge Harry E. Claiborne, a judge of the United States District Court for the District of Nevada, in maintenance and support of its impeachment against him for misbehavior and for high crimes and misdemeanors.

Article I

That Judge Harry E. Claiborne, having been nominated by the President of the United States, and while serving as a judge of the United States District Court for the District of Nevada, was and is guilty of misbehavior and of high crimes and misdemeanors in office in a manner and form as follows:

On or about June 15, 1980, Judge Harry E. Claiborne did willfully and knowingly make and subscribe a United States Individual Income Tax Return for the calendar year 1979, which return was verified by a written declaration that the return was made under penalties of perjury; which return was filed with the Internal Revenue Service; and which return Judge Harry E. Claiborne did not believe to be true and correct as to every material matter in that the return reported total income in the amount of $80,227.04 whereas, as he then and there well knew and believed, he received and failed to report substantial income in addition to that stated on the return in violation of section 7206(1) of title 26, United States Code.

The facts set forth in the foregoing paragraph were found beyond a reasonable doubt by a twelve-person jury in the United States District Court for the District of Nevada.

Wherefore, Judge Harry E. Claiborne was and is guilty of misbehavior and was and is guilty of a high crime and misdemeanor and, by such conduct, warrants impeachment and trial and removal from office.

Article II

That Judge Harry E. Claiborne, having been nominated by the President of the United States, confirmed by the Senate of the United States, and while serving as a judge of the United States Court for the District of Nevada, was and is guilty of misbehavior and of high crimes and misdemeanors in office in a manner and form as follows:

On or about June 15, 1981, Judge Harry E. Claiborne did willfully and knowingly make and subscribe a United States Individual Income Tax Return for the calendar year 1980, which return was verified by a written declaration that the return was made under penalties of perjury; which return was filed with the Internal Revenue Service; and which return Judge Harry E. Claiborne did not believe to be true and correct as to every material matter in that the return reported total income in the amount of $54,251 whereas, as he then and there well knew and believed, [h]e received and failed to report substantial income in addition to that stated on the return in violation of section 7206(1) of title 26, United States Code.

The facts set forth in the foregoing paragraph were found beyond a reasonable doubt by a twelve-person jury in the United States District Court for the District of Nevada.

Wherefore, Judge Harry E. Claiborne was and is guilty of misbehavior and was and is guilty of a high crime and misdemeanor and, by such conduct, warrants impeachment and trial and removal from office.

Article III

That Judge Harry E. Claiborne having been nominated by the President of the United States, confirmed by the Senate of the United States, and while serving as a judge of the United States District Court for the District of Nevada, was and is guilty of misbehavior and of high crimes in office in a manner and form as follows:

On August 10, 1984, in the United States District Court for the District of Nevada, Judge Harry E. Claiborne was found guilty by a twelve-person jury of making and subscribing a false income tax return for the calendar years 1979 and 1980 in violation of section 7206(1) of title 26, United States Code.

Thereafter, a judgement of conviction was entered against Judge Harry E. Claiborne for each of the violations of section 7206(1) of title 26, United States Code, and a sentence of two years imprisonment for each violation was imposed, to be served concurrently, together with a fine of $5000 for each violation.

Wherefore, Judge Harry E. Claiborne was and is guilty of misbehavior and was and is guilty of high crimes.

Article IV

That Judge Harry E. Claiborne, having been nominated by the President of the United States, confirmed by the Senate of the United States, and while serving as a judge of the United States District Court for the District of

Nevada, was and is guilty of misbehavior and of misdemeanors in office in a manner and form as follows:

Judge Harry E. Claiborne took the oath for the office of judge of the United States and is required to discharge and perform all the duties incumbent on him and to uphold and obey the Constitution and laws of the United States.

Judge Harry E. Claiborne, by virtue of his office, is required to uphold the integrity of the judiciary and to perform the duties of his office impartially.

Judge Harry E. Claiborne, by willfully and knowingly falsifying his income on his Federal tax returns for 1979 and 1980, has betrayed the trust of the people of the United States and reduced confidence in the integrity and impartiality of the judiciary, thereby bringing disrepute on the Federal courts and the administration of justice by the courts.

Wherefore, Judge Harry E. Claiborne was and is guilty of misbehavior and was and is guilty of misdemeanors and, by such conduct, warrants impeachment and trial and removal from office.

≼ 22 ≽

District Judge Alcee L. Hastings

(1988–1989)

WITHIN MONTHS OF REMOVING Judge Harry E. Claiborne from office, Congress again set the impeachment machinery in motion against another district court judge, Judge Alcee L. Hastings, who had been the subject of a criminal trial. In his court trial, however, Hastings had been acquitted of the charge of conspiring to solicit a bribe and had returned to the bench. Unlike with Claiborne, then, Congress could not brandish a conviction to argue for impeachment. Congress also had to contend with Judge Hastings's claim of double jeopardy. Having been cleared in court, Hastings argued it was unfair that Congress take up the same matter in its congressional investigation. This "feels like double jeopardy," he said. The African American judge also claimed that the investigation was racially motivated. He did not get very far on either count.

The Senate was also beginning to feel a bit overwhelmed by impeachment cases. Hastings's Senate trial, as with Claiborne's, was conducted under Senate Rule XI, which provided that evidence be heard by a committee. The committee had not even begun hearing evidence when a House

---

DISTRICT JUDGE ALCEE L. HASTINGS   Convicted

CHARGES: Conspiring to solicit a bribe; lying and fabricating evidence in his criminal trial; leaking confidential wiretap information; and bringing disrepute on the federal courts.

MAJOR ISSUE: Whether impeachment and trial in the Senate after acquittal in a criminal trial constitutes double jeopardy.

HOUSE VOTE ON IMPEACHMENT: 413–3

SENATE VOTE FOR CONVICTION:

	Guilty	Not Guilty
Article 1	69	26
Article 2	68	27
Article 3	69	26
Articles 4–5	67	28
Article 6	48	47
Article 7	69	26
Article 8	68	27
Article 9	70	25
Articles 10–15	(No vote on these articles by agreement)	
Article 16	0	95
Article 17	60	35

---

delegation again appeared before the Senate to impeach another district court judge, Walter Nixon (see Document 35, p. 309). Nixon, like Claiborne, had been convicted in a criminal trial and had refused to resign on entering jail. After not hearing an impeachment case for fifty years, the Senate was faced with three impeachment trials within three years—two of which were going on simultaneously!

After hearing all the evidence during the course of the summer of 1989, several senators on Hastings's evidentiary committee believed that acquittal was appropriate. When the vote came up before the whole Senate in October 1989, however, the majority did not agree. Hastings was removed from office. Although the Senate could have also disqualified Hastings from future office holding, it did not do so. Three years after Congress impeached and removed Hastings from his office as federal judge, he returned to Washington to take his seat in the House as a representative from Florida. He would later join in introducing an impeachment resolution of his own, calling for the removal of Whitewater independent counsel Kenneth Starr. The resolution was tabled by the House in 1998, never reaching a vote in the 105th Congress.

ARTICLES OF IMPEACHMENT

Resolved, That Alcee L. Hastings, a judge of the United States District Court for the Southern District of Florida, be impeached for high crimes and misdemeanors and that the following articles of impeachment be exhibited to the Senate:

Articles of impeachment exhibited by the House of Representatives of the United States of America in the name of itself and all of the people of the United States of America, against Alcee L. Hastings, a judge of the United States District Court for the Southern District of Florida, in maintenance and support of its impeachment against him for high crimes and misdemeanors.

Article I

From some time in the first half of 1981 and continuing through October 9, 1981, Judge Hastings and William Borders, then a Washington, D.C. attorney, engaged in a corrupt conspiracy to obtain $150,000 from defendants in United States v. Romano, a case tried before Judge Hastings, in return for the imposition of sentences which would not require incarceration of the defendants.

Wherefore, Judge Alcee L. Hastings is guilty of an impeachable offense warranting removal from office.

Article II

From January 18, 1983, until February 4, 1983, Judge Hastings was a defendant in a criminal case in the United States District Court for the Southern District of Florida. In the course of the trial of that case, Judge Hastings, while under oath to tell the truth, the whole truth, and nothing but the truth, did knowingly and contrary to that oath make a false statement which was intended to mislead the trier of fact.

The false statement was, in substance, that Judge Hastings and William Borders, of Washington, D.C., never made any agreement to solicit a bribe from defendants in United States v. Romano, a case tried before Judge Hastings.

Wherefore, Judge Alcee L. Hastings is guilty of an impeachable offense warranting removal from office.

Article III

From January 18, 1983, until February 4, 1983, Judge Hastings was a defendant in a criminal case in the United States District Court for the Southern District of Florida. In the course of the trial of that case, Judge Hastings, while under oath to tell the truth, the whole truth, and nothing but the truth, did knowingly and contrary to that oath make a false statement which was intended to mislead the trier of fact.

The false statement was, in substance, that Judge Hastings never agreed with William Borders, of Washington, D.C., to modify the sentences of defendants in United States v. Romano. a case tried before Judge Hastings, from a term in the Federal penitentiary to probation in return for a bribe from those defendants.

Wherefore, Judge Alcee L. Hastings is guilty of an impeachable offense warranting removal from office.

Article IV

From January 18, 1983, until February 4, 1983, Judge Hastings was a defendant in a criminal case in the United States District Court for

Alcee L. Hastings

the Southern District of Florida. In the course of the trial of that case, Judge Hastings, while under oath to tell the truth, the whole truth, and nothing but the truth, did knowingly and contrary to that oath make a false statement which was intended to mislead the trier of fact.

The false statement was, in substance, that Judge Hastings never agreed with William Borders, of Washington, D.C., in connection with a payment on a bribe, to enter, within 10 days of that payment, an order returning a substantial amount of property to the defendants in United States v. Romano, a case tried before Judge Hastings. Judge Hastings had previously ordered that property forfeited.

Wherefore, Judge Alcee L. Hastings is guilty of an impeachable offense warranting removal from office.

Article V

From January 18, 1983, until February 4, 1983, Judge Hastings was a defendant in a criminal case in the United States District Court for the Southern District of Florida. In the course of the trial of that case, Judge Hastings, while under oath to tell the truth, the whole truth, and nothing but the truth, did knowingly and contrary to that oath make a false statement which was intended to mislead the trier of fact.

The false statement was, in substance, that Judge Hastings' appearance at the Fontainebleau Hotel in Miami Beach, Florida, on September 16, 1981, was not part of a plan to demonstrate his participation in a bribery scheme with William Borders of Washington, D.C., concerning United States v. Romano, a case tried before Judge Hastings, and that Judge Hastings expected to meet Mr. Borders at that place and on that occasion.

Wherefore, Judge Alcee L. Hastings is guilty of an impeachable offense warranting removal from office.

Article VI

From January 18, 1983, until February 4, 1983, Judge Hastings was a defendant in a criminal case in the United States District Court for the Southern District of Florida. In the course of the trial of that case, Judge Hastings, while under oath to tell the truth, the whole truth, and nothing but the truth, did knowingly and contrary to his oath make a false statement which was intended to mislead the trier of fact.

The false statement was, in substance, that Judge Hastings did not expect William Borders, of Washington, D.C., to appear at Judge Hastings' room in the Sheraton Hotel in Washington, D.C., on September 12, 1981.

Wherefore, Judge Alcee L. Hastings is guilty of an impeachable offense warranting removal from office.

Article VII

From January 18, 1983, until February 4, 1983, Judge Hastings was a defendant in a criminal case in the United States District Court for the Southern District of Florida. In the course of the trial of that case, Judge Hastings, while under oath to tell the truth, the whole truth, and nothing but the truth, did knowingly and contrary to his oath, make a false statement which was intended to mislead the trier of fact.

The false statement concerned Judge Hastings' motive for instructing a law clerk, Jeffrey Miller, to prepare an order on October 5, 1981, in United States v. Romano, a case tried before Judge Hastings, returning a substantial portion of property previously ordered forfeited by Judge Hastings. Judge Hastings stated in substance that he so instructed Mr. Miller primarily because Judge Hastings was concerned that the order would not be completed before Mr. Miller's scheduled departure, when in fact the instruction on October 5, 1981, to prepare such order was in furtherance of a bribery scheme concerning that case.

Wherefore, Judge Alcee L. Hastings is guilty of an impeachable offense warranting removal from office.

Article VIII

From January 18, 1983, until February 4, 1983, Judge Hastings was a defendant in a criminal case in the United States District Court for the Southern District of Florida. In the course of the trial of that case, Judge Hastings, while under oath to tell the truth, the whole truth, and nothing but the truth, did knowingly and contrary to his oath make a false statement which was intended to mislead the trier of fact.

The false statement was, in substance, that Judge Hastings' October 5, 1981, telephone conversation with William Borders, of Washington, D.C., was in fact about writing letters to solicit assistance for Hemphill Pride of Columbia, South Carolina, when in fact it was a coded conversation in furtherance of a conspiracy with Mr. Borders to solicit a bribe from defendants in United States v. Romano, a case tried before Judge Hastings.

Wherefore, Judge Alcee L. Hastings, is guilty of an impeachable offense warranting removal from office.

Article IX

From January 18, 1983, until February 4, 1983, Judge Hastings was a defendant in a criminal case in the United States District Court for the Southern District of Florida. In the course of the trial of that case, Judge Hastings, while under oath to tell the truth, the whole truth, and nothing but the truth, did knowingly and contrary to his oath make a false statement which was intended to mislead the trier of fact.

The false statement was, in substance, that three documents that purported to be drafts of letters to assist Hemphill Pride, of Columbia, South Carolina, had been written by Judge Hastings on October 5, 1981, and were the letters referred to by Judge Hastings in his October 5, 1981, telephone conversation with William Borders, of Washington, D.C.

Wherefore, Judge Alcee L. Hastings is guilty of an impeachable offense warranting removal from office.

Article X

From January 18, 1983, until February 4, 1983, Judge Hastings was a defendant in a criminal case in the United States District Court for the Southern District of Florida. In the course of the trial of that case, Judge Hastings, while under oath to tell the truth, the whole truth, and nothing but the truth, did knowingly and contrary to that oath, make a false statement which was intended to mislead the trier of fact.

The false statement was, in substance, that on May 5, 1981, Judge Hastings talked to Hemphill Pride by placing a telephone call to 803-758-8825 in Columbia, South Carolina.

Wherefore, Judge Alcee L. Hastings is guilty of an impeachable offense warranting removal from office.

Article XI

From January 18, 1983, until February 4, 1983, Judge Hastings was a defendant in a criminal case in the United States District Court for the Southern

District of Florida. In the course of the trial of that case, Judge Hastings, while under oath to tell the truth, the whole truth, and nothing but the truth, did knowingly and contrary to that oath make a false statement which was intended to mislead the trier of fact.

The false statement was, in substance, that on August 2, 1981, Judge Hastings talked to Hemphill Pride by placing a telephone call to 803-782-9387 in Columbia, South Carolina.

Wherefore, Judge Alcee L. Hastings is guilty of an impeachable offense warranting removal from office.

Article XII

From January 18, 1983, until February 4, 1983, Judge Hastings was a defendant in a criminal case in the United States District Court for the Southern District of Florida. In the course of the trial of that case, Judge Hastings, while under oath to tell the truth, the whole truth, and nothing but the truth, did knowingly and contrary to that oath make a false statement which was intended to mislead the trier of fact.

The false statement was, in substance, that on September 2, 1981, Judge Hastings talked to Hemphill Pride by placing a telephone call to 803-758-8825 in Columbia, South Carolina.

Wherefore, Judge Alcee L. Hastings is guilty of an impeachable offense warranting removal from office.

Article XIII

From January 18, 1983, until February 4, 1983, Judge Hastings was a defendant in a criminal case in the United States District Court for the Southern District of Florida. In the course of the trial of that case, Judge Hastings, while under oath to tell the truth, the whole truth, and nothing but the truth, did knowingly and contrary to that oath make a false statement which was intended to mislead the trier of fact.

The false statement was, in substance, that 803-777-7716 was a telephone number at a place where Hemphill Pride could be contacted in July 1981.

Wherefore, Judge Alcee L. Hastings is guilty of an impeachable offense warranting removal from office.

Article XIV

From January 18, 1983, until February 4, 1983, Judge Hastings was a defendant in a criminal case in the United States District Court for the Southern District of Florida. In the course of the trial of that case, Judge Hastings, while under oath to tell the truth, the whole truth, and nothing but the truth, did knowingly and contrary to that oath make a false statement which was intended to mislead the trier of fact.

The false statement was, in substance, that on the afternoon of October 9, 1981, Judge Hastings called his mother and Patricia Williams from his hotel room at the L'Enfant Plaza Hotel in Washington, D.C.

Wherefore, Judge Alcee L. Hastings is guilty of an impeachable offense warranting removal from office.

Article XV

From January 18, 1983, until February 4, 1983, Judge Hastings was a defendant in a criminal case in the United States District Court for the Southern District of Florida. In the course of the trial of that case, Judge Hastings, while under oath to tell the truth, the whole truth, and nothing but the truth, did knowingly and contrary to that oath make a false statement which was intended to mislead the trier of fact concerning his motives for taking a plane on October 9, 1981, from Baltimore-Washington International Airport rather than from Washington National Airport.

Wherefore, Judge Alcee L. Hastings is guilty of an impeachable offense warranting removal from office.

Article XVI

From July 15, 1985, to September 15, 1985, Judge Hastings was the supervising judge of a wiretap instituted under chapter 119 of title 18, United States Code (added by title III of the Omnibus Crime Control and Safe Streets Act of 1968). The wiretap was part of certain investigations then being conducted by law enforcement agents of the United States.

As supervising judge, Judge Hastings learned highly confidential information obtained through the wiretap. The documents disclosing this information, presented to Judge Hastings as the supervising judge, were Judge Hastings' sole source of the highly confidential information.

On September 6, 1985, Judge Hastings revealed highly confidential information that he learned as the supervising judge of the wiretap, as follows: On the morning of September 6, 1985, Judge Hastings told Stephen Clark, the Mayor of Dade County, Florida, to stay away from Kevin "Waxy" Gordon, who was "hot" and was using the Mayor's name in Hialeah, Florida.

As a result of this improper disclosure, certain investigations then being conducted by law enforcement agents of the United States were thwarted and ultimately terminated.

Wherefore, Judge Alcee L. Hastings is guilty of an impeachable offense warranting removal from office.

Article XVII

Judge Hastings, who as a Federal judge is required to enforce and obey the Constitution and laws of the United States, to uphold the integrity of the Judiciary, to avoid impropriety and the appearance of impropriety, and to perform the duties of his office impartially, did, through—

(1) a corrupt relationship with William Borders of Washington, D.C.;

(2) repeated false testimony under oath at Judge Hastings' criminal trial;

(3) fabrication of false documents which were submitted as evidence at his criminal trial; and

(4) improper disclosure of confidential information acquired by him as supervisory judge of a wiretap;

undermine confidence in the integrity and impartiality of the judiciary and betray the trust of the people of the United States, thereby bringing disrepute on the Federal courts and the administration of justice by the Federal courts.

Wherefore, Judge Alcee L. Hastings is guilty of an impeachable offense warranting removal from office.:

Mr. RODINO (during the reading). Mr. Speaker, I ask unanimous consent that the resolution be considered as read and printed in the RECORD.

The SPEAKER pro tempore. Is there objection to the request of the gentleman from New Jersey?

There was no objection.

≈ 23 ≈

District Judge Walter L. Nixon

(1989)

THE IMPEACHMENT OF Walter L. Nixon brought a sense of crisis to both houses of Congress. Just days after Nixon's conviction, Sen. Howell Heflin sponsored a proposal to amend the Constitution to deal with an impeachment clause that Heflin along with many others thought was "cumbersome and out of date." The impeachments and trials of Judges Harry E. Claiborne (see Document 21, p. 168), Alcee L. Hastings (see Document 22, p. 172), and Walter L. Nixon, occurred within a span of three years in the late 1980s, after a fifty-year hiatus from any impeachment trials in Congress. These three trials seemed to represent a significant transformation in Congress's approach to the impeachment process, at least as it applies to federal judges. In all three cases the judges were impeached only after they had already been tried in the courts.

The House presented the Senate with articles of impeachment against Judge Nixon (charging him with the perjury he had been criminally con-

---

DISTRICT JUDGE WALTER L. NIXON   Convicted

CHARGES: Perjury before a federal grand jury; bringing disrepute on the federal judiciary.

MAJOR ISSUE: Whether removal is unavoidable when an officer is a convicted felon and serving time, even if the Senate were to believe that the officer is innocent.

HOUSE VOTE ON IMPEACHMENT: 417–0

SENATE VOTE FOR CONVICTION:

	Guilty	Not Guilty
Article I	89	8
Article II	78	19
Article III	57	40

---

victed of, and with bringing disrepute on the federal judiciary), even before the trial of Judge Hastings had begun. Senate impeachment Rule XI made the nearly concurrent evidentiary hearings against the two judges possible by assigning the task to committees rather than the full Senate. Nixon would challenge this delegation in a lawsuit that claimed it was a violation of the Senate's constitutional duty to "try" all impeachments (see Document 35, p. 309). Significantly, three of the eight "not guilty" votes that Nixon received on the first article of impeachment came from senators who sat on the evidentiary committee. Five of the nineteen "not guilty" votes on the second article again came from the only senators who heard all of the evidence in the case. Nixon was convicted on the first two articles and removed from office.

In two other cases that occurred during the same general time period, Congress refrained from investigating or moving against judges that the Justice Department had brought criminal indictments against, either because the House was unaware of the situation, or because it seemed expedient to await the judicial outcome before beginning the impeachment process. District Judge Robert Collins, as with Judge Claiborne, had spent time in jail drawing his salary after his criminal conviction. Unlike Claiborne, who insisted on going through the entire process, Collins ultimately resigned when Congress finally made a credible threat to impeach him. Judge Robert Aguilar was convicted of five criminal counts in 1990. His convictions were all overturned on appeal, and he resumed his office. At no point did Congress initiate impeachment proceedings against Aguilar.

Congress arguably had saved itself the time and expense of engaging in two out of five impeachments by effectively, although not explicitly, delegating the investigatory portion of its impeachment power to the criminal justice system—that is, to the other two branches of government. But Congress's failure to act in all of these cases as they traveled through the courts raised serious and troubling questions about the impeachment process. Among them was the question of whether, as a matter of policy, Congress *should* effectively delegate the removal power to the courts.

Congress responded to the impeachment onslaught with a flurry of reform proposals, mostly involving amendments to the Constitution. Sen. Trent Lott of Mississippi and Rep. Henry Hyde of Illinois were among those proposing reforms. Sen. Arlen Specter of Pennsylvania was among those who disagreed with the need to change. Although he recognized the enormous time and effort involved in the three recent impeachments, Specter nevertheless concluded that "there is an overriding value in the Senate continuing to act as the body that tries the impeachment of all federal officials including federal judges."

Two representatives from Texas, Jack Brooks and John Bryant, concluded that "efforts to change the system, whether by statutes or constitutional amendment, are ill-advised as a matter of constitutional principle and national policy." Instead of the drastic measure of amending the Constitution, Congress chose instead to create the National Commission on Judicial Discipline and Removal—know as the Kastenmeier Commission, after its chair, former Rep. Robert Kastenmeier of Wisconsin. The commission would eventually recommend against altering our fundamental charter in favor of leaving in place the two-hundred-year-old means for removing misbehaving public officials.

ARTICLES OF IMPEACHMENT

The SPEAKER pro tempore. The Clerk will report the committee amendment in the nature of a substitute.

The Clerk read as follows:

Committee amendment in the nature of a substitute: Strike out all after the resolving clause and insert the following:

That Walter L. Nixon, Jr., a judge of the United States District Court for the Southern District of Mississippi, be impeached for high crimes and misdemeanors, and that the following articles of impeachment be exhibited to the Senate:

Articles of impeachment exhibited by the House of Representatives of the United States of America in the name of itself and all of the People of the United States of America, against Walter L. Nixon, Jr., a judge of the United States District Court for the Southern District of Mississippi, in maintenance and support of its impeachment against him for high crimes and misdemeanors.

Article I

On July 18, 1984, Judge Nixon testified before a Federal grand jury empaneled in the United States District Court for the Southern District of Mississippi (Hattiesburg Division) to investigate Judge Nixon's business relationship with Wiley Fairchild and the handling of the criminal prosecution of Fairchild's son, Drew Fairchild, for drug smuggling. In the course of his grand jury testimony and having duly taken an oath that he would tell the truth, the whole truth, and nothing but the truth, Judge Nixon did knowingly and contrary to his oath make a material false or misleading statement to the grand jury.

The false or misleading statement was, in substance, that Forrest County District Attorney Paul Holmes never discussed the Drew Fairchild case with Judge Nixon.

Wherefore, Judge Walter L. Nixon, Jr., is guilty of an impeachable offense and should be removed from office.

Article II

On July 18, 1984, Judge Nixon testified before a Federal grand jury empaneled in the United States District Court for the Southern District of Mississippi to investigate Judge Nixon's business relationship with Wiley Fairchild and the handling of the prosecution of Fairchild's son, Drew Fairchild, for drug smuggling. In the course of his grand jury testimony and having duly taken an oath that he would tell the truth, the whole truth, and nothing but the truth, Judge Nixon did knowingly and contrary to his oath make a material false or misleading statement to the grand jury.

The false or misleading statement was, in substance, that Judge Nixon had nothing whatsoever officially or unofficially to do with the Drew Fairchild case in Federal court or State court; and that Judge Nixon "never handled any part of it, never had a thing to do with it at all, and never talked to anyone, State or Federal, prosecutor or judge, in any way influence anybody" with respect to the Drew Fairchild case.

Wherefore, Judge Walter L. Nixon, Jr., is guilty of an impeachable offense and should be removed from office.

Article III

By virtue of his office as a judge of the United States District Court for the Southern District of Mississippi, Judge Nixon is required to uphold the integrity of the judiciary, to avoid impropriety and the appearance of impropriety, and to obey the laws of the United States.

Judge Nixon has raised substantial doubt as to his judicial integrity, undermined confidence in the integrity and impartiality of the judiciary, betrayed the trust of the people of the United States, disobeyed the laws of the United States and brought disrepute on the Federal courts and the administration of justice by the Federal courts by the following:

After entering into an oil and gas investment with Wiley Fairchild, Judge Nixon conversed with Wiley Fairchild, Carroll Ingram, and Forrest County District Attorney Paul Holmes concerning the State criminal drug conspiracy prosecution of Drew Fairchild, the son of Wiley Fairchild, and thereafter concealed those conversations as follows:

(1) Judge Nixon concealed those conversations through one or more material false or misleading statements knowingly made to an attorney from the United States Department of Justice and a special agent of the Federal Bureau of Investigation during an interview of Judge Nixon conducted in Biloxi, Mississippi, on April 19, 1984. The substance of the false or misleading statements included the following:

(A) Judge Nixon never discussed with Wiley Fairchild anything about Wiley's son's case.

(B) Wiley Fairchild never brought up his son's case.

(C) At the time of the interview Judge Nixon had no knowledge of the Drew Fairchild case and did not even know Drew Fairchild existed, except for what the judge previously read in the newspaper and what he learned from the questioners in the interview.

(D) Nothing was done or nothing was ever mentioned about Wiley Fairchild's son.

(E) Judge Nixon had never heard about the Drew Fairchild Case, except what he told the questioners in the interview, and certainly had nothing to do with the case.

(F) Judge Nixon had done nothing to influence the Drew Fairchild case.

(G) State prosecutor Paul Holmes never talked to Judge Nixon about the Drew Fairchild case.

(2) Judge Nixon further concealed his conversations with Wiley Fairchild, Paul Holmes, and Carroll Ingram concerning the Drew Fairchild case by knowingly giving one or more material false or misleading statements to a

Federal grand jury during testimony under oath in Hattiesburg, Mississippi, on July 18, 1984. The substance of the false or misleading statements included the following:

(A) Paul Holmes never discussed the Drew Fairchild case with Judge Nixon.

(B) To the best of his knowledge and recollection, Judge Nixon did not know of any reason he would have met with Wiley Fairchild after the Nixon-Fairchild oil and gas investment was finalized in February 1981.

(C) Judge Nixon gave the grand jury all the information that he had and that he could, and had withheld nothing during grand jury testimony.

(D) Judge Nixon had nothing whatsoever unofficially to do with the Drew Fairchild criminal case in State court.

(E) Judge Nixon never talked to anyone, including the State prosecutor, about the Drew Fairchild case.

(F) Judge Nixon never had a thing to do with the Drew Fairchild case at all.

(G) Judge Nixon "never talked to anyone, State or Federal, prosecutor or judge, in any way influence anybody" with respect to the Drew Fairchild case.

Wherefore, Judge Walter L. Nixon, Jr., is guilty of an impeachable offense and should be removed from office.

JUDICIAL CENSURE

THE CONSTITUTION GIVES Congress the power to "punish its members for disorderly behavior, and, with the concurrence of two-thirds, expel a member." However, with the exception of the impeachment clause and the limitation of punishment to removal and disqualification, the Constitution is silent on what measures Congress might take short of removal to punish the "disorderly behavior" of other civil officers. Over the course of the nineteenth century, Congress investigated numerous judges but impeached only four. The low impeachment rate may have been due in part to the fact that several of the investigated judges resigned rather than face impeachment. In other cases, no impeachment resulted because the particular Congress ended without House action, or because the charges were unsubstantiated. Whatever the cause, most judicial investigations ended short of impeachment.

Beginning in the 1890s, however, the House Judiciary Committee or its subcommittees began reporting back to the House about judges whose behavior should be condemned or otherwise rebuked, but who did not seem to warrant impeachment. On occasion a member would rise to protest such reports, raising similar concerns to those raised by Andrew Jackson in 1837 (see Document 26, p. 204). That is, the argument went, by censuring behavior, the House was condemning behavior without opportunity for refutation.

The extent of House action seems to have been limited to voting to accept a report in which a committee condemns or recommends condemnation of a judge's behavior. It is not clear that the House has ever explicitly debated using censure as an alternative to impeachment for federal judges. Certainly many members have assumed its availability as a device to express congressional displeasure with a judge's behavior. In the case of Judge Harold Louderback in the 1930s, the committee considered the charges and the evidence and recommended that Louderback be censured rather than impeached. The House rejected the committee's recommendation, voting for impeachment. The Senate concurred with the committee's assessment that Louderback had not committed impeachment-level offenses, at least to the extent of failing to muster two-thirds for Louderback's removal.[1]

The document presented here is an excerpt from *Hind's Precedents of the House of Representatives,* a summary and compendium of House and Senate actions. Judge Aleck Boarman was first investigated in 1890, and the Judiciary Committee recommended impeachment to the House. This was at the end of the session, however, and although the sentiment seemed to be in favor of impeachment, the House did not act on an impeachment resolution before adjournment. The next session of Congress renewed the investigation of Boarman and concluded that his behavior was censurable, but not impeachable.

In 1980 Congress acknowledged the need for some mechanism short of the "hundred ton gun" of impeachment to discipline judicial misbehavior that does not rise to the level of "high crime or misdemeanor," with passage of the Judicial Councils Reform and Judicial Conduct and Disability Act of 1980. Disapproval of judicial behavior not meriting removal can now be addressed through disciplinary actions by Chief Judges and the Judicial Councils.

❧ 24 ❧

Synopsis of House Action on
Judge Aleck Boarman

(1890)

The investigation into the conduct of Aleck Boarman, United States judge for the western district of Louisiana.

A Member of the House presented specific charges against Judge Boarman to the Judiciary Committee, which had been empowered to investigate the judiciary generally.

A subcommittee visited Louisiana and took testimony against and for Judge Boarman.

The Member who lodged charges against Judge Boarman conducted the case against him before the subcommittee.

Judge Boarman made a sworn statement or answer to the committee investigating his conduct in 1890, but did not testify.

The inquiry of 1890 into the conduct of Judge Boarman was conducted according to the established rules of evidence.

In 1890 the Judiciary Committee concluded that Judge Boarman should be impeached for an act in violation of the statute.

On March 1, 1890, Mr. William C. Oates, of Alabama, from the Committee on the Judiciary, to whom had been referred, on February 18, 1890, a resolution providing for an investigation of "the practice of certain United States district courts and other officers in criminal cases," reported the resolution with an amendment in the nature of a substitute. To show the desirability of such investigation the report cites a letter from the Attorney-General to the chairman of the committee and letters from the Commissioner of Internal Revenue and one of the Auditors of the Treasury. In addition to these letters numerous complaints had been made by persons seeming to be well informed and reputable; and also there had been complaints in the newspaper. Therefore an investigation seemed to the committee desirable, and they recommended a substitute amendment providing for a general investigation, including "maladministration or corrupt official conduct of any of the officers connected with the judicial department of the Government."

On April 1 the House agreed to the resolution with the proposed amendment; and on September 16 the committee was given authority to continue its investigation through the recess of Congress.

On February 17, 1891, Mr. Albert C. Thompson, of Ohio, submitted the report of the committee. This report dealt generally with the subject referred to the committee, and also presented an ascertainment of fact in relation to Aleck Boarman, district judge for the western district of Louisiana. The report states that while the committee were investigating the general subject a letter was, in May, 1890, addressed to the chairman of the committee by Mr. C. J. Boatner, Member of the House from the Fifth District of Louisiana, preferring seven specific charges against Judge Boarman, and asking that a date be fixed when the charges might be substantiated by witnesses. Thereupon a subcommittee of the Committee on the Judiciary visited Shreveport and New Orleans and took testimony relating to the charges. Both Judge Boarman and Mr. Boatner were present at Shreveport, but neither attended at New Orleans. Mr. Boatner conducted the examination of witnesses called to sustain the charges, and Mr. Albert H. Leonard appeared as counsel for Judge Boarman. The report further says:

The subcommittee before whom the testimony was taken aimed to admit nothing inadmissible under the well-established rules of evidence, but, notwithstanding the care exercised, much is found in the record that is not legal evidence. In reaching the conclusions, however, hereinafter stated, the committee endeavor to eliminate from their consideration those matters that are plainly hearsay and neighborhood gossip, and base their judgment, it is believed, upon substantial and trustworthy evidence.

Judge Boarman did not testify before the subcommittee, nor did he introduce any oral testimony whatever, except that of Mr. Albert H. Leonard and a "statement" made by Mr. M. C. Elstner, the latter being entirely personal to Mr. Elstner himself and having no bearing upon any of the issues raised. The answer of Judge Boarman, hereinbefore referred to, is given its full legal effect, as an answer, and is taken to be true except in those particulars wherein its averments are overcome by countervailing legal testimony.

The answer of Judge Boarman, filed at the first meeting of the committee, is printed in the report, and begins as follows:

In the matter of certain charges and complaints made by C. J. Boatner against Aleck Boarman, judge, western district of Louisiana, to the subjudiciary committee of the House of Representatives, sitting at Shreveport, La., the Hon. A. C. Thompson, chairman.

Respondent, in answer to said charges, respectfully makes the following answer and statements under oath:

He denies each and every allegation made against him, except what is hereinafter admitted.

First charge. Respondent denies, etc.

* * *

Respondent submits this answer to said charges, and respectfully asks now, as he has, to the knowledge of the committee, heretofore done, that such a thorough investigation shall be made as will best subserve the public interest.

ALECK BOARMAN.

Sworn to and subscribed before me this November 17, 1890.

[SEAL.]J. B. BEATTIE, *Clerk*

Upon the filing of the answer Mr. Boatner asked and was granted leave to amend the charges against Judge Boarman by the addition of another specification.

The committee concluded as to all the charges except the fourth that while there was much in the testimony warranting severe criticism of his acts yet he should be acquitted; but on the fourth charge the committee were unanimous that he should be impeached. This charge was that he had "used for his own purposes the funds paid into the registry of his court, and has unlawfully and corruptly failed and refused to decide causes in which the funds in dispute were or should have been in the registry of his court, and also (additional charge) that the respondent repeatedly borrowed money from the marshal of this court, contrary to law." The report quotes sections 995, 996, and 5505 of the Revised Statutes and rule 42 governing district courts in admiralty cases, and says:

The committee profoundly regret that from the evidence taken and fully appearing in the record, there appears to have been no attempt on the part of Judge Boarman to comply with the statute and the rules of court as to moneys paid to the clerk. His practice in this regard, if not criminal, is reprehensible in the extreme.

Therefore the committee, without dissent, reported this resolution:

Resolved, That Aleck Boarman, judge of the United States district court for the western district of Louisiana, be impeached of high crimes and misdemeanors.

The House considered the resolution on February 28, which was next to the last legislative day of the Congress, but the debate, which was entirely in favor of impeachment, was not concluded, and the resolution failed to be acted on.

In 1892 the House referred to the Judiciary Committee the evidence taken in the Boarman investigation of 1890 as material in a new investigation.

At the investigation of 1892 Judge Boarman testified and was cross-examined before the committee.

The second investigation of Judge Boarman having revealed an absence of bad intent in his censurable acts, the committee and the House decided against impeachment.

A Member who had preferred charges against Judge Boarman declined, as a member of the Judiciary Committee, to vote on his case.

In the first session of the next Congress, on January 13, 1892, Mr. Boatner submitted a resolution directing an investigation of the charges against Judge Boarman and it was referred to the Committee on the Judiciary.

On January 30 Mr. Oates reported from the committee, in lieu of that resolution, a preamble reciting the proceedings in the former Congress, especially citing the fact that the evidence taken was not ex parte, and that the respondent had been present in person or by counsel when it was taken, and a resolution referring the report made in the last Congress, the charges and the evidence, to the Committee on the Judiciary, with instructions to investigate the same thoroughly, and further providing: "And for the purpose of making the investigation hereby ordered the said Committee on the Judiciary may adopt and use as legal evidence the testimony taken as aforesaid," and "may take and consider any additional and explanatory evidence of a legal character which may be offered either for or against said judge."

This resolution was agreed to, and the committee made the investigation.

On June 1, Mr. Oates submitted the report of the committee.

As to the manner of investigation the report shows that it was conducted by a subcommittee, and says:

Your committee found it unnecessary to take any additional testimony after having adopted that taken by its predecessor in the Fifty-first Congress. Upon due inquiry it was found that there were no other witnesses to be examined in behalf of the Government touching the said charges, and therefore the said judge was notified that if he had any exculpatory or explanatory evidence which he wished to offer that he should have the opportunity of doing so. He then came to Washington, appeared before said special subcommittee, and gave his testimony.

A reference to the printed testimony shows that Judge Boarman testified at length and was then cross-examined by members of the committee. He explained his conduct as to the various charges.

The committee investigated the seven former charges and one new one. The committee found in favor of the judge as to the new charge; and also found in his favor as to the old charges, including that numbered four, on which the committee had found against him in the preceding Congress. As to the fourth charge the report says:

It will be seen in this testimony that the judge claims to have been entirely ignorant of the existence of this statute. (Sec. 5505 relating to receiving from the clerk money belonging to the registry.) He says that it looks like a humiliating confession for a judge to make, and the committee agree with him in that statement. Ignorantia legis non excusat is a maxim of the law, applicable alike to the ignorant and the learned. It can not, therefore, be taken as any excuse whatever for his conduct in this case. He is, by his own confession, technically guilty of embezzlement. There are, however, extenuating circumstances. Wheaton, the clerk, was upon his death bed when he gave the judge the orders * * * for this money. He told the judge that he was going to die, and that this money belonged in the registry of the court, and he did not wish it to go into his succession or estate. The judge swears that his motive in receiving the money was to preserve it unincumbered for the suitors who would be entitled to it when the distribution was decreed; and while he admits that he may have converted a part of it to his own use, if he did he replaced it with the new clerk, and thus those who were entitled to it received their money. While, therefore, the taking of the money by the judge was a statutory embezzlement, it can not be said from the evidence that he took it lucri causa, or with dishonest intent.

The committee find the second branch of the fourth charge—relating to corrupt failure to decide cases—not sustained.

The committee found that judge Boarman's conduct had not been such as to absolve him from censure, but they failed to find that he "had been influenced by corrupt or dishonest motives." Therefore they asked to be discharged from further consideration of the case.

The report also says:

Hon. C. J. Boatner, now a member of this committee, having preferred the charges against Judge Boarman in the Fifty-first Congress, declined to vote on any of the propositions embraced in the foregoing report.

The report of the committee was concurred in by the House without division.

Note

1. Article I, Section 5, Paragraph 2.

IMPEACHMENT OF CABINET OFFICIALS

❧ 25 ❧

Secretary of War William W. Belknap
(1876)

THE ADMINISTRATION OF President Ulysses S. Grant during the 1870s was marked with corruption and scandal. Although Grant himself was innocent of any personal wrongdoing, he surrounded himself with venal and avaricious men and maintained his loyalty to them despite the damage they wrought to the government. Officials at all levels of government, including the secretary of the Treasury, secretary of the navy, attorney general, and postmaster general, were accused of feeding at the public trough. Railroad corruption reached deep into the Congress, with House and Senate committees voting to eject three of their members—including the House minority leader. Although these recommendations would be transformed into votes of censure when the matters reached the full House

---

SECRETARY OF WAR WILLIAM W. BELKNAP   Acquitted

CHARGES: Selling appointments under his control.

MAJOR ISSUE: Whether the Senate can convict a private citizen to disqualify that person from holding future office.

HOUSE VOTE ON IMPEACHMENT: Voice Vote

SENATE VOTE FOR ACQUITTAL:

	Guilty	Not Guilty
Article 1	35	25
Article 2	36	25
Article 3	36	25
Article 4	36	25
Article 5	37	25

(The Senate voted 37–29 to retain jurisdiction over Belknap in spite of his resignation.)

---

and Senate, all three members would later leave office in disgrace. *The Nation* tallied up the costs of the scandal as "Total loss, one Senator . . . badly damaged and not serviceable for future political use, two Vice-Presidents and eight Congressmen."

Congress investigated more judges during this decade than at any other time in U.S. history. Of the eight judges investigated, four resigned before the House could vote to impeach, and a fifth, Mark Delahay (see Document 15, p. 119), resigned after being impeached, but before his Senate trial.

President Grant's supervisor of internal revenue, Gen. John A. McDonald, ran a vast enterprise of bribery and blackmail in which he extorted more than $2.5 million from liquor distillers. When his involvement in the so-called "Whiskey Ring" came to light, McDonald resigned only to be indicted by a federal grand jury. The grand jury would subsequently return indictments against two hundred or more distillers and government officials, of whom some 120 would plead guilty or be convicted, and another dozen would flee the country.

It was against this backdrop of pervasive scandal and wrongdoing that Secretary of War William W. Belknap appeared in Grant's office one day, highly agitated and asking if he could resign immediately. The president accepted his resignation "with regret," only later to find that Belknap's haste stemmed from a futile attempt to avoid impeachment. Informed by a friend that the House was about to impeach him, Belknap rushed to resign at ten o'clock in the morning of March 2, 1876; the House impeached him by voice vote at around three o'clock that afternoon. Belknap claimed that he could not be tried, since he was no longer an "officer of the United States." The Senate disagreed, voting thirty-seven to twenty-nine to continue with his trial.

Belknap was accused of accepting payments in return for giving out an appointment to a lucrative army post tradership, an office that gave its possessor a monopoly over provisioning soldiers at a particular western fort. Given that more than one-third of the Senate registered their conviction that they lacked the power to try Belknap, and that two-thirds would be required to convict, it was puzzling why the Senate moved ahead with the trial. At the conclusion of the trial, thirty-seven senators thought that Belknap was guilty of the bribery charges that had been leveled against him. Two of those senators voting guilty did not believe the Senate had jurisdiction to try the case, but they thought the issue had been settled by the vote on jurisdiction. Belknap was acquitted on all the articles because twenty-five senators voted not guilty. While only three of those twenty-five thought him innocent of the charges, the rest believed, notwithstanding the earlier vote, that the Senate had no jurisdiction to try him after his resignation.

ARTICLES OF IMPEACHMENT

Mr. Manager Lord rose and read the articles of impeachment, as follows:

Articles exhibited by the House of Representatives of the United States of America in the names of themselves and of all the people of the United States of America, against William W. Belknap, late Secretary of War, in maintenance and support of their impeachment against him for high crimes and misdemeanors while in said office.

Article I

That William W. Belknap, while he was in office as Secretary of War of the United States of America, to wit, on the 8th day of October, 1870, had the power and authority, under the laws of the United States, as Secretary of War, as aforesaid, to appoint a person to maintain a trading establishment at Fort Sill, a military post of the United States; that said Belknap, as Secretary of

War, as aforesaid, on the day and year aforesaid, promised to appoint one Caleb P. Marsh to maintain said trading establishment at said military post; that thereafter, to wit, on the day and year aforesaid, the said Caleb P. Marsh and one John S. Evans entered into an agreement in writing substantially as follows, to wit:

Articles of agreement made and entered into this 8th day of October, A.D. 1870, by and between John S. Evans, of Fort Sill, Indian Territory, United States of America, of the first part, and Caleb P. Marsh, of No. 51 West Thirty-fifth street, of the city, county, and State of New York, of the second part, witnesseth, namely:

"Whereas the said Caleb P. Marsh has received from Gen. William W.

William W. Belknap

Belknap, Secretary of War of the United States, the appointment of posttrader at Fort Sill, aforesaid; and whereas the name of said John S. Evans is to be filled into the commission of appointment of said posttrader at Fort Sill, aforesaid, by permission and at the instance and request of said Caleb P. Marsh and for the purpose of carrying out the terms of this agreement; and whereas said John S. Evans is to hold said position of posttrader, as aforesaid, solely as the appointee of said Caleb P. Marsh and for the purposes hereinafter stated:

"Now, therefore, said John S. Evans, in consideration of said appointment and the sum of $1 to him in hand paid by said Caleb P. Marsh, the receipt of which is hereby acknowledged, hereby covenants and agrees to pay to said Caleb P. Marsh the sum of $12,000 annually, payable quarterly in advance, in the city of New York, aforesaid; said sum to be so payable during the first year of this agreement absolutely and under all circumstances, anything hereinafter contained to the contrary notwithstanding; and thereafter said sum shall be so payable, unless increased or reduced in amount, in accordance with the subsequent provisions of this agreement.

"In consideration of the premises, it is mutually agreed between the parties aforesaid as follows, namely:

"First. This agreement is made on the basis of seven cavalry companies of the United States Army, which are now stationed at Fort Sill aforesaid.

"Second. If at the end of the first year of this agreement the forces of the United States Army stationed at Fort Sill, aforesaid, shall be increased or diminished not to exceed one hundred men, then this agreement shall remain in full force and unchanged for the next year. If, however, the said forces shall be increased or diminished beyond the number of one hundred men, then the amount to be paid under this agreement by said John S. Evans to said Caleb P. Marsh shall be increased or reduced in accordance therewith and in proper proportion thereto. The above rule laid down for the continuation of this agreement at the close of the first year thereof shall be applied at the close of each succeeding year so long as this agreement shall remain in force and effect.

"Third. This agreement shall remain in force and effect so long as said Caleb P. Marsh shall hold or control, directly or indirectly, the appointment and position of posttrader at Fort Sill, aforesaid.

"Fourth. This agreement shall take effect from the date and day the Secretary of War, aforesaid, shall sign the commission of posttrader at Fort Sill, aforesaid, said commission to be issued to said John S. Evans at the instance and request of said Caleb P. Marsh and solely for the purpose of carrying out the provisions of this agreement.

"Fifth. Exception is hereby made in regard to the first quarterly payment under this agreement, it being agreed and understood that the same may be paid at any time within the next thirty days after the said Secretary of War shall sign the aforesaid commission of posttrader at Fort Sill.

"Sixth. Said Caleb P. Marsh is at all times, at the request of said John S. Evans, to use any proper influence he may have with said Secretary of War for the protection of said John S. Evans while in the discharge of his legitimate duties in the conduct of the business as posttrader at Fort Sill, aforesaid.

"Seventh. Said John S. Evans is to conduct the said business of posttrader at Fort Sill, aforesaid, solely on his own responsibility and in his own name, it being expressly agreed and understood that said Caleb P. Marsh shall assume no liability in the premises whatever.

"Eighth. And it is expressly understood and agreed that the stipulations and covenants aforesaid are to apply to and bind the heirs, executors, and administrators of the respective parties.

"In witness whereof the parties to these presents have hereunto set their hands and seals the day and year first above written.

"JOHN S. EVANS. [SEAL.]
"C. P. MARSH. [SEAL.]

"Signed, sealed, and delivered in presence of—
"E. T. BARTLETT"

That thereafter, to wit, on the 10th day of October, 1870, said Belknap, as Secretary of War, aforesaid, did, at the instance and request of said Marsh, at the city of Washington, in the District of Columbia, appoint said John S. Evans to maintain said trading establishment at Fort Sill, the military post aforesaid, and in consideration of said appointment of said Evans, so made by him as Secretary of War, as aforesaid, the said Belknap did, on or about the 2d day of November, 1870, unlawfully and corruptly receive from said Caleb P. Marsh the sum of $1,500, and that at divers times thereafter, to wit, on or about the 17th of January, 1871, and at or about the end of each three months during the term of one whole year, the said William W. Belknap, while still in office as Secretary of War, as aforesaid, did unlawfully receive from said Caleb P. Marsh like sums of $1,500, in consideration of the appointment of the said John S. Evans by him, the said Belknap, as Secretary of War, as aforesaid, and in consideration of his permitting said Evans to continue to maintain the said trading establishment at said military post during that time; whereby the said William W. Belknap, who was then Secretary of War, as aforesaid, was guilty of high crimes and misdemeanors in office.

Article II

That said William W. Belknap, while he was in office as Secretary of War of the United States of America, did, at the city of Washington, in the District of Columbia, on the 4th day of November, 1873, willfully, corruptly, and unlawfully take and receive from one Caleb P. Marsh the sum of $1,500, in consideration that he would continue to permit one John S. Evans to maintain a trading establishment at Fort Sill, a military post of the United States, which said establishment said Belknap, as Secretary of War, as aforesaid, was authorized by law to permit to be maintained at said military post, and which the said Evans had been before that time appointed by said Belknap to maintain; and that said Belknap, as Secretary of War, as aforesaid, for said consideration, did corruptly permit the said Evans to continue to maintain the said trading establishment at said military post. And so the said Belknap was thereby guilty, while he was Secretary of War, of a high misdemeanor in his said office.

Article III

That said William W. Belknap was Secretary of War of the United States of America before and during the month of October, 1870, and continued in office as such Secretary of War until the 2d day of March, 1876; that as Secretary of War as aforesaid said Belknap had authority, under the laws of the United States, to appoint a person to maintain a trading establishment at Fort Sill, a military post of the United States, not in the vicinity of any city or town; that on the 10th day of October, 1870, said Belknap, as Secretary of War as aforesaid, did, at the city of Washington, in the District of Columbia, appoint one

John S. Evans to maintain said trading establishment at said military post; and that said John S. Evans, by virtue of said appointment, has since, till the 2d day of March, 1876, maintained a trading establishment at said military post, and that said Evans, on the 8th day of October, 1870, before he was so appointed to maintain said trading establishment as aforesaid, and in order to procure said appointment and to be continued therein, agreed with one Caleb P. Marsh that, in consideration that said Belknap would appoint him, the said Evans, to maintain said trading establishment at said military post, at the instance and request of said Marsh, he, the said Evans, would pay to him a large sum of money, quarterly, in advance, from the date of his said appointment by said Belknap, to wit, $12,000 during the year immediately following the 10th day of October, 1870, and other large sums of money, quarterly, during each year that he, the said Evans, should be permitted by said Belknap to maintain said trading establishment at said post; that said Evans did pay to said Marsh said sum of money quarterly during each year after his said appointment, until the month of December, 1875, when the last of said payments was made; that said Marsh, upon the receipt of each of said payments, paid one-half thereof to him, the said Belknap. Yet the said Belknap, well knowing these facts, and having the power to remove said Evans from said position at any time, and to appoint some other person to maintain said trading establishment, but criminally disregarding his duty as Secretary of War, and basely prostituting his high office to his lust for private gain, did unlawfully and corruptly continue said Evans in said position and permit to maintain said establishment at said military post during all of said time, to the great injury and damage of the officers and soldiers of the Army of the United States stationed at said post, as well as of emigrants, freighters, and other citizens of the United States, against public policy, and to the great disgrace and detriment of the public service.

Whereby the said William W. Belknap was, as Secretary of War as aforesaid, guilty of high crimes and misdemeanors in office.

Article IV

That said William W. Belknap, while he was in office and acting as Secretary of War of the United States of America, did, on the 10th day of October, 1870, in the exercise of the power and authority vested in him as Secretary of War as aforesaid by law, appoint one John S. Evans to maintain a trading establishment at Fort Sill, a military post of the United States, and he, the said Belknap, did receive, from one Caleb P. Marsh, large sums of money for and in consideration of his having so appointed said John S. Evans to maintain said trading establishment at said military post, and for continuing him therein, whereby he has been guilty of high crimes and misdemeanors in his said office. . . .

Article V

That one John S. Evans was, on the 10th day of October, in the year 1870, appointed by the said Belknap to maintain a trading establishment at Fort Sill, a military post on the frontier, not in the vicinity of any city or town, and said Belknap did, from that day continuously to the 2d day of March, 1876, permit said Evans to maintain the same; and said Belknap was induced to make said appointment by the influence and request of one Caleb P. Marsh; and said Evans paid to said Marsh, in consideration of such influence and request and in consideration that he should thereby induce said Belknap to make said appointment, divers large sums of money at various times, amounting to about $12,000 a year from the date of said appointment to the 25th day of March, 1872, and to about $6,000 a year thereafter until the 2d day of March, 1876, all which said Belknap well knew; yet said Belknap did, in consideration that he would permit said Evans to continue to maintain said trading establishment and in order that said payments might continue and be made by said Evans to said Marsh as aforesaid, corruptly receive from said Marsh, either to his, the said Belknap's, own use or to be paid over to the wife of said Belknap, divers large sums of money at various times . . . all of which acts and doings were while the said Belknap was Secretary of War of the United States, as aforesaid, and were a high misdemeanor in said office.

And the House of Representatives by protestation, saving to themselves the liberty of exhibiting at any time hereafter any further articles of accusation or impeachment against the said William W. Belknap, late Secretary of War of the United States, and also of replying to his answers which he shall make unto the articles herein preferred against him, and of offering proof to the same and every part thereof, and to all and every other article, accusation, or impeachment which shall be exhibited by them, as the case shall require, do demand that the said William W. Belknap may be put to answer the high crimes and misdemeanors in office herein charged against him, and that such proceedings, examinations, trials, and judgments may be thereupon had and given as may be agreeable to law and justice.

MICHAEL C. KERR,
Speaker of the House of Representatives.

Attest:

GEO. M. ADAMS,
Clerk of the House of Representatives.

Part V

THE PRESIDENT: OFFENSES SUBJECT TO IMPEACHMENT OR CENSURE

THE MOST VISIBLE AND DRAMATIC IMPEACHMENTS involve the president of the United States. In 1998 the House launched impeachment hearings to consider the conduct of President Bill Clinton. Although this was only the third serious presidential impeachment attempt in history, it, along with the previous two, has riveted the country as no others have, with the possible exception of the impeachment of Supreme Court Justice Samuel Chase in 1804. The documents in this section, including some of the articles of impeachment voted against Andrew Johnson in 1868, and the articles of impeachment voted on by the House Judiciary Committee against Richard Nixon in 1974, provide the only direct congressional precedents available for assessing what behavior by a president is subject to impeachment.

In addition to the three presidential impeachment investigations, there have been three presidential censures in U.S. history. The Senate censured Andrew Jackson, the House censured John Tyler, and both houses condemned President James K. Polk as part of a resolution praising General Zachary Taylor. This section also contains documents relating to congressional censure of the president—offering evidence that Congress at an earlier period believed it had the power to censure the president and offering evidence of what behavior Congress has historically regarded as meriting rebuke, but not removal, of the president.

It is tempting to regard the scope of impeachable conduct for the president as being on a footing so fundamentally different from that for other civil officers as to render the precedents developed in the latter context largely superfluous when applied to the occupant of the White House. On the one hand, it is argued that the president should be more readily subject to impeachment than other civil officers, because the president is the political, and some would add moral, leader of the nation who should be held to a higher standard of conduct. On the other hand, it is also argued that the president should be less readily subject to impeachment, because the impeachment of presidents, unlike judges, calls upon Congress to override the democratic process by removing the people's chosen leader. In any case, the argument goes, impeachment of the president is fundamentally different from all other impeachments.

It is undeniable that because of the visibility and power of the office, the impeachment of the president is considerably more spectacular than similar action against comparatively anonymous civil officers. Spectacle aside, however, the fact remains that the Constitution does not distinguish between the president and other civil officers when it comes to the scope of impeachable conduct. Beyond the limited U.S. experience with proceedings against Presidents Andrew Johnson and Richard Nixon and the fragmentary writings of the framers on impeachment, the only other impeachment precedents available are those established in nonpresidential cases. Functional differences in the nature of presidential impeachments may counsel caution in the application of precedents derived from other contexts, but to ignore such precedent would be to cut impeachment loose from the constitutional moorings that Congress has struggled for two centuries to maintain.

PRESIDENTIAL CENSURE

O N AUGUST 2, 1974, Reps. Paul Findley of Illinois and Delbert L. Latta of Ohio, both conservative Republicans, introduced a resolution to censure President Richard Nixon for negligence and maladministration of his office. Both men hoped to persuade the House to censure Nixon, rather than impeach him.[1] Nixon's resignation a week later, on August 9, ended any chance of an official censure. However, the idea of censuring the president was not new. Though not mentioned in the Constitution, Congress has debated the censure or condemnation of a number of presidents. Moreover, in the 1830s and 1840s Congress condemned and censured Andrew Jackson, John Tyler, and James K. Polk. In all three cases, members of Congress deeply opposed the president's policies but did not believe the president's actions were impeachable, thought they lacked the votes to bring about an impeachment, or believed that an impeachment, while jus-

tified, would not be in the best interest of the nation.

Taken together, these three censures provide a powerful precedent
for congressional censure of the
president. Such a censure, as these
three cases indicate, can take place
without a formal trial or even
allowing the president to present a
defense. Censure carries no penalty,
other than the embarrassment of a
formal condemnation by Congress.
That public condemnation, however, can have a powerful impact
on the president's standing within
the nation.

Andrew Jackson

The most significant of these
condemnations was the Senate's

Andrew Jackson

censure of President Jackson and his response (Document 27, p. 205). Jackson's censure resulted from his removal of the federal deposits from the
Second Bank of the United States. Congress had chartered the Bank in
1816, authorized it to print and circulate currency everywhere in the nation, and to open branches throughout the country. The stability of both
the Bank and the nation's monetary system was reinforced by making the
Bank the official depository for money held by the U.S. government, including all taxes paid to the national government.

In 1832 Jackson vetoed a bill to recharter the Bank. Following his reelection in November of that year, Jackson ordered Secretary of the Treasury Louis McLane to remove all federal deposits from the Bank. Believing, correctly as it turned out, that such an action would cause a major
economic collapse, McLane refused Jackson's order. Jackson then fired
McLane. Jackson's new Treasury secretary, William J. Duane, also refused
to remove the deposits, so Jackson sacked him as well. With Congress out
of session Jackson made an interim appointment of Roger B. Taney to Treasury. In the fall of 1833 Taney began to remove the federal deposits from
the Bank and by December had withdrawn virtually all federal moneys.

While this satisfied Jackson's desire to destroy the Bank, the national economy collapsed into recession as credit everywhere disappeared.

Jackson's war on the Bank was both political and personal, and had almost nothing to do with sound economic policy. Indeed, his actions precipitated the worst financial collapse in U.S. history until the Great Depression of the 1930s. These circumstances led Sen. Henry Clay of Kentucky, Jackson's foremost opponent in Congress, to offer a resolution of censure, declaring that Jackson had "assumed upon himself authority and power not conferred by the constitution and laws, but in derogation of both." (See Document 26, p. 204.) In 1834 the Senate endorsed this resolution by a vote of 26 to 20.

By a vote of 28 to 18 the Senate also adopted a resolution declaring that "the reasons assigned by the Secretary of the Treasury for the removal of the public deposits from the Bank of the United States are insufficient and unsatisfactory." After these votes Jackson wrote a defense of his actions and a condemnation of the censure. In part, Jackson argued that the Senate had no constitutional power to censure him. Jackson asked the Senate to enter his protest into the official record, but the Senate refused to do so.

In January 1837, with less than two months left in Jackson's term of office, the Senate formally expunged its censure from the record. The resolution to expunge was sponsored by Thomas Hart Benton of Missouri, Jackson's most loyal ally and friend in the Senate. Benton's resolution, which passed 24 to 19, asserted that the censure

was not warranted by the constitution, and was irregularly and illegally adopted by the Senate, in violation of the rights of defence which belong to every citizen, and in subversion of the fundamental principles of law and justice; because President Jackson was adjudged and pronounced to be guilty of an impeachable offence, and a stigma place upon him, as a violator of his oath of office, and of the laws and constitution which he was sworn to preserve, protect, and defend, without going through the forms of an impeachment, and without allowing him the benefits of a trial, or the means of defence.

Significantly, the Senate resolution expunging the censure did not assert that a censure was unconstitutional *per se*. Rather, the expunging resolution attacked the process in the Senate that had led to the censure. Among those voting against this resolution to expunge the censure were some of the greatest senators of the era, including Henry Clay, Daniel Webster, John C. Calhoun, and John Crittenden.

John Tyler

In 1842 the House of Representatives condemned President Tyler for his veto of a tariff bill and for the tone of his veto message. A special House committee chaired by John Quincy Adams, the former president who had been elected to Congress from Massachusetts after leaving the White House, attacked Tyler's official conduct and charged him with numerous offenses. A majority of the committee felt that Tyler should be impeached, but they did not recommend that course of action because there was not enough political support for impeachment in the House or the Senate. In addition, Adams believed an impeachment would not be in the best interest of the nation. The House adopted the committee report, condemning Tyler, by a vote of 98 to 90.

Tyler responded with a protest to the House on August 30, 1842. Tyler asked that his statement be entered into the House journal. The House rejected this request and instead adopted three new resolutions condemning Tyler.

James K. Polk

In 1846 President Polk sent U.S. soldiers into disputed territory along the Mexican border. Polk's aggressive policies eventually provoked Mexican forces into firing on American troops. This led to the Mexican-American War, which was enormously unpopular in much of the country. Throughout the war many members of Congress attacked the president in speeches. Democratic Sen. John C. Calhoun of South Carolina, who was a member of Polk's party, was particularly active in proposing various censure resolutions condemning Polk's policies. Congress did not adopt any of Calhoun's resolutions, but Calhoun's attacks on the president set the stage for an eventual resolution condemning Polk.

In May 1848, Congress passed a joint resolution "giving thanks of Congress to Major General Zachary Taylor." The resolution also contained a statement that Taylor's great victory was "in a war unnecessarily and unconstitutionally begun by the President of the United States."

Note

1. Congressional Quarterly, *Watergate: Chronology of a Crisis* (Washington, D.C.: Congressional Quarterly, 1973), 760.

❧ 26 ❧
Resolution of Censure Against
President Andrew Jackson
(1834)

Mr. CLAY then resumed his speech begun yesterday; and on concluding he offered the following modification of his second resolution, and asked the yeas and nays on both;

Resolved, That the President, in the late executive proceeding in relation to the public revenue, has assumed upon himself authority and power not conferred by the Constitution and laws, but in derogation of both.

Mr. MOORE then rose, and briefly explained the reasons why he should vote against both the resolutions, and was followed by

Mr. MCKEAN, who said he thought it his duty to give, in one word, his reasons for the same vote. He considered the resolutions as purely censorious in their character, and the adoption of them would be no remedy whatever for the prevailing distress of the country. But he thought it right to say, that the vote he would give was not to be considered decisive evidence of what his course might be when decisive measures of relief should be proposed.

The question being upon the adoption of the resolution reported by the Committee on Finance, that "the reasons assigned by the Secretary of the Treasury for the removal of the public deposites from the Bank of the United States are insufficient and unsatisfactory," it was decided in the affirmative, as follows, to wit:

YEAS—Messrs. Bibb, Black, Calhoun, Clay, Clayton, Ewing, Frelinghuysen, Hendricks, Kent, King of Georgia, Knight, Leigh, Mangum, Naudain, Poindexter, Porter, Prentiss, Preston, Robbins, Silabee, Smith, Southard, Sprague, Swift, Tomlinson, Tyler, Waggaman, and Webster—28.

NAYS—Messrs. Benton, Brown, Forsyth, Grundy, Hill, Kane, King of Alabama, Linn, McKean, Moore, Morris, Robinson, Shepley, Tallmadge, Tipton, White, Wilkins, and Wright—18.

The question being on Mr. CLAY's second resolution, as modified, was also decided in the affirmative, as follows, to wit:

YEAS—Messrs. Bibb, Black, Calhoun, Clay, Clayton, Ewing, Frelinghuysen, Kent, Knight, Leigh, Mangum, Naudain, Poindexter, Porter, Prentiss, Preston, Robbins, Silabee, Smith, Southard, Sprague, Swift, Tomlinson, Tyler, Waggaman, and Webster—26.

NAYS—Messrs. Benton, Brown, Forsyth, Grundy, Hendricks, Hill, Kane, King of Alabama, King of Georgia, Linn, McKean, Moore, Morris, Robinson, Shepley, Tallmadge, Tipton, White, Wilkins, and Wright—20.

Mr. WAGGAMAN moved, that when the Senate adjourns, it adjourn until Monday.

On a division, the motion was lost—yeas 21, nays 22.

On the motion of Mr. NAUDAIN,

The Senate adjourned.

⊰ 27 ⊱
Jackson's Protest of His Censure
(1834)

IN 1834 THE U.S. SENATE formally censured President Andrew Jackson for removing federal funds from the Bank of the United States and, in the process, pushing the nation into the greatest economic crisis of the century. The Senate censure had no practical effect. Unlike an impeachment and conviction, Jackson did not lose his office or his right to hold any other office under the Constitution. The censure was in fact simply an enormous slap at Jackson's reputation and ego. A former general with a highly developed—perhaps overdeveloped—sense of honor and pride, Jackson was deeply stung by the censure. His protest, printed below, illustrates this.

While complaining that his honor and character have been unfairly impugned, the bulk of Jackson's protest is formal and legalistic. This is perhaps not surprising, since it was drafted by Attorney General Benjamin F. Butler.[1] In the protest Jackson asserts he has been unfairly and unconstitutionally convicted of an impeachable offense without the benefit of a trial. Jackson also denies that the Senate has any constitutional power to censure him. But, he also complains about the form of the accusations, the lack of specificity of the charges, and the failure of the Senate to allow him to present his case. Furthermore, he argues that this is the action of only one House of Congress, and such unilateral action is impermissible. Jackson also complains that the vote on the censure was less than the two-thirds required to convict him in an impeachment trial. For Jackson this was further evidence that a censure by the Senate was unconstitutional.

Jackson asked that his protest "be entered at length on the journals of the Senate," but after some debate the Senate refused to do this. However, in 1837, just weeks before Jackson's term of office ended, the Senate voted to expunge its censure from the record. In what must have been a truly bizarre pseudo-ceremony, the Senate took a copy of its printed journal and drew lines through the original censure.

Jackson's protest raises a fundamental question about censure: Would a censure be more legitimate if it was specific; if it was endorsed by more than 50 percent of the House and two-thirds of the Senate; and if the president was allowed to present a defense? In other words, might Congress vote to censure rather than vote to impeach? And if Congress does vote to censure, must Congress give the president due process rights to defend his good name? One argument is that if Congress can remove a president from office, then it also has the power to condemn and censure the president without removing him from office. That Congress can choose to pass a resolution of censure without impeaching the president is illustrated by the censures of Jackson, Tyler, and Polk, and the proposed censure of Nixon.

Protest

APRIL 15, 1834.

To the Senate of the United States:

It appears by the published Journal of the Senate that on the 26th of December last a resolution was offered by a member of the Senate, which after a protracted debate was on the 28th day of March last modified by the mover and passed by the votes of twenty-six Senators out of forty-six who were present and voted, in the following words, viz:

Resolved, That the President, in the late Executive proceedings in relation to the public revenue, has assumed upon himself authority and power not conferred by the Constitution and laws, but in derogation of both.

Having had the honor, through the voluntary suffrages of the American people, to fill the office of President of the United States during the period which may be presumed to have been referred to in this resolution, it is sufficiently evident that the censure it inflicts was intended for myself. Without notice, unheard and untried, I thus find myself charged on the records of the

"*Symptoms of a Locked Jaw,*" *a contemporary cartoon inspired by Henry Clay's censure of Andrew Jackson.*

Senate, and in a form hitherto unknown in our history, with the high crime of violating the laws and Constitution of my country.

It can seldom be necessary for any department of the Government, when assailed in conversation or debate or by the strictures of the press or of popular assemblies, to step out of its ordinary path for the purpose of vindicating its conduct or of pointing out any irregularity or injustice in the manner of the attack; but when the Chief Executive Magistrate is, by one of the most important branches of the Government in its official capacity, in a public manner, and by its recorded sentence, but without precedent, competent authority, or just cause, declared guilty of a breach of the laws and Constitution, it is due to his station, to public opinion, and to a proper self-respect that the officer thus denounced should promptly expose the wrong which has been done.

In the present case, moreover, there is even a stronger necessity for such a vindication. By an express provision of the Constitution, before the President of the United States can enter on the execution of his office he is required to take an oath or affirmation in the following words:

I do solemnly swear (or affirm) that I will faithfully execute the office of President of the United States and will to the best of my ability preserve, protect, and defend the Constitution of the United States.

The duty of defending so far as in him lies the integrity of the Constitution would indeed have resulted from the very nature of his office, but by thus expressing it in the official oath or affirmation, which in this respect differs from that of any other functionary, the founders of our Republic have attested their sense of its importance and have given to it a peculiar solemnity and force. Bound to the performance of this duty by the oath I have taken, by the strongest obligations of gratitude to the American people, and by the ties which unite my every earthly interest with the welfare and glory of my country, and perfectly convinced that the discussion and passage of the above-mentioned resolution were not only unauthorized by the Constitution, but in many respects repugnant to its provisions and subversive of the rights secured by it to other coordinate departments, I deem it an imperative duty to maintain the supremacy of that sacred instrument and the immunities of the department intrusted to my care by all means consistent with my own lawful powers, with the rights of others, and with the genius of our civil institutions. To this end I have caused this my *solemn protest* against the aforesaid proceedings to be placed on the files of the executive department and to be transmitted to the Senate.

It is alike due to the subject, the Senate, and the people that the views which I have taken of the proceedings referred to, and which compel me to regard them in the light that has been mentioned, should be exhibited at length, and with the freedom and firmness which are required by an occasion so unprecedented and peculiar.

Under the Constitution of the United States the powers and functions of the various departments of the Federal Government and their responsibilities for violation or neglect of duty are clearly defined or result by necessary inference. The legislative power is, subject to the qualified negative of the President, vested in the Congress of the United States, composed of the Senate and House of Representatives; the executive power is vested exclusively in the President, except that in the conclusion of treaties and in certain appointments to office he is to act with the advice and consent of the Senate; the judicial power is vested exclusively in the Supreme and other courts of the United States, except in cases of impeachment, for which purpose the accusatory power is vested in the House of Representatives and that of hearing and determining in the Senate. But although for the special purposes which have been mentioned there is an occasional intermixture of the powers of the different departments, yet with these exceptions each of the three great departments is independent of the others in its sphere of action, and when it deviates from that sphere is not responsible to the others further than it is expressly made so in the Constitution. In every other respect each of them is the coequal of the other two, and all are the servants of the American people, without power or right to control or censure each other in the service of their common superior, save only in the manner and to the degree which that superior has prescribed.

The responsibilities of the President are numerous and weighty. He is liable to impeachment for high crimes and misdemeanors, and on due conviction to removal from office and perpetual disqualification; and notwithstanding such conviction, he may also be indicted and punished according to law. He is also liable to the private action of any party who may have been injured by his illegal mandates or instructions in the same manner and to the same extent as the humblest functionary. In addition to the responsibilities which may thus be enforced by impeachment, criminal prosecution, or suit at law, he is also accountable at the bar of public opinion for every act of his Administration. Subject only to the restraints of truth and justice, the free people of the United States have the undoubted right, as individuals or collectively, orally or in writing, at such times and in such language and form as they may think proper, to discuss his official conduct and to express and promulgate their opinions concerning it. Indirectly also his conduct may come under review in either branch of the Legislature, or in the Senate when acting in its executive capacity, and so far as the executive or legislative proceedings of these bodies may require it, it may be exercised by them. These are believed to be the proper and only modes in which the President of the United States is to be held accountable for his official conduct.

Tested by these principles, the resolution of the Senate is wholly unauthorized by the Constitution, and in derogation of its entire spirit. It assumes that a single branch of the legislative department may for the purposes of a public censure, and without any view to legislation or impeachment, take up, consider, and decide upon the official acts of the Executive. But in no part of the Constitution is the President subjected to any such responsibility, and in no part of that instrument is any such power conferred on either branch of the Legislature.

The justice of these conclusions will be illustrated and confirmed by a brief analysis of the powers of the Senate and a comparison of their recent proceedings with those powers.

The high functions assigned by the Constitution to the Senate are in their nature either legislative, executive, or judicial. It is only in the exercise of its judicial powers, when sitting as a court for the trial of impeachments, that the Senate is expressly authorized and necessarily required to consider and decide upon the conduct of the President or any other public officer. Indirectly, however, as has already been suggested, it may frequently be called on to perform that office. Cases may occur in the course of its legislative or executive proceedings in which it may be indispensable to the proper exercise of its powers that it should inquire into and decide upon the conduct of the President or other public officers, and in every such case its constitutional right to do so is cheerfully conceded. But to authorize the Senate to enter on such a task in its legislative or executive capacity the inquiry must actually grow out of and tend to some legislative or executive action, and the decision, when expressed, must take the form of some appropriate legislative or executive act.

The resolution in question was introduced, discussed, and passed not as a joint but as a separate resolution. It asserts no legislative power, proposes no legislative action, and neither possesses the form nor any of the attributes of a legislative measure. It does not appear to have been entertained or passed with any view or expectation of its issuing in a law or joint resolution, or in the repeal of any law or joint resolution, or in any other legislative action.

Whilst wanting both the form and substance of a legislative measure, it is equally manifest that the resolution was not justified by any of the executive powers conferred on the Senate. These powers relate exclusively to the consideration of treaties and nominations to office, and they are exercised in secret session and with closed doors. This resolution does not apply to any treaty or nomination, and was passed in a public session.

Nor does this proceeding in any way belong to that class of incidental resolutions which relate to the officers of the Senate, to their Chamber and other appurtenances, or to subjects of order and other matters of the like nature, in all which either House may lawfully proceed without any cooperation with the other or with the President.

On the contrary, the whole phraseology and sense of the resolution seem to be judicial. Its essence, true character, and only practical effect are to be found in the conduct which it charges upon the President and in the judgment which it pronounces on that conduct. The resolution, therefore, though discussed and adopted by the Senate in its legislative capacity, is in its office and in all its characteristics essentially judicial.

That the Senate possesses a high judicial power and that instances may occur in which the President of the United States will be amenable to it is undeniable; but under the provisions of the Constitution it would seem to be equally plain that neither the President nor any other officer can be rightfully subjected to the operation of the judicial power of the Senate except in the cases and under the forms prescribed by the Constitution. . . .

The resolution above quoted charges, in substance, that in certain proceedings relating to the public revenue the President has usurped authority and power not conferred upon him by the Constitution and laws, and that in doing so he violated both. Any such act constitutes a high crime—one of the highest, indeed, which the President can commit—a crime which justly exposes him to impeachment by the House of Representatives, and, upon due conviction, to removal from office and to the complete and immutable disfranchisement prescribed by the Constitution. The resolution, then, was in substance an impeachment of the President, and in its passage amounts to a declaration by a majority of the Senate that he is guilty of an impeachable offense. As such it is spread upon the journals of the Senate, published to the nation and to the world, made part of our enduring archives, and incorporated in the history of the age. The punishment of removal from office and future disqualification does not, it is true, follow this decision, nor would it have followed the like decision if the regular forms of proceeding had been pursued, because the requisite number did not concur in the result. But the moral influence of a solemn declaration by a majority of the Senate that the accused is guilty of the offense charged upon him has been as effectually secured as if the like declaration had been made upon an impeachment expressed in the same terms. Indeed, a greater practical effect has been gained, because the votes given for the resolution, though not sufficient to authorize a judgment of guilty on an impeachment, were numerous enough to carry that resolution.

That the resolution does not expressly allege that the assumption of power and authority which it condemns was intentional and corrupt is no answer to the preceding view of its character and effect. The act thus condemned necessarily implies volition and design in the individual to whom it is imputed, and, being unlawful in its character, the legal conclusion is that it was prompted by improper motives and committed with an unlawful intent. The charge is not of a mistake in the exercise of supposed powers, but of the assumption of powers not conferred by the Constitution and laws, but in derogation of both, and nothing is suggested to excuse or palliate the turpitude of the act. In the absence of any such excuse or palliation there is only room for one inference, and that is that the intent was unlawful and corrupt. Besides, the resolution not only contains no mitigating suggestions, but, on the contrary, it holds up the act complained of as justly obnoxious to censure and reprobation, and thus as distinctly stamps it with impurity of motive as if the strongest epithets had been used.

The President of the United States, therefore, has been by a majority of his constitutional triers accused and found guilty of an impeachable offense, but in no part of this proceeding have the directions of the Constitution been observed.

The impeachment, instead of being preferred and prosecuted by the House of Representatives, originated in the Senate, and was prosecuted without the aid or concurrence of the other House. The oath or affirmation prescribed by the Constitution was not taken by the Senators, the Chief Justice did not preside, no notice of the charge was given to the accused, and no opportunity afforded him to respond to the accusation, to meet his accusers face to face, to cross-examine the witnesses, to procure counteracting testimony, or to be heard in his defense. The safeguards and formalities which the Constitution has connected with the power of impeachment were doubtless supposed by the framers of that instrument to be essential to the protection of the public servant, to the attainment of justice, and to the order, impartiality, and dignity of the procedure. These safeguards and formalities were not only practically disregarded in the commencement and conduct of these proceedings, but in their result I find myself convicted by less than two-thirds of the members present of an impeachable offense.

In vain may it be alleged in defense of this proceeding that the form of the resolution is not that of an impeachment or of a judgment thereupon, that the punishment prescribed in the Constitution does not follow its adoption, or that in this case no impeachment is to be expected from the House of Representatives. It is because it did not assume the form of an impeachment that it is the more palpably repugnant to the Constitution, for it is through that form only that the President is judicially responsible to the Senate; and though neither removal from office nor future disqualification ensues, yet it is not to be presumed that the framers of the Constitution considered either or both of those results as constituting the whole of the punishment they prescribed. The judgment of *guilty* by the highest tribunal in the Union, the stigma it would inflict on the offender, his family, and fame, and the perpetual record on the Journal, handing down to future generations the story of his disgrace, were doubtless regarded by them as the bitterest portions, if not the very essence, of that punishment. So far, therefore, as some of its most material parts are concerned, the passage, recording, and promulgation of the resolution are an attempt to bring them on the President in a manner unauthorized by the Constitution. To shield him and other officers who are liable to impeachment from consequences so momentous, except when really merited by official delinquencies, the Constitution has most carefully guarded the whole process of impeachment. A majority of the House of Representatives must think the officer guilty before he can be charged. Two-thirds of the Senate must pronounce him guilty or he is deemed to be innocent. Forty-six Senators appear by the Journal to have been present when the vote on the resolution was taken. If after all the solemnities of an impeachment thirty of those Senators had voted that the

President was guilty, yet would he have been acquitted; but by the mode of proceeding adopted in the present case a lasting record of conviction has been entered up by the votes of twenty-six Senators without an impeachment or trial, whilst the Constitution expressly declares that to the entry of such a judgment an accusation by the House of Representatives, a trial by the Senate, and a concurrence of two-thirds in the vote of guilty shall be indispensable prerequisites.

Whether or not an impeachment was to be expected from the House of Representatives was a point on which the Senate had no constitutional right to speculate, and in respect to which, even had it possessed the spirit of prophecy, its anticipations would have furnished no just ground for this procedure. Admitting that there was reason to believe that a violation of the Constitution and laws had been actually committed by the President, still it was the duty of the Senate, as his sole constitutional judges, to wait for an impeachment until the other House should think proper to prefer it. The members of the Senate could have no right to infer that no impeachment was intended. On the contrary, every legal and rational presumption on their part ought to have been that if there was good reason to believe him guilty of an impeachable offense the House of Representatives would perform its constitutional duty by arraigning the offender before the justice of his country. The contrary presumption would involve an implication derogatory to the integrity and honor of the representatives of the people. But suppose the suspicion thus implied were actually entertained and for good cause, how can it justify the assumption by the Senate of powers not conferred by the Constitution?

. . . The constitutional mode of procedure on an impeachment has not only been wholly disregarded, but some of the first principles of natural right and enlightened jurisprudence have been violated in the very form of the resolution. It carefully abstains from averring in *which* of "the late proceedings in relation to the public revenue the President has assumed upon himself authority and power not conferred by the Constitution and laws." It carefully abstains from specifying *what laws* or *what parts* of the Constitution have been violated. Why was not the certainty of the offense—"the nature and cause of the accusation"—set out in the manner required in the Constitution before even the humblest individual, for the smallest crime, can be exposed to condemnation? Such a specification was due to the accused that he might direct his defense to the real points of attack, to the people that they might clearly understand in what particulars their institutions had been violated, and to the truth and certainty of our public annals. As the record now stands, whilst the resolution plainly charges upon the President at least one act of usurpation in "the late Executive proceedings in relation to the public revenue," and is so framed that

those Senators who believed that one such act, and only one, had been committed could assent to it, its language is yet broad enough to include several such
acts, and so it may have been regarded by some of those who voted for it. But
though the accusation is thus comprehensive in the censures it implies, there is
no such certainty of time, place, or circumstance as to exhibit the particular
conclusion of fact or law which induced any one Senator to vote for it; and it
may well have happened that whilst one Senator believed that some particular
act embraced in the resolution was an arbitrary and unconstitutional assumption of power, others of the majority may have deemed that very act both constitutional and expedient, or, if not expedient, yet still within the pale of the
Constitution; and thus a majority of the Senators may have been enabled to
concur in a vague and undefined accusation that the President, in the course of
"the late Executive proceedings in relation to the public revenue," had violated
the Constitution and laws, whilst if a separate vote had been taken in respect to
each particular act included within the general terms the accusers of the President might on any such vote have been found in the minority.

Still further to exemplify this feature of the proceeding, it is important to
be remarked that the resolution as originally offered to the Senate specified
with adequate precision certain acts of the President which it denounced as a
violation of the Constitution and laws, and that it was not until the very close
of the debate, and when perhaps it was apprehended that a majority might not
sustain the specific accusation contained in it, that the resolution was so modified as to assume its present form. A more striking illustration of the soundness
and necessity of the rules which forbid vague and indefinite generalities and require a reasonable certainty in all judicial allegations, and a more glaring instance of the violation of those rules, has seldom been exhibited.

In this view of the resolution it must certainly be regarded not as a vindication of any particular provision of the law or the Constitution, but simply as
an official rebuke or condemnatory sentence, too general and indefinite to be
easily repelled, but yet sufficiently precise to bring into discredit the conduct
and motives of the Executive. But whatever it may have been intended to accomplish, it is obvious that the vague, general, and abstract form of the resolution is in perfect keeping with those other departures from first principles
and settled improvements in jurisprudence so properly the boast of free coun-
tries in modern times. And it is not too much to say of the whole of these proceedings that if they shall be approved and sustained by an intelligent people,
then will that great contest with arbitrary power which had established in
statutes, in bills of rights, in sacred charters, and in constitutions of government the right of every citizen to a notice before trial, to a hearing before conviction, and to an impartial tribunal for deciding on the charge have been
waged in vain.

. . . Thus it was settled by the Constitution, the laws, and the whole prac-tice of the Government that the entire executive power is vested in the Presi-dent of the United States; that as incident to that power the right of appoint-ing and removing those officers who are to aid him in the execution of the laws, with such restrictions only as the Constitution prescribes, is vested in the President; that the Secretary of the Treasury is one of those officers; that the custody of the public property and money is an Executive function which, in relation to the money, has always been exercised through the Secretary of the Treasury and his subordinates; that in the performance of these duties he is subject to the supervision and control of the President, and in all important measures having relation to them consults the Chief Magistrate and obtains his approval and sanction; that the law establishing the bank did not, as it could not, change the relation between the President and the Secretary—did not re-lease the former from his obligation to see the law faithfully executed nor the latter from the President's supervision and control; that afterwards and before the Secretary did in fact consult and obtain the sanction of the President to transfers and removals of the public deposits, and that all departments of the Government, and the nation itself, approved or acquiesced in these acts and principles as in strict conformity with our Constitution and laws.

During the last year the approaching termination, according to the provi-sions of its charter and the solemn decision of the American people, of the Bank of the United States made it expedient, and its exposed abuses and cor-ruptions made it, in my opinion, the duty of the Secretary of the Treasury, to place the moneys of the United States in other depositories. The Secretary did not concur in that opinion, and declined giving the necessary order and direc-tion. So glaring were the abuses and corruptions of the bank, so evident its fixed purpose to persevere in them, and so palpable its design by its money and power to control the Government and change its character, that I deemed it the imperative duty of the Executive authority, by the exertion of every power confided to it by the Constitution and laws, to check its career and lessen its ability to do mischief, even in the painful alternative of dismissing the head of one of the Departments. At the time the removal was made other causes suffi-cient to justify it existed, but if they had not the Secretary would have been dismissed for this cause only.

His place I supplied by one whose opinions were well known to me, and whose frank expression of them in another situation and generous sacrifices of interest and feeling when unexpectedly called to the station he now occupies ought forever to have shielded his motives from suspicion and his character from reproach. In accordance with the views long before expressed by him he proceeded, with my sanction, to make arrangements for depositing the moneys of the United States in other safe institutions.

The resolution of the Senate as originally framed and as passed, if it refers to these acts, presupposes a right in that body to interfere with this exercise of Executive power. If the principle be once admitted, it is not difficult to perceive where it may end. If by a mere denunciation like this resolution the President should ever be induced to act in a matter of official duty contrary to the honest convictions of his own mind in compliance with the wishes of the Senate, the constitutional independence of the executive department would be as effectually destroyed and its power as effectually transferred to the Senate as if that end had been accomplished by an amendment of the Constitution. But if the Senate have a right to interfere with the Executive powers, they have also the right to make that interference effective, and if the assertion of the power implied in the resolution be silently acquiesced in we may reasonably apprehend that it will be followed at some future day by an attempt at actual enforcement. The Senate may refuse, except on the condition that he will surrender his opinions to theirs and obey their will, to perform their own constitutional functions, to pass the necessary laws, to sanction appropriations proposed by the House of Representatives, and to confirm proper nominations made by the President. It has already been maintained (and it is not conceivable that the resolution of the Senate can be based on any other principle) that the Secretary of the Treasury is the officer of Congress and independent of the President; that the President has no right to control him, and consequently none to remove him. With the same propriety and on similar grounds may the Secretary of State, the Secretaries of War and the Navy, and the Postmaster-General each in succession be declared independent of the President, the subordinates of Congress, and removable only with the concurrence of the Senate. Followed to its consequences, this principle will be found effectually to destroy one coordinate department of the Government, to concentrate in the hands of the Senate the whole executive power, and to leave the President as powerless as he would be useless—the shadow of authority after the substance had departed.

The time and the occasion which have called forth the resolution of the Senate seem to impose upon me an additional obligation not to pass it over in silence. Nearly forty-five years had the President exercised, without a question as to his rightful authority, those powers for the recent assumption of which he is now denounced. The vicissitudes of peace and war had attended our Government; violent parties, watchful to take advantage of any seeming usurpation on the part of the Executive, had distracted our councils; frequent removals, or forced resignations in every sense tantamount to removals, had been made of the Secretary and other officers of the Treasury, and yet in no one instance is it known that any man, whether patriot or partisan, had raised his voice against it as a violation of the Constitution. The expediency and justice of such changes in reference to public officers of all grades have frequently been the topic of discussion, but the constitutional right of the President to appoint, control, and remove the head of the Treasury as well as all other Departments seems to have been universally conceded. And what is the occasion upon which other principles have been first officially asserted? The Bank of the United States, a great moneyed monopoly, had attempted to obtain a renewal of its charter by controlling the elections of the people and the action of the Government. The use of its corporate funds and power in that attempt was fully disclosed, and it was made known to the President that the corporation was putting in train the same course of measures, with the view of making another vigorous effort, through an interference in the elections of the people, to control public opinion and force the Government to yield to its demands. This, with its corruption of the press, its violation of its charter, its exclusion of the Government directors from its proceedings, its neglect of duty and arrogant pretensions, made it, in the opinion of the President, incompatible with the public interest and the safety of our institutions that it should be longer employed as the fiscal agent of the Treasury. A Secretary of the Treasury appointed in the recess of the Senate, who had not been confirmed by that body, and whom the President might or might not at his pleasure nominate to them, refused to do what his superior in the executive department considered the most imperative of his duties, and became in fact, however innocent his motives, the protector of the bank. And on this occasion it is discovered for the first time that those who framed the Constitution misunderstood it; that the First Congress and all its successors have been under a delusion; that the practice of near forty-five years is but a continued usurpation; that the Secretary of the Treasury is not responsible to the President, and that to remove him is a violation of the Constitution and laws for which the President deserves to stand forever dishonored on the journals of the Senate.

. . . The dangerous tendency of the doctrine which denies to the President the power of supervising, directing, and controlling the Secretary of the Treasury in like manner with the other executive officers would soon be manifest in practice were the doctrine to be established. The President is the direct representative of the American people, but the Secretaries are not. If the Secretary of the Treasury be independent of the President in the execution of the laws, then is there no direct responsibility to the people in that important branch of this Government to which is committed the care of the national finances. And it is in the power of the Bank of the United States, or any other corporation, body of men, or individuals, if a Secretary shall be found to accord with them in opinion or can be induced in practice to promote their views, to control through him the whole action of the Government (so far as it is exercised by his Department) in defiance of the Chief Magistrate elected by the people and responsible to them.

But the evil tendency of the particular doctrine adverted to, though sufficiently serious, would be as nothing in comparison with the pernicious consequences which would inevitably flow from the approbation and allowance by the people and the practice by the Senate of the unconstitutional power of arraigning and censuring the official conduct of the Executive in the manner recently pursued. Such proceedings are eminently calculated to unsettle the foundations of the Government, to disturb the harmonious action of its different departments, and to break down the checks and balances by which the wisdom of its framers sought to insure its stability and usefulness.

The honest differences of opinion which occasionally exist between the Senate and the President in regard to matters in which both are obliged to participate are sufficiently embarrassing; but if the course recently adopted by the Senate shall hereafter be frequently pursued, it is not only obvious that the harmony of the relations between the President and the Senate will be destroyed, but that other and graver effects will ultimately ensue. If the censures of the Senate be submitted to by the President, the confidence of the people in his ability and virtue and the character and usefulness of his Administration will soon be at an end, and the real power of the Government will fall into the hands of a body holding their offices for long terms, not elected by the people and not to them directly responsible. If, on the other hand, the illegal censures of the Senate should be resisted by the President, collisions and angry controversies might ensue, discreditable in their progress and in the end compelling the people to adopt the conclusion either that their Chief Magistrate was unworthy of their respect or that the Senate was chargeable with calumny and injustice. Either of these results would impair public confidence in the perfection of the system and lead to serious alterations of its framework or to the practical abandonment of some of its provisions.

The influence of such proceedings on the other departments of the Government, and more especially on the States, could not fail to be extensively pernicious. When the judges in the last resort of official misconduct themselves overleap the bounds of their authority as prescribed by the Constitution, what general disregard of its provisions might not their example be expected to produce? And who does not perceive that such contempt of the Federal constitution by one of its most important departments would hold out the strongest temptations to resistance on the part of the State sovereignties whenever they shall suppose their just rights to have been invaded? Thus all the independent departments of the Government, and the States which compose our confederated Union, instead of attending to their appropriate duties and leaving those who may offend to be reclaimed or punished in the manner pointed out in the Constitution, would fall to mutual crimination and recrimination and give to the people confusion and anarchy instead of order and law, until at length some form of aristocratic power would be established on the ruins of the Constitution or the States be broken into separate communities.

Far be it from me to charge or to insinuate that the present Senate of the United States intend in the most distant way to encourage such a result. It is not of their motives or designs, but only of the tendency of their acts, that it is my duty to speak. It is, if possible, to make Senators themselves sensible of the danger which lurks under the precedent set in their resolution, and at any rate to perform my duty as the responsible head of one of the coequal departments of the Government, that I have been compelled to point out the consequences to which the discussion and passage of the resolution may lead if the tendency of the measure be not checked in its inception. It is due to the high trust with which I have been charged, to those who may be called to succeed me in it, to the representatives of the people whose constitutional prerogative has been unlawfully assumed, to the people and to the States, and to the Constitution they have established that I should not permit its provisions to be broken down by such an attack on the executive department without at least some effort "to preserve, protect, and defend" them. With this view, and for the reasons which have been stated, I do hereby *solemnly protest* against the aforementioned proceedings of the Senate as unauthorized by the Constitution, contrary to its spirit and to several of its express provisions, subversive of that distribution of the powers of government which it has ordained and established, destructive of the checks and safeguards by which those powers were intended on the one hand to be controlled and on the other to be protected, and calculated by their immediate and collateral effects, by their character and tendency, to concentrate in the hands of a body not directly amenable to the people a degree of influence and power dangerous to their liberties and fatal to the Constitution of their choice.

The resolution of the Senate contains an imputation upon my private as well as upon my public character, and as it must stand forever on their journals, I can not close this substitute for that defense which I have not been allowed to present in the ordinary form without remarking that I have lived in vain if it be necessary to enter into a formal vindication of my character and purposes from such an imputation. In vain I do bear upon my person enduring memorials of that contest in which American liberty was purchased; in vain have I since periled property, fame, and life in defense of the rights and privileges so dearly bought; in vain am I now, without a personal aspiration or the hope of individual advantage, encountering responsibilities and dangers from which by mere inactivity in relation to a single point I might have been exempt, if any serious doubts can be entertained as to the purity of my purposes and motives. If I had been ambitious, I should have sought an alliance with that powerful institution which even now aspires to no divided empire. If I had been venal, I should have sold myself to its designs. Had I preferred personal comfort and official ease to the performance of my arduous duty, I should have ceased to molest it. In the history of conquerors and usurpers, never in the fire of youth nor in the vigor of manhood could I find an attraction to lure me from the path of duty, and now I shall scarcely find an inducement to commence their career of ambition when gray hairs and a decaying frame, instead of inviting to toil and battle, call me to the contemplation of other worlds, where conquerors cease to be honored and usurpers expiate their crimes. The only ambition I can feel is to acquit myself to Him to whom I must soon render an account of my stewardship, to serve my fellowmen, and live respected and honored in the history of my country. No; the ambition which leads me on is an anxious desire and a fixed determination to return to the people unimpaired the sacred trust they have confided to my charge; to heal the wounds of the Constitution and preserve it from further violation; to persuade my countrymen, so far as I may, that it is not in a splendid government supported by powerful monopolies and aristocratical establishments that they will find happiness or their liberties protection, but in a plain system, void of pomp, protecting all and granting favors to none, dispensing its blessings, like the dews of Heaven, unseen and unfelt save in the freshness and beauty they contribute to produce. It is such a government that the genius of our people requires; such an one only under which our States may remain for ages to come united, prosperous, and free. If the Almighty Being who has hitherto sustained and protected me will but vouchsafe to make my feeble powers instrumental to such a result, I shall anticipate with pleasure the place to be assigned me in the history of my country, and die contented with the belief that I have contributed in some small degree to increase the value and prolong the duration of American liberty.

To the end that the resolution of the Senate may not be hereafter drawn into precedent with the authority of silent acquiescence on the part of the executive department, and to the end also that my motives and views in the Executive proceedings denounced in that resolution may be known to my fellow-citizens, to the world, and to all posterity, I respectfully request that this message and protest may be entered at length on the journals of the Senate.

ANDREW JACKSON.

Note

1. This man should not be confused with the Massachusetts politician of the same name, who was a leader in the movement to impeach Andrew Johnson.

❧ 28 ❧
Impeachment of Andrew Johnson
(1868)

O N FEBRUARY 25, 1868, Reps. Thaddeus Stevens of Pennsylvania and
John Bingham of Ohio appeared in an unaccustomed place—the U.S.
Senate. Stevens announced to his colleagues in the other house of Congress
that "In obedience to the order of the House of Representatives and all the
people of the United States we do impeach Andrew Johnson, President of
the United States, of high crimes and misdemeanors in office." On March 4
the managers of the impeachment, led by Bingham, presented the Senate
with eleven articles of impeachment. The trial began on March 23 and continued until May 16, when the Senate rendered a verdict on the eleventh
article of impeachment.

The eleven charges against Johnson fall into two categories. Articles 1
through 9 and 11 charged Johnson with violating the Tenure of Office Act
and the Army Appropriations Act and urging and ordering civilians and
military personnel to do the same. Article 10 catalogued Johnson's impetu-
ous, undignified "utterances, declarations, threats, and harangues" against
Congress and against specific members of Congress.

In the end, thirty-nine senators—all Republicans—voted to convict
Johnson, while nineteen senators, twelve Democrats and seven Republicans
voted for acquittal. This was one vote short of the two-thirds majority necessary for conviction. The vote was probably not as close as it appears. For
political reasons, at least four Republican senators voted for conviction, but
were prepared to vote for acquittal, if their votes were needed.[1] Nevertheless the vote was close, and the sentiment in the House and Senate was
overwhelmingly against Johnson.

Background to the Impeachment

Johnson's problems with Congress were a result of his views on race, Reconstruction, and the meaning of the Civil War. These problems were com-

plicated by his personality, his lack of sophistication, his generally crude behavior, and the circumstances of his ascension to the White House.

Before the Civil War, Johnson was a slaveholding Democratic senator from Tennessee. In the 1860 presidential election he supported John C. Breckinridge, the southern Democrat in the four-way contest won by Abraham Lincoln. Throughout his political career he had always supported slavery, and in 1860, as a U.S. senator, he voted for the adoption of a slave code for the federal territories. He personally believed blacks were inferior to whites and better off as slaves, and as late as 1865 took this position. During Reconstruction he denounced congressional actions designed to protect black rights as laws "to protect niggers."[2]

Johnson was not, however, a secessionist. And, when eleven states, including his own Tennessee, left the Union, Johnson remained in the Senate. Tennessee was one of the most divided states in the Confederacy, with strong Union support in its mountainous eastern third. During the Civil War President Lincoln appointed Johnson as the military governor of Tennessee. In this position he vigorously prosecuted the war, always considering secessionists to be traitors. In 1864 Lincoln shrewdly chose this Southerner and Democrat as his running mate on what was called a "Union" ticket.

From the moment Johnson took office Republicans began to have doubts about the new vice president. Johnson was drunk at his inauguration. Whether his inebriated state was a result of illness and fatigue, as his supporters claimed, or because he was in fact a drunkard, as his opponents claimed, was irrelevant to the issue. He had three glasses of whiskey before walking to take his oath of office and gave a rambling and offensive harangue. This was hardly an auspicious beginning. At a party following the inauguration, he made racist statements about the presence of Frederick Douglass. Had Lincoln not been assassinated, these events and actions would have been mere footnotes to history. But Lincoln's martyrdom placed Johnson in the White House. By any measure he was truly the wrong man, in the wrong place, at the wrong time. His presidency was a catastrophe.

The majority of Congress favored a Reconstruction program that would accomplish, at minimum, four things: black suffrage; substantial equality for former slaves; physical and political protection for former slaves, Southern unionists, and Northerners who had moved to the South in the wake of the war; and a remaking of the South that would exclude former Confederate civilian and military leaders from public office. The motivations for these goals were mixed. By the end of the war most Republicans believed in black suffrage as a matter of justice, as well as good politics, since they understood the freedmen would likely support their party. Similarly, it was hard to deny at least fundamental equality to blacks, especially the 150,000 or so surviving black veterans of the U.S. army and navy. The necessity of protecting free blacks and white unionists was obvious to even the most conservative Northerners. So too was the desire to prevent Confederates from controlling politics in the South. Finally, many congressional Republicans, perhaps a majority, favored changes in property relations in the South to facilitate land ownership by former slaves.

Johnson emphatically opposed all these plans. Although he had opposed secession, Johnson was also a former slaveowner who had never rejected slavery itself. He was thoroughly racist and intent on preventing blacks from taking part in governing the nation. He was particularly offended at the idea of blacks helping to govern Southern whites. Thus, Johnson returned twenty-one bills to Congress with a veto on them during the nearly four years he served in office. This compares with a total of thirty-six direct vetoes by all previous presidents combined. More significantly, Congress overrode fifteen of Johnson's vetoes, which represents more veto overrides of any single president in American history, before or since Johnson's term. Before Johnson took office Congress had only overridden a total of six presidential vetoes.[3] Among the laws passed over Johnson's veto were the Freedman's Bureau Act and the Civil Rights Act of 1866.

Johnson also obstructed the enforcement of any laws he opposed. He continuously undermined congressional attempts to protect the lives and liberties of former slaves, Union military veterans, and white unionists living in the South. In the face of terrorism by former Confederates, Johnson shuffled military commanders, put pressure on U.S. military and civilian officials to placate former Confederate leaders, and denounced congressional actions to use the army to preserve public order and black freedom. Johnson ignored statutes that prohibited former Confederate military and civilian leaders from holding public office and installed ex-rebels in high positions of power. He frustrated the intent of the Freedman's Bureau by refusing to allow officials to claim land and redistribute it to former slaves. He issued wholesale pardons of former Confederate leaders in direct opposition to congressional policy and existing statutes. Congress wanted the army to enforce its Reconstruction acts, while Johnson, as commander-in-chief, did his best to prevent the army from doing so. Similarly, he used presidential patronage to obstruct enforcement of existing laws, reverse congressional actions in the former Confederate states, and pressure Northern politicians to oppose the Fourteenth Amendment, which was designed, in part, to give full citizenship rights to all blacks.[4]

As early as 1866 some Radicals[5] in Congress called for Johnson's impeachment claiming, absurdly, that he was involved in the conspiracy to assassinate President Lincoln. Congress ignored these calls, but on March 2, 1867, Congress passed the Tenure of Office Act over Johnson's veto. This law prohibited the president from removing officeholders appointed during his term, without Senate approval. The law was in part designed to prevent Johnson from replacing loyal Republican appointees with Democrats, conservatives, and even former Confederate officeholders. The issue here was not merely political patronage, but rather the implementation of Reconstruction policy. In some states Johnson removed from office any federal official, including local postmasters, who supported the Fourteenth Amendment. The other goal was to ensure that Secretary of War Edwin Stanton, a Radical stalwart, remained in office and thus in control of the army. On March 2, 1867, Congress also passed the Command of the Army Appropriation Act, which required that all orders of the President or the Secretary of War had to be "issued through the General of the army," and at the same time prevented the removal of the "General of the army" without the approval of the Senate. The "General of the army" at this time was Ulysses S. Grant. While not a Radical, Grant was clearly aligned with those Republicans dedicated to black rights and a new political order in the South.

In July 1867, with Congress in recess, Johnson suspended Stanton until Congress could vote on the president's proposed removal of his Secretary of War. This was within the letter of the Tenure of Office Act, which allowed for a recess suspension. In fact, Johnson's action could be interpreted as an indication of his willingness to work with Congress, rather than against Congress. However, on February 21, 1868, Johnson unilaterally fired Stanton after the Senate refused to approve his removal under the Tenure of Office Act. The House of Representatives immediately moved to impeach Johnson for this violation of the act.

Trial in the Senate

At his trial Johnson claimed the Tenure of Office Act was unconstitutional, and that he had violated it merely to test it in court. This, however,

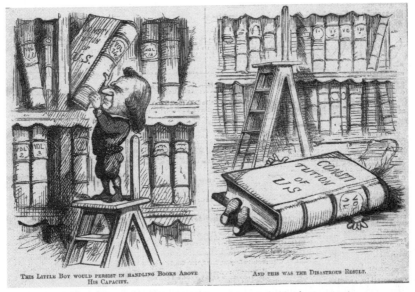

A contemporary cartoon of Andrew Johnson being crushed by the Constitution.

does not explain why he followed the law in the summer of 1867 when he suspended Stanton, and in February 1868 when he asked the Senate to approve Stanton's removal.

The impeachment trial, like the articles of impeachment themselves, was highly legalistic and avoided the key issue of the age. As Republicans saw it, Johnson, the accidental president, was attempting to undermine the victory in the Civil War by doing everything he could to obstruct Congress's Reconstruction policies. Johnson's policies endangered the very lives of white Southern unionists, Northerners living in the South, and millions of ex-slaves. Most of all, his actions threatened black Union veterans, who were being attacked by white mobs and terrorist groups, such as the Ku Klux Klan, which had been organized by a former Confederate general. Instead of protecting these "heroes" of the nation, Johnson was trying to put back in power the very white leaders who had started the war in the first place.

These were, of course, political arguments. Congress could have, and probably should have, framed articles of impeachment that detailed Johnson's malfeasance in office, his obstruction of congressional policy, and his high-handed unilateral actions that may very well have gone beyond the legitimate scope of presidential power. Had the House impeached Johnson for these reasons, at least the trial would have been about the issues that truly mattered. Instead, the trial was about the legality of the Tenure of

---

PRESIDENT ANDREW JOHNSON   Acquitted

CHARGES: Violation of the Tenure of Office Act; encouraging others to violate the Tenure of Office Act; violation of the Command of Army Appropriations Act; encouraging others to violate the Command of Army Appropriations Act; and insulting Congress.

MAJOR ISSUES: Whether violation of an act of Congress by the president in order to test its constitutionality constitutes a high crime and misdemeanor.

HOUSE VOTE ON IMPEACHMENT: 126–47

SENATE VOTE FOR ACQUITTAL:

	Guilty	Not Guilty
Articles I–III	35	19

Office Act and the right of the president to blatantly flaunt statutes passed by Congress.

While Johnson was acquitted, it is not clear what his acquittal meant. Some senators may have voted against conviction because they did not believe Johnson had actually violated the law. Stanton's status under the act was unclear, because Lincoln, not Johnson, had appointed him. Some senators believed that the Tenure of Office Act was unconstitutional, and thus voted for acquittal. But, the most important reason for the acquittal was political. The seven Republicans who voted to acquit Johnson agreed with William M. Evarts, the conservative Republican lawyer hired to defend the president, who argued that "the present situation" was better than "the change proposed."[6] In effect Evarts argued that however bad Johnson was, the situation of the nation would be worse if he was removed from office and replaced by the next-in-line for the presidency, the president pro-tempore of the Senate.

Johnson had succeeded to the presidency after the assassination of President Lincoln. Today, under the Twenty-fifth Amendment to the Constitution, if the office of vice president is vacant, the president appoints a vice president, who must be confirmed by both houses of Congress. But when Johnson became president there was no such mechanism in place, and Johnson had no vice president serving under him. Thus, if the Senate had convicted Johnson and removed him from office the president pro-tempore of the Senate, Benjamin F. Wade of Ohio, would have become president.

Wade was an uncompromising Radical; he opposed Johnson's Reconstruction program while favoring black equality and a thorough remaking of the South. He was a powerful spokesman for the Radicals and even the mainstream of his party, but at the same time he offended many moderate and conservative Republicans, and even a few Radicals. Chief Justice Salmon P. Chase, also a Radical, who presided over the impeachment, personally despised Wade. While commanding the respect and loyalty of a majority of the Republicans in the Senate, Wade also had a number of opponents within his party who, for political and personal reasons, preferred to have Johnson continue in office for another year than see Wade move into the White House. Rep. Thaddeus Stevens, the most important supporter of impeachment, believed that Wade's enemies would in the end vote against impeachment to avoid elevating the Ohio senator to the presidency.[7]

A second reason for the acquittal was the impending end of Johnson's term. By the time of his trial Johnson had less than a year to go in his term. He was hamstrung by a veto-proof Republican majority, and was politically crippled throughout most of the nation. The Republicans who voted against conviction wanted General Grant to be their party's presidential candidate. If Wade succeeded Johnson, this might not happen. Thus, politics that had so devastated Johnson also saved his presidency.

What follows are Articles of Impeachment I–III and IX–XI, voted against President Andrew Johnson by the House of Representatives. The Senate voted on Articles I–III, and in each case the vote was 35 to 19, one vote short of the necessary two-thirds majority to convict the president. Articles IV–VIII, not reprinted here, dealt with the same issues as Articles I–III. Articles IX–XI are substantially different, and while never voted on, are essential for understanding the House's view of what constituted an impeachable offense. Following these articles of impeachment is an excerpt of the closing argument in the trial by Rep. John Bingham of Ohio (Document 29, p. 236). Bingham articulates well the view of the House that Johnson's blatant refusal to follow the Tenure of Office Act was an impeachable offense, *even* if the Supreme Court eventually held the law to be unconstitutional. As Bingham argued, the president was obligated to enforce the national laws, and if he could choose which laws to enforce, and which to reject, then the rule of law itself would disappear. Also central to Bingham's argument was the belief that an impeachable offense need not be a criminal offense but rather was an offense against the public and the public laws.

ARTICLES OF IMPEACHMENT

IN THE HOUSE OF REPRESENTATIVES, UNITED STATES,

March 2, 1868

ARTICLES EXHIBITED BY THE HOUSE OF REPRESENTATIVES OF THE UNITED STATES, IN THE NAME OF THEMSELVES AND ALL THE PEOPLE OF THE UNITED STATES, AGAINST ANDREW JOHNSON, PRESIDENT OF THE UNITED STATES, IN MAINTENANCE AND SUPPORT OF THEIR IMPEACHMENT AGAINST HIM FOR HIGH CRIMES AND MISDEMEANORS IN OFFICE.

Article I

That said Andrew Johnson, President of the United States, on the 21st day of February, A.D. 1868, at Washington, in the District of Columbia, unmindful of the high duties of his office, of his oath of office, and of the requirement of the Constitution that he should take care that the laws be faithfully executed, did unlawfully and in violation of the Constitution and laws of the United States issue an order in writing for the removal of Edwin M. Stanton from the office of Secretary for the Department of War, said Edwin M. Stanton having been theretofore duly appointed and commissioned, by and with the advice and consent of the Senate of the United States, as such Secretary; and said Andrew Johnson, President of the United States, on the 12th day of August, A.D. 1867, and during the recess of said Senate, having suspended by his order Edwin M. Stanton from said office, and within twenty days after the first day of the next meeting of said Senate—that is to say, on the 12th day of December, in the year last aforesaid—having reported to said Senate such suspension, with the evidence and reasons for his action in the case and the name of the person designated to perform the duties of such office temporarily until the next meeting of the Senate; and said Senate thereafterwards, on the 13th day of January, A.D. 1868, having duly considered the evidence and reasons reported by said Andrew Johnson for said suspension, and having refused to concur in said suspension, whereby and by force of the provisions of an act entitled "An act regulating the tenure of certain civil offices," passed March 2, 1867, said Edwin M. Stanton did forthwith resume the functions of his office, whereof the said Andrew Johnson had then and there due notice; and said Edwin M. Stanton, by reason of the premises, on said 21st day of February, being lawfully entitled to hold said office of Secretary for the Department of War; which said order for the removal of said Edwin M. Stanton is in substance as follows; that is to say:

"EXECUTIVE MANSION,
"*Washington, D.C., February 21, 1868.*

"SIR: By virtue of the power and authority vested in me as President by the Constitution and laws of the United States, you are hereby removed from office as Secretary for the Department of War, and your functions as such will terminate upon the receipt of this communication.

"You will transfer to Brevet Major-General Lorenzo Thomas, Adjutant-General of the Army, who has this day been authorized and empowered to act as secretary of War ad interim, all records, books, papers, and other public property now in your custody and charge.

"Respectfully, yours,   ANDREW JOHNSON.

"HON. EDWIN M. STANTON, *Washington, D.C.*

Which order was unlawfully issued with intent then and there to violate the act entitled "An act regulating the tenure of certain civil offices," passed March 2, 1867, and with the further intent, contrary to the provisions of said act, in violation thereof, and contrary to the provisions of the Constitution of the United States, and without the advice and consent of the Senate of the United States, the said Senate then and there being in session, to remove said Edwin M. Stanton from the office of Secretary for the Department of War, the said Edwin M. Stanton being then and there Secretary for the Department of War, and being then and there in the due and unlawful execution and discharge of the duties of said office; whereby said Andrew Johnson, President of the United States, did then and there commit and was guilty of a high misdemeanor in office. . . .

Article II

That on said 21st day of February, in the year of our Lord 1868, at Washington, in the District of Columbia, said Andrew Johnson, President of the United States, unmindful of the high duties of his office, of his oath of office, and in violation of the Constitution of the United States, and contrary to the provisions of an act entitled "An act regulating the tenure of certain civil offices," passed March 2, 1867, without the advice and consent of the Senate of the United States, said Senate then and there being in session, and without authority of law, did, with intent to violate the Constitution of the United States and the act aforesaid, issue and deliver to one Lorenzo Thomas a letter of authority, in substance as follows, that is to say:

EXECUTIVE MANSION,
Washington, D.C., February 21, 1868.

"SIR: Hon. Edwin M. Stanton having been this day removed from office as Secretary for the Department of War, you are hereby authorized and empowered to act as Secretary of War ad interim, and will immediately enter upon the discharge of the duties pertaining to that office.

"Mr. Stanton has been instructed to transfer to you all the records, books, papers, and other public property now in his custody and charge.

"Respectfully, yours,   ANDREW JOHNSON.

"To Brevet Maj. Gen. LORENZO THOMAS,
  Adjutant-General United States Army, Washington, D.C."

Then and there being no vacancy in said office of Secretary for the Department of War, whereby said Andrew Johnson, President of the United States, did then and there commit, and was guilty of a high misdemeanor in office.

Article III

That said Andrew Johnson, President of the United States, on the 21st day of February, in the year of our Lord 1868, at Washington, in the District of Columbia, did commit and was guilty of a high misdemeanor in office in this, that, without authority of law, while the Senate of the United States was then and there in session, he did appoint one Lorenzo Thomas to be Secretary for the Department of War ad interim, without the advice and consent of the Senate and with intent to violate the Constitution of the United States, no vacancy having happened in said office of Secretary for the Department of War during the recess of the Senate, and no vacancy existing in said office at the time, and which said appointment, so made by said Andrew Johnson, of said Lorenzo Thomas, is in substance as follows, that is to say:

EXECUTIVE MANSION,
Washington, D.C., February 21, 1868.

"SIR: Hon. Edwin M. Stanton having been this day removed from office as Secretary for the Department of War, you are hereby authorized and empowered to act as Secretary of War ad interim, and will immediately enter upon the discharge of the duties pertaining to that office.

"Mr. Stanton has been instructed to transfer to you all the records, books, papers, and other public property now in his custody and charge.

"Respectfully, yours,   ANDREW JOHNSON.

"To Brevet Maj. Gen. LORENZO THOMAS,
  "Adjutant-General United States Army, Washington, D.C.

Article IX

That said Andrew Johnson, President of the United States, on the 22d day of February, A.D. 1868, at Washington, in the District of Columbia, in disregard of the Constitution and the laws of the United States duly enacted, as Commander in Chief of the Army of the United States, did bring before himself then and there William H. Emory, a major-general by brevet in the Army of the United States, actually in command of the Department of Washington and the military forces thereof, and did then and there, as such Commander in

Chief, declare to and instruct said Emory that part of a law of the United States, passed March 2, 1867, entitled "Act making appropriations for the support of the Army for the year ending June 30, 1868, and for other purposes," especially the second section thereof, which provides, among other things, that "all orders and instructions relating to military operations issued by the President or Secretary of War shall be issued through the General of the Army, and in case of his inability through the next in rank," was unconstitutional and in contravention of the commission of said Emory, and which said provision of law had been theretofore duly and legally promulgated by general order for the government and direction of the Army of the United States, as the said Andrew Johnson then and there well knew, with intent thereby to induce said Emory, in his official capacity as commander of the Department of Washington, to violate the provisions of said act and to take and receive, act upon, and obey such orders as he, the said Andrew Johnson, might make and give, and which should not be issued through the General of the Army of the United States, according to the provisions of said act, and with the further intent thereby to enable him, and said Andrew Johnson, to prevent the execution of the act entitled "An act regulating the tenure of certain civil offices," passed March 2, 1867, and to unlawfully prevent Edwin M. Stanton, then being Secretary for the Department of War, from holding said office and discharging the duties thereof; whereby said Andrew Johnson, President of the United States, did then and there commit and was guilty of a high misdemeanor in office.

And the House of Representatives, by protestation, saving to themselves the liberty of exhibiting at any time hereafter any further articles or other accusation or impeachment against the said Andrew Johnson, President of the United States, and also of replying to his answers which he shall make unto the articles herein preferred against him, and of offering proof to the same, and every part thereof, and to all and every other article, accusation, or impeachment which shall be exhibited by them, as the case shall require, do demand that the said Andrew Johnson may be put to answer the high crimes and misdemeanors in office here-in charged against him, and that such proceedings, examinations, trials, and judgments may be thereupon had and given as may be agreeable to law and justice.

SCHUYLER COLFAX,
Speaker of the House of Representatives
EDWARD MCPHERSON,
Clerk of the House of Representatives

Attest:
The following additional articles of impeachment were agreed to viz:

IN THE HOUSE OF REPRESENTATIVES, UNITED STATES
March 3, 1868

Article X

That said Andrew Johnson, President of the United States, unmindful of the high duties of his office and the dignity and proprieties thereof, and of the harmony and courtesies which ought to exist and be maintained between the executive and legislative branches of the Government of the United States, designing and intending to set aside the rightful authority and powers of Congress, did attempt to bring into disgrace, ridicule, hatred, contempt, and reproach the Congress of the United States and the several branches thereof, to impair and destroy the regard and respect of all the good people of the United States for the Congress and legislative power thereof (which all officers of the Government ought inviolably to preserve and maintain) and to excite the odium and resentment of all the good people of the United States against Congress and the laws by it duly and constitutionally enacted; and, in pursuance of his said design and intent, openly and publicly, and before divers assemblages of the citizens of the United States, convened in divers parts thereof to meet and receive said Andrew Johnson as the Chief Magistrate of the United States, did, on the 18th day of August, A.D. 1866, and on divers other days and times, as well before as afterwards, make and deliver with a loud voice certain intemperate, inflammatory, and scandalouse harangues, and did therein utter loud threats and bitter menaces, as well against Congress as the laws of the United States, duly enacted thereby, amid the cries, jeers, and laughter of the multitudes then assembled and in hearing, which are set forth in the several specifications hereinafter written, in substance and effect, that is to say:

Specification first.—In this, that at Washington, in the District of Columbia in the Executive Mansion, to a committee of citizens who called upon the President of the United States, speaking of and concerning the Congress of the United States, said Andrew Johnson, President of the United States, heretofore, to wit, on the 18th day of August, in the year of our Lord 1866, did, in a loud voice, declare in substance and effect, among other things, that is to say:

"So far as the executive department of the Government is concerned, the effort has been made to restore the Union, to heal the breach, to pour oil into the wounds which were consequent upon the struggle, and (to speak in common phrase) to prepare, as the learned and wise physician would, a plaster healing in character and coextensive with the wound. We thought, and we think, that we had partially succeeded; but as the work progresses, as reconstruction seemed to be taking place and the country was becoming reunited, we found a disturbing and marring element opposing us. In alluding to that element, I shall go no further than your convention and the distinguished gentleman who had delivered to me the report of its proceedings. I shall make no reference to it that I do not believe the time and the occasion justify.

"We have witnessed in one department of the Government every endeavor to prevent the restoration of peace, harmony, and union. We have seen hanging upon the verge of the Government, as it were, a body called, or which assumes to be, the Congress of the United States, while in fact it is a Congress of only a part of the States. We have seen this Congress pretend to be for the Union when its every step and act tended to perpetrate disunion and make a disruption of the States inevitable. We have seen Congress gradually encroach step by step upon constitutional rights and violate, day after day and month after month, fundamental principles of the Government. We have seen a Congress that seemed to forget that there was a limit to the sphere and scope of legislation. We have seen a Congress in a minority assume to exercise power which, allowed to be consummated, would result in despotism or monarchy itself."

Specification second.—In this, that at Cleveland, in the State of Ohio, heretofore, to wit, on the 3d day of September, in the year of our Lord 1866, before a public assemblage of citizens and others, said Andrew Johnson, President of the United States, speaking of and concerning the Congress of the United States did, in a loud voice, declare in substance and effect among other things, that is to say:

"I will tell you what I did do. I called upon your Congress that is trying to break up the Government.

"In conclusion, beside that, Congress had taken much pains to poison their constituents against him. But what had a Congress done? Have they done anything to restore the Union of these States? No; on the contrary, they had done everything to prevent it; and because he stood now where he did when the rebellion commenced he had been denounced as a traitor. Who had run greater risks or made greater sacrifices than himself? But Congress, factious and domineering, had undertaken to poison the minds of the American people."

Specification third.—In this, that at St. Louis, in the State of Missouri, heretofore, to wit, on the 8th day of September, in the year of our Lord 1866, before a public assemblage of citizens and others, said Andrew Johnson, President of the United States, speaking of and concerning the Congress of the United States, did, in a loud voice, declare, in substance and effect, among other things, that is to say:

"Go on. Perhaps if you had a word or two on the subject of New Orleans, you might understand more about it than you do. And if you will go back—if you will go back and ascertain the cause of the riot at New Orleans, perhaps you will not be so prompt in calling out 'New Orleans.' If you will take up the riot at New Orleans and trace it back to its source or its immediate cause, you will find out who was responsible for the blood that was shed there. If you will take up the riot at New Orleans and trace it back to the Radical Congress, you will find that the riot at New Orleans was substantially planned. If you will take up the proceedings in their caucuses, you will understand that they there knew that a convention was to be called which was extinct by its power having expired; that it was said that the intention was that a new government was to be organized, and on the organization of that government the intention was to enfranchise one portion of the population, called the colored population, who had just been emancipated, and at the same time disenfranchise white men. When you design to talk about New Orleans you ought to understand what you are talking about. When you read the speeches that were made, and take up the facts on the Friday and Saturday before that convention sat, you will find that speeches were made incendiary in their character, exciting that portion of the population, the black population, to arm themselves and prepare for the shedding of blood. You will also find that that convention did assemble in violation of law, and the intention of that convention was to supersede the reorganized authorities in the State government of Louisiana, which had been recognized by the Government of the United States; and every man engaged in that rebellion in that convention, with the intention of superseding and upturning the civil government which had been recognized by the Government of the United States, I say that he was a traitor to the Constitution of the United States, and hence you find that another rebellion was commenced having its origin in the Radical Congress.

"So much for the New Orleans riot. And there was the cause and the origin of the blood that was shed; and every drop of blood that was shed is upon their skirts, and they are responsible for it. I could test this thing a little closer, but will not do it here tonight. But when you talk about the causes and consequences that resulted from proceedings of that kind, perhaps as I have been introduced here and you have provoked questions of this kind, though it does not provoke me, I will tell you a few wholesome things that have been done by this Radical Congress in connection with New Orleans and the extension of the elective franchise.

"I know that I have been traduced and abused. I know it has come in advance of me here, as elsewhere, that I have attempted to exercise an arbitrary power in resisting laws that were intended to be forced upon the Government; that I had abandoned the party that elected me, and that I was a traitor because I exercised the veto power in attempting and did arrest for a time a bill that was called a 'Freedman's Bureau' bill; yes, that I was a traitor. And I have been traduced, I have been slandered, I have been maligned, I have been called Judas Iscariot, and all that. Now, my countrymen here tonight, it is very easy to indulge in epithets; it is easy to call a man a Judas and cry out traitor; but when he is called upon to give arguments and facts he is very easy to indulge in epithets; it is easy to call a man a Judas and he was one of the twelve apostles. Oh yes, the twelve apostles had a Christ. The twelve apostles had a Christ, and he never could have had a Judas unless he had had twelve apostles. If I have played the Judas, who has been my Christ that I have played the Judas with? Was it Thad. Stevens? Was it Wendell Philips? Was it Charles Sumner? These are the men that stop and compare themselves with the Saviour; and everybody that differs with them in opinion, and to try and stay and arrest the diabolical and nefarious policy, is to be denounced as a Judas.

"Well, let me say to you, if you will stand by me in this action; if you will stand by me in trying to give the people a fair chance, soldiers and citizens, to participate in these offices, God being willing, I will kick them out, I will kick them out just as fast as I can.

"Let me say to you, in concluding that what I have said I intended to say. I was not provoked into this, and I care not for their menaces, the taunts, and the jeers, I care not for threats, I do not intend to be bullied by my enemies nor overawed by my friends. But, God willing, with your help I will veto their measures whenever any of them come to me.". . .

Article XI

That said Andrew Johnson, President of the United States, unmindful of the high duties of his office and of his oath of office, and in disregard of the Constitution and laws of the United States, did heretofore, to wit, on the 18th day of August, A.D. 1866, at the city of Washington, in the District of Columbia, by public speech, declare and affirm in substance that the Thirty-ninth Congress of the United States was not a Congress of the United States authorized by the Constitution to exercise legislative power under the same, but, on the contrary, was a Congress of only part of the States; thereby denying and intending to deny that the legislation of said Congress was valid or obligatory upon him, the said Andrew Johnson, except in so far as he saw fit to approve the same, and also thereby denying and intending to deny the power of the said Thirty-ninth Congress to propose amendments to the Constitution of the United States; and in pursuance of said declaration the said Andrew Johnson, President of the United States, afterwards, to wit, on the 21st day February, A.D. 1868, at the city of Washington, in the District of Columbia, did unlawfully, and in disregard of the requirement of the Constitution that he should take care that the laws be faithfully executed, attempt to prevent the execution of an act entitled "An act regulating the tenure of certain civil offices," passed March 2, 1867, by unlawfully devising and contriving, and attempting to devise and contrive, means by which he should prevent Edwin M. Stanton from forthwith resuming the functions of the office of Secretary for the Department of War, notwithstanding the refusal of the Senate to concur in the suspension theretofore made by said Andrew Johnson of said Edwin M. Stanton from said office of Secretary for the Department of War, and also by further unlawfully devising and contriving, and attempting to devise and contrive, means then and there to prevent the execution of an act entitled "An act making appropriations for the support of the Army for the fiscal year ending June 30, 1868 and for other purposes," approved March 2, 1867, and also to prevent the execution of an act entitled "An act to provide for the more efficient government of the rebel States," passed March 2, 1867, whereby the said Andrew Johnson, President of the United States, did then, to wit, on the 21st day of February, A.D. 1868, at the city of Washington, commit and was guilty of a high misdemeanor in office.

SCHUYLER COLFAX,
Speaker of the House of Representatives
EDWARD MCPHERSON,
Clerk of the House of Representatives

Notes

1. Hans L. Trefousse, *Impeachment of a President: Andrew Johnson, the Blacks, and Reconstruction* (Knoxville: University of Tennessee Press, 1975), 169.

2. Trefousse, 5.

3. Johnson also had eight pocket vetoes for a total of twenty-nine vetoes. No other president had used the pocket veto as often either. Pocket vetoes cannot be overridden and thus cannot be used to measure the depth of congressional opposition to the president.

4. See, generally, Michael Les Benedict, *The Impeachment and Trial of Andrew Johnson* (New York: Norton, 1973), 26–60.

5. The term "Radical" defies easy definition and scholars have spent a great deal of effort trying to determine who was a Radical and who was not. Generally speaking, the Radical Republicans wanted to grant blacks equal rights in most areas of life, including suffrage, and to punish or at least restrict the political lives of former Confederate leaders. Some Radicals wanted full racial equality in all aspects of American life. A few suggested redrawing the maps of the Southern states, to destroy the political and social power of the men who had started the war by seceding from the Union. Many Radicals also favored wholesale land redistribution to give blacks economic power and to compensate them for centuries of slavery.

6. Eric Foner, *Reconstruction: America's Unfinished Revolution, 1863–1877* (New York: Harper & Row, 1988), 386.

7. Trefousse, 61–64.

❧ 29 ❧

John Bingham on Impeachment of Johnson

(1868)

R EPRESENTATIVE JOHN BINGHAM, Chair of the Managers of Andrew Johnson's impeachment, gave the closing argument in the Senate. His argument lasted almost three full days, contains just under 50,000 words, and runs about seventy-five pages in small type. Bingham cited English and American history, compared President Johnson to King

George III and King James II, and evoked the memory of many of the Founders of the nation, including Patrick Henry, John Marshall, and Alexander Hamilton. Bingham also tied his argument to more recent political leaders, including Daniel Webster, James Kent, and, of course, Abraham Lincoln. Bingham argued that the Tenure of Office Act was constitutional; his theory was that if Congress can create offices, including Cabinet positions, and the Senate can confirm officeholders, then Congress can also limit when a president can remove officeholders. Bingham also made an argument that Johnson had in fact acknowledged the validity of the law up to the point when he removed Secretary of War Stanton in violation of the law. Bingham's strongest legal argument was based on the notion that the President could not violate the law, even to test it. Although that would seem unconvincing to modern ears, it was in fact consistent with much constitutional theory and precedent at the time. Most important, of course, was Bingham's political argument, that Johnson was reversing the result of the Civil War itself by thwarting and obstructing the efforts of Congress to reconstruct the Union on a basis of substantive racial equality.

Closing Argument of Rep. John Bingham

Mr. PRESIDENT AND SENATORS: . . . [I]n no mere partisan spirit, in no spirit of resentment or prejudice do I come to the argument of this grave issue. . . . [I]n the name of the people, and for the supremacy of their Constitution and laws, I this day speak. I pray you, senators, "hear me for my cause."[1] But yesterday the supremacy of the Constitution and laws was challenged by armed rebellion; to-day the supremacy of the Constitution and laws is challenged by executive usurpation, and is attempted to be defended in the presence of the Senate of the United States.

For four years millions of men disputed by arms the supremacy of American law on American soil. Happily for our common country, happily for our common humanity, on the 9th day of April, in the year of our Lord 1865, the broken battalions of treason and armed resistance to law surrendered to the victorious legions of the republic. On that day, not without sacrifice, not without suffering, not without martyrdom, the laws were vindicated. On that day the word went out all over our own sorrow-stricken land and to every nationality that the republic, the last refuge of constitutional liberty, the last sanctuary of an inviolable justice, was saved by the virtue and valor of its children.

On the 14th day of April, in the year of our Lord 1865, amid the joy and gladness of the people for their great deliverance, here in the capital, by an assassin's hand fell Abraham Lincoln, President of the United States, slain not for his crimes, but for his virtues, and especially for his fidelity to duty—that highest word revealed by God to man.

Upon the death of Abraham Lincoln, Andrew Johnson . . . became President of the United States, upon taking the prescribed oath that he would faithfully execute the office of President, and preserve, protect, and defend the Constitution of the United States. The people, bowing with uncovered head in the presence of the strange, great sorrow which had come upon them, forgot for the moment the disgraceful part which Andrew Johnson had played here[2] upon the tribune of the Senate on the 4th day of March, 1865, and accepted the oath thus taken by him as the successor of Abraham Lincoln as confirmation and assurance that he would take care that the laws be faithfully executed. It is with the people an intuitive judgment, the highest conviction of the human intellect, that the oath faithfully to execute the office of President, and to preserve, protect, and defend the Constitution of the United States, means, and must forever mean—while the Constitution remains as it is—that the President will himself obey, and compel others to obey, the laws enacted by the legislative department of the government, until the same shall have been repealed or reversed. This, we may assume, for the purpose of this argument, to be the general judgment of the people of this country. Surely it is the pride of every intelligent American that none are above and none beneath the laws; that the President is as much the subject of law as the humblest peasant on the remotest frontier of our ever advancing civilization. Law is the only sovereign, save God, recognized by the American people; . . . it binds alike each and all, the official and the unofficial, the citizen and the great people themselves. . . .

I refer now to a still higher authority, which is the expression of the collective power and will of the whole people of the United States, in which it is asserted that—

This Constitution, and the laws made in pursuance thereof, and all treaties made or which shall be made by the authority of the United States, shall be the supreme law of the land; and the judges in every State shall be bound thereby, anything in the constitution and laws of any State to the contrary notwithstanding.

That is the solemn declaration of the Constitution itself; and pending this trial, without a parallel in the history of the nation, it should be written upon these walls.

How are these propositions, so plain and simple, . . . met by the retained counsel who appear to defend this treason of the President, this betrayal of the great trusts of the people? The proposition is met by stating to the Senate, with an audacity that has scarcely a parallel in the history of judicial proceedings, that every official may challenge at pleasure the supreme law of the land, and especially that the President of the United States, charged by his oath, charged by the express letter of the Constitution, that "he shall take care that the laws be faithfully executed," is nevertheless invested with the power to interpret the Constitution for himself, and to determine judicially—senators, I use the word used by the learned gentleman who opened the case for the accused—to determine judicially whether the laws declared by the Constitution to be supreme are after all not null and void, because they do not happen to accord with his judgment.

This is the defence which is presented here before the Senate of the United States, and upon which they are asked to deliberate, that the Executive is clothed with power judicially—I repeat their own word, and I desire that it may be burned into the brain of senators when they come to deliberate upon this question—that the President may judicially construe the Constitution for himself, and judicially determine finally for himself whether the laws, which by your Constitution are declared to be supreme, are not, after all, null and void and of no effect, and not to be executed, because it suits the pleasure of his highness, Andrew Johnson, first king of the people of the United States, in imitation of George III, to suspend their execution. He ought to remember, when he comes with such a defence as that before the Senate of the United States, that it was said by one of those mighty spirits who put the Revolution in motion and who contributed to the organization of this great and powerful people, that Caesar had his Brutus, Charles I had his Cromwell, and George III should profit by their example.[3] Nevertheless—and this is the central point of this entire discussion—the position is assumed here in the presence of the Senate, in the presence of the people of the United States . . . that the President of the United States is invested with the judicial power to determine the force and effect of the Constitution, of his own obligations under it, and the force and effect of every law passed by the Congress of the United States. It must be conceded, if every official may challenge the laws as unconstitutional, and especially if the President may, at his pleasure, declare any act of Congress unconstitutional, reject, disregard, and violate its provisions, and this, too, by the authority of the Constitution, that instrument is itself a Constitution of anarchy, not of order, a Constitution authorizing a violation of law, not enjoining obedience to law. Senators, establish any such rule as this for official conduct, and you will have proved yourselves the architects of your country's ruin; you will have converted this land of law and order, of light and knowledge, into a land of darkness. . . .

The whole defence of the President rests upon the simple but startling proposition that he cannot be held to answer for any violation of the written Constitution and laws of the United States, because of his asserted right under the Constitution, and by the Constitution, to interpret for himself and execute or disregard, at his election, any provision either of the Constitution or statutes of the United States.

. . . That is the issue. It is all there is of it. It is what is embraced in the articles of impeachment. It is all that is embraced in them. In spite of the technicalities, in spite of the lawyer's tricks, in spite of the futile pleas that have been interposed here in the President's defence, that is the issue. It is the head and front of Andrew Johnson's offending, that he has assumed to himself the executive prerogative of interpreting the Constitution and deciding upon the validity of the laws at his pleasure, and suspending them and dispensing with their execution.

. . . [T]he position assumed in this defence for the accused that he may suspend the laws, dispense with their execution, and interpret and construe the Constitution for himself to the hurt of the republic, without peril to his official position, if he accompanies it either at the time or after the fact with a statement that his only object in violating the Constitution or in suspending the laws and dispensing with their execution was to obtain at some future day a judicial construction of the one or a judicial decision upon the validity of the other, the Senate is not to hold him to answer upon impeachment for high crimes and misdemeanors, does involve the proposition, and no man can get away from it, that the courts at last have a supervising power over this unlimited and unrestricted power of impeachment vested by the people in the House of Representatives, and this unrestricted power to try all impeachments vested by the people in the Senate. On this proposition I am willing to stand, defying any man here or elsewhere to challenge it successfully. The position assumed by the accused means that or it means nothing. . . .

Just nothing. Now, I ask you, senators, what colorable excuse is there for presenting any such monstrous proposition as this to the consideration of the Senate of the United States? I think myself in this presence justified in reiterating the words of John Marshall [in *Marbury v. Madison*]. . . .

It is the duty of the Secretary of State to conform to the law, and in this he is an officer of the United States, bound to obey the laws. He acts in this respect, as has been very properly stated at the bar, under the authority of law and not by the instructions of the President.

If he should disobey the law, does it not logically result that the President's commands cannot excuse him; that the people might well depose him from his office whether the President willed it or not? It only illustrates the proposition with which I started out, that neither the President nor his Secretaries are above the Constitution or above the laws which the people enact.

As for the . . . proposition, senators, attempted to be set up here for this accused and guilty President, that he may with impunity, under the Constitution and laws of the United States, interpret the Constitution and sit in judicial judgment . . . that question has also been ruled in the Supreme Court of the United States, and from that hour to this has never been challenged. . . . I say that the position assumed for the President by all his counsel that he is to

judicially interpret the Constitution for himself; that he is to judicially determine the validity of laws, and execute them or suspend them and dispense
with their execution at his pleasure, and defy the power of the people to bring
him to trial and judgment, was settled against him thirty years ago by the
Supreme Court of the United States, and that decision has never been questioned since by any authoritative writer upon your Constitution or by any subsequent decision in your tribunals of justice. . . .

[Next Bingham quoted from *Kendall v. The United States,* which denied the
President could order his postmaster general to disregard an act of Congress.]

It was urged at the bar that the Postmaster General was alone subject to the direction
and control of the President with respect to the execution of the duty imposed upon
him by this law; and this right of the President is claimed as growing out of the
obligation imposed upon him by the Constitution to take care that the laws be faithfully executed. This is a doctrine that cannot receive the sanction of this court. It
would be vesting in the President a *dispensing power,* which has no countenance for its
support in any part of the Constitution, and is asserting a principle which, if carried
out in its results to all cases falling within it, would be clothing the President with a
power entirely to control the legislation of Congress and paralyze the administration
of justice.

To contend that the obligation imposed on the President to see the laws faithfully
executed implies a power to forbid their execution, is a novel construction of the
Constitution, and entirely inadmissible. . . .

I ask you, senators, to consider whether . . . it was a tax upon one's patience
to sit here and listen from day to day and from week to week to these learned
arguments made in defence of the President, all resting upon his asserted executive prerogative to dispense with the execution of the laws and protect himself from trial and conviction before this tribunal, because he said that he only
violated the laws in order to test their validity in the Supreme Court, when
that court had already decided thirty years ago that any such assumed prerogative in the President enabled him to sweep away all the legislation of Congress
and prevent the administration of justice itself, and found no countenance in
the Constitution? . . .

[T]he tenure-of-office law which is called in question here this day leaves no
discretion whatever in the Executive, as to removals or suspensions during the
session of the Senate . . . [and] the President has no excuse whatever for attempting to interfere with and set aside the plain mandates and requirements
of the law. There was no discretion left in him whatever; and even his counsel
had not the audacity to argue here before the Senate that the act of 1867 which
is called in question by this Executive, who has violated its provisions, dis-
pensed with its execution, and defied its authority, left any discretion in him.
The point they make is that it is unconstitutional and no law; and that is the

Thaddeus Stevens and John A. Bingham argue for the impeachment of Andrew Johnson before the Senate, in a magazine cover dated March 14, 1868.

very point settled in Kendall *vs.* The United States, that the power vested in the President "to take care that the laws be faithfully executed" vests in him no power to set aside a law of the United States, and to direct the head of a department to disobey it, and authorize the head of the department to plead his royal mandate in a court of justice in excuse and justification of his refusal to obey the plain requirement of the law. It is written in the Constitution that "he shall take care that the laws be faithfully executed." Are we to mutilate the Constitution, and for the benefit of the accused to interpolate into the Constitution a word which is not there and the introduction of which would annihilate the whole system; that is to say, that "the President shall take care that the laws which he approves, and only the laws which he approves, shall be faithfully executed?" This is at last the position assumed for the President by himself in his answer, and assumed for him by his counsel in his defence; and the assumption conflicts with all that I have already read from the Constitution, with all that I have already read of its judicial interpretation and construction; and it conflicts as well with all that remains of the instrument itself. It is useless to multiply words to make plain a self-evident proposition; it is useless to imply this power in the President to set aside and dispense with the execution of the laws in the face of the express words of the Constitution, that "all legislative power granted by this Constitution shall be vested in a Congress which shall consist of a Senate and a House of Representatives," that he shall be sworn "faithfully to execute the office of President," and therefore faithfully to discharge every obligation which the Constitution enjoins, first and foremost of which obligations is thus written on the very fore-front of the instrument, that he shall take care that the laws enacted by the people's representatives in Congress assembled shall be faithfully executed—not some of the laws; not the laws which he approves; but the laws shall be executed until the same shall have been duly repealed by the power that made them, or shall have been constitutionally reversed by the Supreme Court of the United States acting within the limitations and under the restrictions of the Constitution itself.

. . . You have listened in vain, senators, for a single citation of a single instance in the history of the republic where there was an open violation of the written law of this land, either by the Executive, by States, or by combinations of men, which the people did not crush at the outset and put down. That is a fact in our history creditable to the American people, and a fact that ought to be considered by the Senate when they come to sit in judgment upon this case now made before them for the first time under the Constitution of the United States, whether the President is above the laws and can dispense with their execution with impunity in the exercise of what is adroitly called his judicial power of interpretation.

I need not remind senators of that fact in our early history, when, by insurrection, a certain act was attempted to be resisted in the State of Pennsylvania, when Washington promptly took measures to crush this first uprising of insurrection against the supremacy of the laws. The gentlemen have attempted to summon to their aid the great name of the hero of New Orleans. It is fresh within the recollection of senators, as it is fresh within the recollection of millions of people of this country, that when the State of South Carolina, in the exercise of what she called her sovereign power as a State, by ordinance attempted to set aside the laws of the United States for the collection of customs, the President of the United States, Andrew Jackson, not unmindful of his oath—although the law was distasteful to him, and it is a fact that has passed into history that he even doubted its constitutionality—yet, nevertheless, issued his proclamation to the insurgents, and, lifting his hand, swore "by the Eternal the Union must and shall be preserved." There was no recognition here of the right either in himself or in a State to set aside the laws.

Gentlemen, there is a case still fresher within the recollection of senators, and still fresher in the recollection of the people of this country, that attests more significantly than any other the determination of the people to abide by their laws enacted by their Congress, whatever the law may be and however odious it may be. The gentleman from New York[4] . . . took occasion to refer to the fugitive slave law of 1850; a law which was disgraceful, (and I say it with all respect to the Congress that enacted it;) a law which was in direct violation of the letter and the spirit of the Constitution; a law of which I can say, at least . . . that it never found an advocate in me; a law of which Webster spoke when he said, "My judgment always was, and that is my opinion to-day, that it is unwarranted by the Constitution;"[5] a law which offered a bribe out of the common treasury of the nation to every magistrate who sat in judgment upon the right of a flying bondman to that liberty which was his by virtue of the same creative energy which breathed into his nostrils the breath of life and he became a living soul; a law which offered a reward to the ministers of justice to shorten the judgment of the poor; a law which, smiting the conscience of the American people and the conscience of the civilized world, made it a crime to give shelter to the houseless and, in obedience to the utterances of our divine Master, to give a cup of water to him that was ready to perish; a law enacted for the purpose of sustaining that crime of crimes, that sum of all villanies, which made merchandise of immortality, which transformed a man into a chattel, a thing of trade, which, for want of a better word, we call a slave, with no acknowledged rights in the present, with no hope of a heritage in the great hereafter, to whose darkened soul, under this crushing bondage, the universe was voiceless, and God himself seemed silent; . . . a law sustained by the American people even on that day when Anthony Burns walked in chains under the shadow of Bunker Hill, "where every sod's a soldier's sepulchre," and where sleeps the first great martyr in the cause of American independence,[6] to be tried by a magistrate in a temple of justice girdled itself with chains and guarded by bayonets; and yet the people stood by and said let the law be executed until it be repealed.

Gentlemen talk about the American people recognizing the right of any President to set aside the laws! Who does not know that two years after this enactment, in 1852, the terrible blasphemy was mouthed in Baltimore by the

representatives of that same party that to-day insists upon the executive prerogative to set aside your laws and annihilate your government, touching this
fugitive-slave law, that all discussion in Congress and out of Congress should
be suppressed? . . . When that party passed that resolution they nominated
their candidate,[7] he accepted its terms; and he was carried to the presidential
chair by the votes of all the States of this Union, except four, upon the basis
that he would execute the laws, however odious they might be, however offensive they might be to the judgment and conscience of the people of the United
States and of the civilized world.

And now, with such a record as this, these gentlemen dare to come before
the Senate and tell the Senate that it is the traditional policy of the American
people to allow their own laws to be defied by their own Executive. I deny it.
There is not a line in your history but gives a flat denial to the assumption. It
has never been done.

In this connection, senators, I feel . . . compelled to depart from the direct
line of my argument to notice another point that was made by the gentleman
in order to bolster up this assumption, made for the first time, as I insist, in our
history, of the right of the Executive, by his executive prerogative, to suspend
and dispense with the execution of the laws, and that was the reference which
was made to your lamented and martyred President, Abraham Lincoln. In
God's name, senators, was it not enough that he remembered in the darkest
hours of your trial, and when the pillars of your holy temple trembled in the
storm of battle, that oath which, in his own simple words, was "registered in
heaven," and which he must obey on peril of his soul? . . . I deny that, for a single moment, he was regardless of the obligations of his oath or of the requirements of the Constitution. I deny that he ever violated your laws. I deny that
he ever assumed to himself the power claimed by this apostate President this
day to suspend your laws and dispense with their execution. Though dead, he
yet speaks from the grave; and I ask senators when they come to consider this
accusation against their murdered President, to ponder upon the words of his
first inaugural, when manifestly alluding to the fugitive slave law, which violated every conviction of his nature, from which he went back with abhorrence;
he nevertheless in that inaugural said to the American people, however much
we may dislike certain laws upon our statute-books, we are not at liberty to
defy them, nor to disregard them, nor to set them aside; but we must await the
action of the people and their repeal through the law-making power. I do not
quote the exact words, but I quote the substance; I doubt not they are as familiar to the minds of senators as they are to me.

Oh, but, said the gentleman, he suspended the *habeas corpus* act. The gentleman was too learned not to know that it has been settled law from the earliest

times to this hour that in the midst of arms the laws are silent, and that it is
written in the Constitution that "the privilege of the writ of *habeas corpus* shall
not be suspended unless when in cases of rebellion or invasion the public safety
may require it." It was not Mr. Lincoln that suspended the *habeas corpus* act; it
was that great public, solemn, civil war that covered your heavens with black-
ness and filled the habitations of your people with mourning and lamentation
for their beautiful slain upon the high places of the land. Senators, the best
answer that I can make to this assertion that your murdered President was
responsible for what necessarily resulted from this atrocious and unmatched
rebellion . . . You cannot prosecute war by a magistrate's warrant and a consta-
ble's staff. Abraham Lincoln simply followed the accepted law of the civilized
world in doing what he did. I answer further, for I leave no part of it unanswered, I would count myself dishonored, being able to speak here for him
who cannot speak for himself, if I left any colorable excuse for this assault upon
his character unanswered and unchallenged. . . .

I ask the senators to please note in this controversy between the representatives of the people and the advocates of the President that it is there written in
the Constitution so plainly that no mortal man can gainsay it, that every bill
which shall have passed the Congress of the United States and been presented
to the President and shall have received his signature shall be a law; that it further provides that every bill which he shall disapprove and return to the house
in which it originated with his objections, if reconsidered and passed by the
Congress of the United States by a two-thirds vote, shall become a law; . . . it
shall be a law if he disapproves it and the Congress pass it over his veto; it shall
be a law if he retain it for more than ten days during the session of Congress,
Sundays excepted. In each such case it shall be a law. It is in vain, altogether in
vain, against this bulwark of the Constitution, that gentlemen come, not with
their rifled ordnance, but with their small arms playing upon it, and telling
the Senate of the United States and the people of the United States in the face
of the plain words of the Constitution that it shall not be a law. The people
meant precisely what they said, that it shall be a law; though the President
give never so many reasons, by veto, why he deems it unconstitutional, nevertheless, if Congress by a two-thirds vote pass it over his veto, it shall be the
law. That is the language of the Constitution.

What is their answer? "It is not to be a law unless in pursuance of the Constitution." An unconstitutional law, they say, is no law at all. We agree to that; but
the executive—and that is the point in controversy here—is not the department
of the government to determine that issue between the people and their representatives; and the man is inexcusable, absolutely inexcusable, who ever had the
advantage of common schools and learned to read the plain text of his native ver-

nacular, who dares to raise the issue in the light of the plain text of the Constitution that the President, in the face of the Constitution, is to say it shall not be a law, though the Constitution says expressly IT SHALL BE A LAW. I admit that when an enactment of Congress shall have been set aside by the constitutional authority of this country it thenceforward ceases to be law, and the President himself might well be protected for not thereafter recognizing it as law. . . .

[T]he Constitution . . . grant[s] to the President of the United States no legislative nor judicial power. Both of these powers, legislative and judicial, are necessarily involved in the defence this day attempted to be set up by the Executive; first, in the words of his own counsel, that he may judicially interpret the Constitution for himself and judicially determine upon the validity of every enactment of Congress; and second, in the position assumed by himself, and for which he stands charged here at your bar as a criminal, to repeal—I use the word advisedly and considerately—to repeal by his own will and pleasure the laws enacted by the representatives of the people. This power of suspending the laws, of dispensing with their execution until such time as it may suit his pleasure to test their validity in the courts, is a repeal for the time being, and, if it be sustained by the Senate, may last during his natural life, if so be the American people should so long tolerate him in the office of Chief Magistrate of the nation. Why should I stop to argue the question whether such a power as this, legislative and judicial, may be rightfully assumed by the President of the United States, under the Constitution, when that Constitution expressly declares that all legislative power granted by this Constitution shall be vested in Congress, and that all judicial power shall be vested in a Supreme Court and in such inferior courts as the Congress may by law establish, subject, nevertheless, to the limitations and definitions of power embraced in the Constitution itself? The assumption upon which the defence of the President rests, that he shall only execute such laws as he approves or deems constitutional, is an assumption which invests him with legislative and judicial power in direct contravention of the express words of the Constitution.

If the President may dispense with one act of Congress upon his own discretion, may he not in like manner dispense with every act of Congress? I ask you, Senators, whether this conclusion does not necessarily result, as necessarily as effect follows efficient cause? If not, pray why not? Is the Senate of the United States, in order to shelter this great criminal, to adopt the bold assumption of unrestricted executive prerogative, the wild and guilty fantasy that the king can do no wrong, and thereby clothe the Executive of the American people with power to suspend and dispense with the execution of their laws at his pleasure, to interpret their Constitution for himself, and thereby annihilate their government? . . .

Senators, if he has the power to sit in judgment judicially—and I use the word of his advocate—upon the tenure-of-office act of 1867, he has like power to sit in judgment judicially upon every other act of Congress; and in the event of the President of the United States interfering with the execution of a judiciary act establishing for the first time, if you please, in your history, or for the second time, if you please, if by some strange intervention of Providence the existing judges should perish from the earth, I would like to know what becomes of this naked and bald pretence (unfit to be played with by children, much less by full-grown men) of the President, that he only violates the laws innocently and harmlessly, to have the question decided in the courts, when he arrogates to himself the power to prevent any court sitting in judgment upon the question? . . .

Again, a President of the United States to execute the laws of the people enacted by their representatives in Congress assembled, cannot be chosen without legislation. Are we again to be told that the President at every step is vested with authority to dispense with the execution of the law and to suspend its operation till he can have a decision, if you please, in the courts of justice? Revenue cannot be raised, in the words of the Constitution, to provide for the common defence and general welfare without legislation. Is the President to intervene with his executive prerogative to declare that your revenue laws do not meet his approval, and in the exercise of his independent co-ordinate power as one of the departments of this government if he chooses to suspend the law and dispense with its execution? If the President may set aside all laws and suspend their execution at pleasure, it results that he may annul the Constitution and annihilate the government, and that is the issue before the American Senate. I do not go outside of his answer to establish it, as I shall show before I have done with this controversy.

The Constitution itself, according to this assumption, is at his mercy, as well as the laws, and the people of the United States are to stand by and be mocked and derided in their own Capitol when, in accordance with the express provision of their Constitution, they bring him to the bar of the Senate to answer for such a crime than which none greater ever was committed since the day when the first crime was committed upon this planet as it sprung from the hand of the Creator; that crime which covered one manly brow with the ashy paleness and terrible beauty of death, and another with the damning blotch of fratricide! The people are not to be answered at this bar that it is in vain that they have put into the hands of their representatives the power to impeach such a malefactor, and by the express words of their Constitution they have put the power into the hands of the Senate, the exclusive power, the sole power to try him for his high crimes and misdemeanors.

The question touches the nation's life. . . . The vital principle of your Constitution and laws is that they shall be the supreme law of the land—supreme in every State, supreme in every Territory, supreme in every rood of the republic, supreme upon every deck covered by your flag, in every zone of the globe. And yet we are debating here to-day whether a man whose breath is in his nostrils, the mere servant of the people, may not suspend the execution both of the Constitution and of the laws at his pleasure, and defy the power of the people. The determination, Senators, of all these questions is involved in this issue, and it is for the Senate, and the Senate alone, to decide them and to decide them aright.

. . . If I am right in the position that the acts of Congress are law, binding upon the President and to be executed by him until repealed by Congress or actually reversed by the courts, it results that the wilful violation of such acts of Congress by the President, and the persistent refusal to execute them, is a high crime or misdemeanor, within the terms of the Constitution, for which he is impeachable, and of which, if he be guilty, he ought to be convicted and removed from the office that he has dishonored. It is not needful to inquire whether only crimes or misdemeanors specifically made such by the statutes of the United States are impeachable, because by the laws of the United States all crimes and misdemeanors at the common law, committed within the District of Columbia, are made indictable. I believe it is conceded on every hand that a crime or misdemeanor made indictable by the laws of the United States, when committed by an officer of the United States in his office, in violation of his sworn duty, is a high crime and misdemeanor within the meaning of the Constitution. At all events, if that be not accepted as a true and self-evident proposition by Senators, it would be in vain that I should argue further with them. And I might as well expect to kindle life under the ribs of death as to persuade a Senate, so lost to every sense of duty and to the voice of reason itself, which comes to the conclusion that after all it is not a high crime and misdemeanor under the Constitution for a President of the United States deliberately and purposely, in violation of his oath, in violation of the plain letter of the Constitution that he shall take care that the laws be faithfully executed, to set aside the laws and defiantly declare that he will not execute them. . . .

This is all, Senators, that I deem it important at present to say upon the impeachable character of the offences specified in the articles against the President, further than to remark that although the question does not arise upon this trial for the reasons already stated, a crime or misdemeanor committed by a civil officer of the United States, not indictable by our own laws or by any laws, has never yet been decided not to be impeachable under the Constitution of the United States; nor can that question ever be decided save by the Senate of the United States. I do not propose to waste words, if the Senate please, in noticing what, but for the respect I bear him, I would call the mere lawyer's *quirk* of the learned counsel from Massachusetts upon the defence, [Mr. Curtis,][8] that even if the President be guilty of the crimes laid to his charge in the articles presented by the House of Representatives, they are not high crimes and misdemeanors within the meaning of the Constitution, because they are not kindred to the great crimes of treason and bribery. It is enough, Senators, for me to remind you of what I have already said, that they are crimes which touch the nation's life, which touch the stability of your institutions; they are crimes which, if tolerated by this highest judicial tribunal in the land, vest the President by solemn judgment with the power under the Constitution to suspend at pleasure all the laws upon your statute-book, and thereby overturn your government. They have heretofore been held crimes, and crimes of such magnitude that they have cost the perpetrators their lives—not simply their offices, but their lives. . . .

But I return to my proposition. The defence of the President is not whether indictable crimes or offences are laid to his charge, but it rests upon the broad proposition, as already said, that impeachment will not lie against him for any violation of the Constitution and laws because of his asserted constitutional right to judicially interpret every provision of the Constitution for himself, and also to interpret for himself the validity of every law and execute or disregard upon his election any provision of either the Constitution or the laws, especially if he declare at or after the fact that his only purpose in violating the one or the other was to have a true construction of the Constitution in the one case, and a judicial determination of the validity of the law in the other, in the courts of the United States. . . .

I ask, Senators, in all candor, if the President of the United States, by force of the Constitution, as the learned counsel argue, is vested with judicial authority thus to interpret the Constitution and decide upon the validity of any law of Congress. . . , what is there to hinder the President from saying this of every law of the land; that it cuts off some power confided to him by the people? . . .

Senators, that all that I have said in this general way of the power assumed and exercised by the President and attempted to be justified here is directly involved in this issue, and underlies this whole question between the people and this guilty President, no man can gainsay.

1. He stands charged with a misdemeanor in office in that he issued an order in writing for the removal of the Secretary of War during the session of the Senate, without its advice and consent, in direct violation of express law, and with intent to violate the law.

2. He stands charged, during the session of the Senate, without its advice or consent, in direct violation of the express letter of the Constitution and of the act of March 2, 1867, with issuing a letter of authority to one Lorenzo Thomas, authorizing him and commanding him to assume and exercise the functions of Secretary for the Department of War.

3. He stands charged with an unlawful conspiracy to hinder the Secretary of War from holding the office, in violation of the law, in violation of the Constitution, in violation of his own oath, and with the further conspiracy to prevent the execution of the tenure-of-office act, in direct violation of his oath as well as in direct violation of the express provisions of your statute; and to prevent, also, the Secretary of War from holding the office of Secretary for the Department of War; and with the further conspiracy, by force, threat, or intimidation, to possess the property of the United States and unlawfully control the same contrary to the act of July 20, 1861.

He stands charged further with an unlawful attempt to influence Major General Emory to disregard the requirements of the act making appropriations for the support of the army, passed March 2, 1867, and which expressly provides that a violation of its provisions shall be a high crime and misdemeanor in office.

He stands further charged with a high misdemeanor in this, that on the 18th day of August, 1866, by public speech he attempted to excite resistance to the thirty-ninth Congress and to the laws of its enactment.

He stands further charged with a high misdemeanor in this, that he did affirm that the thirty-ninth Congress was not a Congress of the United States, thereby denying and intending to deny the validity of its legislation except in so far as he saw fit to approve it, and denying its power to propose an amendment to the Constitution of the United States; with devising and contriving means by which he should prevent the Secretary of War, as required by the act of the 2d March, 1867, from resuming forthwith the functions of his office, after having suspended him and after the refusal of the Senate to concur in the suspension; and with further devising and contriving to prevent the execution of an act making appropriations for the support of the army, passed March 3, 1867, and further to prevent the execution of the act to provide for the more efficient government of the rebel States.

That these several acts so charged are impeachable has been shown. To deny that they are impeachable is, as I have said, to place the President above the Constitution and the laws, to change the servant of the people into their master, the executor of their laws into the violator of their laws. . . .

And what answer is made when we come to your bar to impeach them; when we show him guilty of maladministration as no man ever was before in this country; when we show that he has violated your Constitution; when we show that he has violated your laws; when we show that he has defied the power of the Senate even after they had admonished him of the danger that was impending over him? The answer is, that he is vested with an unlimited prerogative to decide all these questions for himself, and to suspend even your power of impeachment in the courts of justice until some future day, which day may never come, when it will suit his convenience to test the validity of your laws and consequently the uprightness of his own conduct before the Supreme Court of the United States. . . .

I have said enough and more than enough to show that the matter charged against the President is impeachable. I waste no words upon the frivolous questions whether the articles have the technical requisites of an indictment. There is no law anywhere that requires it. There is nothing in the precedents of the Senate of the United States, sitting as a high court of impeachment, but condemns any suggestion of the kind. I read, however, for the perfection of my argument rather than for the instruction of the Senate, from the text of Rawle of the Constitution, in which he declares "that articles of impeachment need not be drawn up with the precision and strictness of indictments. It is all-sufficient that the charges be distinct and intelligible." They are distinct and intelligible; they are well enough understood, even by the children of the land who are able to read their mother tongue, that the President stands charged with usurpation of power in violation of the Constitution, in violation of his oath, in violation of the laws; that he stands charged with an attempt to subvert the Constitution and laws, and usurp to himself all the powers of the government vested in the legislative and judicial, as well as in the executive departments.

Notes

1. This was a quotation from Daniel Webster's famous "Seventh of March Speech," given in support of the Compromise of 1850. It is one of Bingham's many attempts to tie his summation to the icons of American history.

2. Johnson was extremely intoxicated on the day of his inauguration as Vice President, and gave a rambling, insulting, and barely coherent speech to the Senate.

3. The reference is to a speech by Patrick Henry on the eve of the Revolution.

4. William Evarts, one of the President's attorneys.

5. The allusion to Webster here is somewhat disingenuous, since Webster in fact voted for and supported the Fugitive Slave Law of 1850.

6. The Anthony Burns case (1854) was the most famous return of a fugitive slave in the 1850s.

7. Franklin Pierce.

8. Benjamin R. Curtis, a former U.S. Supreme Court Justice best known for his dissent in *Dred Scott v. Sandford* (1857), was one of the attorneys defending Johnson.

❦ 30 ❧
Impeachment Investigation of Richard Nixon
(1974)

IN NOVEMBER 1972 Richard Nixon was reelected president, winning forty-nine of fifty states. Less than two years later, on July 27, 1974, the House Judiciary Committee adopted three articles of impeachment against the president. All three articles dealt with his misuse of the office of the presidency to cover up various criminal conspiracies and to harass private citizens who opposed his administration. These articles concerned behavior implicating Nixon's public role as president.

The committee rejected two other charges. One charge involved Nixon's bombing of Cambodia during the Vietnam War. A majority of the committee members thought this charge was inappropriate, given the nature of modern foreign policy and the consistent refusal of Congress to assert itself by developing a national policy on southeast Asia. Another proposed article, also defeated, accused Nixon of tax evasion and personally enriching himself through illegal use of government money to improve the value of his private residences in Florida and California. A majority of the committee argued that these were "private" crimes, and that impeachment was not proper for the punishment of private conduct. As one Democrat on the committee, who voted for the other four articles declared, "I don't find this an abuse of power," even though it was illegal.

How had Nixon gone from the greatest landslide victory of the modern presidency to the verge of impeachment? The drama began during the election campaign itself, when a security guard at the Watergate Hotel and office complex in Washington, D.C., noticed that the lock on a door had been taped open one night. He removed the tape, but when he found the tape back on the door a little later, he called the police. Thus began "Watergate" and the eventual end of the Nixon administration.

The Watergate Break-In: "A Third Rate Burglary"

On June 17, 1972, officers arrested five men who had broken into the Democratic National Headquarters in the Watergate Hotel in Washington, D.C. Four were Cuban immigrants involved in various anti-Castro activities and with shadowy ties to various American intelligence agencies. The leader of the team was James McCord, a former Central Intelligence Agency (CIA) agent. These five burglars were employed by the Committee to Re-elect the President (CREEP), an organization set up on behalf of President Nixon and run by his closest associates, including former attorney general John Mitchell. The five burglars had broken into the Democratic headquarters to adjust electronic eavesdropping equipment that they had planted in an earlier, undetected, break-in. In the earlier break-in the men had also illegally copied Democratic Party documents. The break-ins were part of an illegal "intelligence gathering" operation funded and planned by Nixon's reelection campaign. Also implicated and arrested were two other CREEP employees, former CIA agent, E. Howard Hunt, and ex-FBI agent, G. Gordon Liddy. On June 20, President Nixon learned of the connection between his campaign and the burglars. Three days later, on June 23, Nixon began to take steps to cover up the connection to his campaign organization.

The Cover-Up

Initially Nixon attempted to get the CIA to prevent any serious investigation of the crime by informing the Washington, D.C., police and the FBI that the break-in was a "national security" operation. The CIA, quite properly, refused to join in the cover-up. Even without the CIA's help, the prosecution moved slowly during the summer of 1972, and the break-in was not a factor in the November election, in which Nixon won a landslide victory over South Dakota senator George McGovern, the Democratic candidate.

From June until the election Nixon and his close associates, including Mitchell, White House aides John Ehrlichman and H. R. "Bob" Haldeman, and Counsel to the President John W. Dean III, developed an elaborate cover-up of the administration's involvement in the Watergate burglary. The cover-up held throughout the summer and into November.

However, even before the election investigators were moving toward exposing the cover-up. Shortly after the break-in the FBI took over the case, beginning a methodical investigation of the burglars and their immediate superiors, Hunt and Liddy. Large sums of cash found in the possession of the burglars led to an investigation by the House Banking and Currency Committee, chaired by Rep. Wright Patman of Texas.

In August and September Nixon refused to allow subordinates, including Mitchell, Dean, and Secretary of Commerce Maurice Stans, to testify before Patman's committee. Nevertheless, on October 31, 1972, Patman's committee staff released a report accusing the White House of erecting a "curtain of secrecy" over the relationship between the president's reelection committee, the White House, and the break-in.

Burglars on Trial

In January 1973 four of the burglars and Hunt pled guilty to breaking and entering before U.S. District Court Judge John Sirica, while Liddy and McCord were convicted for their role in the break-in. The five defendants who pled guilty expected light sentences, as did the two who were convicted. Instead, Judge Sirica, long known as "maximum John," let it be known he was prepared to hand down very stiff sentences. Sirica believed the trial was a sham because the burglars offered no defense, and thus the prosecution was unable to get at the cause of the break-in, or determine who ordered it. Despite his Republican affiliation, Sirica was anxious to get to the bottom of this strange break-in.

On March 20, 1973, James McCord, the leader of the break-in, wrote Sirica a letter, indicating that the defendants had been bribed to plead guilty or to remain silent about their connection to the White House. The next day John Dean told President Nixon there was "a cancer within, close to the Presidency, that is growing." The Watergate cover-up was about to unravel. On March 23, Sirica read McCord's letter in open court. Sirica then handed out maximum sentences to all the defendants. Hunt was sentenced to thirty-five years, Liddy to six to twenty years, and the Cubans to forty years each. Sirica wanted to uncover the true culprits behind this case, and believed, correctly, that such sentences would scare the defendants into cooperation. He told the defendants he would consider a reduction of the sentences if they cooperated with the ongoing grand jury and congressional investigations of the break-in. Eventually Sirica reduced the sentences for all but Liddy, who consistently refused to cooperate.

The Special Prosecutor and the Ervin Committee

In the spring and summer of 1973 two separate investigations of "Watergate," as the scandal was now being called, emerged. On May 18, 1973, Attorney General Elliot Richardson appointed Harvard law professor Archibald Cox to lead the Watergate Special Prosecution Task Force. Cox had served as solicitor general in the Kennedy administration, and although he was a Democrat, Cox was seen as nonpartisan and thoroughly scrupulous in his adherence to professional ethics. (Interestingly, Cox was the great-grandson of William Evarts, one of the lawyers who defended President Andrew Johnson at his impeachment trial.) Cox was authorized to determine the extent to which the Nixon reelection committee had been involved in the burglary and cover-up.

Meanwhile, the Senate Select Committee on Presidential Campaign Activities began to investigate the nature of the break-in and its connection to campaign financing and fund raising. Chairing the committee was a conservative North Carolina Democrat, Sam Ervin. From the beginning the Ervin Committee was cordial and bipartisan, with no hint it would ultimately help bring down Nixon's presidency. Indeed, Senator Ervin declared it was "simply inconceivable" to think that the president would be implicated by the investigation. The ranking Republican on the committee, Howard Baker of Tennessee, became famous throughout the nation for his constant refrain in televised hearings, "What did the President know, and when did he know it?" The eventual answers to that question would force Nixon to resign.

On April 30, 1973, Nixon fired Haldeman, Ehrlichman, Mitchell, and Dean, although in a nationally televised speech that night the president made clear that he blamed only Dean for the emerging scandal. On May 22 Nixon told the nation that the four men had indeed been involved in a cover-up of the White House connection to the break-in, but Nixon claimed to know nothing about it. From June 25 to 29 John Dean testified before the Ervin Committee and accused the president of being deeply involved in the cover-up. Dean also revealed that Nixon had compiled an "enemies list," which included journalists, politicians, intellectuals, and entertainers. Dean also told the committee about illegal use of tax audits and other forms of harassment aimed at Nixon's enemies. Eventually, evidence would emerge that those arrested at the Watergate had previously been involved in other burglaries and were known within the White House as "the plumbers unit," because they were delegated to stop "leaks" of information Nixon considered hostile to his policies and his presidency.

The Ervin Committee hearings were televised throughout the summer of 1973, and rebroadcast at night on public television to allow greater public access to them. As the evidence about the origin of the break-in, and especially the origin of the cover-up, increasingly led to the White House and the Oval Office, the public lost confidence in the president. In July,

Alexander Butterfield, a White House aide, casually revealed to the Ervin Committee that Nixon had a voice-activated tape recording system in his office, and thus all his conversations about Watergate had been recorded. Both the Ervin Committee and special prosecutor Cox soon sought these tapes, which President Nixon refused to turn over.

The Saturday Night Massacre

On Saturday, October 20, 1973, Cox subpoenaed evidence from

"Now where?" Cartoon by Le Pelley.

Nixon, including audio tapes of Oval Office conversations. In an effort to avoid turning over the tapes, which later proved that Nixon had been involved in a massive conspiracy, the president ordered Attorney General Richardson to fire Cox. When Richardson refused this order, Nixon removed him from office. Deputy Attorney General William D. Ruckelshaus also refused to fire Cox, and Nixon fired him as well. Finally, Acting Attorney General Robert Bork fired Cox. These events, known as the "Saturday night massacre," profoundly undermined confidence in the president, who appeared to be using his powers in a high-handed, and perhaps illegal, attempt to prevent a full investigation of Watergate.[1]

Rather than relieve pressure on the White House, the "Saturday night massacre" simply increased it. Nixon reluctantly agreed to turn over nine of the subpoenaed tapes to Judge Sirica, who was supervising the Watergate grand jury. But it turned out that two of the tapes were missing and a third had an unexplained eighteen-and-one-half-minute gap, which the FBI later determined was caused by repeated erasures of that section of the tape. The erasures were designed to obliterate any trace of the conversation recorded on it. Meanwhile, under great pressure, the Nixon Justice Department appointed Leon Jaworski, a conservative Texas lawyer, to replace Cox, whom Nixon had always disliked because of his eastern establishment credentials and his ties to the Kennedys.

A New Special Prosecutor

Nixon, however, got no relief as the new special prosecutor pressed the investigation forward. Jaworski investigated a number of issues including the Watergate break-in and the cover-up, other break-ins by White House operatives ("the plumbers"), illegal campaign contributions to the Nixon reelection campaign, illegal interference from the White House with an antitrust case involving International Telephone and Telegraph (ITT), and Nixon's evasion of income taxes.

By early 1974 Jaworski's grand jury was ready to bring indictments against high level members of the administration. In February Jaworski concluded:

beginning no later than March 21, 1973, the President joined an ongoing criminal conspiracy to obstruct justice, obstruct a criminal investigation, and commit perjury (which included payment of cash to Watergate defendants to influence their testimony, making and causing to be made false statements, and declarations, making offers of clemency and leniency, and obtaining information from the Justice Department to thwart its investigation) and that the President is also liable for substantive violations of various criminal statutes.

Eventually evidence would show that Nixon's involvement in the conspiracy began as early as June 23, 1972.

Impeachment Hearings

On October 30, 1973, the House Judiciary Committee, chaired by Rep. Peter W. Rodino Jr. of New Jersey, began a preliminary inquiry into Watergate and in April the committee began impeachment hearings. On July 24, 1974, the U.S. Supreme Court, in *United States v. Nixon,* ordered the president to turn over a number of additional White House tapes to the impeachment committee. On July 27 the House Judiciary Committee voted out three articles of impeachment all dealing with Nixon's public behavior as president for his involvement in the Watergate cover-up. Significantly, the committee rejected a proposed impeachment article that dealt with Nixon's private conduct. The rejected article charged Nixon with evasion of taxes and illegally using government funds to improve the value of his private residences in Florida and California. Proponents of the article argued that Nixon knew his taxes would not be carefully scrutinized because he was the president, and that he had thus misused the office to personally enrich himself. However, a majority of the committee, including a number

---

RICHARD NIXON   Resigned

CHARGES: [Considered by the House Judiciary Committee] Obstruction of justice; abuse of power; contempt of Congress; illegal war-making in Cambodia during Vietnam War; and income tax evasion and illegal use of federal funds to enhance the value of his private residences in Florida and California.

MAJOR ISSUES: Whether illegal acts of a private nature, such as tax evasion, constitute impeachable offenses, and whether public acts which are not criminal are impeachable?

HOUSE JUDICIARY COMMITTEE VOTE:

	For	Against
Article 1 (obstruction of justice)	27	11
Article 2 (abuse of power)	28	10
Article 3 (contempt of Congress)	21	17
Article 4 (income tax evasion)	12	26
Article 5 (Cambodia bombing)	12	26

(The full House did not vote because Nixon resigned.)

---

of Democrats, believed that Congress could only impeach for actions against the government and against the political system—in a sense "public" crimes—and that while Nixon might be guilty of the felony of tax evasion or misuse of government funds, these were personal and private crimes, not crimes against the Constitution or the nation. Thus, in the view of the committee, they were not impeachable offenses.

The three articles the committee did approve were for (1) obstruction of justice; (2) abuse of power; and (3) contempt of Congress. The first passed 27 to 11 with 6 Republicans and 21 Democrats in the majority. The second passed 28 to 10 and the third 21 to 17.

The first article dealt with the White House cover-up of the break-in. After the committee voted on this article new evidence emerged, and today scholars almost universally recognize that Nixon in fact participated in the cover-up. Eventually the Watergate grand jury, operating under Leon Jaworski, named Nixon an unindicted co-conspirator for his role in the cover-up.

The second article dealt with what was perhaps the most frightening aspect of Watergate. It charged that during his presidency Nixon had misused the Internal Revenue Service (IRS), the FBI, the Secret Service, and other federal agencies to harass his "enemies" and other private citizens who had spoken out against the administration. In addition, the White House had authorized its "plumbers unit"—the same men who broke into the Watergate Hotel—to burglarize private citizens who opposed the administration. The charges sounded like the machinations of a tyrannical dictator, not the leader of the Free World. This article gained the support of one more Republican, leading to a vote of 28 to 10.

The last article charged Nixon with contempt of Congress for stonewalling on the investigation and attempting to prevent the investigation from going forward. Only two Republicans supported this article, and two Democrats also voted no, leading to a vote of 21 to 17. Opponents of this article argued that Nixon had a right to defend himself and his administration and that such a defense was not equivalent to obstruction of justice. Moreover, as Democratic Rep. Walter Flowers of Alabama argued, contempt of Congress "doesn't stand on its own as an impeachable offense." Similarly, Republican Rep. Delbert Latta of Ohio asserted that this article would be "a long step toward further diminishing the power of the President."[2]

Resignation

From July 27 until August 9 the nation watched in awe, as the constitutional process moved toward a full debate in the House. Two Representatives, Paul Findley of Illinois and Delbert L. Latta of Ohio, proposed that Congress censure the president, but such a move, which might have saved Nixon's presidency earlier on, was no longer tenable. On August 5 Nixon released the contents of a new batch of tapes. The transcript of a conversation with Haldeman on June 23, 1972—just days after the break-in—revealed a "smoking gun"—uncontrovertible evidence of Nixon's personal involvement in the cover-up. Among other things, on the tape Nixon suggested using the CIA to help with the cover-up. At this point many Republicans on the House Judiciary Committee, who had previously voted against impeachment, indicated they would vote for impeachment.

On August 9, 1974, Nixon resigned. The full House of Representatives never had an opportunity to consider or vote on the articles of impeachment. Vice President Gerald R. Ford was sworn in as president. On September 8, 1974, President Ford pardoned Nixon for all federal crimes.

Richard Nixon hugs daughter Julie the day of his resignation. Daughter Tricia and her husband Edward Cox are in the background.

PROPOSED ARTICLES OF IMPEACHMENT CONSIDERED BY THE HOUSE JUDICIARY COMMITTEE

Impeaching Richard M. Nixon, President of the United States, of high crimes and misdemeanors.

Resolved, That Richard M. Nixon, President of the United States, is impeached for high crimes and misdemeanors, and that the following articles of impeachment be exhibited to the Senate:

Articles of impeachment exhibited by the House of Representatives of the United States of America in the name of itself and of all of the people of the United States of America, against Richard M. Nixon, President of the United States of America, in maintenance and support of its impeachment against him for high crimes and misdemeanors.

Article I

In his conduct of the office of President of the United States, Richard M. Nixon, in violation of his constitutional oath faithfully to execute the office of President of the United States and, to the best of his ability, preserve, protect, and defend the Constitution of the United States, and in violation of his con-

stitutional duty to take care that the laws be faithfully executed, has prevented, obstructed, and impeded the administration of justice, in that:

On June 17, 1972, and prior thereto, agents of the Committee for the Reelection of the President committed unlawful entry of the headquarters of the
Democratic National Committee in Washington, District of Columbia, for the
purpose of securing political intelligence. Subsequent thereto, Richard M.
Nixon, using the powers of his high office, engaged personally and through his
subordinates and agents, in a course of conduct or plan designed to delay, impede, and obstruct the investigation of such unlawful entry; to cover up, conceal and protect those responsible; and to conceal the existence and scope of
other unlawful covert activities.

The means used to implement this course of conduct or plan included one
or more of the following:

(1) making or causing to be made false or misleading statements to lawfully
authorized investigative officers and employees of the United States;

(2) withholding relevant and material evidence or information from lawfully authorized investigative officers and employees of the United States;

(3) approving, condoning, acquiescing in, and counseling witnesses with
respect to the giving of false or misleading statements to lawfully authorized
investigative officers and employees of the United States and false or misleading testimony in duly instituted judicial and congressional proceedings;

(4) interfering or endeavoring to interfere with the conduct of investigations by the Department of Justice of the United States, the Federal Bureau of
Investigation, the Office of Watergate Special Prosecution Force, and Congressional Committees;

(5) approving, condoning, and acquiescing in, the surreptitious payment of
substantial sums of money for the purpose of obtaining the silence or influencing the testimony of witnesses, potential witnesses or individuals who participated in such unlawful entry and other illegal activities;

(6) endeavoring to misuse the Central Intelligence Agency, an agency of the
United States;

(7) disseminating information received from officers of the Department of
Justice of the United States to subjects of investigations conducted by lawfully
authorized investigative officers and employees of the United States, for the
purpose of aiding and assisting such subjects in their attempts to avoid criminal liability;

(8) making false or misleading public statements for the purpose of deceiv-
ing the people of the United States into believing that a thorough and complete investigation had been conducted with respect to allegations of misconduct on the part of personnel of the executive branch of the United States and

Members of the House Judiciary Committee meet in 1974 to consider impeaching Richard Nixon.

personnel of the Committee for Re-election of the President, and that there was no involvement of such personnel in such misconduct; or

(9) endeavoring to cause prospective defendants, and individuals duly tried and convicted, to expect favored treatment and consideration in return for their silence or false testimony, or rewarding individuals for their silence or false testimony.

In all of this, Richard M. Nixon has acted in a manner contrary to his trust as President and subversive of constitutional government, to the great prejudice of the cause of law and justice and to the manifest injury of the people of the United States.

Wherefore Richard M. Nixon, by such conduct, warrants impeachment and trial, and removal from office.

Article II

Using the powers of the office of President of the United States, Richard M. Nixon, in violation of his constitutional oath faithfully to execute the office of President of the United States and, to the best of his ability, preserve, protect, and defend the Constitution of the United States, and in disregard of his constitutional duty to take care that the laws be faithfully executed, has repeatedly engaged in conduct violating the constitutional rights of citizens, impairing the due and proper administration of justice and the conduct of lawful inquiries, or contravening the laws governing agencies of the executive branch and the purposes of these agencies.

This conduct has included one or more of the following:

(1) He has, acting personally and through his subordinates and agents, endeavored to obtain from the Internal Revenue Service, in violation of the constitutional rights of citizens, confidential information contained in income tax returns for purposes not authorized by law, and to cause, in violation of the constitutional rights of citizens, income tax audits or other income tax investigations to be initiated or conducted in a discriminatory manner.

(2) He misused the Federal Bureau of Investigation, the Secret Service, and other executive personnel, in violation or disregard of the constitutional rights of citizens, by directing or authorizing such agencies or personnel to conduct or continue electronic surveillance or other investigations for purposes unrelated to national security, the enforcement of laws, or any other lawful function of his office; he did direct, authorize, or permit the use of information obtained thereby for purposes unrelated to national security, the enforcement of laws, or any other lawful function of his office; and he did direct the concealment of certain records made by the Federal Bureau of Investigation of electronic surveillance.

(3) He has, acting personally and through his subordinates and agents, in violation or disregard of the constitutional rights of citizens, authorized and permitted to be maintained a secret investigative unit within the office of the President, financed in part with money derived from campaign contributions, which unlawfully utilized the resources of the Central Intelligence Agency, engaged in covert and unlawful activities, and attempted to prejudice the constitutional right of an accused to a fair trial.

(4) He has failed to take care that the laws were faithfully executed by failing to act when he knew or had reason to know that his close subordinates endeavored to impede and frustrate lawful inquiries by duly constituted executive, judicial, and legislative entities concerning the unlawful entry into the headquarters of the Democratic National Committee, and the cover-up thereof, and concerning other unlawful activities, including those relating to the confirmation of Richard Kleindienst as Attorney General of the United States, the electronic surveillance of private citizens, the break-in into the offices of Dr. Lewis Fielding, and the campaign financing practices of the Committee to Re-elect the President.

(5) In disregard of the rule of law, he knowingly misused the executive power by interfering with agencies of the executive branch, including the Federal Bureau of Investigation, the Criminal Division, and the Office of Watergate Special Prosecution Force, of the Department of Justice, and the Central

Intelligence Agency, in violation of his duty to take care that the laws be faithfully executed.

In all of this, Richard M. Nixon has acted in a manner contrary to his trust as President and subversive of constitutional government, to the great prejudice of the cause of law and justice and to the manifest injury of the people of the United States.

Wherefore Richard M. Nixon, by such conduct, warrants impeachment and trial, and removal from office.

Article III

In his conduct of the office of President of the United States, Richard M. Nixon, contrary to his oath faithfully to execute the office of President of the United States and, to the best of his ability, preserve, protect, and defend the Constitution of the United States, and in violation of his constitutional duty to take care that the laws be faithfully executed, has failed without lawful cause or excuse to produce papers and things as directed by duly authorized subpoenas issued by the Committee on the Judiciary of the House of Representatives on April 11, 1974, May 15, 1974, May 30, 1974, and June 24, 1974, and willfully disobeyed such subpoenas. The subpoenaed papers and things were deemed necessary by the Committee in order to resolve by direct evidence fundamental, factual questions relating to Presidential direction, knowledge, or approval of actions demonstrated by other evidence to be substantial grounds for impeachment of the President. In refusing to produce these papers and things, Richard M. Nixon, substituting his judgment as to what materials were necessary for the inquiry, interposed the powers of the Presidency against the lawful subpoenas of the House of Representatives, thereby assuming to himself functions and judgments necessary to the exercise of the sole power of impeachment vested by the Constitution in the House of Representatives.

In all of this, Richard M. Nixon has acted in a manner contrary to his trust as President and subversive of constitutional government, to the great prejudice of the cause of law and justice, and to the manifest injury of the people of the United States.

Wherefore Richard M. Nixon, by such conduct, warrants impeachment and trial, and removal from office.

Article IV

In his conduct of the office of President of the United States, Richard M. Nixon, in violation of his constitutional oath faithfully to execute the office of President of the United States and, to the best of his ability, preserve, protect, and defend the Constitution of the United States, and in disregard of his constitutional duty to take care that the laws be faithfully executed, did receive emoluments from the United States in excess of the compensation provided by law pursuant to Article II, Section 1, Clause 7 of the Constitution, and did willfully attempt to evade the payment of a portion of Federal income taxes due and owing by him for the years 1969, 1970, 1971, and 1972, in that:

(1) He, during the period for which he has been elected President, unlawfully received compensation in the form of government expenditures at and on his privately-owned properties located in or near San Clemente, California, and Key Biscayne, Florida.

(2) He knowingly and fraudulently failed to report certain income and claimed deductions in the year 1969, 1970, 1971, and 1972 on his Federal income tax returns which were not authorized by law, including deductions for a gift of papers to the United States valued at approximately $576,000.

In all of this Richard M. Nixon has acted in a manner contrary to his trust as President and subversive of constitutional government, to the great prejudice of the cause of law and justice and to the manifest injury of the people of the United States.

Wherefore Richard M. Nixon, by such conduct, warrants impeachment and trial, and removal from office.

Article V

In his conduct of the office of President of the United States, Richard M. Nixon, in violation of his constitutional oath faithfully to execute the office of President of the United States and, to the best of his ability, preserve, protect, and defend the Constitution of the United States, and in disregard of his constitutional duty to take care that the laws be faithfully executed, on and subsequent to March 17, 1969, authorized, ordered, and ratified the concealment from the Congress of false and misleading statements concerning the existence, scope and nature of American bombing operations in Cambodia in derogation of the power of the Congress to declare war, to make appropriations and to raise and support armies, and by such conduct warrants impeachment and trial and removal from office.

Notes

1. A court later ruled in *Nadar v. Bork* that this act was in fact illegal.

2. Congressional Quarterly, *Watergate: Chronology of a Crisis* (Washington, D.C.: Congressional Quarterly, 1973).

❧ 31 ❧

Impeachment Investigation of Bill Clinton

(1998)

T HE IMPEACHMENT INVESTIGATION of President Bill Clinton may pass into history as a blight on the administration of a single president, or may turn out to be a transformative event in the evolution of the American presidency. Unlike the impeachment of Andrew Johnson, it has not been about high politics and clashes between branches over issues of great national importance. Unlike the impeachment proceedings against Richard Nixon, it has not been about a threat to the very constitutional order of the nation. From one perspective, it was about public integrity and whether the president committed perjury and obstructed justice. However, from another perspective, it has not even been about the president's public conduct of his office or anything directly connected to his official duties. It began as an investigation about financial transactions that took place more than a decade before Clinton was elected president, and it was transformed into an investigation about his relationship with a White House intern.

The Whitewater Affair

In January 1994 Attorney General Janet Reno appointed a special prosecutor, Robert Fiske Jr., to investigate what has since become known as the "Whitewater Affair." In August 1994 a three-judge panel replaced Fiske with Kenneth W. Starr, a former federal judge, a former Republican solicitor general, and a member of a Chicago law firm.

Whitewater was a failed resort built in Arkansas while Clinton was governor of that state. Many of Clinton's close friends, political allies, and business associates had invested in the project. Prosecutors ultimately determined that the failed Whitewater project involved numerous illegal transactions, including the fraudulent use of banks. By the end of 1998, nine individuals had pled guilty to various crimes and three others had been convicted by juries, while two prosecutions had ended in acquittals or mistrials.

Throughout the investigation many observers questioned Starr's tactics. Most troubling were grand jury leaks to the press that appeared to come from Starr's office. Many of the president's supporters as well as nonpartisan observers saw Starr in sharp contrast with both Archibald Cox and Leon Jaworski in their investigations of President Nixon. While investigating Nixon both men avoided any partisan political activities and did everything possible to prevent leaks about the investigation. The Starr investigation, on the other hand, had acquired overtones of political motivation. Thus, even as Starr brought charges against President Clinton, the White House called for an investigation of the investigator.

The Paula Jones Lawsuit

While Starr's investigation was progressing without much public interest, the president faced a civil lawsuit brought by Paula Jones, a former state employee in Arkansas. She alleged that in May 1991 Clinton had invited her to a hotel room in Little Rock where he made a crude sexual advance. Jones did not make any legal claim at the time of this alleged incident or during the next two years while Clinton ran for president and won election. In May 1994, however, she filed a sexual harassment suit against the president. Clinton argued he was immune from civil suits while in office, but in early 1997 the Supreme Court ruled against him. In *Clinton v. Jones* the Court unanimously held that the president was not immune from a civil lawsuit while in office. Ironically, as it turned out, the Court noted that such a suit would not affect the president's ability to govern or perform the duties of his office.

After this favorable ruling, Jones's lawyers began taking videotaped depositions from the president at the White House. Many of the questions focused on whether Clinton had sexual relations with or had sexually harassed White House employees. During these depositions Clinton was asked about his relationship to a White House intern named Monica Lewinsky, and whether he had ever had "sexual relations" with Lewinsky. Jones's lawyers asked poorly worded questions and Judge Susan Webber Wright agreed to a narrow definition of "sexual relations." Clinton denied having a "sexual relationship" with Lewinsky. Eventually the judge ruled that questions about Clinton and Lewinsky were not necessary to Jones's suit. Subsequently Judge Webber Wright dismissed the suit, explaining that even if all of Jones's allegations were true, she did not have any grounds to sue Clinton. Jones's lawyers appealed that decision.

The Lewinsky Matter

Meanwhile, independent counsel Starr obtained tapes of telephone conversations between Lewinsky and Linda Tripp, a former White House em-

In 1998 Bill Clinton became only the third president in U.S. history to have Congress begin formal impeachment proceedings against him.

ployee and onetime confidant of Lewinsky. Without Lewinsky's knowledge, Tripp secretly taped conversations concerning Lewinsky's relationship with President Clinton and her hopes that the president would pull strings to get her a job. The supposed connection between Lewinsky and the White-water investigation lay in the implication that the president might be obstructing justice by asking Lewinsky to lie in the Jones case in return for a job. On this basis Attorney General Reno agreed to let Starr expand his probe into the Jones case.

Over the spring and summer of 1998 Tripp, Lewinsky, Lewinsky's mother, the president's personal secretary, dozens of White House aides, and eventually the president were called to testify before the Whitewater grand jury. At the heart of this investigation was whether the president had committed perjury when being deposed by Jones's lawyers, whether he had attempted to obstruct justice by influencing Lewinsky and others to lie about his relationship with Lewinsky, and whether he had tried to hide evidence about his relationship with Lewinsky.

What had begun as an investigation about a land deal gone sour had turned into a scandal involving the president and a young White House intern. Throughout the first seven months of 1998 the president publicly denied any involvement with Lewinsky, misleading his friends, supporters, and even his own family.

The Response to Starr and the Lewinsky Scandal

On August 17, 1998, President Clinton gave videotaped testimony from the White House to Starr's grand jury. That night the president addressed the nation, admitting to an inappropriate relationship with Lewinsky and apologizing for misleading the nation about his relationship with her. Clinton asserted that his earlier answers to Paula Jones's lawyers had been "legally accurate" but that he "did not volunteer information." He admitted his relationship with Lewinsky "was not appropriate. In fact, it was wrong." He declared it was "a critical lapse in judgment and a personal failure" for which he took sole responsibility. He apologized for his public statements denying the affair.

In addition to apologizing for his behavior, Clinton attacked Starr and those behind the Jones lawsuit. He asserted that the Jones case was a "politically inspired lawsuit" and that the Whitewater investigation had found "no evidence of wrongdoing by me or my wife." Clinton reminded the nation that the independent counsel investigation had failed to find anything illegal about Clinton's relationship to Whitewater, and so the "investigation moved on to my staff and friends, then into my private life." Clinton told the nation that "even presidents have private lives" and it was "time to stop the pursuit of personal destruction and the prying into private lives and get on with our national life."

Reaction to the speech was mixed. Many in Congress thought the president should have been more contrite, more apologetic, and less critical of Starr. But polls showed the majority of Americans, while disappointed and upset with the president, did not believe he should be impeached for his behavior. With a robust economy and virtually full employment, support for Clinton's handling of the job as president remained strong. Despite the scandal, and a more than 15 percent drop in the stock market during the next month, the president's popularity remained high. Americans seemed ready to distinguish between Clinton's public handling of the job and this appalling failure in his personal life.

Shortly before the 1998 congressional elections Starr handed his report to the House of Representatives. On the basis of his investigation, Starr found eleven possible grounds for impeachment (see p. 272). None were about Whitewater or any connected illegal transactions. All involved the president's sexual behavior with Monica Lewinsky and accusations that he had obstructed justice in trying to keep his behavior secret. Starr included the president's claims of executive privilege, and Secret Service claims of a new privilege for secret service agents within his charges of abuse of power and obstruction of justice.

The Republican majority in the House with the support of thirty-one Democrats immediately voted to implement procedures for an open-ended impeachment investigation of the president. Holding an eleven-seat majority in the House, a vote to impeach the president seemed likely. The committee soon released the Starr report, which contained numerous details about Clinton's sexual relationship with Lewinsky. The report was available over the Internet, sold in bookstores, and excerpted in newspapers. At times salacious, at times boring, the report again seemed to have little effect on the president's popular standing.

Shortly after releasing the report, the Republican majority on the Judiciary Committee voted to release the tape of Clinton's grand jury testimony. Despite widespread expectations, the release of the tape had no profound impact on public attitudes toward the impeachment inquiry. Public opinion continued to reject President Clinton's removal from office.

The 1998 Election: The People Speak

During the last weeks of the 1998 congressional campaigns, the Republican Party tried to focus debate on the Lewinsky scandal with a multimillion-dollar advertising campaign in key congressional races. Speaker of the House Newt Gingrich predicted the Republicans would gain thirty seats in the House and a few in the Senate. In every midterm election since 1934 the party in the White House had lost seats in Congress; this made Gingrich's prediction seem plausible. However, breaking this sixty-four-year trend, the Democrats picked up five seats in the House and held their own in the Senate. Two incumbent Republicans lost their Senate seats, while only one incumbent Democratic senator was defeated.

Less than one week after the election, Rep. Henry Hyde, Chairman of the Judiciary Committee, announced that he would severely limit the impeachment investigation, and that he would call Starr as one of the few witnesses. Meanwhile, in the face of Republican losses in the election, Gingrich announced he would not seek another term as Speaker of the House and that he would resign from Congress before his newly elected term would begin. Also that week, the president and Jones's lawyers reached an out-of-court settlement finally ending the Jones sexual harassment case. The president agreed to pay Jones $850,000 but would not apologize to her (something that had been a stumbling block to an earlier settlement).

The Hyde committee pressed forward, holding its first impeachment hearings on November 19, 1998. Confusion over the reach of the phrase "high Crimes and Misdemeanors" reigned. On the one hand, numerous legal scholars and 400 leading historians sent signed petitions to Congress asserting that whatever President Clinton had done, it was not an impeachable offense. On the other hand some scholars argued that lying under oath, even in a civil lawsuit, was enough to make the case for impeachment.

Relying on history, such as the material found in this book, some scholars testifying before a subcommittee of the House Judiciary Committee in November 1998 offered conflicting views as to whether Congress has the power to censure the president given that censure by Congress of any officials other than members of Congress is not found in the Constitution. Whether censure is an appropriate response to President Clinton's behavior—or whether impeachment will in the end prove to be the direction Congress moves—will in part be determined by how Congress and the American people view the traditions and precedents of our political system.

STARR RECOMMENDATIONS

THERE IS SUBSTANTIAL AND CREDIBLE INFORMATION THAT PRESIDENT CLINTON COMMITTED ACTS THAT MAY CONSTITUTE GROUNDS FOR AN IMPEACHMENT

Introduction

Pursuant to Section 595(c) of Title 28, the Office of Independent Counsel (OIC) hereby submits substantial and credible information that President Clinton obstructed justice during the *Jones v. Clinton* sexual harassment lawsuit by lying under oath and concealing evidence of his relationship with a young White House intern and federal employee, Monica Lewinsky. After a federal criminal investigation of the President's actions began in January 1998, the President lied under oath to the grand jury and obstructed justice during the grand jury investigation. There also is substantial and credible information that the President's actions with respect to Monica Lewinsky constitute an abuse of authority inconsistent with the President's constitutional duty to faithfully execute the laws.

There is substantial and credible information supporting the following eleven possible grounds for impeachment:

1. President Clinton lied under oath in his civil case when he denied a sexual affair, a sexual relationship, or sexual relations with Monica Lewinsky.

2. President Clinton lied under oath to the grand jury about his sexual relationship with Ms. Lewinsky.

3. In his civil deposition, to support his false statement about the sexual relationship, President Clinton also lied under oath about being alone with Ms. Lewinsky and about the many gifts exchanged between Ms. Lewinsky and him.

4. President Clinton lied under oath in his civil deposition about his discussions with Ms. Lewinsky concerning her involvement in the *Jones* case.

5. During the *Jones* case, the President obstructed justice and had an understanding with Ms. Lewinsky to jointly conceal the truth about their relationship by concealing gifts subpoenaed by Ms. Jones's attorneys.

6. During the *Jones* case, the President obstructed justice and had an understanding with Ms. Lewinsky to jointly conceal the truth of their relationship from the judicial process by a scheme that included the following means: (i) Both the President and Ms. Lewinsky understood that they would lie under oath in the *Jones* case about their sexual relationship; (ii) the President suggested to Ms. Lewinsky that she prepare an affidavit that, for the President's purposes, would memorialize her testimony under oath and could be used to prevent questioning of both of them about their relationship; (iii) Ms. Lewinsky signed and filed the false affidavit; (iv) the President used Ms. Lewinsky's false affidavit at his deposition in an attempt to head off questions about Ms. Lewinsky; and (v) when that failed, the President lied under oath at his civil deposition about the relationship with Ms. Lewinsky.

7. President Clinton endeavored to obstruct justice by helping Ms. Lewinsky obtain a job in New York at a time when she would have been a witness harmful to him were she to tell the truth in the *Jones* case.

8. President Clinton lied under oath in his civil deposition about his discussions with Vernon Jordan concerning Ms. Lewinsky's involvement in the *Jones* case.

9. The President improperly tampered with a potential witness by attempting to corruptly influence the testimony of his personal secretary, Betty Currie, in the days after his civil deposition.

10. President Clinton endeavored to obstruct justice during the grand jury investigation by refusing to testify for seven months *and* lying to senior White House aides with knowledge that they would relay the President's false state-

ments to the grand jury—and did thereby deceive, obstruct, and impede the grand jury.

11. President Clinton abused his constitutional authority by (i) lying to the public and the Congress in January 1998 about his relationship with Ms. Lewinsky; (ii) promising at that time to cooperate fully with the grand jury investigation; (iii) later refusing six invitations to testify voluntarily to the grand jury; (iv) invoking Executive Privilege; (v) lying to the grand jury in August 1998; and (vi) lying again to the public and Congress on August 17, 1998—all as part of an effort to hinder, impede, and deflect possible inquiry by the Congress of the United States.

The first two possible grounds for impeachment concern the President's lying under oath about the nature of his relationship with Ms. Lewinsky. The details associated with those grounds are, by their nature, explicit. The President's testimony unfortunately has rendered the details essential with respect to those two grounds, as will be explained in those grounds.

❧ 32 ☙

Majority Counsel's Charges Against Clinton
(1998)

AFTER INDEPENDENT COUNSEL Kenneth W. Starr handed over to Congress on September 9, 1998, dozens of boxes of evidence obtained through the investigation of President Bill Clinton, the members and staff of the House Judiciary Committee took several weeks to sift through the mountainous amount of material. On October 5, 1998, David P. Schippers, the majority counsel on the House Judiciary Committee, reported to the committee that there was "substantial and credible evidence" to support an inquiry into possible impeachable conduct by the president.

Schippers took Starr's eleven original suggested counts, dropped one (abuse of power) and added or redefined several others. In total he found fifteen possible counts of impeachable behavior. The minority counsel for the committee, Democrat Abbe Lowell, disagreed. Whether there were eleven or fifteen counts was irrelevant, Lowell argued, because the underlying facts contained in Starr's report simply did not rise to the level of impeachable offenses. The following document is Schippers's expanded list of fifteen grounds for possible impeachment of President Clinton.

I

There is substantial and credible evidence that the President may have been part of a conspiracy with Monica Lewinsky and others to obstruct justice and the due administration of justice by:

(A) Providing false and misleading testimony under oath in a civil deposition and before the grand jury;

(B) Withholding evidence and causing evidence to be withheld and concealed; and

(C) Tampering with prospective witnesses in a civil lawsuit and before a federal grand jury.

The President and Ms. Lewinsky had developed a "cover story" to conceal their activities. (M. L. 8/6/98 GJ, at pp. 54-55, 234). On December 6, 1997, the President learned that Ms. Lewinsky's name had appeared on the *Jones v. Clinton* witness list. (Clinton GJ, p. 84). He informed Ms. Lewinsky of that fact on December 17, 1997, and the two agreed that they would employ the same cover story in the *Jones* case. (M. L. 8/6/98 GJ, pp. 122-123; M. L. 2/1/98 Proffer). The President at that time suggested that an affidavit might be enough to prevent Ms. Lewinsky from testifying. (M. L. 8/6/98 GJ, pp. 122-123). On December 19, 1997, Ms. Lewinsky was subpoenaed to give a deposition in the *Jones* case. (M. L. 8/6/98 GJ, p. 128).

Thereafter, the record tends to establish that the following events took place:

1) In the second week of December, 1997, Ms. Lewinsky told Ms. Tripp that she would lie if called to testify and tried to convince Ms. Tripp to do the same. (M. L. 8/6/98 GJ, p. 127).

2) Ms. Lewinsky attempted on several occasions to get Ms. Tripp to contact the White House before giving testimony in the *Jones* case. (Tripp 7/16/98 GJ, p. 75; M. L. 8/6/98 GJ, p. 71).

3) Ms. Lewinsky participated in preparing a false and intentionally misleading affidavit to be filed in the *Jones* case. (M. L. 8/6/98 GJ, pp. 200-203).

4) Ms. Lewinsky provided a copy of the draft affidavit to a third party for approval and discussed changes calculated to mislead. (M. L. 8/6/98 GJ, pp. 200-202).

Chairman Henry Hyde (center) and other members of the House Judiciary Committee receive Kenneth W. Starr's summary report on the investigation of President Bill Clinton.

5) Ms. Lewinsky and the President talked by phone on January 6, 1998, and agreed that she would give false and misleading answers to questions about her job at the Pentagon. (M. L. 8/6/98 GJ, p. 197).

6) On January 7, 1998, Ms. Lewinsky signed the false and misleading affidavit. (M. L. 8/6/98 GJ, p. 203). Conspirators intended to use the affidavit to avoid Ms. Lewinsky's giving a deposition. (M. L. 8/6/98 GJ, pp. 122-123; M. L. 2/1/98 Proffer).

7) After Ms. Lewinsky's name surfaced, conspirators began to employ code names in their contacts. (M. L. 8/6/98 GJ, pp. 215-217).

8) On December 28, 1997, Ms. Lewinsky and the President met at the White House and discussed the subpoena she had received. Ms. Lewinsky suggested that she conceal the gifts received from the President. (M. L. 8/6/98 GJ, p. 152).

9) Shortly thereafter, the President's personal secretary, Betty Currie, picked up a box of the gifts from Ms. Lewinsky. (Currie 5/6/98 GJ, pp. 107-108; M. L. 8/6/98 GJ, pp. 154-156).

10) Betty Currie hid the box of gifts under her bed at home. (Currie 5/6/98 GJ, pp. 107-108; Currie 1/27/98 GJ, pp. 57-58).

11) The President gave false answers to questions contained in Interrogatories in the *Jones* case. (V2-DC-53; V2-DC-104).

12) On December 31, 1997, Ms. Lewinsky, at the suggestion of a third party, deleted 50 draft notes to the President. (M. L. 8/1/98 OIC Interview, p. 13). She had already been subpoenaed in the *Jones* case.

13) On January 17, 1998, the President's attorney produced Ms. Lewinsky's false affidavit at the President's deposition and the President adopted it as true.

14) On January 17, 1998, in his deposition, the President gave false and misleading testimony under oath concerning his relationship with Ms. Lewinsky about the gifts she had given him and several other matters. (Clinton Dep., pp. 49-84; M. L. 7/27/98 OIC Interview, pp. 12-15).

15) The President, on January 18, 1998, and thereafter, coached his personal secretary, Betty Currie, to give a false and misleading account of the Lewinsky relationship if called to testify. (Currie 1/27/98 GJ, pp. 71-74, 81).

16) The President narrated elaborate detailed false accounts of his relationship with Monica Lewinsky to prospective witnesses with the intention that those false accounts would be repeated in testimony. (Currie 1/27/98 GJ, pp. 71-74, 81; Podesta 6/16/98 GJ, pp. 88-92; Blumenthal 6/4/98 GJ, pp. 49-51; Blumenthal 6/25/98 GJ, p. 8; Bowles 4/2/98 GJ, pp. 83-84; Ickes 6/10/98 GJ, p. 73; Ickes 8/5/98 GJ, p. 88).

17) On August 17, 1998, the President gave false and misleading testimony under oath to a federal grand jury on the following points: his relationship with Ms. Lewinsky, his testimony in the January 17, 1998 deposition, his conversations with various individuals and his knowledge of Ms. Lewinsky's affidavit and its falsity. . . .

II

There is substantial and credible evidence that the President may have aided, abetted, counseled, and procured Monica Lewinsky to file and caused to be filed a false affidavit in the case of *Jones v. Clinton, et al.,* in violation of 18 U.S.C. 1623 and 2.

The record tends to establish the following:

In a telephone conversation with Ms. Lewinsky on December 17, 1997, the President told her that her name was on the witness list in the *Jones* case. (M. L. 8/6/98 GJ, p.123). The President then suggested that she might submit an affidavit to avoid testimony. (Id.). Both the President and Ms. Lewinsky knew that the affidavit would need to be false in order to accomplish that result. In that conversation, the President also suggested "You know, you can always say you were coming to see Betty or that you were bringing me letters." (M. L. 8/6/98

GJ, p.123). Ms. Lewinsky knew exactly what he meant because it was the same "cover story" that they had agreed upon earlier. (M. L. 8/6/98 GJ, p.124).

Thereafter, Ms. Lewinsky discussed the affidavit with and furnished a copy to a confidant of the President for approval. (M. L. 8/6/98 GJ, pp. 200-202). Ms. Lewinsky signed the false affidavit and caused her attorney to provide it to the President's lawyer for use in the *Jones* case.

III

There is substantial and credible evidence that the President may have aided, abetted, counseled, and procured Monica Lewinsky in obstruction of justice when she executed and caused to be filed a false affidavit in the case of *Jones v. Clinton, et al.,* with knowledge of the pending proceedings and with the intent to influence, obstruct or impede that proceeding in the due administration of justice, in violation of 18 U.S.C. 1503 and 2.

The record tends to establish that the President not only aided and abetted Monica Lewinsky in preparing, signing and causing to be filed a false affidavit, he also aided and abetted her in using that false affidavit to obstruct justice.

Both Ms. Lewinsky and the President knew that her false affidavit would be used to mislead the Plaintiff's attorneys and the court. Specifically, they intended that the affidavit would be sufficient to avoid Ms. Lewinsky being required to give a deposition in the *Jones* case. Moreover, the natural and probable effect of the false statement was interference with the due administration of justice. If the court and the *Jones* attorneys were convinced by the affidavit, there would be no deposition of Ms. Lewinsky, and the Plaintiff's attorneys would be denied the ability to learn about material facts and to decide whether to introduce evidence of those facts.

Mr. Clinton caused his attorney to employ the knowingly false affidavit not only to avoid Ms. Lewinsky's deposition, but to preclude the attorneys from interrogating the President about the same subject. (Clinton Dep., p. 54).

IV

There is substantial and credible evidence that the President may have engaged in misprision of Monica Lewinsky's felonies of submitting a false affidavit and of obstructing the due administration of justice both by taking affirmative steps to conceal those felonies, and by failing to disclose the felonies though under a constitutional and statutory duty to do so, in violation of 18 U.S.C. 4.

The record tends to establish the following:

Monica Lewinsky admitted to the commission of two felonies: Signing a false affidavit under oath (M. L. 8/6/98 GJ, pp. 204-205) and endeavoring to obstruct justice by using the false affidavit to mislead the court and the lawyers in the *Jones* case so that she would not be deposed and be required to give evidence concerning her activities with the President. (M. L. 8/6/98 GJ, pp. 122-123; M. L. 2/1/98 Proffer). In addition, the President was fully aware that those felonies had been committed when he gave his deposition testimony on January 17, 1998. (Clinton Dep., p. 54).

Nonetheless, Mr. Clinton took affirmative steps to conceal these felonies, including allowing his attorney, in his presence, to use the affidavit and to suggest that it was true. (Clinton Dep., p. 54). More importantly, the President himself, while being questioned by his own counsel referring to one of the clearly false paragraphs in Ms. Lewinsky's affidavit, stated, "That is absolutely true." (Clinton Dep., p. 203).

More importantly, the President is the chief law enforcement officer of the United States. He is under a Constitutional duty to take care that the laws be faithfully executed. When confronted with direct knowledge of the commission of a felony, he is required by his office, as is every other law enforcement officer, agent or attorney, to bring to the attention of the appropriate authorities the fact of the felony and the identity of the perpetrator. If he did not do so, the President could be guilty of misprision of felony.

V

There is substantial and credible evidence that the President may have testified falsely under oath in his deposition in *Jones v. Clinton, et al.* on January 17, 1998 regarding his relationship with Monica Lewinsky, in violation of 18 U.S.C. 1621 and 1623.

The record tends to establish the following:

There are three instances where credible evidence exists that the President may have testified falsely about this relationship:

(1) when he denied a "sexual relationship" in sworn Answers to Interrogatories (V2-DC-53 and V2-DC-104);

(2) when he denied having an "extramarital sexual affair" in his deposition (Clinton Dep., p. 78); and

(3) when he denied having "sexual relations" or "an affair" with Monica Lewinsky in his deposition. (Clinton Dep., p. 78).

When the President denied a sexual relationship he was not bound by the definition the court had provided. There is substantial evidence obtained from

Ms. Lewinsky, the President's grand jury testimony, and DNA test results that Ms. Lewinsky performed sexual acts with the President on numerous occasions. Those terms, given their common meaning, could reasonably be construed to include oral sex. The President also denied having sexual relations with Ms. Lewinsky (Clinton Dep., p. 78), as the court defined the term. (Clinton Dep., Ex. 1). In the context of the lawsuit and the wording of that definition, there is substantial evidence that the President's explanation given to the grand jury is an afterthought and is unreasonably narrow under the circumstances. Consequently, there is substantial evidence that the President's denial under oath in his deposition of a "sexual relationship", a "sexual affair" or "sexual relations" with Ms. Lewinsky was not true.

VI

There is substantial and credible evidence that the President may have given false testimony under oath before the federal grand jury on August 17, 1998 concerning his relationship with Monica Lewinsky, in violation of 18 U.S.C. 1621 and 1623.

The record tends to establish the following:

During his grand jury testimony, the President admitted only to "inappropriate intimate contact" with Monica Lewinsky. (Clinton GJ, p. 10). He did not admit to any specific acts. He categorically denied ever touching Ms. Lewinsky on the breasts or genitalia for the purpose of giving her sexual gratification. There is, however, substantial contradictory evidence from Ms. Lewinsky. She testified at length and with specificity that the President kissed and fondled her breasts on numerous occasions during their encounters, and at times there was also direct genital contact. (M. L. 8/26/98 Dep., pp. 30-38, 50-53). Moreover, her testimony is corroborated by several of her friends. (Davis 3/17/98 GJ, p. 20; Erbland 2/12/98 GJ, p. 29, 45; Ungvari 3/19/98 GJ, pp. 23-24; Bleiler 1/28/98 OIC Interview, p. 3).

The President described himself as a non-reciprocating recipient of Ms. Lewinsky's services. (Clinton GJ, p. 151). Therefore, he suggested that he did not engage in "sexual relations" within the definition given him at the *Jones* case deposition. (Id). He also testified that his interpretation of the word "cause" in the definition meant the use of force or contact with the intent to arouse or gratify. (Clinton GJ., pp. 17-18). The inference drawn by the Independent Counsel that the President's explanation was merely an afterthought, calculated to explain away testimony that had been proved false by Ms. Lewinsky's evidence, appears credible under the circumstances.

VII

There is substantial and credible evidence that the President may have given false testimony under oath in his deposition given in *Jones v. Clinton, et al.* on January 17, 1998 regarding his statement that he could not recall being alone with Monica Lewinsky and regarding his minimizing the number of gifts that they had exchanged in violation of 18 U.S.C. 1621 and 1623.

The record tends to establish the following:

President Clinton testified at his deposition that he had "no specific recollection" of being alone with Ms. Lewinsky in any room at the White House. (Clinton Dep., p. 59). There is ample evidence from other sources to the contrary. They include: Betty Currie (1/27/98 GJ, pp. 32-33; 5/6/98 GJ, p. 98; 7/22/98 GJ, pp. 25-26); Monica Lewinsky (M. L. 2/1/98 Proffer; M. L. 8/26/98 GJ); several Secret Service Agents and White House logs. Moreover, the President testified in the grand jury that he was "alone" with Ms. Lewinsky in 1996 and 1997 and that he had a "specific recollection" of certain instances when he was alone with her. (Clinton GJ, pp. 30-32). He admitted to the grand jury that he was alone with her on December 28, 1997, only three weeks prior to his deposition testimony. (Clinton GJ, p. 34).

The President was also asked at this deposition whether he had ever given gifts to Ms. Lewinsky. He responded, "I don't recall." He then asked the *Jones* attorney if he knew what they were. After the attorney named specific gifts, the President finally remembered giving Ms. Lewinsky something from the Black Dog. (Clinton Dep., p. 75). That testimony was given less than three weeks after Ms. Currie had picked up a box of the President's gifts and hid them under her bed. (Currie 1/27/98 GJ, pp. 57-58; Currie 5/6/98 GJ, pp. 107-108).

In his grand jury testimony nearly seven months later, he admitted giving Ms. Lewinsky Christmas gifts on December 28, 1997 (Clinton GJ, p. 33) and "on other occasions." (Clinton GJ, p. 36). When confronted with his lack of memory at his deposition, the President responded that his statement "I don't recall" referred to the identity of specific gifts, not whether or not he actually gave her gifts. (Clinton GJ, p. 52).

The President also testified at his deposition that Ms. Lewinsky gave him gifts "once or twice." (Clinton Dep., pp. 76-77). Ms. Lewinsky says that she gave a substantial number of gifts to the President. (M. L. 8/6/98 GJ, pp. 27-28, Ex. M. L.-7). This is corroborated by gifts turned over by Ms. Lewinsky to the Independent Counsel and by a letter to the Independent Counsel from the President's attorney. Thus, there is substantial and credible evidence that the President may have testified falsely about being alone with Monica Lewinsky and the gifts he gave to her.

VIII

There is substantial and credible evidence that the President may have testified falsely under oath in his deposition given in *Jones v. Clinton* on January 17, 1998, concerning conversations with Monica Lewinsky about her involvement in the *Jones* case, in violation of 18 U.S.C. 1621 and 1623.

The record tends to reflect the following:

The President was asked at his deposition if he ever talked to Ms. Lewinsky about the possibility that she would testify in the *Jones* case. He answered, "I'm not sure." He then related a conversation with Ms. Lewinsky where he joked about how the *Jones* attorneys would probably subpoena every female witness with whom he has ever spoken. (Clinton Dep., p. 70). He was also asked whether Ms. Lewinsky told him that she had been subpoenaed. The answer was, "No, I don't know if she had been." (Clinton Dep., p. 68).

There is substantial evidence—much from the President's own grand jury testimony—that those statements are false. The President testified before the grand jury that he spoke with Ms. Lewinsky at the White House on December 28, 1997 about the "prospect that she might have to give testimony." (Clinton GJ, p. 33). He also later testified that Vernon Jordan told him on December 19, 1997 that Ms. Lewinsky had been subpoenaed. (Clinton GJ, p. 42). Mr. Jordan also recalled telling the same thing to the President twice on December 19, 1997, once over the telephone and once in person. (Jordan 5/5/98 GJ, p. 145; Jordan 3/3/98 GJ, pp. 167-170). Despite his deposition testimony, the President admitted that he knew Ms. Lewinsky had been subpoenaed when he met her on December 28, 1997. (Clinton GJ, p. 36). There is substantial and credible evidence that his statement that he was "not sure" if he spoke with Ms. Lewinsky about her testimony is false.

IX

There is substantial and credible evidence that the President may have endeavored to obstruct justice by engaging in a pattern of activity calculated to conceal evidence from the judicial proceedings in *Jones v. Clinton, et al.,* regarding his relationship with Monica Lewinsky, in violation of 18 U.S.C. 1503.

The record tends to establish that on Sunday, December 28, 1997, the President gave Ms. Lewinsky Christmas gifts in the Oval Office during a visit arranged by Ms. Currie. (M. L. 8/6/98 GJ, pp. 149-150). According to Ms. Lewinsky, when she suggested that the gifts he had given her should be concealed because they were the subject of a subpoena, the President stated, "I don't know" or "Let me think about that." (M. L. 8/6/98 GJ, p. 152).

Ms. Lewinsky testified that Ms. Currie contacted her at home several hours later and stated, "I understand you have something to give me" or "the President said you have something to give me." (M. L. 8/6/98 GJ, pp. 154-155). Later that same day, Ms. Currie picked up a box of gifts from Ms. Lewinsky's home. (M. L. 8/6/98 GJ, pp. 156-158; Currie 5/6/98 GJ, pp. 107-108).

The evidence indicates that the President may have instructed Ms. Currie to conceal evidence. The President has denied giving that instruction, and he contended under oath that he advised Ms. Lewinsky to provide all of the gifts to the *Jones* attorneys pursuant to the subpoena. (Clinton GJ, pp. 44-45). In contrast, Ms. Lewinsky testified that the President never challenged her suggestion that the gifts should be concealed. (M. L. 8/26/98 Dep., pp. 58-59).

X

There is substantial and credible evidence that the President may have endeavored to obstruct justice in the case of *Jones v. Clinton, et al.,* by agreeing with Monica Lewinsky on a cover story about their relationship, by causing a false affidavit to be filed by Ms. Lewinsky and by giving false and misleading testimony in the deposition given on January 17, 1998, in violation of 18 U.S.C. 1503.

The record tends to establish that the President and Ms. Lewinsky agreed on false explanations for her private visits to the Oval Office. Ms. Lewinsky testified that when the President contacted her and told her that she was on the *Jones* witness list, he advised her that she could always repeat these cover stories, and he suggested that she file an affidavit. (M. L. 8/6/98 GJ, p. 123). After this conversation, Ms. Lewinsky filed a false affidavit. The President learned of Ms. Lewinsky's affidavit prior to his deposition in the *Jones* case. (Jordan 5/5/98 GJ, p. 24-25).

Subsequently, during his deposition, the President stated that he never had a sexual relationship or affair with Ms. Lewinsky. He further stated that the paragraph in Ms. Lewinsky's affidavit denying a sexual relationship with the President was "absolutely true," even though his attorney had argued that the affidavit covered "sex of any kind in any manner, shape or form." (Clinton Dep., pp. 54, 104).

XI

There is substantial and credible evidence that the President may have endeavored to obstruct justice by helping Monica Lewinsky to obtain a job in New York City at a time when she would have given evidence adverse to Mr.

Clinton if she told the truth in the case of *Jones v. Clinton, et al.,* in violation of 18 U.S.C. 1503 and 1512.

The record tends to establish the following:

In October, 1997, the President and Ms. Lewinsky discussed the possibility of Vernon Jordan assisting Ms. Lewinsky in finding a job in New York. (M. L. 8/6/98 GJ, pp. 103-104). On November 5, 1997, Mr. Jordan and Ms. Lewinsky discussed employment possibilities, and Mr. Jordan told her that she came "highly recommended." (M. L. 7/31/98 Int., p. 15; e-mail from Lewinsky to Catherine Davis, 11/6/97).

However, no significant action was taken on Ms. Lewinsky's behalf until December, when the *Jones* attorneys identified Ms. Lewinsky as a witness. Within days, after Mr. Jordan again met with Ms. Lewinsky, he contacted a number of people in the private sector who could help Ms. Lewinsky find work in New York. (Jordan 3/3/98 GJ, pp. 48-49).

Additional evidence indicates that on the day Ms. Lewinsky signed a false affidavit denying a sexual relationship with the President, Mr. Jordan contacted the President and discussed the affidavit. (Jordan 5/5/98 GJ, pp. 223-225). The next day, Ms. Lewinsky interviewed with MacAndrews & Forbes, an interview arranged with Mr. Jordan's assistance. (M. L. 8/6/98 GJ, pp. 205-206). When Ms. Lewinsky told Mr. Jordan that the interview went poorly, Mr. Jordan contacted the CEO of MacAndrews & Forbes. (Perelman 4/23/98 Dep., p. 10; Telephone Calls, Table 37, Call 6). The following day, Ms. Lewinsky was offered the job, and Mr. Jordan contacted the White House with the message "mission accomplished." (Jordan 5/28/98 GJ, p. 39).

In sum, Mr. Jordan secured a job for Ms. Lewinsky with a phone call placed on the day after Ms. Lewinsky signed a false affidavit protecting the President. Evidence indicates that this timing was not coincidental.

XII

There is substantial and credible evidence that the President may have testified falsely under oath in his deposition given in *Jones v. Clinton, et al.* on January 17, 1998, concerning his conversations with Vernon Jordan about Ms. Lewinsky, in violation of 18 U.S.C. 1621 and 1623.

The record tends to establish that Mr. Jordan and the President discussed Ms. Lewinsky on various occasions from the time she was served until she fired Mr. Carter and hired Mr. Ginsburg. This is contrary to the President's deposition testimony. The President was asked in his deposition whether anyone besides his attorney told him that Ms. Lewinsky had been served. "I don't think so," he responded. He then said that Bruce Lindsey was the first person who told him. (Clinton Dep., pp. 68-69). In the Grand Jury, the President was specifically asked if Mr. Jordan informed him that Ms. Lewinsky was under subpoena. "No sir," he answered. (Clinton GJ, p. 40). Later in that testimony, when confronted with a specific date (the evening of December 19, 1997), the President admitted that he spoke with Mr. Jordan about the subpoena. (Clinton GJ, p. 42; Jordan 5/5/98 GJ, p. 145; Jordan 3/3/98 GJ, pp. 167-170). Both the President and Mr. Jordan testified in the Grand Jury that Mr. Jordan informed the President on January 7 that Ms. Lewinsky had signed the affidavit. (Clinton GJ, p. 74; Jordan 5/5/98 GJ, 222-228). Ms. Lewinsky said she too informed the President of the subpoena. (M. L. 8/20/98 GJ, p. 66).

The President was also asked during his deposition if anyone reported to him within the past two weeks (from January 17, 1998) that they had a conversation with Monica Lewinsky concerning the lawsuit. The President said, "I don't think so." (Clinton Dep., p. 72). As noted, Mr. Jordan told the President on January 7, 1998, that Ms. Lewinsky signed the affidavit. (Jordan 5/5/98 GJ, pp. 222-228). In addition, the President was asked if he had a conversation with Mr. Jordan where Ms. Lewinsky's name was mentioned. He said yes, that Mr. Jordan mentioned that she asked for advice about moving to New York. Actually, the President had conversations with Mr. Jordan concerning three general subjects: Choosing an attorney to represent Ms. Lewinsky after she had been subpoenaed (Jordan 5/28/98 GJ, p. 4); Ms. Lewinsky's subpoena and the contents of her executed Affidavit (Jordan 5/5/98 GJ, pp. 142-145; Jordan 3/3/98 GJ, pp. 167-172; Jordan 3/5/98 GJ, pp. 24-25, 223, 225); and Vernon Jordan's success in procuring a New York job for Ms. Lewinsky. (Jordan 5/28/98 GJ, p. 39).

XIII

There is substantial and credible evidence that the President may have endeavored to obstruct justice and engage in witness tampering in attempting to coach and influence the testimony of Betty Currie before the grand jury, in violation of 18 U.S.C. 1512.

The record tends to establish the following:

According to Ms. Currie, the President contacted her on the day he was deposed in the *Jones* case and asked her to meet him the following day. (Currie 1/27/98 GJ, pp. 65-66). The next day, Ms. Currie met with the President, and he asked her whether she agreed with a series of possibly false statements, including, "We were never really alone," "You could always see and hear everything," and "Monica came on to me and I never touched her, right?" (Currie 1/27/98 GJ, pp. 71-74). Ms. Currie stated that the President's tone and demeanor indicated that he wanted her to agree with these statements. (Currie 1/27/98 GJ, pp. 73-74). According to Ms. Currie, the President called her into the Oval Office several days later and reiterated his previous statements using the same tone and demeanor. (Currie 1/27/98 GJ, p. 81). Ms. Currie later stated that she felt she was free to disagree with the President. (Currie 7/22/98 GJ, p.23).

The President testified concerning those statements before the grand jury, and he did not deny that he made them. (Clinton 8/17/98 GJ, pp. 133-139). Rather, the President testified that in some of the statements he was referring only to meetings with Ms. Lewinsky in 1997, and that he intended the word "alone" to mean the entire Oval Office Complex. (Clinton 8/17/98 GJ, pp. 133-139).

XIV

There is substantial and credible evidence that the President may have engaged in witness tampering by coaching prospective witnesses and by narrating elaborate detailed false accounts of his relationship with Ms. Lewinsky as if those stories were true, intending that the witnesses believe the story and testify to it before a grand jury, in violation of 18 U.S.C. 1512.

The record tends to establish the following:

John Podesta, the President's Deputy Chief of Staff, testified that the President told him that he did not have sex with Ms. Lewinsky "in any way whatsoever" and "that they had not had oral sex." (Podesta 6/16/98 GJ, p. 92). Mr. Podesta repeated these statements to the grand jury. (Podesta 6/23/98 GJ, p. 80).

Sidney Blumenthal, an Assistant to the President, said that the President told him more detailed stories. He testified that the President told him that Ms. Lewinsky, who the President claimed had a reputation as a stalker, came at him, made sexual demands of him, and threatened him, but he rebuffed her. (Blumenthal 6/4/98 GJ, pp. 46-51). Mr. Blumenthal further testified that the President told him that he could recall placing only one call to Ms. Lewinsky. (Blumenthal 6/25/98 GJ, p. 27). Mr. Blumenthal mentioned to the President that there were press reports that he, the President, had made telephone calls to Ms. Lewinsky, and also left voice mail messages. The President then told Mr. Blumenthal that he remembered calling Ms. Lewinsky after Betty Currie's brother died. (Blumenthal 6/4/98 GJ, p. 50).

XV

There is substantial and credible evidence that the President may have given false testimony under oath before the federal grand jury on August 17, 1998 concerning his knowledge of the contents of Monica Lewinsky's affidavit and his knowledge of remarks made in his presence by his counsel in violation of 18 U.S.C. 1621 and 1623.

The record tends to establish the following:

During the deposition, the President's attorney attempted to thwart questions pertaining to Ms. Lewinsky by citing her affidavit and asserting to the court that the affidavit represents that there "is absolutely no sex of any kind, manner, shape or form, with President Clinton." (Clinton Dep., p. 54). At several points in his grand jury testimony, the President maintained that he cannot be held responsible for this representation made by his lawyer because he was not paying attention to the interchange between his lawyer and the court. (Clinton GJ, pp. 25-26, 30, 59). The videotape of the deposition shows the President apparently listening intently to the interchange. In addition, Mr. Clinton's counsel represented to the court that the President was fully aware of the affidavit and its contents. (Clinton Dep., p. 54).

The President's own attorney asked him during the deposition whether Ms. Lewinsky's affidavit denying a sexual relationship was "true and accurate." The President was unequivocal; he said, "This is absolutely true." (Clinton Dep., p. 204). Ms. Lewinsky later said the affidavit contained false and misleading statements. (M. L. 8/6/98 GJ, pp. 204-205). The President explained to the grand jury that Ms. Lewinsky may have believed that her affidavit was true if she believed "sexual relationship" meant intercourse. (Clinton GJ, pp. 22-23). However, counsel did not ask the President if Ms. Lewinsky thought it was true; he asked the President if it was, in fact, a true statement. The President was bound by the court's definition at that point, and under his own interpretation of that definition, Ms. Lewinsky engaged in sexual relations. An affidavit denying this, by the President's own interpretation of the definition, is false.

That is my report to this Committee. The guiding object of our efforts over the past three weeks has been to search for the truth. We felt it our obligation to follow the facts and the law wherever they might lead, fairly and impartially. If this Committee sees fit to proceed to the next level of inquiry, we will continue to do so under your guidance.

❧ 33 ❧
Clinton's Defense
(1998)

IN SEPTEMBER 1998 independent counsel Kenneth Starr submitted to Congress his findings that there was evidence of possible impeachable conduct by President Bill Clinton. Congress voted to release his summary report to the public, before any member of Congress or Clinton's defense team had an opportunity to read it, and then referred the matter to the House Judiciary Committee. As the committee geared up to hold its first hearing on October 5, 1998, the president's lawyers, anticipating the public disclosure, released the following document in defense of the president. This document, which was a combined effort by Clinton's private lawyers, under the direction of David E. Kendall, and lawyers from the Office of the White House Counsel, headed by Charles Ruff, did not address the individual charges against the president but discussed how the case against Clinton went against the impeachment precedents found in U.S. history.

MEMORANDUM REGARDING STANDARDS FOR IMPEACHMENT

Oct 2, 1998

Early next week the Members of the Judiciary Committee will cast their first votes as participants in a "grand inquest" charged with responsibility for the most grave of constitutional proceedings. They will do so in circumstances unlike those in any proceeding that they have experienced in their professional careers. They will be asked to judge whether the evidence before them (untested by the usual adversarial process) provides any reason to believe that the President has violated a standard of conduct that they have made no effort to define.

No Member ever has ventured, or seen others venture, into any legal process without some understanding of the standards to be applied. Before a prosecutor would even open a grand jury investigation, he would test the information he had against the criminal code to determine whether there was any possibility that a crime actually had been committed. Before a plaintiff's lawyer would file a complaint, she would test the facts her client gave her against the law to determine whether there was a valid claim. Yet, the Members of the Commit-

Independent counsel Kenneth W. Starr (standing lower left) takes oath before testifying before the House Judiciary Committee, which was investigating possible impeachable conduct of President Bill Clinton.

tee are being asked to vote on whether there is any basis for believing that the President has committed impeachable offenses—but are being told that nothing will be done to define those offenses until after they have voted.

We submit that no lawyer would follow such a course in dealing with any other matter. We submit, as well, that nothing in this unique proceeding— even acknowledging its special political nature—should lead the Members of this distinguished body, who should serve as models for other lawyers to emulate, to abandon the principles of fairness and due process that lie at the heart of their profession.

That said, we are convinced that, if the Committee does adopt a definition of impeachable offenses consistent with the clear historical precedents and equally clear intent of the Framers underlying Section 4 of Article II, as well as the standards applied during the Nixon proceedings twenty-four years ago, it will conclude that nothing in the Starr Referral is remotely sufficient to warrant an impeachment inquiry.

Apart from a declaration of war, the most solemn and important responsibility Congress bears is to wield the power of impeachment wisely. The significance of this process can scarcely be overstated. As Prof. Charles Black has noted, "[t]he presidency is a prime symbol of our national unity. The election of the president (with his alternate, the vice-president) is the only political act that we perform together as a nation; voting in the presidential election is certainly the political choice most significant to the American people, and most closely attended to by them." It is therefore critical that the process of impeachment, through which 535 people may undo a national decision, both be fair and be perceived to be fair.

Fundamental fairness requires that the House Committee on the Judiciary clarify and define the standard of impeachability that will be applicable to this case before voting to proceed with an inquiry. We respectfully submit that the Starr Referral, salacious and prejudicial as it may be, cannot meet any standard that is defined in conformity with precedent, constitutional tradition, and the express intent of the Framers.

I. The Committee on the Judiciary Should Define What an "Impeachable Offense" Is Before It Votes to Authorize an Impeachment Inquiry.

The Committee on the Judiciary should first determine what constitutes an "impeachable offense" before it votes on whether to authorize an impeachment inquiry. As we will demonstrate, the Framers of the Constitution did not intend for the definition of "Treason, Bribery or other high Crimes or Misdemeanors" to be open-ended. Even if the standard chosen by the Committee is somewhat abstract, it is important that it be agreed upon in advance of voting whether to go forward with an impeachment inquiry. The Committee has a responsibility to measure the allegations and weigh the evidence against an established standard. If the Committee instead seeks to shape the standard to fit the allegations, the public will surely see it as a partisan effort to drive the President from office.

If the rule of law means anything, it means that legal rules and standards are ascertainable in advance of their application to evidence. This basic principle underlies our entire legal system. The Framers of the Constitution explicitly forbade Congress from enacting *ex post facto* laws and bills of attainder, and they also guaranteed due process of law before life, liberty, or property could be forfeited to the government. Indeed, fair notice is a fundamental component of the Constitutional guarantee of due process. In civil suits and criminal trials, the applicable law and the governing standards are known in advance, and even wide-ranging grand jury investigations are conducted to ascertain whether there is probable cause to believe that specific statutes have been violated.

Impeachment is not, of course, a judicial proceeding. But because of its dramatic potential to reverse a democratic election and overturn the will of the people, due process and fundamental fairness are as plainly required as in any court proceeding. One of the former staff lawyers for the 1974 House Impeachment Inquiry has emphasized the "overarching requirement of fairness to the President in an impeachment proceeding. The proceeding [is] one against the President, and his right to procedural fairness [has] to be recognized. . . . Whether or not impeachment is a 'criminal' proceeding, it is an accusatory one. . . ."

The basic requirement that proceedings with such significant consequences not be initiated or progress in the absence of clearly defined rules is reflected in various doctrines governing the conduct of court proceedings. The judicial system recognizes that power exercised arbitrarily is power abused, and that rules and procedures defined in advance go a long way toward assuring both the appearance and the reality of fairness. It is inconceivable that the courts would permit the filing of a civil complaint, or the return of an indictment, based merely on the promise that the plaintiff or the government would decide along the way what the rules should be, whether those rules were violated, and what burdens of proof and other standards should govern the proceedings as they progressed.

As the Supreme Court has stated, "a law fails to meet the requirements of the Due Process Clause if it is so vague and standardless that it . . . leaves judges and jurors to decide, without any legally fixed standards, what is prohibited and what is not in each particular case." *Giaccio* v. *Pennsylvania,* 382 U.S. 399, 402-03 (1966). Such ad hoc decision-making is necessarily suspect because it creates a strong potential for decisions based on a desired result, not on principled reasoning. These core constitutional doctrines, repeatedly reaffirmed by the Supreme Court and the lower courts, reflect a fundamental belief of our system of justice that the only way to assure that power—and especially the power to punish—is exercised fairly and without bias or improper motive is to establish the rules at the outset and to remain faithful to them throughout the process. The fairness of the process legitimizes both the process itself and the outcome. These principles necessarily must guide the actions of the Committee in a decision of the historical and constitutional magnitude that it confronts. A decision by the Committee to vote whether an impeachment inquiry is warranted without first establishing the legal standards which will apply directly contravenes these principles in a deeply disturbing manner.

The need for a working definition of the term "impeachable offense" is underlined by the inflammatory and one-sided presentation of "facts" in the Starr Referral. While that document states that "[i]t is not the role of this Office to determine whether the President's actions warrant impeachment by the House and removal by the Senate," Ref. 5, the OIC, purporting to act under his statutory mandate to submit "substantial and credible information" that "may constitute grounds for an impeachment," 28 U.S.C. §595(c), has in fact submitted a "brief." The document is one-sided, tendentious, and loaded with unnecessary and prejudicial graphic detail. Independent Counsel Starr finds room for hundreds of salacious details but could not find space to quote Ms. Lewinsky's closing comment to the grand jury (elicited by a grand juror, not by the prosecutors): "I would just like to say that no one ever asked me to lie and I was never promised a job for my silence." App. 1161. His failure to explain how the details of the Referral could be deemed relevant to anything this Committee might consider is simply perverse.

Nor did the judicial assent (such as it was) sought by the Independent Counsel prior to sending the Referral to Congress do anything to assure fairness. The contrast to the Watergate experience could not be more striking. In that earlier case, it will be recalled, the Watergate Special Prosecution Force did not send to Congress an argumentative or inflammatory document but rather a simple "road map" which merely summarized and identified the location of relevant evidence. Moreover, this document was submitted for review to Judge Sirica, the supervising judge of the grand jury, before it was sent to the House of Representatives. Counsel for President Nixon was given notice and an opportunity to be heard before the report was sent to Congress. Judge Sirica carefully reviewed the report, explicitly finding that it constituted a fair summary of the grand jury's evidence:

"It draws no accusatory conclusions. . . . It contains no recommendations, advice or statements that infringe on the prerogatives of other branches of government. . . . It renders no moral or social judgments. The Report is a simple and straightforward compilation of information gathered by the Grand Jury, and no more. . . . [The special prosecutor] has obviously taken care to assure that its Report contains no objectionable features, and has throughout acted in the interest of fairness."

In this case, on the other hand, the Independent Counsel went not to the supervising grand jury judge, Chief Judge Norma Holloway Johnson, but rather to the Special Division for the Purpose of Appointing Independent Counsels of the United States Court of Appeal for the District of Columbia Circuit, which had appointed him Independent Counsel almost exactly four years earlier. There was no notice to counsel for the President, and no opportunity for counsel to be heard on the propriety or fairness of any referral to Congress. Nor did the Independent Counsel submit any report for the Special Division to review, if it had been so inclined. Instead, the Independent Counsel sought—and received—a blank check from the Special Division to include in its referral (which would not be drafted and submitted to Congress until two months later) "all grand jury material *that the independent counsel deems necessary* to comply with the requirements of § 595(c)." App. 10 (emphasis added).

Against this backdrop, it is critical that the Committee on the Judiciary define the standard of impeachable conduct. Otherwise, a vote to proceed with a full-scale impeachment inquiry will have all the intelligibility of the Roman Emperor's thumb in the gladiatorial arena. The vote will signal no agreement, bipartisan or otherwise, on whether the national trauma of impeachment hearings is justified on other than purely partisan grounds.

II. The Conduct Alleged in the Starr Referral Does Not, Under Any
Reasonable Standard, Constitute an Impeachable Offense.

The Constitution provides that the President shall be removed from office
only upon "Impeachment for, and Conviction of, Treason, Bribery, or other
high Crimes and Misdemeanors." U.S. Const. Art. II, § 4. Of course, there is
no suggestion of treason or bribery present here. Therefore, the question con-
fronting the Committee is whether the acts of the President alleged in the
Starr Referral could conceivably amount to "high Crimes and Misdemeanors."
The Committee has an obligation to consider, before it embarks upon an impeachment inquiry, whether the allegations here could possibly meet that very
stringent Constitutional standard.

The Committee's deliberations should be guided by two considerations.
First, for reasons going to the very structure of our government, the Framers
made the standard of impeachable offenses an especially high one, requiring a
showing of injury to our very system of government. Second, historical precedents from the last presidential impeachment inquiry show that only the
gravest public offenses can be considered impeachable.

A. The Framers Did Not Intend that Impeachment Be Used Easily.

The Framers included specific provisions for impeachment in the Constitution because they understood that only the most serious forms of public
wrongdoing warranted the most severe political remedy. Impeachment is a
basic constitutional safeguard, designed both to correct harms to the system of
government itself and to protect the people from serious malfeasance in the
carrying out of public functions. Nothing less than the gravest executive
wrongdoing can justify impeachment. The Constitution leaves lesser wrongs
to the political process and to public opinion.

1. To the Framers, Impeachment Was an Important but Necessarily Limited
Remedy.

The English precedents illustrate that impeachment was understood to
apply only to fundamental offenses against the system of government. In English practice, the term "high crimes and misdemeanors" had been applied to
offenses, the common elements of which were their severity and the fact that
the wrongdoing was directed against the state. The English cases included
misappropriation of public funds, interfering in elections, accepting bribes,
and various forms of corruption. *Ibid.* These offenses all affected the discharge
of public duties by public officials. In short, under the English practice, "the
critical element of injury in an impeachable offense was *injury to the state.*"

The notion that "injury to the state" was the distinctive mark of the impeachable offense was also shared by the Staff of the Impeachment Inquiry when it researched the issue in connection with the investigation of President Nixon in 1974. In early English impeachments, the Staff concluded, "the thrust of the charge was damage to the state. . . . Characteristically, impeachment was used in individual cases to reach offenses, as perceived by Parliament, *against the system of government."*

The constitutional and ratification debates confirm that impeachment was limited to only the gravest political wrongs. The Framers plainly intended the impeachment standard to be a high one. They rejected a proposal that the President be impeachable for "maladministration," for, as James Madison pointed out, such a standard would "be equivalent to a tenure during the pleasure of the Senate." The Framers plainly did not intend to permit Congress to debilitate the executive by authorizing impeachment for something short of the most serious harm to the state. In George Mason's apt language, impeachment was thought necessary to remedy "great and dangerous offenses" not covered by "Treason" or "Bribery" such as "[a]ttempts to subvert the Constitution."

That is why, at the time of the ratification debates, Alexander Hamilton described impeachment as a "method of NATIONAL INQUEST into the conduct of public men." No act touches more fundamental questions of constitutional government than does the process of Presidential impeachment. No act more directly affects the public interest. No act presents the potential for greater injustice—injustice both to the Chief Executive and to the people who elected him—and the Framers were fully aware of this.

The specific harms the Framers sought to redress by impeachment are far more serious than those presented here. During the ratification debates, a number of the Framers addressed the Constitution's impeachment provisions. The following is a list of wrongs they believed the impeachment power was intended to address:

- receipt of emoluments from a foreign power in violation of Article I, section 9;
- using the pardon power to pardon the President's own crimes or crimes he advised;
- summoning the representatives of only a few states to ratify a treaty;
- concealing information from or giving false information to the Senate so as to cause it to take measures they otherwise would not have taken injurious to the country;
- general failure to perform the duties of the Executive.

The history on which they relied, the arguments they made in Convention, the specific ills they regarded as redressable—all these establish that the

Framers believed that impeachment must be reserved for only the most serious forms of wrongdoing. They believed, in short, that impeachment "reached offenses against the government, and especially abuses of constitutional duties." Fidelity to that understanding requires the Committee to formulate an appropriately high standard to guide its decision whether to launch an inquiry with such potentially grave national consequences.

2. Impeachment Requires a Very High Standard Because Ours Is a Presidential and Not a Parliamentary System.

Ours is a written constitution of separated powers. In that Constitution, the President does not serve at the will of Congress, but as the directly elected, solitary head of the Executive Branch. The Constitution reflects a judgment that a strong executive, executing the law independently of legislative will, was a necessary protection for a free people.

These elementary facts of constitutional structure underscore the need for a very high standard of impeachable offenses. It was emphatically not the intention of the Framers that the President should be subject to the will of the dominant legislative party. Our system of government does not permit Congress to unseat the President merely because it disagrees with his behavior or his policies. The Framers' decisive rejection of parliamentary government is one reason why they caused the phrase "Treason, Bribery or other high Crimes and Misdemeanors" to appear in the Constitution itself. They chose to specify those categories of offenses subject to the impeachment power, rather than leave that judgment to the unfettered whim of the legislature.

Although the Committee need not set forth the concept of "impeachable offense" with scientific precision, that concept must be made sufficiently clear and its substance made sufficiently demanding to ensure that any subsequent impeachment inquiry will be reasonably viewed by the public as arising in one of those rare cases when the legislature is compelled to stand in for all the people and remove a President whose continuation in office threatens grave harm to the Republic. Any "standard" short of that will effectuate both a legislative usurpation of a power belonging only to the people (the power to choose and "depose" Presidents by election) and a legislative encroachment on the power of the Executive. The Committee must articulate such a standard here. It must say just what it is about the alleged conduct in the Starr Referral that amounts to a "great offense[] against the Constitution." If it does not posit such a standard and if, in addition, it cannot say clearly and forcefully why such a high standard is conceivably met here, there is no plausible justification for proceeding with an impeachment inquiry. To proceed without such a clear standard is to weaken the President in the absence of the only justification our Constitution permits for such a step—a demonstrated need to protect the people themselves.

3. Impeachment Requires a Very High and Very Clear Standard Because It Nullifies the Popular Will.

The Framers made the President the sole nationally elected public official, responsible to all the people. He is the only person whose mandate is country-wide, extending to all citizens, all places, and all interests. He is the people's choice.

Therefore, when the issue of impeachment is raised, the House (and ultimately the Senate) confront[s] this inescapable question: is the alleged misconduct so profoundly serious, so malevolent, that it justifies undoing the people's decision? Is the wrong alleged of a sort that not only demands removal of the President before the ordinary electoral cycle can do its work, but also justifies the national trauma that accompanies the impeachment process itself?

The wrongdoing alleged here does not remotely meet that standard.

B. Impeachment Is a Remedy Only for Public Wrongdoing.

1. The Framers Believed that Impeachment Redresses Wrongful Conduct that Is Public.

The remedy of impeachment was designed for only those very grave harms not otherwise politically redressable. As James Wilson wrote, "our President . . . is amenable to [the laws] in his private character as a citizen, and in his public character by *impeachment*." That is why Justice Story described the harms to be reached by impeachment as those "offensive acts which do not properly belong to the judicial character in the ordinary administration of justice, and are far removed from the reach of municipal jurisprudence."

For these reasons, impeachment is limited to only certain forms of potential wrongdoing and it is intended to redress only certain kinds of harms. Again, in Hamilton's words:

the subjects of [the Senate's impeachment] jurisdiction are those offenses which proceed from the misconduct of public men, or in other words from the abuse o[r] violation of some public trust. They are of a nature which may with peculiar propriety be denominated POLITICAL, as they relate chiefly to injuries done to the society itself.

The Framers and early commentators on the Constitution are in accord on the question of impeachment's intended purpose. In Justice James Wilson's words, impeachments are "proceedings of a political nature . . . confined to political characters" charging only "political crimes and misdemeanors" and culminating only in "political punishments." And as Justice Story put the matter, "the [impeachment] power partakes of a political character, as it respects injuries to the society in its political character." In short, impeachment was not thought to be a remedy for private wrongs—or even for most public wrongs. Rather, the Framers "intended that a president be removable from office for the commission of great offenses against the Constitution." Impeachment therefore addresses public wrongdoing, whether denominated a "political crime[] against the state," or "an act of malfeasance or abuse of office," or a "great offense[s] against the federal government." Ordinary civil wrongs can be addressed through ordinary civil processes. And ordinary political wrongs can be addressed at the ballot box and by public opinion. Impeachment is reserved for the most serious public misconduct, those aggravated abuses of executive power that, given the President's four-year term, might otherwise go unchecked.

That impeachment was reserved for serious public wrongdoing of a serious political nature was no mere abstraction to the authors of the Constitution. The ink on the Constitution was barely dry when Congress was forced to investigate wrongdoing by one of the Framers. In 1792–93, Congress investigated then-Secretary of the Treasury Alexander Hamilton for alleged financial misdealings with James Reynolds, a convicted securities swindler. Hamilton was interviewed by members of Congress, including the House Speaker and James Monroe, the future President. Hamilton admitted to making secret payments to Reynolds whose release from prison the Treasury Department had authorized. Hamilton acknowledged that he had made the payments but explained that he had committed adultery with Reynolds' wife; that he had made payments to Reynolds to cover it up; that he had had Mrs. Reynolds burn incriminating correspondence; and that he had promised to pay the Reynolds' travel costs if they would leave town.

The Members of Congress who heard Hamilton's confession concluded that the matter was private, not public; that as a result no impeachable offense had occurred; and that the entire matter should remain secret. Although President Washington, Vice-President Adams, Secretary of State Jefferson and House Minority leader James Madison (two of whom had signed the Constitution) all eventually became aware of the affair, they too maintained their silence. And even after the whole matter became public knowledge some years later, Hamilton was appointed to the second highest position in the United States Army and was speedily confirmed by the Senate.

It is apparent from the Hamilton case that the Framers did not regard private sexual misconduct as creating an impeachable offense. It is also apparent that efforts to cover up such private behavior, including even paying hush money to induce someone to destroy documents, did not meet the standard. Neither Hamilton's very high position, nor the fact that his payments to a securities swindler created an enormous "appearance" problem, were enough to implicate the standard. These wrongs were real, and they were not insubstantial, but to the Framers they were essentially private and therefore *not* impeachable.

Some have responded to the argument that the conduct at issue in the Referral is private by contending that the President is charged with faithfully executing the laws of the United States and that perjury would be a violation of that duty. That argument, however, proves far too much. Under that theory, any violation of federal law would constitute an impeachable offense, no matter how minor and no matter whether it arose out of the President's private life or his public responsibilities. Thus, lying in a deposition in a private lawsuit would, for constitutional purposes, be the equivalent of lying to Congress about significant conduct of the Executive Branch—surely a result those advocates do not contemplate. More importantly, we know from the bipartisan defeat of the tax fraud Article against President Nixon, see Part II.C, *infra,* that the "faithfully execute" theory has been flatly rejected by this Committee.

2. Contemporary Scholars Agree That Impeachment Is Justified Not for Private Wrongs But Only for Political Offenses Against the State Itself.

Impeachable acts need not be criminal acts. As Professor Black has noted, it would probably be an impeachable act for a President to move to Saudi Arabia so he could have four wives while proposing to conduct the Presidency by mail and wireless from there; or to announce and adhere to a policy of appointing no Roman Catholics to public office; or to announce a policy of granting full pardons, in advance of indictment or trial, to federal agents or police who killed anyone in the line of duty in the District of Columbia. None of these acts would be crimes, but all would be impeachable. This, because they are all "serious assaults on the integrity of government." And all of these acts are public acts having public consequences.

But the reverse is not true: criminal acts are not necessarily impeachable. Holders of public office should not be impeached for conduct (even criminal conduct) that is essentially private. That is why scholars and other disinterested observers have consistently framed the test of impeachable offenses in terms of some fundamental attack on our system of government, describing impeachment as being reserved for:

- "offenses against the government";
- "political crimes against the state";

- "serious assaults on the integrity of the processes of government";
- "such crimes as would so stain a president as to make his continuance in office dangerous to public order";
- "wrongdoing convincingly established [and] so egregious that [the President's] continuation in office is intolerable";
- "malfeasance or abuse of office," bearing a "functional relationship" to public office;
- "great offense[s] against the federal government";
- "acts which, like treason and bribery, undermine the integrity of government."

Allegations concerning private sexual conduct and efforts to conceal that private conduct simply do not implicate high crimes or misdemeanors.

Private misconduct, or even public misconduct short of an offense against the state, is not redressable by impeachment because that solemn process, in Justice Story's words, addresses "offences[] which are committed by public men in violation of their public trust and duties." Impeachment is a political act in the sense that its aims are public; it attempts to rein in abuses of the public trust committed by public officeholders in connection with conduct in public office. The availability of the process is commensurate with the gravity of the harm. As one scholar has put it, "[t]he nature of [impeachment] proceedings is dictated by the harms sought to be redressed—'the misconduct of public men' relating to the conduct of their public office—and the ultimate issue to be resolved—whether they have forfeited through that conduct their right to continued public trust."

C. There Is No Impeachable Offense Here Under the "Nixon Standard."

When the House Judiciary Committee investigated President Nixon in the 1970's, it too confronted the question of just what constitutes an "impeachable offense."

1. In the Nixon Matter, the Majority and Minority Agreed on a High Standard of Impeachable Offenses.

One of the first tasks assigned to the staff of the Judiciary Committee when it began its investigation of President Nixon was to prepare a legal analysis of the grounds for impeachment of a President. The staff concluded that:

"Impeachment is a constitutional remedy addressed to *serious offenses against the system of government.* . . . It is not controlling whether treason and bribery are criminal. More important, they are *constitutional wrongs that subvert the structure of government, or under-*

mine the integrity of office and even the Constitution itself, and thus are 'high' offenses in the sense that word was used in English impeachments. . . . The emphasis has been on the significant effects of the conduct—*undermining the integrity of office, disregard of constitutional duties and oath of office, arrogation of power, abuse of the governmental process, adverse impact on the system of government.* . . . Because impeachment of a President is a grave step for the nation, it is to be predicated only upon *conduct seriously incompatible with either the constitutional form and principles of our government or the proper performance of constitutional duties* of the president['s] office."

The minority staff of the Nixon impeachment inquiry prepared a memorandum in response to a request by the Republicans on the Judiciary Committee that argued for the notion that only serious misconduct with the appropriate criminal intent was sufficient for impeachment. They stated as follows:

"It is *not* a fair summary . . . to say that the Framers were principally concerned with reaching a course of conduct, whether or not criminal, generally inconsistent with the proper and effective exercise of the office of the presidency. They were concerned with preserving the government from being overthrown by the treachery or corruption of one man. . . . [I]t is our judgment, based upon this constitutional history, that the Framers of the United States Constitution intended that the President should be removable by the legislative branch only for *serious misconduct dangerous to the system of government established by the Constitution.*"

Notwithstanding their many differences, the Judiciary Committee investigating President Nixon was in substantial agreement on the question posed here: an impeachable wrong is an offense against our very system, a constitutional evil subversive of the government itself.

That demanding standard is not remotely implicated by the wrongs alleged in the Starr Referral. Nor was it met by all the charges against President Nixon.

2. In the Nixon Matter, the Majority and Minority Applied a Demanding Standard to Preclude Impeachment for Grounds Analogous to Those Presented Here.

Among the charges in the Starr Referral, the one most insistently repeated is the allegation that the President has committed perjury. The historically accepted standard of "high Crimes and Misdemeanors" has particular application to the perjury charge because it closely resembles a similar charge alleged— but not finally approved—against President Nixon in 1974.

The Judiciary Committee proposed five articles of impeachment against President Nixon. Three were approved for transmission to the full House, and two were voted down. One of the defeated articles alleged the signing by the

President, under oath, of a false tax return. The President was alleged to have failed to report certain income, to have taken improper tax deductions, and to have manufactured (himself or by his agents) false documents to support the deductions taken.

By a bipartisan vote greater than a 2-1 margin, the Judiciary Committee rejected the tax-evasion article. Democrats and Republicans alike, all of whom eventually approved at least one other article of impeachment, spoke against the idea that tax evasion constituted an impeachable offense. Congressman Railsback (R-IL) opposed the article saying that "there is a serious question as to whether something involving his personal tax liability has anything to do with [the] conduct of the office of the President." Congressman Owens (D-UT) stated that, even assuming the charges were true in fact, "on the evidence available, these offenses do not rise, in my opinion, to the level of impeachment." Congressman Hogan (R-MD) did not believe tax evasion an impeachable offense because the Constitution's phrase "high crime signified a crime against the system of government, not merely a serious crime." And Congressman Waldie (D-CA) spoke against the article, saying that "there had not been an enormous abuse of power," notwithstanding his finding "the conduct of the President in these instances to have been shabby, to have been unacceptable, and to have been disgraceful even."

These voices, and the overwhelming vote against the tax evasion article, underscore the fact that the 1974 Judiciary Committee's judgment was faithful to its legal conclusions. It would not (and did not) approve an article of impeachment for anything short of a fundamental offense against our very system of government. This Committee should observe no less stringent a standard.

D. History and Experience Require the Committee to Stay Its Hand.

Cognizant of the enormous harm that the very initiation of an impeachment inquiry would engender, the House should pursue such an inquiry if and only if there is an allegation of actions which would constitute fundamental injuries to the governmental process. In the words of Sen. William Pitt Fessenden, one of the seven Senate Republicans who voted against the conviction of President Andrew Johnson, an impeachable offense must be "of such a character to commend itself at once to the minds of all right thinking men, as beyond all question, an adequate cause for impeachment. It should leave no reasonable ground of suspicion upon the motives of those who inflict the penalty."

The Committee should vote to launch an impeachment inquiry only if it concludes that the Starr Referral has alleged acts which, if proven, would so seriously threaten the integrity of governmental processes as to have made the

President's continuation in office a threat to the public order. Impropriety falling short of that high standard does not meet the constitutional measure. It must be left to the court of public opinion and the judgment of history.

Conclusion

The Judiciary Committee is poised to vote on a resolution calling for the formal commencement of impeachment proceedings without having offered any benchmark (or indeed any approximation) for impeachable offenses. To proceed in this way is to subordinate the constitutional objective of addressing impeachable wrongs to the partisan political objective of embarking on an open-ended, undefined roving inquiry of the President. As Justice Jackson noted in an analogous setting, "it is a question of picking the man and then searching the law books, or putting investigators to work, to pin some offense on him." Such a procedure would be unfair in a prosecutor and here it would be deeply unfair and destructive of our constitutional structure.

Three conclusions follow from a failure to set out the standard of impeachable offenses before voting to initiate an impeachment inquiry:

• First, that failure portends a dangerous, standardless inquiry, a kind of roving commission by the majority to inflict partisan injury on the minority. The majority would thereby signal its willingness to damage the President, distract government from its proper business, and waste enormous time and resources, with absolutely no off-setting benefit to the people.

• Second, in view of our history's repeated lesson that the standard for impeachable offenses is a very high one, the failure to articulate such a standard necessarily bespeaks an awareness that the material presented in the Starr Referral does not approach that high threshold. Even assuming that every allegation in the one-sided Referral were true, there is simply nothing there that approaches any great offense against the Constitution. The decision to proceed without acknowledging this standard confirms this conclusion.

• Finally, the failure reflects a process that is politically irresponsible because it ducks any effective oversight by the public (at the polls or otherwise) of the reasons why those who vote to launch such an unjustifiable inquiry have done so. Unable to justify its actions under the Constitution, the majority will instead choose to launch its own Starr-like, open-ended, expensive, intrusive and wasteful inquiry for no stated reason at all.

As then-Representative and later President Gerald Ford once expressed the issue, a President can only be removed for "crimes of the magnitude of treason and bribery." The Referral alleges no wrongs of that magnitude. The Committee should decline to proceed further.

Part VI

IMPEACHMENT IN THE COURTS

BY 1936, THE IMPEACHMENT MECHANISM had been fully used—from accusation through trial—only eleven times. When the Senate convicted and removed District Judge Halsted L. Ritter that year, he became only the fourth federal official in U.S. history to suffer that fate. He would become the first to challenge his ouster in a court of law. His challenge went directly to the legitimacy of the Senate's interpretation of "high crimes and misdemeanors." More than fifty years later, after becoming only the seventh officer in more than two hundred years to be removed on an impeachment, District Judge Walter L. Nixon likewise sought relief in the courts in a case that reached the Supreme Court. Although the challenge to his removal concerned the procedures the Senate used to try him, the Court, as did the earlier Court of Claims in *Ritter*, addressed the fundamental question of whether there is any checking control over Congress during *any* stage in the removal process.

In both *Ritter* and *Nixon* the courts based their refusal to examine the actions of Congress on a constitutional doctrine known as the *separation of powers* doctrine. The phrase "separation of powers" does not appear in the Constitution. It is, however, inherent in the governmental structure that the Constitution created. The framers feared that tyranny would surely result if any one person or group of people should acquire too much power. One of the barriers they created to block dangerous concentrations of governmental power was to separate the powers of government into three categories and allocate them to three separate branches of government. Thus the legislature, or Congress, was given the power to make laws; the executive, or the president, was given the power to carry out the laws; and the judiciary was given the power to decide disputes under the laws.

The framers did not, however, believe that separation of powers either could or should be rigid and absolute, because unfettered power, even if separated, could lead to tyranny. So the framers also created a system of checks and balances intended to keep power between the branches in equilibrium. Thus, the president's power to execute the laws and the judiciary's power to decide cases (including the Supreme Court's power to interpret the Constitution) is kept in check by Congress's power to remove officers of either branch who abuse their authority through the commission of high crimes and misdemeanors. But what if Congress abuses its removal power, by defining high crimes and misdemeanors as any behavior that a majority of members of Congress do not like, thus arbitrarily removing officers of the government? The following documents address that question.

◄ 34 ►

Ritter v. U.S. and Judicial Review

(1936)

IN *RITTER V. U.S.* District Judge Halsted L. Ritter filed suit to recover back pay on the grounds that Congress had illegally removed him from office. (See Document 20, p. 157.) The House had brought seven articles of impeachment against Judge Ritter in 1936. The first six articles charged him with specific misdeeds; the seventh collected all of the previous charges together and accused the judge of bringing disrepute on his court by his behavior. The Senate acquitted the judge on all six of the specific charges but then convicted him on the final collective charge. Judge Ritter challenged the Senate's right to remove him, claiming that none of the charges amounted to "high crimes and misdemeanors" and that it had been improper to convict him on the aggregated charges in the last article after he had been acquitted of each of the individual charges.

In every case that comes before a court of law, the first question the court must answer, either explicitly or implicitly, is whether it has "jurisdiction" to hear the case. That is, the court must determine whether it has the *authority* to render a judgment in the case before it. In *Ritter,* the U.S. Court of Claims refused to consider Judge Ritter's claim that he had been unconstitutionally removed, because the court determined that it had no authority to review the Senate's actions. According to the court's reading of the Constitution, Congress had the *sole* and *final* authority to determine the meaning of "high crimes and misdemeanors" and to apply the meaning determined upon to the facts of individual cases.

GREEN, Judge, delivered the opinion of the court:

The plaintiff, who had been appointed a Judge of a District Court of the United States, brings this suit to recover the salary appurtenant to this office from April 1, 1936, to and including April 30, 1936, in the sum of $833.33 which has not been paid to him. In his petition the plaintiff sets out the commission which he had received appointing him a District Judge signed by the President on February 15, 1929, and alleges that he performed the duties of his office until prevented from so doing by reason of impeachment proceedings against him. The petition shows that in March 1936 the House of Representatives of the United States adopted articles of impeachment against him which were duly presented to the Senate of the United States. The articles of impeachment are also set out and the action taken by the Senate thereon, showing that the plaintiff was adjudged "not guilty" on all of said articles except the seventh; that as to the seventh article the plaintiff had moved to dismiss the same on the ground that it constituted an accumulation and combination of all the charges in preceding articles upon which the Senate must first pass; that this motion was overruled by the Court of Impeachment; and that plaintiff answered denying the jurisdiction of the Senate to consider the seventh article, denied the allegations contained therein, and severally denied the allegations of paragraph 3 thereof.

The petition further shows that the United States Senate, after having acquitted the plaintiff on the first six articles of impeachment, proceeded to try him on the seventh article and found him guilty of the charge contained therein, and that thereafter a judgment was entered by the Senate ordering that the plaintiff be removed from his office as judge of a United States District Court.

It is further alleged in the petition that the attempted and purported removal of plaintiff from the office of Judge of the United States District Court by the Senate of the United States sitting as high Court of Impeachment was illegal, unconstitutional, and void, and did not constitute a removal from such office or deprive him of the emoluments thereof, for the reason that the charges made in the articles of impeachment do not constitute a high crime or misdemeanor within the meaning of the Constitution; that the seventh article of impeachment upon which the plaintiff was found guilty was but a restatement of portions of prior articles as to which plaintiff was adjudged "not guilty"; that the Senate had no jurisdiction to try the plaintiff upon any of the articles of impeachment; and that after it had found the plaintiff "not guilty" on the first six articles, it had no jurisdiction to try the plaintiff upon the seventh article, which charged only matters which were contained in the prior articles.

For the reasons stated above, the plaintiff alleges that the judgment and conviction rendered against him by the Senate was an unconstitutional exercise of authority and is utterly void and of no effect. . . .

In stating the issues in the case, we have not set out the articles of impeachment containing the charges made against the plaintiff, nor have we referred to the testimony introduced in support of them, for the reason that in the view which we take of the case it is not necessary to consider either of these matters.

It will be observed that the plaintiff bases his claim that the Senate acted without jurisdiction on two allegations: first, that the charges made in the articles of impeachment did not constitute im-

Halsted L. Ritter

peachable offenses under the Constitution; and second, that having been acquitted on the first six articles, the Senate had no jurisdiction to try him under the seventh article which merely restated the matters charged in the previous articles. But this is not the question first to be determined in the case. Before we consider whether the Senate acted within its jurisdiction in its proceedings, we must first decide whether this court has jurisdiction to review the action of the Senate and pass on this matter. . . .

It is not contended there is any provision in the Constitution which authorizes a review of the proceedings had and judgment rendered by the Senate in impeachment cases, but it is said the Senate acts as a high court of impeachment and that, being for the purposes of impeachment trials a court, if it acts without constitutional authority its judgments are a nullity. But what court is authorized to review its judgments and set them aside? The writers on constitutional law are unanimous in holding that there is none. . . .

While the question now being considered has never been presented to a Federal Court in relation to the impeachment of a Federal officer, there are several decisions of the State courts relating to the finality of judgments rendered upon impeachment trials under constitutional provisions similar to those contained in the Constitution of the United States.

In *State v. Chambers* . . . in passing upon an incidental question arising in the impeachment trial of Governor J. C. Walton of that State, the Supreme Court of Oklahoma held that the legislature had exclusive jurisdiction over matters of impeachment.

The Supreme Court of Texas in two cases has held that the courts have no right to review collaterally a judgment of impeachment, and while in its opinion in the first case, *Ferguson v. Maddox,* . . . the language used is not entirely harmonious, its conclusion was:

As to impeachment, it is a court of original, exclusive, and final jurisdiction.

The same rule was laid down in *Ferguson v. Wilcox.* . . .

When we consider the matter now before the court from a historical point of view it is quite evident that there was no thought at the time the constitutional provisions for impeachment were adopted of making the proceedings subject to review by the courts. In the constitutional convention it was proposed by several members that impeachments should be tried by a special court consisting of a judge or judges. Madison preferred the Supreme Court. But these propositions were rejected and while there was some suggestion in the consideration of the matter that the Senate might abuse its power, there was no intimation by anyone that the impeachment proceedings might be reviewed or set aside by the courts. . . .

The first impeachment proceedings were had not long after the Constitution had been adopted in Jefferson's Administration. John Pickering was a Federal District Judge whom historians say at times appeared on the bench in an intoxicated condition and indulged in language incoherent, irrational, and profane, and the proceedings carried on by him were extremely irregular. The House of Representatives voted articles of impeachment against him and the Senate proceeded to try the case. The Judge did not appear either in person or by counsel, but his son presented a petition alleging that when the acts charged against the Judge were committed he was insane and had been insane for two years and was now physically unable to attend the court. The Senate heard the evidence on insanity but nevertheless proceeded to try the Judge on the impeachment charges. He was found guilty and removed from office. . . . After his conviction Pickering was adjudged insane by proper authority. The action of the Senate was characterized by the historian McMaster as "arbitrary", "illegal", and "infamous." We need not consider whether this language was justified. It is sufficient to say that notwithstanding the peculiar circumstances of the case no one at that time or since has suggested that the conviction of Judge Pickering might have been reviewed by the courts.

Judge Story in his work on the Constitution analyzes at great length the provisions with reference to impeachment and considers the objections made to the Senate as the trial body in such proceedings in preference to the courts. But while recognizing that the Senate might err or even abuse its power, he does not suggest that there would be any remedy.

If the impeachment proceedings were reviewable by the courts, a conviction would bring such serious results to the accused that in nearly every case where it so resulted the case would be carried to the superior tribunal. It has already been observed that in *People v. Hayes,* supra, the New York court referring to impeachment proceedings said:

This great power is political. History is replete with illustrations of its use and abuses.

While the Senate in one sense acts as a court on the trial of an impeachment, it is essentially a political body and in its actions is influenced by the views of its members on the public welfare. The courts, on the other hand, are expected to render their decisions according to the law regardless of the consequences. This must have been realized by the members of the Constitutional Convention and in rejecting proposals to have impeachments tried by a court composed of regularly appointed judges we think it avoided the possibility of unseemly conflicts between a political body such as the Senate and the judicial tribunals which might determine the case on different principles.

In the case of *State of Mississippi v. Johnson,* . . . the Chief Justice said with reference to a hypothetical case where the House of Representatives had impeached the President and an injunction was sought to restrain the Senate from sitting as a court of impeachment—

Would the strange spectacle be offered to the public world of the attempt by this court to arrest proceedings in that court?

implying that the Supreme Court would take no such action even though it was claimed that the Senate was acting unconstitutionally.

Our conclusion is that we have no authority to review the impeachment proceedings held in the Senate and decide whether the accusations made against the plaintiff were such that he could properly be impeached thereon, nor can we pass upon the question of whether his acquittal on the first six articles was a bar to prosecution under the seventh. In our opinion, the Senate was the sole tribunal that could take jurisdiction of the articles of impeachment presented to that body against the plaintiff and its decision is final.

Plaintiff's petition must be dismissed and it is so ordered.

WHALEY, Judge; WILLIAMS, Judge; LITTLETON, Judge; and BOOTH, Chief Justice, concur.

❧ 35 ❧
Nixon v. U.S. and Political Question Doctrine
(1993)

DISTRICT JUDGE WALTER L. NIXON of Mississippi was convicted of per-jury and sentenced to prison. He was subsequently impeached by the House. (See Document 23, p. 180.) The Senate then tried him for removal from office, using a rule passed to economize on Senate time. This rule, known as Rule XI, allows the Senate to designate a committee of twelve to hear evidence in an impeachment case and then present that evidence to the full Senate in the form of a report. Nixon was convicted and removed from office by the Senate. He appealed his removal to the courts, contending that the Senate, by delegating the hearing of evidence to a committee, had failed to live up to its constitutional obligation to "try" all impeachments.

The case reached the Supreme Court, and on January 13, 1993, Chief Justice William H. Rehnquist delivered the opinion of the court, which was joined by Justices Sandra Day O'Connor, John Paul Stevens, Antonin Scalia, Anthony M. Kennedy, and Clarence Thomas. Justices Byron White, Harry A. Blackmun, and David H. Souter concurred in the judgment. The majority opinion concluded that under the Constitution, impeachment is a "political question" that is explicitly given to the legislative branch to decide, and that the judiciary is given no authority by the Constitution to review any aspect of Congress's handling of impeachment cases.

To understand the Court's ruling in the Nixon case, it is important to understand the relationship between the three opinions reproduced here. The first opinion is Rehnquist's majority opinion. Judge Nixon had asked the Court to set aside his conviction and removal because the Senate had acted improperly in trying him. The Court's judgment was to let the removal stand, reasoning that it had no authority to even look into the way the Senate conducted an impeachment trial.

The second opinion, by Justices White and Blackmun, is a "concurrence in the judgment," which means that although they agree with the outcome—that is, Judge Nixon's removal should stand—they do not agree with the Court's determination that it has no authority to review the Senate's handling of the matter. Thus, their opinion is an explanation of the reasons they differ from the majority on what the Constitution requires.

In the final opinion—another concurrence in the judgment—Justice Souter agrees that the doctrine of separation of powers requires that the courts refrain from reviewing the Senate's actions in cases like Judge Nixon's. Justice Souter would not make that absolute, however, arguing that if the Senate should act in an egregiously arbitrary way that was clearly "beyond the scope of its constitutional authority"—"convicting, say, upon a coin toss"—so as to have serious "impact on the Republic," the courts might need to step in.

In an interesting historical footnote, the solicitor general who argued before the Court for the Senate's unlimited power to structure impeachment proceedings was Kenneth W. Starr, who would, as independent counsel, recommend the impeachment of President Bill Clinton to the House of Representatives in 1998.

※ ※ ※

Chief Justice REHNQUIST delivered the opinion of the Court.

Petitioner Walter L. Nixon, Jr., asks this Court to decide whether Senate Rule XI, which allows a committee of Senators to hear evidence against an individual who has been impeached and to report that evidence to the full Senate, violates the Impeachment Trial Clause, Art. I, § 3, cl. 6. That Clause provides that the "Senate shall have the sole Power to try all Impeachments." But before we reach the merits of such a claim, we must decide whether it is "justiciable," that is, whether it is a claim that may be resolved by the courts. We conclude that it is not.

Nixon, a former Chief Judge of the United States District Court for the Southern District of Mississippi, was convicted by a jury of two counts of making false statements before a federal grand jury and sentenced to prison. . . . The grand jury investigation stemmed from reports that Nixon had accepted a gratuity from a Mississippi businessman in exchange for asking a local district attorney to halt the prosecution of the businessman's son. Because Nixon refused to resign from his office as a United States District Judge, he continued to collect his judicial salary while serving out his prison sentence. . . .

On May 10, 1989, the House of Representatives adopted three articles of impeachment for high crimes and misdemeanors. The first two articles charged Nixon with giving false testimony before the grand jury and the third article charged him with bringing disrepute on the Federal Judiciary. . . .

After the House presented the articles to the Senate, the Senate voted to invoke its own Impeachment Rule XI, under which the presiding officer appoints a committee of Senators to "receive evidence and take testimony." . . .

The Senate committee held four days of hearings, during which 10 witnesses, including Nixon, testified. . . . Pursuant to Rule XI, the committee presented the full Senate with a complete transcript of the proceeding and a Report stating the uncontested facts and summarizing the evidence on the contested facts. . . . Nixon and the House impeachment managers submitted extensive final briefs to the full Senate and delivered arguments from the Senate floor during the three hours set aside for oral argument in front of that body. Nixon himself gave a personal appeal, and several Senators posed questions directly to both parties. . . . The Senate voted by more than the constitutionally required two-thirds majority to convict Nixon on the first two arti-

Walter L. Nixon

cles. . . . The presiding officer then entered judgment removing Nixon from his office as United States District Judge. . . .

Nixon thereafter commenced the present suit, arguing that Senate Rule XI violates the constitutional grant of authority to the Senate to "try" all impeachments because it prohibits the whole Senate from taking part in the evidentiary hearings. See Art. I, § 3, cl. 6. Nixon sought a declaratory judgment that his impeachment conviction was void and that his judicial salary and privileges should be reinstated. . . .

[1][2] A controversy is nonjusticiable—i.e., involves a political question—where there is "a textually demonstrable constitutional commitment of the issue to a coordinate political department; or a lack of judicially discoverable and manageable standards for resolving it. . . ."

[3] In this case, we must examine Art. I, § 3, cl. 6, to determine the scope of authority conferred upon the Senate by the Framers regarding impeachment. It provides:

"The Senate shall have the sole Power to try all Impeachments. When sitting for that Purpose, they shall be on Oath or Affirmation. When the President of the United States is tried, the Chief Justice shall preside: And no Person shall be convicted without the Concurrence of two thirds of the Members present."

The language and structure of this Clause are revealing. The first sentence is a grant of authority to the Senate, and the word "sole" indicates that this authority is reposed in the Senate and nowhere else. The next two sentences specify requirements to which the Senate proceedings shall conform: The Senate shall be on oath or affirmation, a two-thirds vote is required to convict, and when the President is tried the Chief Justice shall preside.

Petitioner argues that the word "try" in the first sentence imposes by implication an additional requirement on the Senate in that the proceedings must be in the nature of a judicial trial. From there petitioner goes on to argue that this limitation precludes the Senate from delegating to a select committee the task of hearing the testimony of witnesses, as was done pursuant to Senate Rule XI. " '[T]ry' means more than simply 'vote on' or 'review' or 'judge.' In 1787 and today, trying a case means hearing the evidence, not scanning a cold record.". . . Petitioner concludes from this that courts may review whether or not the Senate "tried" him before convicting him.

There are several difficulties with this position which lead us ultimately to reject it. The word "try," both in 1787 and later, has considerably broader meanings than those to which petitioner would limit it. . . . Based on the variety of definitions, however, we cannot say that the Framers used the word "try" as an implied limitation on the method by which the Senate might proceed in trying impeachments. . . .

The Framers labored over the question of where the impeachment power should lie. Significantly, in at least two considered scenarios the power was placed with the Federal Judiciary. . . . Indeed, James Madison and the Committee of Detail proposed that the Supreme Court should have the power to determine impeachments. . . . Despite these proposals, the Convention ultimately decided that the Senate would have "the sole Power to try all Impeachments." Art. I, § 3, cl. 6. According to Alexander Hamilton, the Senate was the "most fit depositary of this important trust" because its Members are representatives of the people. . . . The Supreme Court was not the proper body because the Framers "doubted whether the members of that tribunal would, at all times, be endowed with so eminent a portion of fortitude as would be called for in the execution of so difficult a task" or whether the Court "would possess the degree of credit and authority" to carry out its judgment if it conflicted with the accusation brought by the Legislature—the people's representative. . . . In addition, the Framers believed the Court was too small in number: "The awful discretion, which a court of impeachments must necessarily have, to doom to honor or to infamy the most confidential and the most distinguished characters of the community, forbids the commitment of the trust to a small number of persons." . . .

There are two additional reasons why the Judiciary, and the Supreme Court in particular, were not chosen to have any role in impeachments. First, the Framers recognized that most likely there would be two sets of proceedings for individuals who commit impeachable offenses—the impeachment trial and a separate criminal trial. In fact, the Constitution explicitly provides for two separate proceedings. See Art. I, § 3, cl. 7. The Framers deliberately separated the two forums to avoid raising the specter of bias and to ensure independent judgments:

"Would it be proper that the persons, who had disposed of his fame and his most valuable rights as a citizen in one trial, should in another trial, for the same offence, be also the disposers of his life and his fortune? Would there not be the greatest reason to apprehend, that error in the first sentence would be the parent of error in the second sentence? That the strong bias of one decision would be apt to overrule the influence of any new lights, which might be brought to vary the complexion of another decision?" The Federalist No. 65, p. 442 (J. Cooke ed. 1961).

Certainly judicial review of the Senate's "trial" would introduce the same risk of bias as would participation in the trial itself.

Second, judicial review would be inconsistent with the Framers' insistence that our system be one of checks and balances. In our constitutional system, impeachment was designed to be the only check on the Judicial Branch by the Legislature. On the topic of judicial accountability, Hamilton wrote:

"The precautions for their responsibility are comprised in the article re-specting impeachments. They are liable to be impeached for mal-conduct by the house of representatives, and tried by the senate, and if convicted, may be dismissed from office and disqualified for holding any other. This is the only provision on the point, which is consistent with the necessary independence of the judicial character, and is the only one which we find in our own constitu-tion in respect to our own judges." . . .

Judicial involvement in impeachment proceedings, even if only for pur-poses of judicial review, is counterintuitive because it would eviscerate the "important constitutional check" placed on the Judiciary by the Framers. . . . Nixon's argument would place final reviewing authority with respect to im-peachments in the hands of the same body that the impeachment process is meant to regulate. . . .

Nevertheless, Nixon argues that judicial review is necessary in order to place a check on the Legislature. Nixon fears that if the Senate is given unre-viewable authority to interpret the Impeachment Trial Clause, there is a grave risk that the Senate will usurp judicial power. The Framers anticipated this objection and created two constitutional safeguards to keep the Senate in check. The first safeguard is that the whole of the impeachment power is divided between the two legislative bodies, with the House given the right to accuse and the Senate given the right to judge. . . . The second safeguard is the two-thirds supermajority vote requirement. . . .

In addition to the textual commitment argument, we are persuaded that the lack of finality and the difficulty of fashioning relief counsel against justiciability. . . . We agree with the Court of Appeals that opening the door of judicial review to the procedures used by the Senate in trying impeachments would "expose the political life of the country to months, or perhaps years, of chaos.". . . This lack of finality would manifest itself most dramatically if the President were impeached. The legitimacy of any successor, and hence his effectiveness, would be impaired severely, not merely while the judicial process was running its course, but during any retrial that a differently constituted Senate might conduct if its first judgment of conviction were invalidated. Equally uncertain is the question of what relief a court may give other than simply setting aside the judgment of conviction. Could it order the reinstatement of a convicted federal judge, or order Congress to create an additional judgeship if the seat had been filled in the interim?

Petitioner finally contends that a holding of nonjusticiability cannot be reconciled with our opinion in *Powell v. McCormack* . . . (1969). The relevant issue in *Powell* was whether courts could review the House of Representatives' conclusion that Powell was "unqualified" to sit as a Member because he had been accused of misappropriating public funds and abusing the process of the New York courts. We stated that the question of justiciability turned on whether the Constitution committed authority to the House to judge its Members' qualifications, and if so, the extent of that commitment. . . . Article I, § 5, provides that "Each House shall be the Judge of the Elections, Returns and Qualifications of its own Members." In turn, Art. I, § 2, specifies three requirements for membership in the House: The candidate must be at least 25 years of age, a citizen of the United States for no less than seven years, and an inhabitant of the State he is chosen to represent. We held that, in light of the three requirements specified in the Constitution, the word "qualifications"—of which the House was to be the Judge—was of a precise, limited nature.

Our conclusion in *Powell* was based on the fixed meaning of "[q]ualifications" set forth in Art. I, § 2. The claim by the House that its power to "be the Judge of the Elections, Returns and Qualifications of its own Members" was a textual commitment of unreviewable authority was defeated by the existence of this separate provision specifying the only qualifications which might be imposed for House membership. The decision as to whether a Member satisfied these qualifications was placed with the House, but the decision as to what these qualifications consisted of was not.

In the case before us, there is no separate provision of the Constitution that could be defeated by allowing the Senate final authority to determine the meaning of the word "try" in the Impeachment Trial Clause. We agree with Nixon that courts possess power to review either legislative or executive action that transgresses identifiable textual limits. As we have made clear, "whether the action of [either the Legislative or Executive Branch] exceeds whatever authority has been committed, is itself a delicate exercise in constitutional interpretation, and is a responsibility of this Court as ultimate interpreter of the Constitution.". . . . But we conclude, after exercising that delicate responsibility, that the word "try" in the Impeachment Trial Clause does not provide an identifiable textual limit on the authority which is committed to the Senate.

For the foregoing reasons, the judgment of the Court of Appeals is
Affirmed. . . .

Justice WHITE, with whom Justice BLACKMUN joins, concurring in the judgment.

Petitioner contends that the method by which the Senate convicted him on two articles of impeachment violates Art. I, § 3, cl. 6, of the Constitution, which mandates that the Senate "try" impeachments. The Court is of the view that the Constitution forbids us even to consider his contention. I find no such prohibition and would therefore reach the merits of the claim. I concur in the judgment because the Senate fulfilled its constitutional obligation to "try" petitioner.

I

It should be said at the outset that, as a practical matter, it will likely make little difference whether the Court's or my view controls this case. This is so because the Senate has very wide discretion in specifying impeachment trial procedures and because it is extremely unlikely that the Senate would abuse its discretion and insist on a procedure that could not be deemed a trial by reasonable judges. Even taking a wholly practical approach, I would prefer not to announce an unreviewable discretion in the Senate to ignore completely the constitutional direction to "try" impeachment cases. When asked at oral argument whether that direction would be satisfied if, after a House vote to impeach, the Senate, without any procedure whatsoever, unanimously found the accused guilty of being "a bad guy," counsel for the United States answered that the Government's theory "leads me to answer that question yes.". . . Especially in light of this advice from the Solicitor General, I would not issue an invitation to the Senate to find an excuse, in the name of other pressing business, to be dismissive of its critical role in the impeachment process.

Practicalities aside, however, since the meaning of a constitutional provision is at issue, my disagreement with the Court should be stated.

II

The majority states that the question raised in this case meets two of the criteria for political questions set out in *Baker v. Carr,* 369 U.S. 186, 82 S.Ct. 691, 7 L.Ed.2d 663 (1962). It concludes first that there is " 'a textually demonstrable constitutional commitment of the issue to a coordinate political department.' " It also finds that the question cannot be resolved for " 'a lack of judicially discoverable and manageable standards.' ". . .

Of course the issue in the political question doctrine is not whether the constitutional text commits exclusive responsibility for a particular governmental function to one of the political branches. . . . Rather, the issue is whether the Constitution has given one of the political branches final responsibility for interpreting the scope and nature of such a power. . . .

A

The majority finds a clear textual commitment in the Constitution's use of the word "sole" in the phrase "[t]he Senate shall have the sole Power to try all Impeachments." Art. I, § 3, cl. 6. It attributes "considerable significance" to the fact that this term appears in only one other passage in the Constitution. . . . See Art. I, § 2, cl. 5 (the House of Representatives "shall have the sole Power of Impeachment"). The Framers' sparing use of "sole" is thought to indicate that its employment in the Impeachment Trial Clause demonstrates a concern to give the Senate exclusive interpretive authority over the Clause.

In disagreeing with the Court, I note that the Solicitor General stated at oral argument that "[w]e don't rest our submission on sole power to try.". . . The significance of the Constitution's use of the term "sole" lies not in the infrequency with which the term appears, but in the fact that it appears exactly twice, in parallel provisions concerning impeachment. That the word "sole" is found only in the House and Senate Impeachment Clauses demonstrates that its purpose is to emphasize the distinct role of each in the impeachment process. . . .

The majority also claims support in the history and early interpretations of the Impeachment Clauses, noting the various arguments in support of the current system made at the Constitutional Convention and expressed powerfully by Hamilton in The Federalist Nos. 65 and 66. In light of these materials there can be little doubt that the Framers came to the view at the Convention that the trial of officials' public misdeeds should be conducted by representatives of the people; that the fledgling Judiciary lacked the wherewithal to adjudicate political intrigues; that the Judiciary ought not to try both impeachments and subsequent criminal cases emanating from them; and that the impeachment power must reside in the Legislative Branch to provide a check on the largely unaccountable Judiciary.

The majority's review of the historical record thus explains why the power to try impeachments properly resides with the Senate. It does not explain, however, the sweeping statement that the Judiciary was "not chosen to have any role in impeachments.". . . Not a single word in the historical materials cited by the majority addresses judicial review of the Impeachment Trial Clause. And a glance at the arguments surrounding the Impeachment Clauses negates the majority's attempt to infer nonjusticiability from the Framers' arguments in support of the Senate's power to try impeachments. . . .

What the relevant history mainly reveals is deep ambivalence among many of the Framers over the very institution of impeachment, which, by its nature, is not easily reconciled with our system of checks and balances. As they clearly recognized, the branch of the Federal Government which is possessed of the authority to try impeachments, by having final say over the membership of each branch, holds a potentially unanswerable power over the others. In addition, that branch, insofar as it is called upon to try not only members of other branches, but also its own, will have the advantage of being the judge of its own members' causes.

It is no surprise, then, that the question of impeachment greatly vexed the Framers. The pages of the Convention debates reveal diverse plans for resolving this exceedingly difficult issue. . . .

The historical evidence reveals above all else that the Framers were deeply concerned about placing in any branch the "awful discretion, which a court of impeachments must necessarily have." . . . Viewed against this history, the discord between the majority's position and the basic principles of checks and balances underlying the Constitution's separation of powers is clear. In essence, the majority suggests that the Framers conferred upon Congress a potential tool of legislative dominance yet at the same time rendered Congress' exercise of that power one of the very few areas of legislative authority immune from any judicial review. While the majority rejects petitioner's justiciability argument as espousing a view "inconsistent with the Framers' insistence that our system be one of checks and balances,". . . it is the Court's finding of nonjusticiability that truly upsets the Framers' careful design. In a truly balanced system, impeachments tried by the Senate would serve as a means of controlling the largely unaccountable Judiciary, even as judicial review would ensure that the Senate adhered to a minimal set of procedural standards in conducting impeachment trials.

B

The majority also contends that the term "try" does not present a judicially manageable standard. It notes that in 1787, as today, the word "try" may refer to an inquiry in the nature of a judicial proceeding, or, more generally, to experimentation or investigation. In light of the term's multiple senses, the Court finds itself unable to conclude that the Framers used the word "try" as "an implied limitation on the method by which the Senate might proceed in trying impeachments.". . . Also according to the majority, comparison to the other more specific requirements listed in the Impeachment Trial Clause—that the senators must proceed under oath and vote by two-thirds to convict, and that the Chief Justice must preside over an impeachment trial of the President—indicates that the word "try" was not meant by the Framers to constitute a limitation on the Senate's conduct and further reveals the term's unmanageability. . . .

To begin with, one would intuitively expect that, in defining the power of a political body to conduct an inquiry into official wrongdoing, the Framers used "try" in its legal sense. That intuition is borne out by reflection on the alternatives. The third Clause of Art. I, § 3, cannot seriously be read to mean that the Senate shall "attempt" or "experiment with" impeachments. It is equally implausible to say that the Senate is charged with "investigating" impeachments given that this description would substantially overlap with the House of Representatives' "sole" power to draw up articles of impeachment. . . .

The other variant of the majority position focuses not on which sense of "try" is employed in the Impeachment Trial Clause, but on whether the legal sense of that term creates a judicially manageable standard. The majority concludes that the term provides no "identifiable textual limit." Yet, as the Government itself conceded at oral argument, the term "try" is hardly so elusive as the majority would have it. . . . Were the Senate, for example, to adopt the practice of automatically entering a judgment of conviction whenever articles of impeachment were delivered from the House, it is quite clear that the Senate will have failed to "try" impeachments. . . .

III

The majority's conclusion that "try" is incapable of meaningful judicial construction is not without irony. One might think that if any class of concepts would fall within the definitional abilities of the Judiciary, it would be that class having to do with procedural justice. Examination of the remaining question—whether proceedings in accordance with Senate Rule XI are compatible with the Impeachment Trial Clause—confirms this intuition.

Petitioner bears the rather substantial burden of demonstrating that, simply by employing the word "try," the Constitution prohibits the Senate from relying on a fact-finding committee. . . .

Petitioner argues, however, that because committees were not used in state impeachment trials prior to the Convention, the word "try" cannot be interpreted to permit their use. It is, however, a substantial leap to infer from the absence of a particular device of parliamentary procedure that its use has been forever barred by the Constitution. And there is textual and historical evidence that undermines the inference sought to be drawn in this case. . . .

In short, textual and historical evidence reveals that the Impeachment Trial Clause was not meant to bind the hands of the Senate beyond establishing a set of minimal procedures. Without identifying the exact contours of these procedures, it is sufficient to say that the Senate's use of a factfinding committee under Rule XI is entirely compatible with the Constitution's command that the Senate "try all impeachments." Petitioner's challenge to his conviction must therefore fail.

IV

Petitioner has not asked the Court to conduct his impeachment trial; he has asked instead that it determine whether his impeachment was tried by the Senate. The majority refuses to reach this determination out of a laudable desire to respect the authority of the Legislature. Regrettably, this concern is manifested in a manner that does needless violence to the Constitution. The deference that is owed can be found in the Constitution itself, which provides the Senate ample discretion to determine how best to try impeachments. . . .

Justice SOUTER, concurring in the judgment.

I agree with the Court that this case presents a nonjusticiable political question. Because my analysis differs somewhat from the Court's, however, I concur in its judgment by this separate opinion.

As we cautioned in *Baker v. Carr*, . . . "the 'political question' label" tends "to obscure the need for case-by-case inquiry." The need for such close examination is nevertheless clear from our precedents, which demonstrate that the functional nature of the political question doctrine requires analysis of "the precise facts and posture of the particular case," and precludes "resolution by any semantic cataloguing.". . .

Whatever considerations feature most prominently in a particular case, the political question doctrine is "essentially a function of the separation of powers," ibid., existing to restrain courts "from inappropriate interference in the business of the other branches of Government,". . . and deriving in large part from prudential concerns about the respect we owe the political departments. . . . Not all interference is inappropriate or disrespectful, however, and application of the doctrine ultimately turns, as Learned Hand put it, on "how importunately the occasion demands an answer.". . .

This occasion does not demand an answer. . . .

One can, nevertheless, envision different and unusual circumstances that might justify a more searching review of impeachment proceedings. If the Senate were to act in a manner seriously threatening the integrity of its results, convicting, say, upon a coin toss, or upon a summary determination that an officer of the United States was simply " 'a bad guy,' " . . . judicial interference might well be appropriate. In such circumstances, the Senate's action might be so far beyond the scope of its constitutional authority, and the consequent impact on the Republic so great, as to merit a judicial response despite the prudential concerns that would ordinarily counsel silence. . . .

Selected Bibliography

Benedict, Michael Les. *The Impeachment of Andrew Johnson.* New York: Norton, 1973.

Berger, Raoul. "President, Congress, and the Courts." *Yale Law Journal.* 83 (1974), 1111.

_____. *Impeachment: The Constitutional Problems.* Cambridge, Mass.: Harvard University Press, 1973.

_____. "Impeachment for High Crimes and Misdemeanors." *Southern California Law Review* 44 (1971), 395.

Bushnell, Eleanore. *Crimes, Follies, and Misfortunes: The Federal Impeachment Trials.* Chicago: University of Illinois Press, 1991.

Cannon, Clarence, ed. *Cannon's Precedents of the House of Representatives of the United States, Including References to Provisions of the Constitution, the Laws, and Decisions of the United States Senate.* Vol. VI. Washington, D.C.: Government Printing Office, 1935.

Deschler, Lewis, ed. *Deschler's Precedents of the House of Representatives of the United States, Including References to Provisions of the Constitution, the Laws, and Decisions of the Courts.* Vol. VI. Washington, D.C.: Government Printing Office, 1977.

Elliot, Jonathan. *Debates in the Several State Conventions on the Adoption of the Federal Constitution.* 5 vols. Philadelphia: Lippincott, 1896.

Farrand, Max, ed. *The Records of the Federal Convention of 1787.* 4 vols. New Haven: Yale University Press, 1937.

Freedman, Eric M. "The Law as King and the King as Law: Is a President Immune from Criminal Prosecution Before Impeachment?" *Hastings Constitutional Law Quarterly* 20 (1992), 7.

Gerhardt, Michael J. *The Federal Impeachment Process: A Constitutional and Historical Analysis.* Princeton, N.J.: Princeton University Press, 1996.

_____. "The Constitutional Limits to Impeachment and Its Alternatives." *Texas Law Review* 68 (1989), 1.

Grimes, Warren S. "Hundred-Ton-Gun Control: Preserving Impeachment as the Exclusive Removal Mechanism for Federal Judges." *UCLA Law Review* 38 (1991), 1209.

Hamilton, Alexander, James Madison, and John Jay. *The Federalist.* Cambridge, Mass.: Belknap Press, 1966.

Hinds, Asher C., ed. *Hinds' Precedents of the House of Representatives of the United States, Including References to Provisions of the Constitution, the Laws, and Decisions of the United States Senate.* Vol. III. Washington, D.C.: Government Printing Office, 1907.

Hoffer, Peter Charles, and N. E. H. Hull. *Impeachment in America, 1635–1805.* New Haven, Yale University Press, 1984.

The Impeachment Report: A Guide to Congressional Proceedings in the Case of Richard M. Nixon, President of the United States. New York: New American Library, 1974.

Kurland, Philip B. "Watergate, Impeachment and the Constitution." *Mississippi Law Journal* 45 (1974), 531.

Rehnquist, William H. *Grand Inquests: The Historic Impeachments of Justice Samuel Chase and President Andrew Johnson.* New York: Morrow, 1992.

U.S. Congress. House of Representatives. Committee on the Judiciary. *Constitutional Grounds for Presidential Impeachment: Report by the Staff of the Impeachment Inquiry.* 93rd Cong., 2nd sess., 1984.

_____. *Associate Justice William O. Douglas: Final Report by the Special Subcommittee on House Resolution 920.* 91st Cong., 2nd sess., 1970.

Van Tassel, Emily Field. *Why Judges Resign: Influences on Federal Judicial Service.* Washington, D.C.: Federal Judicial Center, 1993.

_____. "Resignations and Removals: A History of Federal Judicial Service and Disservice— 1789–1992," *University of Pennsylvania Law Review* 142 (1993), 333.

Volcansek, Mary L. *Judicial Impeachment: None Called for Justice.* Chicago, University of Illinois Press, 1993.

Listing of Document Sources

1. U.S. Constitution.

2. Max Farrand, ed. *The Records of the Federal Convention of 1787*. 4 vols. New Haven: Yale University Press, 1937.

3. Alexander Hamilton, James Madison, and John Jay. *The Federalist*. Cambridge, Mass.: Belknap Press, 1966.

4. Alexander Hamilton. *Observations on Certain Documents Contained in No. V & VI of "The History of the United States for the Year 1796," In Which the Charge of Speculation Against Alexander Hamilton, Late Secretary of the Treasury, Is Fully Refuted. Written By Himself.* Philadelphia: John Fenno, 1797.

5. *The Debates and Proceedings in the Congress of the United States.* Washington, D.C.: Government Printing Office, 1849. Col. 903–963 (1793).

6. U.S. Congress. House of Representatives. Committee on the Judiciary. *Associate Justice William O. Douglas: Final Report by the Special Subcommittee on House Resolution 920.* 91st Cong., 2nd sess., 1970.

7. U.S. Congress. House of Representatives. Committee on the Judiciary. *Associate Justice William O. Douglas.*

8. U.S. Congress. House of Representatives. Committee on the Judiciary. *Associate Justice William O. Douglas.*

9. Lewis Deschler, ed. *Deschler's Precedents of the United States House of Representatives.* Vol. III. Washington, D.C.: Government Printing Office, 1977.

10. Asher C. Hinds, ed. *Hinds' Precedents of the House of Representatives of the United States.* Vol. III. Washington, D.C.: Government Printing Office, 1907. Sec. 2294–2318.

11. *Hinds' Precedents.* Vol. III. Sec. 2319–2341.

12. *Hinds' Precedents.* Vol. III. Sec. 2342–2363.

13. *Hinds' Precedents.* Vol. III. Sec. 2364–2384.

14. *Hinds' Precedents.* Vol. III. Sec. 2385–2397.

15. *Hinds' Precedents.* Vol. III. Sec. 2504–2505.

16. *Hinds' Precedents.* Vol. III. Sec. 2469–2485.

17. Clarence Cannon, ed. *Cannon's Precedents of the House of Representatives of the United States.* Vol. IV. Washington, D.C.: Government Printing Office, 1935. Sec. 498–500.

18. *Cannon's Precedents.* Vol. III. Ch. 14, 16.1–16.4.

19. *Cannon's Precedents.* Vol. VI. Sec. 513–514; *Deschler's Precedents.* Vol. III. Ch. 14, 17.1–17.3.

20. *Deschler's Precedents.* Vol. III. Ch. 14, 18.1–18.4.

21. U.S. Congress. House of Representatives. H.R. Rep. No. 688, 99th Cong., 2nd sess. (1986).

22. U.S. Congress. House of Representatives. H.R. Rep. No. 810, 100th Cong., 2nd sess. (1988).

23. U.S. Congress. House of Representatives. H.R. Rep. No. 36, 101th Cong., 1st sess. (1989).

24. *Hinds' Precedents.* Vol. III. Sec. 2517–2518.

25. *Hinds' Precedents.* Vol. III. Sec. 2444–2468.

26. *Congressional Globe.* March 28, 1834.

27. *Message and Papers of the Presidents.* "Protest of President Jackson," April 15, 1834, 1288–1312.

28. *Hinds' Precedents.* Vol. III. Sec. 2408–2443.

29. *Proceedings in the Trial of Andrew Johnson, President of the United States, Before the United States Senate, on Articles of Impeachment Exhibited by the House of Representatives.* Washington, D.C.: F.&J. Rives & Geo. A. Bailey, 1868.

30. U.S. Congress. House of Representatives. *Impeachment of Richard M. Nixon, President of the United States.* H.R. Rep. No. 93-1305, 93rd Cong., 2nd sess.

31. U.S. Congress. House of Representatives. *http://icreport.house.gov/icreport/7grounds.htm*

32. U.S. Congress. House of Representatives. *http://www.house.gov/judiciary/schippers/htm*

33. White House. Press release. October 2, 1998.

34. 84 Court of Claims 293 (1936).

35. 506 U.S. 224 (1993).

Index